McGRAW-HILL SERIES IN EDUCATION

HAROLD BENJAMIN, Consulting Editor

Problems in the Improvement of Reading

This book is produced in full compliance with the government's regulations for conserving paper and other essential materials.

Selected Titles from

McGraw-Hill Series in Education

Harold Benjamin, *Consulting Editor*

Problems in the Improvement of Reading ᷍

BY

CONSTANCE M. McCULLOUGH
Assistant Professor of Education
Western Reserve University

RUTH M. STRANG
Professor of Education, Teachers College,
Columbia University

ARTHUR E. TRAXLER
Associate Director
Educational Records Bureau

First Edition

New York · *London*
MCGRAW-HILL BOOK COMPANY, INC.
1946

THE MAPLE PRESS COMPANY, YORK, PA.

PREFACE

There is no doubt that teachers and administrators need help with the reading problems they encounter in their schools. In considering what kind of book would be most useful, the authors decided that the book that would give the greatest help to those for whom it was designed would start with their point of view, reinforce their conviction of the importance of reading, show them goals toward which they could work, and give them specific suggestions on how to attain these desirable ends.

The book should have some of the features of a manual, giving detailed descriptions of procedure, but it should be much more than a manual. Reading is too complex a subject to be taught by rule of thumb. For this reason, the book should also include principles, derived from experience and experiment, on which sound procedures are based. This background of understanding is necessary to enable the teacher or administrator more intelligently to adapt procedures to his particular school, class, or individual student and to create new methods and materials.

In addition to descriptions of specific procedures and the theory underlying them, the book should contain examples of total approaches to common reading problems—such as improving reading in the school as a whole, forming and conducting remedial reading clubs or classes, working individually with seriously retarded readers. By means of descriptions of work actually done in schools and colleges, the reader may obtain a picture of reading instruction with all its interrelations and ramifications. From this illustrative material he should derive certain generalizations regarding the developmental program, remedial work, and clinical treatment of individuals with reading problems. He should see more clearly what he is trying to do, how he can do it, and whether he has accomplished what he hoped in improving his students' reading. It is a book of this kind that the authors have attempted to write—a book combining the administrative, guidance, and reading-technique approaches.

It is probable that for a number of reasons reading problems in high school and college will increase in this postwar era. An influx of students into junior colleges, colleges, and universities is to be expected. Among these students there will be many who have not been in the

v

habit of acquiring knowledge from printed sources. Yet despite the increasing use of visual and auditory instruction methods, a large proportion of their study time will be devoted to reading. Some men who have served in the fighting forces may have special difficulty in concentrating on college subjects, in reorienting themselves to civilian interests, in overcoming their resistances to "words, words, words," and in rehabilitating reading skills required in college. Moreover, lack of suitable reading material for these retarded readers, a curriculum that offers no incentive for them to put forth the effort that effective reading demands, and lack of facilities for assisting them with their reading problems—all these factors forecast the need for helpful books in this field.

Grateful acknowledgment is made to Dr. Robert S. Woodworth, who read and made helpful comments on the section on the psychology of reading; to James Hayford, who carefully edited the entire manuscript; and to many students at Teachers College, Columbia University, in the authors' classes in The Improvement of Reading in High School and College. Among the students who have contributed descriptions of programs and procedures are Grace Hope Allardice, R. Athelma, Margaret F. Borton, Selena C. Clay, Elizabeth Edmonds, Gladys Fisher, Marilyn Graff, Georgia Lightfoot, Ethel Madden, Sally Prentice, Pauline Stock, Harriet M. Sweetland, Katherine Templeton, and Barbara Van Patten. Needless to say, the authors owe much to many other persons who have described present practice and have reported research in the field. References to many of these investigations are listed at the end of each chapter, so that the student who desires more detail may find it in the original article. The authors wish to make acknowledgment also to the Houghton Mifflin Company for permission to quote selections from *A Survey of European Civilization, Ancient Times to the Present,* by Wallace K. Ferguson and Geoffrey Bruun, and to the Macmillan Company for permission to quote selections from *Foundations of Biology,* by Lorande Loss Woodruff, in Appendix C.

CONSTANCE M. McCULLOUGH.
RUTH M. STRANG.
ARTHUR E. TRAXLER.

May, 1946.

HOW TO READ THIS BOOK

Because this is a practical rather than a theoretical book, it should be approached from the vantage point of the particular experience of each of its readers—from the standpoint of a person who wants to improve his own reading; of a teacher of students who are expected to gain a large proportion of their knowledge through reading; of a parent who is concerned with the success of his children; of an administrator who wants the students in his school to be adequately equipped for the work and the leisure of life; or of a specialist in reading. Whatever your experience has been with reading, you should try to bring it to bear on reading this book.

If you are interested for either personal or professional reasons in making immediate application of this material to the improvement of your own reading, the authors recommend the following procedure, so familiar to experienced teachers but so often neglected even by college and graduate students. First, recall your own experience with reading and your unanswered questions and unsolved problems in the field. Only after you have done this are you ready to explore the book. Reading this preface will acquaint you with the authors' intent and purpose. Reading the table of contents will acquaint you in more detail with the general pattern of the book. These preliminary steps should give you a basis on which to decide whether to read the whole book or to read certain chapters only or to look elsewhere for material more directly relevant to your needs.

If you decide to read the book or at least parts of it, you should be aware of your purpose in doing so. Do you wish to become acquainted with the backgrounds and specific suggestions that the book offers, or do you seek the answer to some specific question or problem presented in a single chapter? If the former is your purpose, self-initiated or imposed by the requirements of a college course, you may as well follow the authors' lead and begin with the first chapter. In either case, before reading a chapter, spend a few minutes formulating what you would have said on the subject if you had been asked to write the chapter. Then take five minutes to skim through the chapter, reading headings and topic sentences here and there to get a general idea of the content of each paragraph and of what the author is trying to do.

Now you are ready to read more carefully. Just how you read will be determined by your specific purpose. If you want to learn the authors' point of view on each major topic so that at the end of each section or chapter you can outline the main pattern of thought, then you will try to boil down the main idea in each paragraph. If the main idea is particularly important to you, you will want to see just how it has been supported and illustrated. If the main idea is not particularly important or is already familiar to you, you only need to glance at the supporting detail. You will be able to remember these central ideas more easily if you relate each to the previous one so as to build an integrated structure of thought as you read rather than merely a collection of isolated ideas.

While you are reading, various bright ideas may occur to you, sometimes closely related to the subject, sometimes not. Good ideas are at a premium, so do not lose them. Jot down a key word or two to remind yourself of them, and consider them later for what they are worth in your personal or professional life.

With the authors' contribution to the subject and your own ideas clearly before you, you are prepared to make whatever applications seem valuable to you. You have reviewed your previous experience, perhaps enriched it by your reading of the chapter, and are now equipped a little more adequately to meet the next situation involving the improvement of your own or your students' reading.

Each chapter, in fact, should give you a fuller background of experience and a stronger foundation on which to build the ideas that you will gain from reading the next chapter. Thus chapter by chapter, your understanding of reading should grow and your ability to deal with the practical problems of reading in school or college or in your personal life should increase. Perhaps you will be interested in further reading and study, for this book provides only one gateway to a vast and complex field of study.

ORGANIZATION

This book is organized, as the title suggests, on a problem basis. In so organizing their book, the authors have encountered the difficulties of duplication. Because problems relating to the school-wide program, reading in specific subjects, remedial reading classes, and individual diagnosis and treatment all have many elements in common, some repetition has been inevitable. To be sure, a certain amount of duplication is desirable for emphasis and for ensuring the retention of important ideas. However, the authors have avoided unnecessary and undesirable duplication by treating fully each important topic, such as testing, diagnostic procedure, and vocabulary, at the place where it could be most appropriately introduced. Subsequently, the topic or phase of the topic thus treated has merely been mentioned. By using the index, a reader who wants more detailed information on any common topic can find the place where that phase of reading is most fully discussed.

An extensive bibliography has been added at the end of each chapter for those students to whom library facilities are easily available and who wish to go more deeply into the research basis for improvement of reading in college and secondary schools. For the benefit of teachers, librarians, and administrators, who are naturally more concerned with practical applications, selected books on methods and articles describing reading programs and procedures have been included.

CONTENTS

CHAPTER I

GLIMPSES OF PRESENT PRACTICE

I should like to know (1) ways in which schools and colleges have attacked the problem of aiding students whose reading skill is inadequate; (2) how I might organize work in my own classes so that students may be helped to improve their reading in my subject; and (3) how to enlist the interest and cooperation of the entire staff in helping students to build a functional vocabulary, a body of meaningful concepts in their content fields, and reading and study skills that will carry over to all activities in which they are needed. I should like to know how to make reading a means of carrying out school enterprises and assignments that seem important and useful to the student.

This point of view expressed by one forward-looking teacher is in the minds of many others. The need for improvement in reading has been frankly recognized by administrators, teachers, counselors, and students. The possibility of improvement has been demonstrated by many programs and experiments. Teachers and administrators, in their own classes and schools, with or without the help of reading experts, have developed various programs and procedures to meet the obvious need. They have employed different methods and have made some attempts to evaluate them. Their experience is helpful to others who are facing somewhat similar situations.

For this reason, before considering systematically the nature of reading and other fundamental and theoretical aspects, we shall present in this introductory chapter a number of snapshots of reading programs. We have selected some of the best attempts to improve reading in a variety of situations covering a range from rural schools to colleges and universities. Instead of describing programs that are representative of instruction in reading now being given, we shall present some procedures that are better than usual practice in schools of these types. This is the best substitute for actual visits to the schools. From the concrete examples the reader may make his own tentative generalizations and obtain suggestions for the reading program in his own class or school.

READING IN RURAL SCHOOLS

In a one-room rural school an exceptionally well-trained and gifted teacher took advantage of many opportunities for the improvement

1

of reading.   Her procedures would interest teachers in other types
schools also.   The grade scores on suitable standardized reading tests
given to all pupils as soon as the teacher had become acquainted with
them, gave a picture of their general reading ability.   Observation
during the test and analysis of each pupil's response supplied additional
information about reading attitudes, errors, and grade level of reading
proficiency.

A library corner with table and chairs and a variety of suitable
books invited pupils to read.   A pupil librarian and committee were
responsible for keeping books in order, for displaying them attractively
on the table, and for checking them in and out.   Older pupils who
needed practice in reading very easy books obtained this practice
without embarrassment by being made responsible for helping younger
children select and read books suitable for them.   The public library
lent books to the school for a 4-week period and the state department
of education lent books for a term or a year.   A library period was
scheduled each day, in which pupils read whatever they chose.   The
teacher discouraged the reading of comics during school hours, except
True Comics.

For the sake of individual satisfaction in accomplishment and of
stimulation to others, pupils kept a record of the books that they read
and of their reaction to them on a wall chart entitled, "Books We Have
Read."

Special instruction to individuals and small groups was an essential
part of the reading program.   Here the one-room school has an
advantage over the larger school.   When the pupils in second or
third grade were ready to learn the vowel sounds, older pupils who
needed this instruction joined the group.   Similarly, practice in
dividing words into syllables and in other methods of recognizing
unfamiliar words was given to all pupils who needed it, regardless of
their age or their grade status.

Part of the last period devoted to supervised study was used for
practice in developing reading skills essential for efficient study of
the day's assignment, one day with one group, another day with
another group.   Thus pupils learned to read for different purposes,
using newspapers and periodicals for practice material as well as their
text and reference books.   The reading of each selection was followed
by a check on comprehension suited to the purpose for which the
reading was done.   New words received attention, pupils sharing
experiences with the word, trying to get its meaning from the context,
and checking their guesses by looking up the word in the dictionary.
Some of these supervised-study periods were used for remedial work

with retarded readers. Individual work was provided through independent word study and workbooks. No less important than specific instruction in reading were informal conversations and games that helped to increase oral-English ability, in which many rural children lag behind city children.

As a future project, the teacher had in mind a school newspaper with pupil editor and editorial committee. Pupils from grades 3 through 8 would participate in this valuable language activity.

Rural children who have had poor opportunities for learning to read at home and in school enter high school, if indeed they attempt further education, seriously retarded in reading. If reading material is limited to the daily paper, the *Farm Journal*, and a few government agricultural leaflets, the children have little incentive to read at home. Even in homes where the cultural level is higher and books are available, children frequently have little time at home for reading. In many parts of the country farm work is an all-year, all-day, wearying job in which children help in greater or less degree from the time they are ten years old or even before that. In one junior high school there were boys of fifteen who arose at 4 A.M. to milk and see that milk was sent to the creamery. By the time they arrived by bus at school, at nine o'clock, many had done 4 hours' work. They did afternoon and evening chores after school. When these chores were finished, it was eight o'clock or later, and few were then interested in reading.

Under these conditions the following provisions for reading were made in the junior high school: In the seventh grade all pupils had three periods a week in which they were free to read books and articles of their own choice. In the eighth grade all pupils had 20 periods of special instruction in reading during the semester, scheduled in any way desired—one period a week, one unit of 20 consecutive periods, or 2 units of 10 periods each. All classes were scheduled during school hours. There was also one activity or club period a week that was frequently devoted to reading. Without such a program, many pupils would have dropped out of school at the end of junior high school, partly because of their inability to read the kind and amount of material required in the higher grades.

INSTRUCTION IN READING IN A JUNIOR HIGH SCHOOL[1]

On the basis of test results, a reading-skill program was organized for one entire junior high school. The students of each grade were

[1] State Street School, Hackensack, N. J. Dr. William Patterson, principal; Lois Sinniger, chairman of the evaluation committee; Louise Whelan, chairman of the reading committee.

divided into high, low, and average groups according to their scores on the Iowa Silent Reading Test, supplemented by the recommendation of teachers and in some cases by the Stanford revision of the Binet scale. These groups had a daily 20-minute reading period presided over by one of their subject teachers. The superior readers broadened their interests and improved their tastes by reading plays, by sharing good books they had read, by reporting on worth-while articles and books, and by spending one period a week in the public library. The average group concentrated on the reading skills in which they were weak. The low group learned how to recognize unfamiliar words, and reading silently, tried to follow the material the teacher read orally with good phrasing and expression. They also read a large number of easy books and did practice exercises on the reading skills needed in their subjects. Three special groups of slow learners—15 in a group—were given still more individualized instruction and reading experiences for the purpose of increasing their self-confidence. Three teachers worked closely with them, each teacher taking each of the groups in rotation for 13 weeks. For these slow learners the goals were immediate and tangible; the activities were simple and concrete and could be finished quickly. Reading grew out of firsthand experiences and was functionally related to their music, arts, shop, physical education, and other classes.

At the end of the year, test results were shown in graphic form, giving percentages of retardation and acceleration in reading for the past two years. In the last year the median ninth-grade student gained 1.4 years; the median eighth-grade student 1.1 years; and the median seventh-grade student 0.7 year. The faculty met in small groups to discuss the progress in reading in each grade, the factors that might account for this progress, as well as for weaknesses and strengths in students' reading skills, and procedures for improvement. The need for improvement in vocabulary in all grades was so evident that the teachers decided to put greater emphasis on the meaning of words through the context and on other methods of word recognition, as well as to give more attention to teaching the specific meanings of unfamiliar words as they were encountered. Another recommendation was that students should have more practice in summarizing and evaluating the material that they had read.

The result of this program, developed cooperatively by the teachers and the principal, was that the teachers became more aware of the need for attention to reading and more expert in giving instruction. When they were made responsible for a 20-minute period of reading each day, they were stimulated to learn more about the teaching of reading. Some joined an extramural university course given at the school and shared their experiences and their newly acquired knowledge. Thus the special reading period served as an in-service education device that might be expected to bring about better teaching of reading in all subjects.

A WORKSHOP TYPE OF PROGRAM

In schools where there are large numbers of pupils who have reading problems, workshop courses and reading laboratories have been introduced into the curriculum. The purpose of these modified classes is to teach to the less gifted pupils reading skills and utility English, as well as literature particularly adapted to the pupils' practical needs. Such a course is a pedagogical hybrid, having characteristics both of a class in English and of a remedial reading group. A report by Elizabeth S. McClure will serve to illustrate this kind of remedial reading program (25, pages 140–144):

The school in which this remedial reading was introduced provides three distinct courses of study to meet the diverse needs of the pupils. An academic course is planned to meet the needs of pupils who intend to go to college; a commercial course is open to recommended pupils after the freshman year; and a civic or social-scientific course is provided for pupils scoring low in scholastic aptitude and having no definite aims in view after high school. The remedial reading reported by Miss McClure was done with low ninth-grade pupils in the last-mentioned group.

Her class consisted of twelve boys and eight girls, all of whom had been cited by their subject teachers as deficient in reading ability. The teachers' judgment was confirmed by the results of tests. Over half of the pupils came from underprivileged homes; many presented serious behavior problems.

As part of the teacher's preliminary preparation, she accompanied the visiting teacher into the homes of the boys and girls in her class. This trip quickened her desire to give these children new horizons through reading. Many of them came from dirty, ramshackle homes in the pine barrens. In a house devoid of any comforts or niceties one could scarcely expect to find books or magazines. And a heritage of ignorance, slovenliness, and indifference could not be expected to have fostered in children a love of reading.

The program for this group was planned primarily to create enjoyment and interest in everyday reading situations. As a first step the cooperation of the other teachers in aiding these pupils and in reporting improvement was enlisted. The next step was to obtain the confidence and good will of the pupils. The approach was somewhat as follows: "We have many clubs in our school, but no reading club. Wouldn't it be fun to form one? Suppose we make a little survey of this class to see how many are interested in books, what books you have at home, and what books you would like to read." This suggestion was sufficient to interest the pupils in preparing a short questionnaire, which they distributed and summarized. The answers and discussion following this questionnaire revealed that several of the pupils frankly disliked reading of any kind and that the others read books and magazines of such poor quality as *True Story*, *Detective Story*, and *Movie Mirror*. It was a real thrill to anticipate putting into the hands of these book-impoverished children good reading material. But this could not be done too abruptly.

The club was organized and a chairman, a secretary, and two librarians were elected. Because the librarians were uncertain as to their duties, the entire club visited the library and spent a period browsing among the books and receiving help from the school librarian in finding books. She agreed to supply the class with interesting bibliographies and to arrange a shelf of books that they might especially enjoy. The town librarian was equally cooperative.

Several very interesting conversational English periods grew out of the visits and the questionnaires. These informal conversations served to establish friendly relations within the group and with the teacher. Several additional periods were spent in administering the Terman Group Test of Mental Ability and the Gray Oral Reading Paragraphs. Thus the first week was spent in organizing the reading club, in testing the pupils, and in acquainting them with the library. The rest of the program evolved week by week as follows:

Feb. 13 to 20.   We Set the Stage

The room in which the club met was given as "bookish" an atmosphere as possible. A few artistically gifted pupils made slogans and posters for the bulletin boards. Others wrote compositions with such titles as "Book Journeys," "Book Friends," and "Movies from Books."

The town library donated dozens of attractive book covers, and publishing houses every month bestowed their discarded colorful displays upon the club representative who called for them. The children enjoyed looking at this material, displayed from time to time on the bulletin boards. "Where can we get that book? Is that picture really about something in the book? What does that word mean? Is that book any good for boys?" These were some of the questions elicited by the displays.

Feb. 20 to Mar. 5.   We Read about the Radio

Since one unit in the ninth-grade civics course is on the radio, the class began to read on this subject. They soon discovered a dearth of material in their school library and suggested collecting magazines and newspapers for the library. So the call went out for magazines old and new, Sunday-supplement sheets, and the radio page in the daily papers. The freshman class heard the appeal and responded by bringing in piles of magazines, many of excellent quality. From these magazines and newspapers the reading group cut all the material pertinent to the subject. They then mounted these clippings, indexed and filed them under such headings as "Broadcasts,"

"Children's Programs," and "Radio Stations." Notwithstanding the difficulty of much of the material in the radio issue of the little magazine *Modern Literature,* the pupils read it with interest.

During this unit the club arranged several imaginary radio programs to give pupils practice in oral reading. One day various pupils prepared themselves to read some material that might be used in a radio broadcast. A screen was placed in the front of the room and the pupils went behind it to read. Having the audience unseen prevented stage fright and added to the fun. Each reader was impressed with the necessity of being a good radio announcer. "You don't want your audience to shut you off," they were told, "so you must try to do these things in your reading:

"1. Read smoothly
"2. Phrase correctly
"3. Enunciate clearly
"4. Pause only in the right places
"5. Read with expression—see the subject so clearly yourself that your audience will see it, too."

Another day they arranged a Professor Quiz program centered on vocabulary. Several pupils prepared vocabulary lists of words taken from their reading. Other pupils were selected to define the words and use them in sentences. If they failed, they heard the gong ring for them. This device aroused interest and stimulated vocabulary study. A similar program was built around questions on material that had been read by all the class.

Mar. 5 to 19. We Visit the Movies

The first day that a movie unit was announced in class, interest ran high. The children brought in a motley assortment of magazines and spent one period in reading and discussing them. The next day they explored the better magazines for movie material and made a file comparable to their radio file. The school librarian provided a copy of *Motion Picture Digest* for everyone in the class. This type of reading was fascinating to the pupils because each had a favorite movie to look up. Unfamiliar words, such as "pathos," "spectacular," and "melodrama," were carefully explained and illustrated by some particular picture which the pupils had seen.

Using the *Motion Picture Digest* as a model, the pupils wrote their own reviews of movies they had seen, marking them + or −, as the case might be, for children, youths, or adults. In writing these reviews they exhibited unusually good critical ability. Undoubtedly reading the *Motion Picture Digest* had helped them formulate their opinions.

During the movie unit each pupil made a notebook in which he put the following material:

1. A movie review
2. A paragraph or two telling why a certain story would make a good movie
3. Clippings and pictures about movies
4. A list of good movie manners
5. Reasons for studying the movies

6. Requirements for a good movie
7. A list of sources of information about the movies
8. A summary of two stories about movies taken from *Adventure Bound*
9. A movie vocabulary

Mar. 20 to Apr. 3. We Read about Our Community

Because the locality is rich in historical lore, the group decided to center some of their reading on the fact and fiction of the community. The school librarian arranged a shelf of books about this section of New Jersey. When the children discovered that two of their number actually lived in farmhouses described in *Old Farmhouses of New Jersey*, they became most enthusiastic about discovering more places of interest in their community. The group visited many places of interest. These excursions stimulated further reading and constructive activities. Students' models of people and places, maps, charts, and pictures were placed in the display case near the school's front entrance and their pride in their achievement was increased still more by a feature article on their exhibit in the school paper. The reading interest aroused extended to books about other communities.

The other units—Hobby Show; We Are Salesmen; We Start Book Lists; We Write Headlines; We Plan an Assembly Program (which took the form of a dramatization of characters about whom they had read, and which stimulated them to read further in order to check on the accuracy of details for costumes); We Take Our Reading Outdoors (which included some choral speaking)—these units were handled in the same ingenious, enthusiastic way as those already described in greater detail.

This program was successful in many ways, not the least of which was the improvement in the pupils' behavior. In cooperation, attentiveness, alertness, and self-confidence the children improved markedly. Three children who had been unable to follow instructions at the beginning of the program overcame their difficulty. One timid little girl chosen as librarian blossomed under her responsibility and became one of the friendliest persons in the room. Before the program was begun, only six books had been borrowed from the library by this group, whereas, at the end of the semester, the librarian reported that a total of 102 books had been withdrawn by children in the Reading Club. Not all of these books were read, perhaps, but at least they were examined. The town librarian likewise reported an increase in the number of books borrowed and the interest shown by members of the Reading Club. Other teachers reported an improvement in their pupils' reading comprehension and interest in every subject. At the close of the experiment the class radiated a certain vitality which was lacking before the work began.

Vitality is the keynote of this program—a vitality achieved by setting in motion activities in which these boys and girls could function successfully. Reading was involved in each on-going activity and motivated by it. Each activity was sufficiently complex and varied in form to provide for individual differences within the group to which the teacher was alert. These are the outstanding features of this successful program.

A PROGRAM ENLISTING THE COOPERATION OF VARIOUS TEACHERS

Under some conditions a limited approach to the reading problem is necessary. This was the case in a tenth-grade class in a school where the principal was not ready to make any fundamental changes.

An analysis of the results of the Traxler test showed that, while there were the usual individual differences, the class as a whole was up to ninth-grade standard on all abilities measured by the test. Further investigation, however, showed that the reading materials available were much too advanced for students in the tenth grade. The principal said that nothing could be done about changing the texts or the supplementary readers, as the courses were rigorously prescribed from above. It was largely a matter of fitting the students to the curriculum. On this basis, their vocabulary was inadequate for much of their reading and the principal felt that something could be done about that phase of the problem.

Exploration of the library revealed that it contained several hundred volumes, most of them donated by public-spirited citizens who had given the school all the books that they themselves did not want to keep on their own shelves. The library was most inadequate indeed, and the prospects looked dark; for years no money had been appropriated for books and none was likely to be available.

The first step was to encourage the use of the public library and to solicit magazines, so as to provide at least a minimum of interesting reading.

The second step was to discuss the problem with the faculty, from the point of view of the various subjects. Not all of these teachers were aware that reading difficulties came within their province, but all were willing to consider the subject. In the end the purpose was achieved. All decided to make lists of words that were peculiar to their own subjects and to consider ways and means of helping the students acquire rich and meaningful associations with these words. In general, this would involve providing firsthand experience with each word whenever possible: *e.g.*, experimenting with a substance in chemistry or a process in physics, or visiting a place of historic or civic interest. These new words were then used frequently in conversation and in assignments, were written on the blackboard and discussed in class. Loose usage or complete misuse of the words was corrected. Thus the entire staff was enlisted in one phase of the reading problem.

The English teacher made a special contribution by introducing a vocabulary unit, which was considered a legitimate part of her work (prescribed curriculum notwithstanding). She explored with her students the origin of language and the sources of words that are in common use today. She undertook to gather lists of difficult words by noting errors in students' themes and conversation, besides unfamiliar words in the required reading. These words were listed in a large class dictionary, to which all members of the class contributed definitions, derivations, and sentences or paragraphs in which the words were used. Each student was encouraged and shown how to build up his own dictionary of difficult words. Sometimes the students invented word games of the Professor Quiz type. A corner of the blackboard was set aside for words having derivations of special interest. These words were frequently changed and seldom failed to attract attention. In such ways the students gained an appreciation of the meanings of many different words that they needed for their reading, writing, and speaking. During the year the English teacher also instructed them on how to use a dictionary and how to get meanings from context; and she gave them practice in these two abilities by means of various exercises that she constructed.

The Latin teacher cooperated by teaching ways of getting the meanings of words from their derivations and provided practice in the use of Latin prefixes, suffixes, and roots in vocabulary building and interpretation.

The English teacher's enthusiasm was contagious; the program brought results that justified repetition of the effort. There was little danger of the students' becoming too word-conscious. However, it may be that they were led to develop too much interest in big and unusual words and tended to overlook the simple, colorful words that make a language strong and vivid.

A READING PROGRAM IN A HIGH SCHOOL OF SUPERIOR STUDENTS

This high school had a student body with an average I.Q. higher than that of public schools—114, as derived from a group intelligence test. The students lived in a residential, English-speaking community. The principal and the head of the English department were desirous of improving their students' reading ability.

The results of the Traxler Silent Reading Test given to grades 7 to 10 indicated a high reading level for these students in general. In every grade the school averages for the total score were higher than the test norms. The members of grade 7 showed the poorest results but were superior in comprehension. Grade 10 rate scores were all higher than the national mean. Ten times a week grade 7 had been having reading periods in which careful reading was emphasized. This emphasis upon care probably accounts for the relatively low score in rate and the higher score in comprehension for that grade. In the tenth grade it may be that pressure resulting from increased length of assignments in literature had helped to develop greater speed.

Although the school average was above the national norms, there were a number of retarded readers in the school. In all grades, from 20 to 29 per cent fell below the national norms for the grade. In total comprehension, 13.3 per cent of the seventh-grade pupils were below the seventh-grade norms, and 25.9 per cent of the tenth-grade pupils were below the norms for grade 10.

To improve the reading efficiency of all students who were not realizing their reading potentialities, the following all-school program was initiated:

1. Students, teachers, and principal worked together to recognize the difficulties and outline purposes and procedures. This cooperation was more effective than a superimposed plan, because it ensured understanding and interest on the part of all concerned.

2. The general plan emphasized vocabulary, wide reading, and reading skills needed in each subject.

3. The English teacher took a part of her period each day for students to read one exercise in *Study Type of Reading Exercises* (26), in order that they might gain ideas about efficient reading and practice reading a study type of material.

4. Every teacher diagnosed errors, noted students' reading interests, and studied students' comprehension of the subject matter studied in her class.

5. Students kept records of their reading, including the results of tests, evidence of progress made, and all voluntary reading.

6. Physical defects were checked and corrections were made.

7. Special classes for students who needed more intensive remedial work were provided.

READING IN A VOCATIONAL HIGH SCHOOL

The backgrounds of the students who attend the vocational high school vary from school to school and within a particular school. The following is a description of a typical student in one city vocational high school.

Marie is fourteen years old and of average intelligence. She lives with a grandmother, her parents, and seven brothers and sisters. Two languages are spoken in the home. Her grandmother is illiterate and her mother semiliterate. Her father reads in his native language and is engaged in skilled labor. One of the brothers works in a store as clerk and another is a machinist's helper. Her older sister is married and lives at home. The other children are still in school. There is a clannish loyalty among the members of the family and their relatives. The father is head of the house and exercises supreme authority.

Marie is friendly with her neighbors as well as with her relatives, and they have good times together. After work they all know how to relax. They sing a great deal. Much of their recreation consists of little gatherings at their respective houses, where they sing, dance, and have a grand time. The radio at home is often tuned in to musical programs. The younger brothers listen to The Lone Ranger, Superman, and other adventure programs.

Marie works in a shop two evenings a week and thus earns some money for the family, for a few clothes, for presents, and for a movie a week. She is well stocked with gadget jewelry. Within the boundaries of her family circle and her neighborhood she has seen a good deal of "life"; but she has never been outside her city or even visited other parts of the city to any extent. She is very hazy about the world and what happened in it before 1930. Her father brings home an Italian paper and her brother sometimes brings in a tabloid. If Marie has any money to spend for magazines, she buys *Look*, *Pic*, *Life*, *True Story*, or *True Confessions*. There is a library in her neighborhood, but she "never has time to go there."

At school, Marie is studying garment-machine operating. She is more interested in dressmaking, but knows that there are more jobs in machine operating. She hopes that she will find a place in a good factory and have pleasant coworkers with whom she can chat as she works. Her school program includes shopwork and subjects related to it—health education, music, social science, and English.

These subjects require considerable reading ability. In the shop courses she has to be able to read the safety rules and to apply them; to understand and follow directions, because precise interpretation is necessary for proper execution; to become familiar with the technical words peculiar to the trade; and to use reference material and library aids. In health education she needs to be able to find facts, to see relationships and draw conclusions, and to understand principles and apply them to life situations.

In related mathematics she needs the ability to interpret the exact meaning of a question or a problem in arithmetic—the computation of salary or of hourly wage, the cost of a certain amount of yardage of a dress, etc. She must be able to recognize what facts are given, to know what is to be found, to know what process should be used to reach a correct solution.

In related art she must use reference books in the library; she must skim books on the history of fashions and hair styles to find facts on a given topic.

In the course in textiles she needs to locate information in periodicals, to find facts of a technical nature, and to grasp and apply principles.

In the music course, oral reading from a book of lyrics is required.

In English the aim is (1) to enable students to read material relating to their vocation—workmen's compensation law, union rules, trade practices and trade ethics, other rulings that affect trades, informative books and articles on employment opportunities, qualifications for jobs, training for various jobs, how to get a job, and similar material; (2) to interest students in reading as a leisure-time activity; and (3) to encourage the students to read material that will help them to understand, appreciate, and work toward the realization of true democracy.

Aside from what must be done in order to meet the immediate requirements of school subjects, Marie obviously feels little need for reading. Her present recreational activities are satisfying and she is looking forward to a similar use of leisure time when she goes to work. While recognizing the apparent lack of need for reading in her life, the school is faced with the question: Shall we accept her present appraisal of reading or shall we help her to acquire reading interests and skills that will enrich her personal life and make her a better parent and citizen? If the second alternative is accepted, Marie must first become aware of her need for reading.

The feeling of need for reading was stimulated in various ways in the vocational school that Marie attended. In each subject informal tests based on the required readings were given, so that the students could see for themselves how little return they got from the time that they spent in reading. This realization of their inadequate reading ability led them to seek help in reading more efficiently. One teacher tested their efficiency in newspaper reading and aroused their interest by giving them a half hour for reading a portion of the daily newspaper and then asking those who got the most value for the time expended to report their reading methods.

Some of the periods of English class realistically resembled leisure time. Thus students obtained experiences in the enjoyable use of leisure, which, it was hoped, would carry over into their out-of-school lives. In these periods they selected literature, of the past and of contemporary life, appropriate to them.[1] From this reading they gained an understanding of people and an insight into their own problems of daily living. In their class discussions of books and articles they had read, they came to appreciate the contribution that reading can make to conversation. In their independent reading they experienced the enjoyment that books can give. For groups that especially enjoyed singing, as Marie did, poetry was introduced in the form of songs. The teacher began by asking students to name the songs that they liked best and to tell why they preferred these. They began to use the terminology of poetry—lyric, ballad, rhythm, etc.—and to find some of their favorite songs in poetry anthologies. In one class they discovered that Freneau's ode, "God save the rights of man," could be sung to the tune of "America," and it became a popular glee-club number. Choral reading was another experience particularly enjoyed by these groups.

In order that a program of this kind might be carried on, the English room was equipped as a reading laboratory, with many books covering a wide variety of interests and a wide range of difficulty— short stories, novels, plays, poems, essays, biographies, histories, newspapers, pamphlets of various kinds, and magazines dealing with current problems. Tables and comfortable chairs were provided. The room was made pleasant and gay with growing plants, hangings, pictures, exhibits of book covers, and in other ways that the students suggested. There were a few study-type exercise books and sets of drill material (see pages 335–347) for those who were having certain reading difficulties that had not been corrected by the general class procedure. A number of different practice books were provided, so that each student could select the kind of practice material that suited his particular need.

The students themselves became interested in selecting appropriate reading material. One brought in a magazine that contained a very exciting story; another contributed pamphlets that he obtained from the company where his father worked; still another brought in the catalogues of schools giving correspondence courses that he would like to take after he began to work. In this way, reading material closely related to the lives of the students was accumulated and evaluated. The bulletin board was an important feature of the reading laboratory. Clippings on personal appearance, music, fashions, and subjects related to the trades were especially interesting to trade-school students like Marie.

[1] For example, see ANZIA, YEZIERSKA, *Children of Loneliness*, and *Hunger*, for foreign-born groups; O. HENRY, *A Service of Love*, K. MANSFIELD, *A Cup of Tea*.

The shops provided an excellent laboratory for reading. Here the students first became acquainted with the objects and the processes of the trade and then naturally learned the printed symbols that were used to represent them. Thus a vocabulary in the trade subjects was built on a foundation of fact and grew up in a solid, coherent way. Since "books are tools of the trade," students learned in the shops to read illustrated operators' manuals, handbooks, and textbooks as sources of technical information, descriptions of processes and machines, and explanations. Trade catalogues familiarized them with tools, machines, and materials. They obtained instruction and practice in reading periodicals and pamphlets for latest developments and trends in the trade. One boy's attitude toward reading changed when he was asked to read the safety rules to a group of his fellow workers each morning before work. This task prompted him to buy a dictionary, learn to pronounce his words correctly, and read up on safety rules. He recognized the need for reading only when he could see what it could contribute to his safety, his job, and his salary.

Younger girls enjoyed making "book jackets"—drawing or pasting an appropriate illustration on the front of each jacket and writing a "blurb" on the flaps that were folded inside the book cover. This provided practice in finding the main idea of a book and in judicious selection of facts that would give other students an interesting and accurate bird's-eye view of its contents.

The librarian of the school, a former teacher as well as an experienced and resourceful librarian, was very skillful in making a wise choice of books for purchase and in helping the pupils who needed guidance. She set up many attractive displays in the showcases and about the room. She assembled a collection of books on aviation. At the beginning of each term she gave lessons on the use of the library, and provided references for special groups. She helped teachers make up bibliographies for particular purposes. She collected and filed a set of brief evaluations of books in the school library that had been made in English classes.

A journalism class was organized for students who showed any unusual ability in writing, and an enriched course of study was offered to those with enough ability to become teachers in trade schools or who for some other good reason wanted to continue their technical and academic training. There were also special small groups in reading for those who were so markedly retarded in reading skills that they could not profit by attendance in regular classes without receiving additional instruction and practice.

In this vocational school, where many students had never read a book, oral reading proved beneficial. One teacher began by telling the class stories and having the students tell him stories. Then, together, they began to look for the simplest adventure stories to read. There was no emphasis on competition or speed, but only on reading itself, as one source of pleasure and recreation. The students enjoyed being read to and, by listening, added to their oral vocabulary. These values seemed to justify stressing enjoyment in listening, even though some students grumbled and groaned when they had to do independent silent reading.

CHICAGO READING PROGRAM (11)

In the Chicago school system the cooperatively developed plan to coordinate the program in all schools was built on two basic principles: the "comprehensiveness of the reading activity influencing every aspect of the school curriculum, and the continuity of growth in reading" (11, page 48). Attention was given to reading, listening, speaking, and writing.

In carrying out this program, the content teachers had the major responsibility. They described the reading skills and techniques needed in their subject and in a laboratory-type reading period gave opportunity for the practical application of these skills and techniques. Students and teachers planned the program together.

The English teacher played an important part. She consulted with other teachers concerning the pupils' specific needs in other subjects and used curriculum materials in each field as practice material in reading. Systematic instruction in reading skills was given to all pupils. As an aid to teachers, special materials were prepared.[1] Emphasis was placed on sensitivity to language and on its variety and depth of meaning.

The units included orientation of students to the school through the reading of school bulletins and other sources of local information, current literature, structure and use of language, understanding of the nature of reading, nature and structure of words and practice in interpretation, location of reading material, making use of visual aids, cooperative living, basic skills of communication. One period a week was devoted to basic reading, but indirect instruction and practice in reading were given in each unit and, more directly, as the need was indicated. Students also spent some time in analyzing their personal reactions to reading.

[1] *A Handbook in Work Reading, Grades 7 and 8*, Chicago Bureau of Curriculum, Board of Education, 1943 (mimeographed); and *Aids to Reading, Grades 7 and 8*, Chicago Bureau of Curriculum, Board of Education, 1943 (mimeographed).

The newspaper—"democracy's textbook"—was extensively used as reading material. News items were read in order that future editorials might be predicted. Exercises were based largely on current material.

In the staff reading room, teachers filed their bibliographies, outlines on reading techniques, and reports on their most successful teaching methods. Many approaches were used and teachers were eager to experiment, to discuss new ideas, and to cooperate in reading activities (11).

Emphasis was placed on purposeful reading, and recreative reading was encouraged; pupils had varied opportunities to enjoy reading as a leisure-time activity. They listened to radio programs such as World of Wings, Let's Tell a Story, and Battle of Books on station WBEZ Chicago. They engaged in cooperative enterprises for Book Week. Records of each pupil's free reading were sent to the next grade, as an aid to the new teacher and as a reference for the pupil.

Coordination of the reading work in the system was of three types—coordination within each school, between a high school and its contributing elementary schools, and among the schools of one district. Within each school a reading committee made contributions to the all-school program. Teachers constructed special drills when suitable material was not available. Principals distributed helpful supervisory bulletins. For in-service education, panel discussions and demonstrations of teaching procedures were used. Teachers throughout the entire system benefited by annotated bibliographies prepared by committees, and by in-service bulletins on significant developments in the program issued by the central office.

PITTSBURGH READING PROGRAM

In the Pittsburgh public schools, some years ago, a reading expert and staff were made available to principals who requested their services. There were four types of remedial reading work—reading home rooms, reading clubs, the reading-readiness program, and clinical treatment of seriously retarded cases.

Reading home rooms or reading clubs were established in response to requests from schools. The home-room reading group met together during half the day; for the rest of the day the students were in other classes. Teachers were first told the nature of the work, so that they would not give the pupils the impression that membership in the reading rooms was undesirable. The testing program was demonstrated to the teacher. Reading tests were then given by teachers, who corrected the papers and sent profiles to the central office. There the cases that seemed to need remedial reading were selected and then further checked by judgment of the teachers. Cases for which prognosis of success was very poor were not included in the class, but some mild cases of reading inability were included to emphasize the flexibility of its membership. As pupils improved, they were returned to regular classes and others on the waiting list were allowed to enter. In some schools the quality of reading instruction in the school as a whole improved so much that the special classes were no longer necessary. Dr. Marion Monroe visited these classes and gave suggestions to the teachers on the basis of her observations.

The reading clubs were more recreational than the reading home rooms; they emphasized reading interests and recreational reading.

The third type of work was the reading-readiness program. This was tried out experimentally in certain schools and proved so successful that it was extended throughout the city. Undoubtedly a good deal of reading difficulty and emotional and social maladjustment will be prevented by forestalling failures in learning to read. Such failures usually result from formal reading instruction before the children can profit by it and from expecting a standard level of achievement for every child in the first grade.

The fourth type of work was the clinical treatment of seriously retarded readers who were referred by teachers through the principal. With the help of the teacher, the principal filled out a form requesting an examination by the reading clinic. Sometimes the mere process of answering the questions gave the principal and the teachers a clear enough picture of the problem so that they could handle it themselves. If the case was referred to the clinic, a psychological examination was given by the psychologist, a physical examination by the physician, and a reading examination by a member of the reading-clinic staff. An interview with the parent was also requested.

After all data had been gathered, a case conference was held, attended by the director of the reading clinic, the reading assistant, the psychologist, the supervisor of reading, the principal, and, whenever possible, the teacher and the home-and-school visitor. They discussed the case, and a stenographic record was made of the recommendations on which they agreed. If the principal or the teacher did not agree with a suggestion made by a specialist, it was not included. Thus the recommendations were made very practical and easy for the teacher to follow with the help of the supervisor. Recommendations varied with the situation: recommendations for a school where modern methods prevail were different from those made for a traditional school. The aim was to avoid giving any teacher a sense of insecurity by forcing him to use methods that he did not understand or that he was afraid to apply. Cases were followed up for the purpose of ascertaining which procedures were most successful with different kinds of cases.

Although at first glance this way of proceeding may seem extremely expensive, it does not appear so when it is viewed not only as a method for helping individual students, but also as a method of in-service education of principals and teachers with respect to reading problems. In fact, everyone who attends a case conference may learn from the exchange of information. Principal and teacher may learn how an expert deals with a reading difficulty, and the experts may learn from each other, besides gaining a more practical approach from the school people.

From the standpoint of general organization, this program is a model that might well be followed in other school systems. The main features are

1. A supervisor who is truly expert in the technical aspects of the field and who is also tactful and skillful

2. Intimate contact of the regular supervisor of reading with the school program and clinic work, so that he may obtain more expert knowledge and skill

3. Initial voluntary participation of principals (A school invites the specialist to work in the school.)

4. The experimental aspect (Various methods are tried in different schools and teachers are encouraged to experiment.)

5. A constructive developmental program as well as the necessary remedial and clinical work

IMPROVEMENT OF READING IN A CLASS OF COLLEGE FRESHMEN

In a college to which many students came from rural schools or from homes with foreign-language backgrounds, the freshman English course included attention to both reading and writing. The students were encouraged through instruction and practice to develop the following reading habits and skills:

1. To read widely—poetry, biography, travel, drama, essays, science, social studies, and other fields as well as fiction; periodicals and newspapers, as well as books; many authors instead of only a few favorites. A two-week unit on newspaper reading was included, during which students learned to appreciate the different styles and problems of newspaper writing and reading. The requirement of six book reviews a year, not more than two of which were fiction, pushed the student into new fields. The instructor was glad to help students in planning their voluntary reading program.

2. To read to understand and apply, not to "cover" material. This attitude toward reading was encouraged in a number of ways. Written reports on books showed the student's insight into the content of the book and the author's purpose, developed habits of synthesis and criticism, and indicated his ability to write. As a class exercise, students were frequently asked to read a short assignment. This was followed by a 10-minute test, either oral or written, which showed the student's grasp of main points and details, his ability to follow the development of the thought in the passage, his understanding of words and phrases, and his appreciation of literary quality. Instruction and practice in outlining, condensing, making abstracts, and writing précis also helped students become more careful, discriminating readers. When different forms of writing were discussed, good examples of each kind were placed in the library for students to read. Time for informal conversation on free reading was also provided. Students were urged to find out about an author so that, before reading his book, they could answer such questions as, "Is he qualified to write on this subject?" "Is he a recognized authority?" "Is he likely to be biased in some respect?" From jackets of books, on contributors' pages of periodicals, and in book reviews, students obtained information about authors. An encyclopedia and *Who's Who* supplied information about well-known writers. Students made immediate use of their reading in class discussion and written compositions, as well as in conversation outside class.

3. To read selectively, guided by one's own purpose in reading and by hints from the preface and an introductory chapter on the author's purpose and method of procedure. By this technique students learned to determine which parts to skim and which to read thoughtfully, as well as to tell how one part is related to another. They were also given practice in finding the theme, or central idea, and formulating it in a concise and useful form, and in tracing the development of the author's main ideas as they read.

4. To interpret figures of speech and other words and phrases that have overtones far removed from their simple sense meaning.

5. To increase the size and richness of one's vocabulary. Students brought up for clarification in class unfamiliar words and references to unfamiliar persons and places. They referred to the context in which the word occurred, pooled experiences with the word, and used illustrative material whenever possible. As their impressions were checked with the actual meaning or range of meaning of a word, they became aware of the fuzziness of their word knowledge and of the importance of knowing key words in order to understand a passage.

6. To improve the quality of oral reading. During the year each student read in class some selection that he thought was particularly well written. The instructor noted any oral reading difficulties and, in an individual conference, gave suggestions for overcoming them.

In this college English course the development of reading interests and skills was the major objective. The students were taught how to read and what to read. In addition to their reading and writing experiences as a class, the students also worked with the instructor individually to develop independence in building better patterns of reading, to correct poor habits of reading, and to acquire more effective reading methods.

IMPROVEMENT OF READING AT THE UNIVERSITY OF MINNESOTA (29)

At the University of Minnesota, as elsewhere, students were found to vary greatly in reading proficiency. Students suspected of having poor reading skills were referred to the reading clinic from various sources on the campus, and the person who made the referral was kept informed of the student's progress during the period of training. Reported deficiencies were checked in the clinic by the use of various standardized tests, by case study procedures, and by careful observation of the student in reading and study situations. On the basis of this diagnosis of difficulties, a tentative remedial program was set up in conference with the student. The plan for remedial work and any new information that became available were reviewed with the student once a week, and modifications and suggestions were made according to his progress.

Two copies of this plan were made. The instructor kept one copy in her confidential file. On this copy she made notes concerning the student's progress. In addition, she kept a careful anecdotal record of his day-to-day behavior in the clinic. The other copy served as the student's guide and was kept in an open file, where the student could have access to it whenever he needed it for reference. Remedial exercises were filed in open bins in the clinic. The student used these exercises according to the plan for remedial work that was recorded on the plan sheet. In many cases, special exercises were constructed to meet the individual needs of students. These were made in standard form and put into the open bins. The student recorded on his copy of the plan sheet his estimate of his progress in the clinical work. Thus he was encouraged to take responsibility for his own progress in reading.

As soon as possible the student was transferred from individual work in conference with the instructor to semi-individual work with other students in the clinic. At all times enough instructors and assistants were available in the clinic to give the students any help that they needed and to review their work as they progressed.

Progress in the clinic was evaluated on the basis of the weekly review of day-to-day remedial work and periodic checking with standardized tests. There was no standard length of time a student had to stay in the clinic. Each was released from his work there by mutual agreement between him and the instructor.

As soon as the student demonstrated that he had acquired adequate essential reading skills, remedial work was based to some extent on course assignments. This helped to ensure the transfer of skills learned in the clinic to college assignments. Actual course assignments were not used immediately because of the possibility that the length or difficulty of such assignments had already created an adverse mental set. It seemed better to determine what the student could do on controlled material rather than on assignments for which he might have inadequate background or which might be too difficult for him with his actual reading skills.

The clinic instructor and the student together determined the best time for transferring to course material. At this time the student conferred with his instructors, told them what he was doing in the reading clinic, and asked for suggestions concerning application of these techniques to course assignments. In this way the instructors felt that they had a part in the student's progress and also became acquainted with techniques used in the reading clinic. Occasionally they discussed some of the reading techniques in their classes.

IMPROVEMENT OF READING AT HIRAM COLLEGE

At Hiram College, Hiram, Ohio, a utility course for college freshmen called "English Conference" has been offered for several years (16). It was developed the first year by Dr. Constance McCullough, and combined work in English, counseling, and specific attention to the improvement of reading. The English Conference group constituted the lowest 40 per cent of the entering freshman class, judged on the basis of the Purdue English Placement Test, the Iowa Silent Reading Test, and an autobiographical essay. The classwork during the first 6 weeks consisted of special instruction focused on the students' immediate needs in their intensive courses. At the end of this initial procedure, the remaining hours of the class were spent in impromptu writing or discussion of written material on topics assigned in other classes and in reading exercises of the study type that provided practice in reading more rapidly, grasping the main ideas, and getting the pattern of the author's thought. In the second semester the class was divided into three groups—a high-comprehension group, a low-comprehension group, and a group whose grammar and mechanics were generally poor. All three groups engaged in a widely varied reading program; each student read a book of his own choice each week. In the first part of the course there were weekly individual conferences—half-hour periods of work with the instructor. During the second semester conferences were held only with students who appeared to have special need of individual work. On the Purdue English Placement Test the average percentile rose from the 36th percentile in September to the 67th percentile in December. The mean score on comprehension in the Iowa Silent Reading Test was raised from 124.6 in September to 132.7 in December, and to 156.3 in May. Thus a total gain of 1½ to 2 years, as measured by the Iowa Silent Reading Test, was secured.

IMPROVEMENT OF READING AT HARVARD COLLEGE (3, 5)

Since 1938 Dearborn and his associates have been experimenting with a remedial reading program that has now become an elective on the part of many freshmen. At first the students were selected for remedial work on the basis of low scores on the scholastic aptitude test; later all freshmen were given a more extensive battery of reading tests and those in the lowest fifth were invited to join the remedial reading group. Six to eight weeks of training brought marked gains in speed, as measured by reading tests, and in words read per minute, as judged by photographic records. At the time of writing, the course is being revised and a report may be forthcoming shortly on the improvements made from the standpoint of materials and methods.

In the third year, 1940–1941, a battery of reading tests, requiring 1½ hours to administer, was given to 1,250 students at Harvard and Radcliffe. The tests used were the Nelson-Denny Reading Test for Colleges and Senior High Schools, the comprehension part of the Cooperative Reading Comprehension Test C2, and the rate test of the Iowa Silent Reading Test. The average total Nelson-Denny score for this group of freshmen was at the 96th percentile. Those ranking in the lowest 20 per cent of the class were invited to attend the remedial classes.

Attendance was voluntary and "carried with it an extra charge and no college credit" (5, page 673). The classes met for three 50-minute periods a week for 6 weeks—18 meetings in all—at 5 P.M., the only time available for this purpose.

During the period of training, the class was given short explanations and hints on reading speed, the factors that condition reading speed, the way to discriminate between main ideas and details, and the psychology of reading. Three types of material were used—the reading films, the reading manual, and speeded reading material. At the beginning of each period one of the films was shown. At first it was run at the rate of 150 words a minute; the speed was increased to 400 words a minute in the last session. The film was followed by a test of comprehension, consisting of 10 multiple-choice questions on its content. The students next read a section of the manual of corrective reading exercises, which was divided into three subject-matter divisions: history, English, and science. The content was similar to what the college student is expected to read. The exercises stressed two types of ability, the ability to draw inferences or conclusions and the ability to use the data presented to solve problems (30). The students recorded the time of reading; instructors occasionally checked their comprehension of the material by asking them to write a summary or to give a headline or a title. The usual daily assignment consisted of three of the selections in the manual.

This group work, related closely to the reading required in college courses, was supplemented by individual conferences concerning the personal problems of the students, as well as their reading and study problems. When difficulty with a course was uncovered, "the student's method of doing assignments was analyzed, and a superior method was discussed, and, in some cases, demonstrated" (5, page 676).

"In summary, it may be said that in general the Harvard remedial group profited markedly from the remedial sessions." Not much gain on the Nelson-Denny test could be expected, because this group initially rated so near the top.

IMPROVEMENT OF READING AT COLUMBIA COLLEGE

The Columbia College reading program, initiated by Dean Hawkes about 10 years ago, has been carried on by four persons in succession— Mrs. Florence C. Rose, Dr. Margaret Martin Conant, Mrs. Elizabeth Samuels Bell, and Mrs. Paul Cherrington. Each was employed by the college on a half-time basis. Although each developed the work in her own way, the main features, which will be described here, have persisted throughout the 10-year period.

Students needing help in reading were selected at the beginning of each term on the basis of test scores, faculty judgment, and marks for the previous term. The Cooperative Reading Test and the Cooperative Test of Literary Appreciation revealed the poor readers. Those who had a total score below the twenty-fifth percentile of the Cooperative Reading Test, or who were low in some specific aspect of reading measured by any of the other tests used, constituted the initial list. To these the dean sent a letter telling them that a remedial reading service was available free of charge and that they had been selected on the basis of their test scores as eligible for this service. In the initial meetings the worker explained the nature of the service, stressing the fact that it was voluntary but that attendance should be maintained once students had started the course.

After the mid-term examinations the dean sent letters to instructors asking them to recommend students who, according to their judgment, should have instruction in reading. As the worker's time was limited, she selected those who seemed most eager to have help.

After the first meeting, time was arranged for further group testing and for discussing the tests. The worker explained the scores and the students studied the reading passages to ascertain what kind of errors they had made. From this discussion the worker obtained some idea of their difficulties and of the extent of their confusion.

Time was then scheduled for two 45-minute periods a week, in which students met in small groups, and a half-hour period once or twice a week for individual conferences. The use of two seminar rooms next to the library, each of which seated about eight students, proved to be the best arrangement.

A few students, after gaining sufficient proficiency, left before the end of the semester, while others continued the work into or through the second semester.

The worker had access to cumulative personnel records in the dean's office, as well as to the admission and test data in the individual students' folders in the registrar's office. If the student showed signs of visual defects, he could have a thorough eye examination at the eye clinic; if the need for additional tests was indicated, these could be obtained from the Columbia Testing Bureau. Scores on the tests given in the fundamental orientation course that forms the core of the freshman program could be obtained from the instructors.

Very few of the students had serious difficulties in the mechanics of reading. Their problem was one of adjustment to college reading requirements. Many of them had been able to meet high-school scholastic requirements with a minimum of reading, but when they first began at college they were faced with an extremely difficult reading program. For example, they had a humanities course meeting four times a week, in which Marcus Aurelius' *Meditations*, Plato, and other erudite authors were discussed. Even the textbooks in the course were difficult. These boys just out of high school had no foothold in experience that enabled them to grasp many of the abstract ideas presented. They lacked general cultural background.

After they had worked a while in the remedial group, their needs became even more apparent. They needed a reorientation toward study in general, an appreciation of the value of reading to them personally, a recognition of the relation of the classics to present conditions.   They needed to take a creative interest in their reading rather than merely to cover one assignment after another.   They needed to learn to recognize and remember the important points instead of getting bogged down in details.   Most of the students had little idea of how to organize their thinking.   They took too many notes.   They had no idea of how a book is organized, of using the table of contents, or of looking for the author's pattern of thought. Some had special problems of vocabulary.   Some had personality difficulties—emotional blocks that interfered with concentration, feelings of insecurity, and lack of self-confidence that colored all their college activities.

The worker tried to meet these needs individually and in small groups.   To supply background in the courses, she obtained the cooperation of the librarians in compiling a special reading list of simpler books giving information about the life and times and contributions of the men they were studying.   For example, when the students were reading Vergil the worker gave each member of the small group 25 minutes to obtain as much information as possible from one of these easier reference books.   She then allowed them 5 minutes more for organizing their notes, after which each presented the facts that he had gained to the other members of the group.

At the beginning of each period, the worker gave the students one exercise in the *Study Type of Reading Exercises* (26) and timed them on the reading.   She used different types of tests of comprehension, depending upon the needs of the group—outline, summary, and essay-type questions, and questions of the short-answer type.   The students, who kept records of their time for each exercise and made their own graphs based on the number of words read per minute, usually were able to explain the vagaries of their speed.   After doing seven or eight exercises, they sometimes turned back to the first and demonstrated to their own satisfaction that they would never again read it so slowly as they had done the first time.

To orient the students to reading and study methods in general, the worker asked them to describe their methods in studying an assignment.   Then she gave them 5 minutes for looking over the pamphlet *How to Read Rapidly and Well* (32), to see how many ideas applicable to themselves they could find.   They discussed the most important points in this pamphlet and considered how to incorporate them into their own reading and study program.   During the next few periods the worker used the students' assignments as practice material.   She asked what the title of a particular chapter meant to them, what they thought the author was going to discuss, what the relation of this chapter was to others so far as they could judge by the table of contents. They spent 5 to 10 minutes finding out what the author was trying to do and getting an idea of the whole structure. After the reading, the group discussed their impressions of the content, raised questions that they thought the assignment would answer, and told how the reading was related to their previous knowledge. Practice in outlining was gained in this connection. The students who had been most successful in getting an accurate impression described their methods of reading. Frequently one member would raise a question and start a lively discussion of the author's point of view. The whole group needed this practice in presenting points orally and in logical form.

Magazine articles were used for the same purpose, and here the students went from a general survey to a rather detailed discussion of the author's style and of his method of organizing his thoughts.

To increase their ability for finding the important ideas in an article or a book, they made a more intensive study of the paragraph —what its main point was, how that main point was related to the previous paragraph, and what were the different types of paragraphs. In this unit the worker used *Writing Good English* (18) and *College Reading Skills* (15).

From the study of paragraphs they turned to specific sentences and their relation to the main topic of the paragraph. They watched for antecedents and for shifts from one group of sentences to another. All the students became more aware of transitional phrases.

If some members of the group finished their reading before the others were ready to discuss the given assignment, they made use of the time by examining especially interesting newspaper clippings for which appropriate comprehension questions had been prepared. These clippings covered a number of areas—drama, science, sports, aviation, Latin America, the Far East, Washington politics, United States foreign policies—and frequently stimulated students to read further along similar lines.

Still using their assignments as practice material, the students studied difficult and unfamiliar words as these were encountered, approaching the meaning of each word through the context. A little book, *Twelve Ways to Build a Vocabulary* (9), proved useful in stimulating the use of precise words in place of blanket terms such as "things."

These periods were kept flexible and were constantly adapted to the various needs and interests of the students, who shared with one another methods that proved successful and summed up the main points of every extended discussion.

In the individual conferences the aim was to treat each case as an individual problem and to deal not so much with a "reading difficulty" as with a "person who had a reading difficulty." These chats with individual students were the most revealing part of the work. The worker did as little talking as possible and the student was encouraged to talk as much as he could or would. He usually showed that something was bothering him—loneliness, inability to make friends, homesickness, the feeling that the challenge of college was too much for him, relations with girls. Usually the student talked casually for about 15 minutes, and then settled down to the necessary study and reading. During the talk the worker usually could catch glimpses of the student's family relationships and general attitudes—the attitudes of the family toward him; his attitude toward college, the war, girls, sports, teachers, work, vocation.

Often the student said at the end of the conference that he had needed someone to talk to. The person who carries on this kind of work is privileged in that respect; students often feel that they cannot talk so freely to a professor, partly because the professor is involved in their success in college, and partly because they realize that they cannot expect him to give individual attention to each of his many students. The worker frequently asked a student how well he had done in the weekly quiz and how he felt about it. Part of the conference time was spent on study of the next day's assignment. For example, if the student had an assignment in reading one of the novels for the humanities course, the worker read a bit with him, discussed the story, the characters, the style, and its relation to the present day. By making a resourceful use of the materials on which the student was engaged, the worker could find out about his reading method, compare it with her own, and discuss with him how they both might improve their methods. In the individual conferences it was possible to establish a relation of warm acceptance of the student (he had enough mentors, as it was) and to give him undivided attention as long as he needed it.

Cooperation with the staff was invaluable. Whenever it was possible, the worker met instructors or advisers and they discussed each case, exchanging information and developing plans. Professors who were interested kept sending their difficult cases to the worker and otherwise cooperated with her.

At the end of the semester the worker gave a second form of the initial reading test. The results of this, plus the comments of the students themselves, their rate-of-reading graphs, and the day-by-day outlines that they had made supplied one basis for the evaluation of the work. Another basis was the students' classwork—oral reports and discussion; evidences of improved organization, comprehension, and word knowledge; better methods of reading and better attitudes toward reading and study; course marks; and other indications of progress noticed by instructors. The worker kept a diary account of the day-by-day group work and a record of the individual students. At the end of each semester she filed in the dean's office a briefer report on each student.

CONCLUDING STATEMENTS

These descriptive accounts illustrate various ways in which different persons have approached actual school and college reading problems. Some have used the environmental approach—placing suitable books where they are easily accessible and creating a school environment that makes improvement in reading desirable and necessary. Others have employed analytical methods—using tests, observation, or other means of detecting reading difficulties, which they then proceed to correct. Others have approached the reading problem through improved teaching, especially in English classes, but ideally in every subject. Still others have scheduled time for reading and have organized special classes for instruction and practice in it. A few have made the improvement of reading part of the counseling program. In relatively few cases, specialists in reading have been employed to organize and supervise the total school program and to give clinical treatment to complex reading cases. Seldom is any one approach used alone; most of the accounts that have been given show a combination of two or more methods.

Varied as the approaches are, the best procedures have certain principles in common:

1. The student should feel a need for improving his reading and take responsibility for making and carrying out an appropriate individual program for improvement.

2. The need for learning to read more effectively arises most naturally out of interesting and valuable school and home activities and out of vital interests of individual students. Adjustment should be made in the total school program for needed instruction and practice in reading.

3. Difficulties that are interfering with a student's reading efficiency must be discovered and specific steps must be taken to correct them.

4. Each class is a reading laboratory, in which the reading attitudes, interests, and abilities required for success in the subject should be developed and suitable reading materials made easily accessible.

5. Special instruction and practice in reading, to be functional, must be geared into the daily reading jobs that individuals have to do or ought to do.

All these principles are important.   All should be incorporated into an adequate reading program.   The tendency has been to swing from one extreme to another—to emphasize interest alone or to overemphasize drill unrelated to vital interests; to neglect diagnosis almost wholly or to spend so much time on diagnosis that none was left for remedial work; to stress a developmental program, ignoring the serious reading difficulties of individuals, or to focus attention on problem cases to the neglect of preventive work.

To avoid these extremes and to build a sound and adequate program, the person interested in the improvement of reading needs a thorough understanding of the nature of reading, of conditions that interfere with good reading development, and of the gain in reading skill that may be expected during elementary, high-school, and college years.   In the following chapters these aspects of reading will be presented more fully and systematically.

References

1. ADAM, HARVEY, "Reading Interests of Boys in a Vocational High School," *High Points*, Vol. 12, pp. 34–38, April, 1940.

2. BARRY, LINDA, and MARJORIE PRATT, "A Remedial-reading Program in a Public High School," *School Review*, Vol. 45, pp. 17–27, January, 1937.

3. BOND, ELDEN A., "The Yale-Harvard Freshman Speed-reading Experiment," *School and Society*, Vol. 54, pp. 107–111, Aug. 16, 1941.

4. Committee on Fundamentals of the North Central Association of Secondary Schools and Colleges, Subcommittee on Reading (Clarence E. Blume, chairman), *Attacking Reading Problems in Secondary Schools*, North Central Association of Colleges and Secondary Schools, 1944, 59 pp.

5. DEARBORN, WALTER F., and S. VINCENT WILKING, "Improving the Reading of College Freshmen," *School Review*, Vol. 49, pp. 668–778, November, 1941.

6. FADIMAN, CLIFTON, *Reading I've Liked*, Simon and Schuster, Inc., New York, 1941, lxiv + 908 pp.

7. FLEMMING, CECILE WHITE, and GRACE L. ALDRICH, "The Development of Study Skills and Work Habits in the Horace Mann School," *Teachers College Record*, Vol. 44, pp. 433–448, March, 1943.

8. GATES, ARTHUR I., and MIRIAM C. PRITCHARD, *Teaching Reading to Slow-learning Pupils*, Bureau of Publications, Teachers College, Columbia University, New York, 1942, 65 pp.

9. HART, ARCHIBALD, *Twelve Ways to Build a Vocabulary*, E. P. Dutton & Company, Inc., New York, 1940, 183 pp.

10. HUDSON, JESS S., "Reading Readiness in Intermediate Grades," *Elementary English Review*, Vol. 19, pp. 134–137, April, 1942.

11. JOHNSON, WILLIAM H., "Our Chicago Developmental Reading Program in Operation," *Elementary English Review*, Vol. 21, pp. 47–53, February, 1944.

12. KOTTMEYER, WILLIAM: "Improving Reading Instruction in the St. Louis Schools," *Elementary School Journal*, Vol. 45, pp. 33–38, September, 1944.

13. KULLER, RUTH, "Occupational Literature for Pupils Deficient in Reading Ability," *Occupations*, Vol. 17, pp. 527–529, March, 1939.

14. McCallister, J. M., "College Instruction in Reading," *Phi Delta Kappan*, Vol. 24, pp. 311–313, April, 1942.
15. McCullough, Constance M., *College Reading Skills*, Western Reserve University Bookstore, Cleveland, Ohio, 1941, v + 60 pp.
16. McCullough, Constance, M., "Proposing an Alternative Miracle," *College English, Vol.* 1, pp. 504–512, March, 1940.
17. National Education Association, Research Division, "Better Reading Instruction," *Research Bulletin of the National Education Association*, Vol. 13, pp. 273–325, November, 1935.
18. Perrin, Porter G., and F. E. Ward, *Writing Good English*, Scott, Foresman and Company, Chicago, 1940.
19. Rasche, William R., "The Work of the Milwaukee Vocational School among Poor Readers," in *Adapting Reading Programs to Wartime Needs* (William S. Gray, editor), pp. 253–257, University of Chicago Press, Chicago, 1943.
20. "Reading and Child Growth," *Elementary English Review*, Vol. 21, pp. 41–78, February, 1944.
21. Richter, Carlton E., and F. W. Parr, "Remedial Reading Instruction in Oregon Secondary Schools," *School Review*, Vol. 50, pp. 368–380, May, 1942.
22. Salisbury, Rachel, *Better Work Habits in Composition*, Scott, Foresman and Company, Chicago, 1935, xviii + 203 pp.
23. Simpson, Ray G., "The Reading Laboratory as a Service Unit in College," *School and Society*, Vol. 55, pp. 621–623, May 30, 1942.
24. Strang, Ruth, "Developing Reading Potentialities of High School Students," *Teachers College Record*, Vol. 43, pp. 468–488, March, 1942.
25. Strang, Ruth, *Problems in the Improvement of Reading in High School and College*, 2d ed., The Science Press Printing Company, Lancaster, Pa., 1940, 423 pp.
26. Strang, Ruth, *Study Type of Reading Exercises*, Bureau of Publications, Teachers College, Columbia University, New York, 1935, 100 pp.
27. Tinker, Miles A., "Recent Trends in Reading Instruction," *Journal of Educational Research*, Vol. 36, pp. 468–480, February, 1943.
28. Triggs, Frances Oralind, *Improve Your Reading*, A Manual of Remedial Reading Exercises, University of Minnesota Press, Minneapolis, 1942, 127 pp.
29. Triggs, Frances Oralind, *Remedial Reading*, The Diagnosis and Correction of Reading Difficulties at the College Level, University of Minnesota Press, Minneapolis, 1943, viii + 219 pp.
30. Wilking, S. Vincent, "The Improvement of Reading Ability in College," *Education*, Vol. 62, pp. 27–31, September, 1941.
31. Wittenborn, John Richard, "Classes in Remedial Reading and Study Habits," *Journal of Educational Research*, Vol. 37, pp. 571–586, April, 1944.
32. Wrenn, C. Gilbert, and Luella Cole, *How to Read Rapidly and Well*, Stanford University Press, Stanford University, Calif., 1935, 16 pp.

CHAPTER II

THE NATURE OF READING

I should like to get perspective on this problem of reading—to see it "steadily and whole," instead of piecemeal. I should like to see more clearly its relation to personality development, to social and civic relationships, and to the everyday lives of my pupils. Is reading really important for them and, if it is, how can I help them realize its importance?

It was a teacher of reading who thus expressed his desire to acquire a knowledge of the purpose and nature of reading, as well as of procedures successfully employed in other institutions.

Reading may be viewed in different ways. It may be described as a means to an end; as a form of experience, which itself depends on previous experience; as an avenue of communication; as a process of interpretation of meaning. Reading may also be explained in terms of psychological theory; it may be analyzed into its constituent elements; and it may be studied with reference to related factors. In this chapter, reading will be viewed in these seven ways.

READING AS A MEANS TO AN END: THE SOCIOLOGY OF READING

Reading is an avenue of learning, a tool, a means to an end. Even recreational or leisure-time reading contributes more than immediate pleasure; it may also give the abiding satisfaction that comes through reflection on what one has read. If reading, then, is a means of reaching a goal, the end or goal, to a considerable extent, determines the nature of the process. As Walter de la Mare said, "Reading may be one of life's inexhaustible pleasures and blessings, but may also become mere habit, an escape from thinking, or a drug."

Effective reading is purposeful. It has personal and social values. It enables a person to "meet the practical needs of life more effectively"—to find his way around, to learn how to make and to do things, to solve daily problems. Reading should serve each person according to his needs. Few persons are interested in reading, per se; the majority of boys and girls want to read about things that are vital to them—animals, model airplanes, radio, electricity, careers. A farm boy may read and comprehend and apply pamphlets on raising cows, on soil and fertilizer, and on how to build a radio, and yet be in a remedial reading class in school. A city boy brought out armfuls of books on aviation to show a visitor and talked intelligently and enthusiastically about them. When she was leaving, he said with a grin, "You know, Miss Jones, I'm supposed to be a nonreader."

The need of high-school students for reading may be illustrated by the following analysis made by a teacher:[1]

The boys and girls of the ninth grade find a good many demands made upon them in the field of reading. To begin with, they could scarcely have reached the last year of junior high school without some proficiency in it. Those who have been unable to master any degree of skill usually drop out after their eighth year of school, when state law no longer makes attendance compulsory. Those who remain in school will vary in ability and skill, but all of them discover certain uses for reading both in activities outside of school and in school. A partial list of the reading skills they need follows:

1. Every young citizen is expected to be able to fill out certain blanks for information. These include employment forms, school information blanks, government questionnaires, post office forms, and the like; and often-times the adults of the family, unable to read or write the English language, ask their children's help with other more complicated forms. Without adequate skill in the interpretation of meaning, these tasks cannot be satisfactorily performed.

2. In these days a good deal of necessary information comes in the form of pamphlets, newspaper articles, and printed material. For instance, when in our part of the country aliens of certain nationalities—Japanese, German, Italian—had to observe the curfew laws, notices were given through printed materials. During our blackout period, regulations, violations of which were punishable by law, were printed in the newspapers. More than one family became involved because of inability to understand, and therefore to comply. The announcement came out last fall that boys and girls could be excused from two weeks of school if they would work on the farms and would fulfill certain stated requirements as given in printed directions. There are literally scores of such everyday needs calling for an ability to read and understand directions.

3. I have often wondered how visitors to New York who do not understand the numerous signs of direction in the Times Square subway station find their way around. In our part of the country boys and girls are expected to be able to read simple road signs, bus signs, danger signals, and other directions to carry on normal living. For a motorist a road map is a convenience only if he can interpret it. Even the menu cards in the restaurants and drugstores demand a certain amount of reading ability.

4. In school, of course, the demands upon students' reading ability increase. For their social science classes, they must be able to read and interpret not only their textbooks, but newspaper and magazine information, encyclopedias, and supplementary books. Part of their course is centered on a school news-

[1] Contributed by Mrs. Amy Dahlgren Fenner, formerly teacher and librarian in McCarver Junior High School, Tacoma, Wash.

paper review.   Failure in reading would mean failure in fulfilling minimum requirements.

5. In science, they are expected to read even more difficult factual material. Since science is a required course for the majority, it is important that they have the necessary reading skill.

6. In English, students need the skill to do extensive outside reading as well as the required class selections.   Even for simple daily tests and exercises in grammar or composition, reading is essential.   While the English class tries to improve reading skill, it demands to a degree a previous mastery of that skill, without which a pupil is lost.

7. Typewriting involves comprehension of material to be typed.   Music demands ability to read and interpret the words.   Mechanical drawing and woodwork shop require a certain familiarity with specifications made in printed form.   There is scarcely a subject in the curriculum, unless it be gym or art, in which there is not a daily need of reading skill.

8. The young boy or girl in our school has presented to him a rich field of leisure activity if he can read with enjoyment and proficiency.   But books, magazines, and newspapers that give him a glimpse into other worlds are of value only if he can make use of them.   Although we must frankly admit that he may not wish to take advantage of this world, it is open to him if he can read.   If he does not, he knows he is missing something other boys and girls find.   To me, this is one of the most potent inducements to strive to teach reading to our boys and girls.   Its delights are a help in keeping them from undesirable leisure activity and in giving purpose, direction, and inspiration to their lives.

The world of books is expanding each year.   The annual issue of new books and new editions of old books has increased from two thousand in 1880 to about ten thousand at the present time.   More than two thousand daily newspapers are published in the United States. In order to keep up with even a small part of the thinking that is going on in the world today, a person needs to read rapidly, efficiently, and with selective judgment.

When adolescents leave school, they usually engage in work that requires varying amounts of reading.   A young person doing routine mechanical work in a factory sees little need for reading anything beyond safety signs, rules, and other regulations.   For these purposes a fourth-grade level of reading ability would suffice.   This level of reading ability has been required by some employers who have traced accidents to employees' failure to read and comprehend signs and directions relating to safety.   In the skilled trades considerable reading is desirable, if not necessary, for the best quality of work.

In business some successful persons read little, relying instead on observation and personal contacts to obtain new ideas.   Others use reading as a means of keeping one jump ahead of present practice.

The professions, of course, all require much reading during the period of preparation, as well as continued reading after graduation, if one is to keep pace with new developments. Too often administrators and teachers do not demonstrate in their own lives the value of a program of efficient reading (55). After they have obtained their degrees, they do not pursue any systematic course of professional reading. Persons in law, engineering, and medicine say that reading is of the utmost importance in their fields and that a professional person cannot be successful if he does not keep up to date. For a few professions, such as library work, writing, and bibliographical research work, extensive reading is absolutely essential.

Thus in some vocations the importance of reading is close to zero, while in others it is close to 100 per cent. Among the values of reading recognized by persons in different vocations, are the following:

To keep up with trends and developments in their field
To acquire a general background in their field and in related world conditions
To gain specific knowledge needed in their work and suggestions concerning efficient methods of doing work
To help in establishing social and business contacts
To enable them to do their day's work, which consists chiefly of reading

Reading is important for the leisure of life, no less than for the work of life; it contributes to personal as well as to professional growth; it helps to make life richer and more meaningful. It provides pleasure and relaxation in leisure time. Reading is a form of experience through which horizons may be expanded and personality may be developed. This personal aspect of reading (treated more fully on pages 37–38 and 60–61) is succinctly summarized in the following quotation (72, page 3):

. . . Language [is] . . . an indispensable, potent, but highly fluid set of symbols by which human beings mentally put their feelings and experiences in order, get and keep in touch with other human beings, and build up new and clearer understanding of the world around them.

In the discharge of his civic responsibilities, the individual depends on the impressions he receives from conversation, newspapers, magazines, books, radio, motion pictures. If the citizen is to make sound judgments he must discern the true meaning of the words that he hears and reads and of the pictures that he sees. Failure to discriminate fact from opinion and to detect and resist subtle influences exerted on him by pressure groups makes him the victim of persons who are seeking their own advancement or the advancement of their group rather than the welfare of all. Effective reading is a weapon to use against exploitation and manipulation.

The role of words in shaping the future is cogently expressed in these words (60, p. 226):

Where we don't put our problems properly into words—and don't have those words truly understood by a large body of our fellow citizens—we are almost sure to be in serious trouble as we face the future. [Democracy demands that we] find words to think with, words to tell others with, words to help shape America's destiny with.

Democracy requires a foundation of widespread knowledge; it cannot succeed when the people are ignorant and cannot or will not think for themselves. The draft figures revealed previously unrecognized ignorance—433,000 men otherwise eligible for service in the Army who could not meet the Army's literacy requirement. Of these, at least 250,000 could be classified as educational deficiencies. A much larger number of persons fall short of an adequate, accurate comprehension of what they read, or habitually distort the author's meaning to make it conform to their prejudices.

Genuine literacy is important to international as well as to national understanding and unity. Reading, radio, motion pictures, and personal contacts may become instruments by means of which peoples learn about one another—their wisdom, their culture, and their aspirations. A just and lasting peace depends upon the universal communication of a new conception of greatness—greatness through cooperation and good will rather than through competition and power. To be sure, every avenue of communication should be employed to build this ideal of personal and national greatness. But communication through the reading of printed material will continue to reinforce and supplement all other means of communication. By reading, the student will become cognizant of historical trends and better able to take advantage of them. By reading, the student will discover that certain principles are common to and accepted by all nations, races, and religions. By reading, the student will be brought into contact with current thinking the world over. Thus if he reads selectively and critically, he will be able to act on sound thinking rather than be swayed by a self-seeking minority. It is obvious that reading is a means toward the realization of the most highly important personal and social goals.

Sometimes it is profitable for teachers, as public servants, to review the specific purposes for which reading is taught. To make such a review sharpens one's awareness of the value of certain current practices and emphases, reinforces arguments for the inclusion of neglected areas. Purposes divorced from an evaluation of practice are meaningless; but practice divorced from a consciousness of purposes is equally meaningless. The following list of purposes for which the public is justified in spending money should be read with current practice in mind and with a view to revision of practice where it seems necessary. Reading instruction should help the student

1. To understand signs essential to everyday living
2. To follow printed directions and learn how to make and to do things
3. To read and interpret maps, charts, graphs, and other pictorial material
4. To evaluate facts, to see relationships, to distinguish between fact and opinion, to recognize distortions of the truth
5. To promote maximum efficiency in reading by developing his ability to determine his purpose in reading a given piece of material, and the method appropriate to accomplishing it
6. To follow and to appraise the logic of printed argument
7. To feel the impetus to make comparisons and draw inferences and conclusions, and to feel the stimulation to think further on a subject
8. To increase his vocational efficiency through skillful reading of material pertaining to that vocation
9. To enrich his personal living by making available the contribution of books to his understanding and appreciation of himself and other persons in an ever-shrinking world
10. To gain pleasure and relaxation in leisure time and to obtain content for intelligent conversation
11. To extend the influence of the ideas contained in books through capable oral reading
12. To share a common reading heritage that will promote national unity through understanding, shared purposes, and a common social philosophy
13. To keep informed concerning current events and points of view
14. To understand printed matter important to local, national, state, and international citizenship

READING AND EXPERIENCE

Reading depends on experience. Words become meaningful to us through our experience. If a word has no roots in our experience, it must be translated into other words that anchor it to realities with which we are familiar. For example, to a person who has never been on a farm, hens might be described as "birds about the size of your head that don't fly very well" (73). Everyone has "wells of meaning" into which he dips when he is confronted with a word.

Part of the teacher's responsibility in the teaching of reading is to foster, broaden, and elevate the personal interests and experiences of his students. He will provide situations that demand effective read-

ing. He will try to find books that relate to individuals' experiences
and that meet some need in their lives. The more the student reads
in order to carry on some activity in which he is interested, the more
clearly he will see the meaning and use of reading in his daily life.

Reading not only depends on experience; it is a form of experience.
Through reading, a person "gets at the realities the writer is attempting
to set forth." It is a creative act. Just as the writer creates a structure of thought, so the reader re-creates for himself the pattern of
thought in any passage. As early as 1916 Kerfoot (34, page 5) wrote,
"Reading, so far from being a receptive act, is a creative process."

Using his own experience as a point of departure, the reader reaches
out to new ideas presented by the author. Thus reading is a means of
extending experience, enabling a person to transcend the limitations
of time and space. As Stevenson said, "Reading takes us out of our
country and ourselves." Through this vicarious experience, the
reader learns. According to Everett Dean Martin, "Anyone who can
learn from life can learn from books."

Reading is an aid to the organizing of experience. The mind,
facing experience, seeks appropriate verbal symbols and organizes
experience around them. Thus patterns of words representing experience form the structure of the individual mind and of civilization.
The cultural level of a people and the quality of the books that they
produce are dependent upon the development of their verbal symbols.

READING AND COMMUNICATION

Reading as communication has two sides—the receiving end and
the transmitting end. The receiving end involves the process of
getting the thought that the author wanted to convey; the transmitting
end involves sharing that thought with others. From the standpoint
of communication, a reader is concerned with how the author expresses
his thoughts, why the author says things in a certain way, and how
he himself can share the author's ideas with others. In order to
convey the correct meaning, a word cannot mean one thing to the
speaker and another thing to the listener. In order for communication to take place, the speaker and the listener must agree on the
meaning of key words.

The improvement of communication from the receiving end
involves the reading process as it is commonly understood. In order
to communicate, one must first comprehend. Thus to have instruction
and practice in comprehending the author's true pattern of thought
is basic to communication.

In many schools and colleges much more attention has been given to measuring students' ability to take in ideas than to ascertaining their ability to communicate with others. The standardized tests of silent reading in common use are, on the whole, poor measures of reading in order to communicate. More valuable for this purpose are informal tests, constructed with composition-type exercises, that encourage communication through written responses. Oral responses to the question, What did the author say? are excellent means of appraising a student's ability to communicate the author's thought in a face-to-face situation.

A procedure for developing this end of the communication process is to take dictaphone or shorthand records of the student's first attempts to communicate to another person what he has gained from reading a passage, and then to have him listen to what he has said and revise it. More evidence should be obtained as to the functioning of reading in students' casual conversation, in their discussion, in oral reports by individuals and by committees, in written reports, and in composition-type examinations. These end results of reading should be carefully evaluated and the findings should be used in the improvement of the transmitting end of communication through reading.

READING AS INTERPRETATION OF MEANING

The present emphasis on semantics—the science of meaning—is closely related to the experience aspect of reading. The word "semantics" is derived from the Greek *semantikos*, "significant," "pertaining to meaning." Psychologically, "semantics" may be described as "an awareness of how words work for us." General semantics has been defined as "the study of word-fact relations."[1]

Direct experience is nonverbal; language is what we say about our experience. A word is never the object, the action, or the event; it is never even a perfect substitute for an object or an action. At best, it can only represent the object, never describe it completely. Consequently, all our writing and speech are abstractions; we never say all. There is always an *et cetera*.

Language is a kind of map that stands for or represents an experience. In this sense, reading is an attempt to reconstruct the facts or the territory that the author's language is mapping out. Many instances of failure to comprehend a descriptive or narrative passage or to follow directions are due to the inadequacy of word-fact relations.

[1] The authors are indebted for much of the material in this section to a lecture given by M. Kendig of the Institute of General Semantics and to the writings of Louis Zahner and I. A. Richards.

If a statement is regarded as a kind of map, the test of its adequacy is the number of persons who reach their destination by means of it.

The further removed a word is from its plain sense meaning, the more is left unsaid. For example, to say, "There is a fire," conveys a definite meaning to the person who is sharing the experience of looking at a pile of burning leaves. If persons could deal only with physical objects and their movements in space, the meanings of these could easily be made clear to others; but human life does not operate on this simple level. It is often necessary to refer to classes of objects. To say "I'd like to sit by the fire" is somewhat indefinite, for the hearer does not know whether the speaker wants to sit by an open fireplace, a stove, or a campfire. To say "Life is a pure flame" requires a complex process of translation, involving an understanding of the particular quality of flame that is being abstracted and the situation in which it is being applied. Metaphors and other figures of speech are found not only in poetry; everyday speech and writing are packed with metaphors. For example, in a list of articles in an issue of the *Reader's Digest* one finds the following titles: "Flood-lighting the Job Market," "New Strength for the Staff of Life," "Stamping Out Starvation," and "Hollywood's New Ghost Voice." In these instances, the common meaning of a word or phrase is replaced by a special or partial meaning.

Words have a wide range of meaning. They wander about within the limits set for them by dictionary definitions (49). For many words these limits are extensive. For instance, *Webster's International Dictionary* gives 16 meanings for "book," 29 meanings for "dust," and 36 meanings for "shade." The *Unabridged Oxford Dictionary* gives as many as 150 meanings for a single word. Even the dictionary does not include all variations of meaning that are in current usage. Moreover, some words, like "force," "mass," and "work," have both a general meaning in common usage and a technical meaning. These words and, in fact, any other words get their peculiar meaning from the context. "Consider what is done to the word 'dog' by putting 'hot' in front of it."

Most uncharted of all are such words as "peace," "democracy," "justice," "meaning," "cause," and "true." These and others like them describe the very structure of society, thought, and feeling; they are, therefore, worthy of having much time spent on them. The territory that each of these words covers is so vast that every person may have a somewhat different view of it. Therefore, for each individual who utters or hears it, the word used has different significance according to that person's own experience.

One of the most important tasks of every teacher is to help his students construct maps of common meanings for these words of world-wide significance.   The class, as a whole, may study each word as it crops up in reading or discussion and may translate it with the aid of concrete experience, thus trying to arrive at the most satisfactory interpretation possible at the time.

The task of interpretation of meaning is made still more complex by the fact that words are constantly changing their meanings.   For example, the word "women," referring to women in 1915, is not the same as "women," referring to 1945, for the status and interests of women have markedly changed during the last 30 years.   Thus one must take into account time and place, the author's intent and purpose, and other factors in making an accurate interpretation of the meaning of a passage.   A person who has acquired the art of reading makes a preliminary survey of the passage and asks and answers questions as he reads: What kind of language is being used?   For what purpose? What does this key word actually mean?   Is this statement a generalization or does it have a specific meaning?   Which meanings or multiple meanings probably give the best interpretation?   Meaning is obtained only from the study of "words in cooperation with each other."

This view of the interpretation of meaning has made the study of vocabulary infinitely more complex.   Vocabulary used to involve merely an assemblage or collection of words that were supposed to be adequately understood from a definition or a synonym.   Richards pointed out that a study of words that leaves students with the impression that a word has only one definite meaning is positively detrimental. Zahner (72, page 7) emphasized the importance of realizing from the beginning

. . . how individual a thing a word as a symbol often is and how, if human communication is not to be a game of blind-man's buff, each individual must stretch his own idea of a symbol's "meaning" to allow for, and discriminate among, the sorts of experience which another individual may attach to the same symbol.

There are some persons who fear that the semantic movement may go to an undesirable extreme of intensive analysis of short passages, to the neglect of extensive reading.   There is little danger, however, of this overemphasis if these principles of interpretation are applied as occasions arise in connection with daily reading activities.   If this is done, considerable time may be given one day to interpreting a metaphor in literature or to gaining a more adequate understanding of a key word in the social sciences, while, on other days, the student may be concerned with larger relationships.

PSYCHOLOGICAL EXPLANATION OF READING

Reading may be described in terms of various psychological theories, each of which throws some light on the nature of reading. According to Hollingworth (30, pages 7, 198–203), improvement in reading may be explained by increased ability to get the meaning of a word or a phrase from a quick perception of some of its parts. Thus details or slight clues are sufficient to give the rapid, experienced reader the thought of the passage as a whole.

The behaviorist has encouraged drill in associating the printed word form with the object or action or with oral or silent verbal explanations of its meaning. The success with which these associations are made depends on a number of factors, among them the person's readiness to respond, the opportunity he has to practice reading, and the degree of satisfaction that accompanies or follows his attempt to learn to read. The conditioned-response school also makes a contribution to the understanding of reading, especially in its emphasis on "reinforcement" as a factor in strengthening and maintaining an activity and on "extinction" where reinforcement is persistently absent. If a reader has a specific purpose, and if he goes after something in a paragraph or a passage and gets it, his reading activity is reinforced. If he aimlessly dawdles through a paragraph, getting nothing in particular from it, he has no reinforcement.

The Gestalt point of view, especially as represented by Lewin, is perhaps the most helpful to present in detail here. Any reading assignment is part of a total situation, including the person himself, his environment, and the reading material. If the student approaches the reading without interest or with an expectation of failure to comprehend, his expenditure of energy is lessened and his performance is below par. He may "stick to it" because of external compulsion or a sense of duty; but his expectation of failure, his inefficient reading methods, the uninteresting nature of the reading material, discomfort due to poor vision, the pull of other interests and distractions—all these lead him to withdraw from the task psychologically, if not physically.

If he is to be induced to expend sufficient effort to comprehend the passage, these negative influences must in some way be neutralized. This may be done in a variety of ways: he may be given a background of meaning in the subject through pictures, discussion, or other experiences; the passage to be read may be associated with some vital interest in his life, such as being in a play or becoming more popular with the opposite sex; elements of interest that he has not noticed in the passage may be called to his attention; suggestions for increasing his comprehension may be given. Unnecessary noise, interruptions, and other distractions may be eliminated during his study period; corrections may be made for visual defects. In these and other ways the nature of the reading experience may be changed for him, and a positive, energy-releasing approach may be substituted for a negative, energy-depleting attitude.

Actually, the influences affecting an individual's reading performance at any one time extend far more widely than has been indicated. They reach back into childhood experiences of failure and inadequacy; they extend into present parent-child and sibling relationships; they are tempered by goals and purposes. No one can really understand a student's reading ability without being cognizant of the complex forces that are influencing him at any one moment.

In the more restricted circle of the reading process itself, the reader's idea of the author's mood and attitude toward his subject and toward the reader influences the way a person reads. The sensitive writer undoubtedly tries to establish rapport with his readers and may subtly convey to them his interest in communicating his point of view. He may be playful, sarcastic, evangelistic, or steadfastly unemotional toward all sides of a question. Another author may seem to write just for himself, and perhaps the reader senses his aloofness. Sometimes the reader feels that the author is talking to someone else and not to him. To an even greater extent the reader's background, intention, and purpose in reading the passage determine the ideas that he selects as important, the interpretation that he gives to the meaning of the writer's statements, and the weight or emphasis that he assigns to each idea in its relationship to the whole.

Thus the author's intention and the reader's intention determine to a great extent what the reader selects, organizes, interprets, infers, appreciates. To do this effectively, the reader needs a mastery of the mechanics of word recognition; and he needs, besides, efficient methods of determining the meaning of unfamiliar words in a particular context, of getting the main ideas of paragraphs and the pattern of thought of the passage as a whole, of getting the literal or sense meaning of the specific statements, and of drawing correct inferences.

All these processes, so necessary for effective reading, are interrelated. Appraisal of a student's reading will reveal specific difficulties for the removal of which practice and instruction can be given. It is at this point that texts on the improvement of reading have been especially weak. They have not given teachers sufficient aid in constructing practice exercises and in instructing students in these essential methods of getting meaning from the printed page.

From all schools of psychology certain common principles of learning emerge. The first is that the condition of the individual—his capacities and predispositions as well as his present physical condition and the desires aroused by his immediate environment—intervenes between the teacher's instruction and the student's learning. For these reasons, learning must be individualized.

The second principle is that learning to read well is not a casual affair. A basis of practice is necessary; no one can learn something that he has never experienced, at least in part. We must, therefore, provide repetition of good reading methods through many natural and planned activities that require reading.

Mere repetition, however, is not enough. Prayers rattled off when we were children may have gained true meaning for us only years later; the words of geometry theorems memorized verbatim for the sake of a perfect recitation in class were not meaningful because they were not our own. If a fact or a procedure is to be truly learned by a student, it must be used by him in a meaningful way and must bring satisfaction. This satisfaction may be immediate and closely associated with the activity itself, or it may be derived from the understanding that this activity, perhaps disagreeable in itself, is important for the realization of a much-to-be-desired larger goal or purpose.

The third factor that influences learning to read more effectively is reflection—*i.e.*, ideas intervening between the stimuli to which the individual is exposed and the responses he makes. An unpublished exploratory study has recently shown that some of the best readers are more aware of the process they use than are the poor readers. When asked to describe their method of reading, the good readers said that they "skimmed rapidly to see what the author was trying to do," "decided on the kind of information that would be most important in that particular article," "looked for main ideas in the first or second sentences of the paragraphs," "related ideas in the article to previous knowledge of the subject," "tried to see whether anything the author said or implied justified his conclusion." The poor readers, on the other hand, tended to be vague and general about their reading processes.

Unless we plan to approach the teaching of reading through avenues appropriate to the individual, provide many natural and significant opportunities for the practice and use of good reading methods, and give specific instruction in efficient methods of reading, both teacher and student are likely to fail.

To summarize, reading is a psychological process in which the reader obtains meaning from printed words. In order to do this, he must be able to see and recognize the symbols (see pages 66–67, 230–231, 235–238, and 249–253). But clear visual images and the recognition of words are not enough; he must determine their meaning in a particular context. Interpretation of meaning involves memory of previous experiences, reasoning, and the reader's purpose and attitude toward the reading situation as a whole. Thus effective reading is a resultant of the complex interaction between a person and an environment in which reading materials, at a particular time, occupy the center of his attention. After he has acquired the meaning of a passage, he may apply the knowledge to problems of daily living, fusing the newly acquired information with previous knowledge obtained from life situations and from other reading. At this stage memory enters in to ensure the retention of ideas for as long a time as the person needs to keep them in mind.

CONSTITUENTS OF THE READING PROCESS

Many attempts have been made to study the constituents of reading. Thus far, a perceptual factor, a word factor, an interpretation-of-language factor, a reasoning factor, and a speed factor have been isolated (12, page 35). The perceptual factor seems to be most closely related to the ability to perceive details. The word, or vocabulary, factor involves fluency in dealing with single words and obviously plays an important part in reading comprehension. The interpretation-of-language factor reflects ability to deal with the interpretation of the meaning of words in context. The reasoning factor involves the ability to see relationships of ideas and to give the proper weight to each element. Lacking this ability, the student tends to take the memorizing attitude, instead of the analyzing attitude (46). Thorndike's classic analysis of reading as a reasoning process (61) calls attention to the constant unconscious evaluation of the relative importance of and interrelation between words and phrases and sentences that is necessary as one reads. Lyman described reading, thinking, and studying as three aspects of one process (39, page 14):

We *read* serious books to get ideas; we *think* about them to see what these ideas mean; we *study* ideas and their meanings, endeavoring to make them our permanent possessions and to get ready to use them in problems of our own.

Horn explained (31, page 154) that the author

. . . does not really convey ideas to the reader; he merely stimulates him to construct them out of his own experience. If the concept is . . . new to the reader, its construction more nearly approaches problem solving than simple association.

Speed of Comprehension.—The speed factor in reading is of special interest because so many poor readers think of "slow rate" as their chief difficulty. As a matter of fact, however, many students read some kinds of books too fast and other kinds too slowly. In the following paragraph Fadiman called attention to the necessity of adjusting speed to the kind of material (15, xlii–xliii):

I do not believe dogmatically either in fast or slow reading. I believe tripe should be read practically with the speed of light and, let us say, Toynbee's *A Study of History* with tortoise deliberation. And most books are nearer to tripe than they are to Toynbee. But the trouble with practically all of us is that we suffer from chronic reverence. We make the unwarranted assumption that because a man is in print he has something to say, and, acting on this assumption, we read his every word with scrupulous care. This may be good manners, but it's a confounded waste of time.

There is no one best rate of reading. The estimates of an average rate of 250 words per minute for high-school students and 350 words per minute for college students give only an approximate idea of the speed with which students should read their assignments.

Many studies of the correlation between speed and comprehension in reading have been made. The results of these studies are extremely varied. Correlations ranging from −.47 to .92 have been reported (6). Some of the highest correlations were obtained from tests in which the comprehension score was, to some extent, a function of rate of reading and in which it was impossible for a slow reader to secure a high comprehension score. Some of the lowest correlations were obtained when speed of reading one kind of passage and comprehension of quite a different kind of material were measured. It is only when similar passages within the reader's educational experience are used that a positive relationship between rate of reading and comprehension may be expected (64). It seems clear that the relation between rate and comprehension varies with conditions of reading and with the types of tests employed (59). On the whole, when independent measurements of rate and comprehension based on the same passages have been made, the correlations have tended to be significantly positive, but low. A correlation of .3 between rate and comprehension is fairly close to an average of the results of all these studies.

The fact that a positive correlation between speed and comprehension has been found in the majority of the studies has led some persons to infer that the more rapidly one reads the better he is likely to comprehend. This conclusion is not justified. Correlations are based on the scores of groups of individuals, and they imply nothing concerning the comprehension of the same individual at different reading speeds. In fact, with some individuals, too much emphasis on speed of reading may result in tension and confusion.

A few attempts have been made with the same individuals to determine the effect upon the comprehension of varying the reading speed. Flanagan (17), for example, reported the results of an experiment with twelfth-grade pupils who were trained to read passages and answer questions on them at three different rates of reading. Comprehension decreased slightly from the slow to the medium rate and much from the medium to the rapid rate. When the group was divided into thirds on the basis of their scores at the slow rate, each group showed about the same decrease from the medium to the rapid rate. This and other investigations suggest that the reading rate of an individual may be increased considerably without noteworthy loss in comprehension, but that when his rate is greatly speeded up his comprehension may be expected to decrease significantly.

Investigations have shown a negative relation between speed and comprehension in certain fields, especially in mathematics and science (3, page 7). Students whose achievement in these subjects was highest made, on the average, the lower scores on general speed of reading tests. Tinker (64) found that the correlation between rate of reading and comprehension is high for easy material and progressively lower with increasingly difficult passages. "Material which requires a special background of training for its interpretation appears to lower the correlation." Anderson's summary of this relationship between rate and comprehension (2) clarifies thinking on this question (2, page 29):

Rate is the necessary outcome of time-consuming processes in reading. All factors which affect the comprehending activities contribute to the time in course of these activities. Thus reading rate will vary as the *result* of variations in the comprehending functions. An alteration in rate which is not adjusted to the difficulty of material, the purpose in reading, and the general ability of the individual will disturb the normal course of the thought processes involved.

The concept of *rate of comprehension* is much more useful than the concept of *rate of reading*. A comparatively slow rate of comprehension for a particular passage may be considered as a symptom—as an indication of underlying difficulties in perception, word knowledge, and comprehension. If visual defects are corrected, if vocabulary is increased and enriched, if more effective methods of comprehension are taught, increase in speed appropriate to the material and the purpose of the reader may be expected.

Ability to Remember.—Wide individual differences are found in ability to remember. In one experiment (14) three factual passages were given to pupils in grades 7 to 9. The pupils were allowed to read the passages at their own rates. A test on comprehension and memory was given immediately after reading and then repeated 1 day later, 14 days later, 30 days later, and 100 days later. Factors found to influence memory were

1. Familiarity of material—familiar material is more easily remembered than new or strange material.

2. Length of time intervening—the rate of forgetting is rapid at first, then slower; but there is a positive correlation between immediate memory and delayed memory.

3. Meaningfulness of the material—the initial forgetting for factual material was less abrupt than for nonsense syllables. The point of complete forgetting is not approximated even after 100 days.

Introspective Reports of the Reading Process.—Perhaps the most revealing information about reading processes can be gained through introspective reports written by students. Certainly, except for records of eye movements or of performances on standardized tests, we have little information about the reading process as it is actually carried on by individuals. Even Dewey's excellent case studies (13) of eighth-grade boys and girls, while supplying significant details as to how a passage may be comprehended, do not give much insight into the methods that may be employed. Introspective reports made by superior graduate students indicate a general tendency to use such cues to the author's organization as table of contents, paragraph headings, topic sentences, and repeated key words. In addition, these superior students employ unique methods, which they have developed for themselves. These methods may not be suitable for other persons. There are excellent readers who show no such idiosyncrasies of eye movements or mental processes. The following account is one student's attempt to describe the mental processes involved in reading a specific assignment:

I start either with great irritation, wishing I could do all the things I want to do instead of this dumb assignment, or with a feeling of satisfaction because during this whole day I do not have to be annoyed by going to any classes or lectures or any special things. I decide from the exterior appearance, and also from the type, spacing, etc., that I like or do not like the book. I abhor long lines and like my spacing between lines to be greater than it usually is.

I do not like to do exactly what I am told. Sometimes I do read the required pages and no more and no less, especially when I expect to get from the reading only familiarity with what it is about, a sort of inventory reading. In that case I skim, with the following eye movements: I see paragraph headings and sometimes parts of first and last sentences. I am confident that any new idea, *if* there is one, will catch my eye and I think the skimming is really rather unnecessarily crooked. I believe I could do it in a straight line just as well if only I dared to be that unconscientious. My subconscious, or my eye, or something, really does pick out anything that is unfamiliar.

In skimming thus, what I read is neither sentences nor phrases but lumps, usually about three lines at a time. The lump that usually has the idea, if there is one, is near the bottom of the page between 1 and 2 in. from the bottom and to the right of the middle. It is here that I pause longest and decide whether or not the book is any good, but I make a shorter pause at other places on the page. Of course, this varies with the density of the material. There is some material that is so thin that I try to use one quick vertical sweep per page or every few pages before I decide that there just isn't anything in the book.

The one assignment I have done this week was a report for psychology. So I had to read it all and stop and take notes. It was *A Child's Approach to Religion* by Reverend H. W. Fox. Here I read about one and one-half to two pages, accompanying the reading with thinking, then reread as in the first type described, then made a note, usually copying a sentence. My thinking was as follows: "How can I report 90 pages in 5 minutes? I wonder if I can get it read in an hour. I hate to take notes, that takes so long. I suppose it will take an hour and a half. Nicely turned phrase, that. H'm. I'll remember that to tell Anna. H'm, he (the author) is really quite advanced! Now that is quite clever. I wonder if he is going to tell how to tell children about the problem not yet mentioned by him, death. (Here I think how Anna tried to keep her little boy from contact with death and remember three jokes about children's sayings about death and heaven.) Now, there he is not quite so advanced. Pretty good, on the whole. I believe I'll buy two copies, one for Anna and one for my sister. Mustn't take too many notes. Oh dear! I do want to hear that lecture and it is time to go. Sigh."

Although this student followed certain approved reading habits—adapting his rate and method to his purpose and to the kind of material and reading with an active, questioning mind—his account of his skimming method would be impossible to verify with an eye-movement camera. In the case of familiar material he may, in a quick glance down the page, catch key words by means of which his active mind quickly constructs the probable content of the page. A person with a less agile mind and less familiarity with the subject would gain nothing but confusion by attempting to read in this way.

Specific habits of reading for different purposes are described by another able student as follows:

Thumbing the pages; zigzag eye sweeping broomlike over the page from the top down; fixation in certain sections of the page while I see at least three lines in depth and a phrase in width with certain marginal width on either side; conversation back and forth in my mind about the ideas including thought about past experiences—a sort of daydreaming all around the ideas presented; stopping to admire clever wording; the use of table of contents, paragraph headings, topic sentences, etc.

This account is another illustration of the idiosyncrasies in reading method that one may find among able students. Like the previously mentioned student, he is describing the reading of familiar material in which he needs only a few ideas in order to reconstruct the trend of the passage.

Another graduate student who scored high on a standardized reading test described his method of getting the structure of the author's thought in this way:

I find my method of gaining ideas from reading is comparable to building a skyscraper. I first read the material through completely and quickly. On the way, I get a general outline or skeleton of the material. After this quick reading I go back and start over more slowly. This time I argue my way through the book and fill in the skeleton which I built the first time. This seems to be my method for reading material which is rather difficult.

This student likewise reads with an active mind and follows the generally effective procedure of getting a sense of structure of the passage as a whole and of what the author is trying to do, before attempting to select important points and details.

Another graduate student gave the following account of his procedure:

Assigned readings are read rapidly but thoroughly and are reread or reskimmed previous to examination. Suggested readings are skimmed or read, depending on the interest. Notes are taken on pertinent sections, diagrams, figures in research-type reading but never on assigned readings unless the exam is essay type, and never copiously in any case. Casual reading of novels, junk, informative books, and newspapers—read for fun—is always done rapidly and in the "skimming" manner.

It is clear that this student had learned to adjust his reading methods to the kind of reading jobs he had to do.

The role of distractions is introspectively reviewed by another student as follows:

I found my eye following the words down the page while I was still thinking of something quite remote suggested in the previous paragraph. When the material was very familiar, I found myself planning my schedule for the next two days. Some noises in the hall and out of doors were distracting; the noise of elevated trains, for example, made me glad I wasn't at the moment being jostled around in a subway as I was yesterday. Vocabulary offered a small difficulty, since I had to look up some words in the dictionary for exact meanings. One article was easiest for me to read because I am interested in the writer, who is a friend of my father. And finally, I had in the back of my mind the question assigned for discussion, namely: To what extent is nationalism rooted in the native constitution of man? And I was looking for possible suggestions to aid our group discussion.

Another introspective report describes the approach to a reading assignment and the peripheral mental activity associated with the reading of the chapters.

There are five chapters to read—that makes 138 pages, and I have 2½ hours before dinner. Shall I take notes now or after I have read the chapters? This assignment looks interesting—defense mechanisms in the psychology of adjustment. Guess I shall enjoy the continuity of the thing and take notes later. . . . The format is pleasing. I like books printed in this type; it is well spaced and clear, and good on the eyes. . . . What does *empirical* mean? (Time out: look it up in dictionary.) That is clear. . . . Well, I didn't understand that part at all. I'd better go back to the beginning of the sentence. . . . No, to the beginning of the paragraph. Oh yes. Now, can I close my eyes and repeat those five defense mechanisms? No, I only remembered four. (Time out: look back over the five again.) . . . Well, 10 pages of very interesting facts. I like this book. Maybe I shall finish it by six o'clock after all. . . . Oh dear, I read every word of that paragraph but my mind was completely disassociated from it. How *can* I do that? And I do it often. How can I *see* the words if I am not thinking about them? . . . I *saw* every single word, didn't I? When did my mind slide off the page? How do I know that I saw every single word? When I reread the paragraph I recognize isolated words, and that sets me to pondering about the strangeness of the phenomenon. . . . This page can be skimmed; it is a simple case study. This page is more detailed and technical, better slow up. . . .

Many more introspective reports combined with electro-ocular-grams of average and superior readers should be obtained before any generalizations as to the reading process can be made. At present successful students seem to be able to meet course requirements by departing widely from commonly accepted reading procedures and they describe eye movements quite different from the orderly progression of fixations across each line of print. From the 50 records collected, it would seem, however, that superior students have these qualities in common: they approach a reading assignment with an inquiring mind; they use whatever aids the book affords for getting the structure of the author's thought; they are mentally active, even to the extent of going off on irrelevant bypaths, and they check their comprehension of the material.   Each reader appears to have certain idiosyncrasies of method that seem to aid him, although they may be quite inappropriate to another student or for use on another kind of material.

The highly intelligent student, like Diana of the Crossways, in order to get the author's thought, needs fewer cues than does a less intelligent student.   Accordingly, the less able student may find it impossible to employ the "flash method," which the brilliant student uses with good results.

The two following reports were written by students who were so much dissatisfied with their reading methods that they voluntarily joined a class in the improvement of reading.   The first represents a difficulty that teachers often fear as a result of too great an emphasis on interest.

Reading has always been one of my chief delights—partly because I was given the proper stimulation to read when I was very young. As both my mother and father enjoy reading and consider it one of life's greatest pleasures, I have been brought up in an atmosphere conducive to reading.   Books have always predominated among my Christmas and birthday gifts, and a large share of my leisure time is spent reading.

The model training school administered by faculty of the Mankato State Teachers College had very "advanced" ideas about reading when I attended that school from first through ninth grades.   We were encouraged to read for enjoyment, to read with no idea of getting facts, but to interpret, in our own words and experiences, what the author said.

Each week we had a library period when we were allowed to spend an hour browsing through books and magazines in the library.   I read so avidly that I soon had "devoured" all the books in the children's library and the librarian gave me permission to use the college library books.   Faculty friends of my father "turned me loose" in their private libraries, and I soon gained the reputation of being a bookworm.

This wide reading, however, encouraged me to skim the books which I failed to find interesting.   When I came to dull books in history during my high-school years, I found myself skimming those too, instead of reading them for factual material.   This same difficulty arose at the university. I postponed reading those textbooks which seemed to me dull—and consequently ran into difficulty at examination time.

While most of the professors here prefer inferential reading to factual, there are still some courses which require a great deal of memorizing of specific facts.   My reading problem arises chiefly when I am reading for these courses. I can't seem to make mere "facts" stick in my mind.   I find it difficult to sit down to a dull book and extract rapidly all the pertinent facts which I must learn.

The second report is an excellent description of reading problems common to many persons.

My main reason for taking this course in the improvement of reading is to speed up my reading rate. Probably one thing which retards it is the fact that I find it difficult to concentrate on the reading matter before me. Therefore, if this course can increase my power of concentration, it will undoubtedly help speed up my reading rate. My fastest rate, when I concentrate as well as I know how, is twenty pages an hour of the average book. Tests do not show up my deficiency because, first of all, tests introduce a special situation in which I am under pressure. I always do anything more efficiently under pressure than when I am left to myself. Secondly, tests usually give short reading passages. It should hardly be surprising, I think, that a person can read a short passage at a much more rapid rate than a long passage. With a short passage there is, you see, no problem of concentration, whereas concentration can become a problem when one has several pages to read at a sitting.

Another aspect of my problem is, I think, that I have only one reading method, the intensive reading method. I suppose that I should have at least two reading methods, the intensive and the extensive. There are times when it is a good thing to read at the rate of twenty pages an hour, for instance, in studying some technical book, making an exhaustive study of any type of book, or in getting the utmost pleasure out of a literary masterpiece. But there are other times when a much more rapid rate would be helpful, for instance, in reading newspapers and magazines.

One reason for my difficulty in concentrating is the fact that I have an imagination which is too active. As I read along in a novel, for instance, I come across a word or a phrase which recalls something in my past experience. I stop to enjoy that sensation and usually the recalled experience will remind me of something else and so on *ad infinitum*. Thus my creative imagination makes of the book a sort of instigator of a series of pleasant, or sometimes unpleasant, memories. This sort of creative or re-creative reading is pleasant, but it uses up precious time when it intrudes into all my reading. And, in extreme cases, it slows up my reading to such an extent that by the time I reach the end I have forgotten the beginning of the book.

Introspective reports of this kind and of a more systematic, analytical type high-light individual differences in the reading process and the extraordinary complexity of the constituent elements in effective reading.

FACTORS RELATED TO READING

All the communication arts are interrelated and some of these relationships have already been mentioned on pages 38–39. Certain phases of the relations between reading and listening are of special interest to educators: Which is the better avenue of learning—listening or reading? Does listening to the radio while reading decrease reading and study efficiency? Does radio make readers?

Listening and Reading.—The correlation between comprehension in reading and comprehension in listening is, in general, high (4, 11, 20, 37, 52). Mispronunciation is frequently accompanied by inaccurate comprehension. In general, if a student can understand what he hears, he may be expected to understand similar material by reading it. Failure to comprehend it through reading may indicate poor vision, bad reading methods, a negative attitude toward reading, or emotional blocking.

The superiority of listening over reading as an avenue of learning decreases as the child gains proficiency in reading. By the time he reaches junior high school he frequently gets more complete and accurate meaning from reading than from listening. This increasing superiority of reading in the upper grades is related to the difficulty of the material and the amount of practice in gaining knowledge through reading. If the material is easy, students are likely to comprehend it as well when listening as when reading. In the case of difficult material, however, students of high scholastic aptitude and reading ability comprehend more efficiently by reading than by listening. The effect of auditory presentation varies with the difficulty of the material, the type of material, the kind of thinking required, and the educational background of the persons (11, page 159).

A wide range of individual differences, however, is found. Auditory defects may tend to make reading a better avenue of learning for some, and visual defects may increase the relative listening efficiency of others. The amount of practice he has had and the kind of instruction he has received may also lead a person to become more proficient in one avenue of learning than in the other.

Reading efficiency may be decreased if one attempts to read and listen to the radio at the same time. Students differ in their opinions about the effect of having the radio turned on while they are studying. Some claim that it increases their reading efficiency; others admit that it distracts their attention. Fendrick (16) concluded from a carefully controlled experiment with two groups of 60 college students that music played while students were studying an assignment in psychology probably decreased their study efficiency and affected the more intelligent students more seriously than it did those of lower mental ability. Loss in efficiency is greatest when the noise begins. After a while, the student tends to ignore it. At that stage, a shift to silence becomes a distraction. Thus the radio, because of its variety, is likely to be more distracting than a monotonous hammering or other constant noises.

There are, of course, individual differences in the degree to which listening to the radio interferes with comprehension in reading. If a student really studies, listening to the radio becomes one of the conditions that affect his study efficiency. If his attention is primarily on the radio, it may seriously increase his tendency to dawdle in his studies. Some persons can concentrate in spite of distracting music, conversation, and noises. Some may even work more intensely because of the distraction; but in the long run, resisting distraction is nerve racking and tends to leave a person tired and irritable. Most persons have experienced a sense of relief in turning off the radio after they have divided their attention for an hour or more between listening and reading.

Part of this problem of the relationship between reading and listening is the influence of the radio on reading interests. There is some evidence that "radio makes readers." Mersand (45) reported that of 150 high-school boys who heard a certain play dramatized over the radio about half read it afterward; and many more read other books because of their interest in the radio dramatizations. We need more information on ways in which listening to the radio, seeing motion pictures, going on excursions, participating in discussions, and engaging in handwork or creative art work may interfere with or facilitate reading.

A number of other factors have been studied with reference to their effect on reading proficiency: visual defects, eye movements, intelligence, spelling and other school achievements, and personality problems.

Visual Defects and Reading.—Visual defects appear to be prevalent among groups of good readers of high-school and college age, as well as among poor readers of the same age. By the time that students have reached college they are likely to have learned to read in spite of visual defects. In certain individual cases, however, visual factors do affect the student's reading ability. Moreover, even though a student may transcend the limitations of visual handicaps during a short period of testing, he needs good vision for sustained effort in reading. Accordingly, visual factors should always be examined in the appraisal of a student's reading. Hearing defects likewise may or may not be the cause of poor reading, but the possibility of hearing loss should at least be investigated.

The relation of eye movements to reading proficiency is more complex than was originally thought. Regressive eye movements seem to occur when the reader's thought is interrupted by the presence of unfamiliar words and by failure to recognize the correct meaning of a word in its context or to relate it to other ideas in the passage; also, when his perception is inadequate and when his eyes move more slowly or more quickly than his thoughts. The photographic record of eye movements represents a complex situation that requires considerable acumen for interpretation. The eye movement patterns of good readers are not always easily distinguished from those of poor readers. On difficult material, the effective reader who is intently trying to comprehend the author's thought or to remember all important details makes eye movements resembling those of a poor reader who is trying to understand an easier passage (2). His eyes tend to pause frequently on each line and occasionally to go back over the line. His eye movements tend to be irregular, though not erratic and inconsistent. On the other hand, when the good reader is reading a selection merely for a general impression, he tends to make "few and short pauses and regular sequences in fixations along the line of print" (2, page 17). Thus the eye-movement record varies with the difficulty of the material and with the purpose, intelligence, and reading habits of the subject.

Eye movements must be regarded as an intrinsic part of the reading process. In general, good readers show greater flexibility in eye movements than do poor readers; they adjust their reading methods to serve their ends.

Irregular eye movements with frequent pauses and backward movements are symptoms of difficulty in comprehension and in adaptability to the demands of various reading situations. For this reason, practice and instruction in getting the author's meaning should improve eye movement as well as general reading ability.

Intelligence and Reading.—One of the most controversial questions in this field is the relation between reading and general intelligence or scholastic aptitude. Although it seems obvious that there must be a positive relationship between general mental ability and ability to read, this relationship is more complex than appears on the surface. The high correlations between reading tests and group verbal intelligence tests give a somewhat misleading idea of the relationship between reading and mental ability, because reading is required in both types of tests. When the intelligence test is divided into linguistic and quantitative parts, the relationship between intelligence and reading breaks down, as is shown by the figures below. Using the California Test of Mental Maturity and two reading tests in examining 74 ninth-grade pupils, Traxler (65) obtained the following coefficients of correlation:

Language factors with Iowa Silent Reading Test..... .685 ± .041
Nonlanguage factors with Iowa Silent Reading Test.. .356 ± .068
Language factors with Traxler Silent Reading Test... .753 ± .034
Nonlanguage factors with Traxler Silent Reading Test. .357 ± .068

Somewhat similar results were obtained in another experiment (57) using the Elementary Series of the California Test of Mental Maturity with children in elementary grades.

Language factors with Thorndike-McCall Reading Test...... .824
Nonlanguage factors with Thorndike-McCall Reading Test... .557
Language factors with Gates Silent Reading Test, Type A..... .805
Nonlanguage factors with Gates Silent Reading Test, Type A. .359
Language factors with Gates Silent Reading Test, Type B..... .799
Nonlanguage factors with Gates Silent Reading Test, Type B. .413
Language factors with Gates Silent Reading Test, Type D.... .844
Nonlanguage factors with Gates Silent Reading Test, Type D.. .514

Each of the four reading tests correlates definitely lower with the nonlanguage than with the language scores of the California Test of Mental Ability. There is some indication that the linguistic and quantitative parts do not measure exactly the same kind of mental ability and that the language type of test may be the better measure of those aspects of mental ability that are basic to schoolwork. Obviously the linguistic intelligence tests and certain reading comprehension tests have in common a considerable amount of this verbal factor. That being the case, it is quite possible for a bright child having reading or general language difficulty to give the impression, on a verbal intelligence test, of having low mental ability.

In an experiment with college students (43) the coefficients of correlation between intelligence-test scores and reading-test scores are reported in Table 1.

Most of the correlations between Iowa comprehension scores and American Council linguistic scores obtained at the Educational Record Bureau are higher than the correlation of .56 reported here.

Evidence is accumulating to indicate that it is not a waste of time to teach reading to students with low scores on intelligence tests. If teachers really teach reading, the less intelligent as well as the more intelligent profit by the instruction, provided that the passages to be read are not too complicated and abstract. If reading is limited to the comprehension of signs, directions, and simple material on the third- and fourth-grade level of difficulty, adolescents with I.Q.'s from 60 to 80 have successfully been taught to "read."

Sears (53) reported a case of a boy sixteen years old who had an I.Q. of 56 and an estimated mental age of 9-0 years, and who made marked progress in reading in 250 periods of individual instruction. At first he was given much practice in tracing and writing separated words; later he was able to learn, by the "look-and-say" method, with some use of phonics, an unlimited number of simple, concrete words related to his experience. Thus he acquired a vocabulary of 500 or 600 common words that were of practical use to him in reading signs and notices, advertisements, labels, and directions for doing elementary work in the trade in which he was interested. His progress during the first 145 lessons was rapid. His score on a battery of reading tests rose from grade 1.2 to grade 2.6—a rate one and one-half times that expected of the normal child. The next 55 lessons added only 2 months' gain, and the last 50 lessons a gain of only 1 month. He had

TABLE 1.—COEFFICIENTS OF CORRELATION BETWEEN INTELLIGENCE-TEST SCORES AND READING SCORES

Iowa Silent Reading Test	American Council on Education Psychological Examination, 48 cases		California Test of Mental Maturity, 45 cases	
	Linguistic score	Quantitative score	Linguistic score	Quantitative score
Comprehension scores:				
Initial test................	.56	.27	.45	.14
Final test................	.57	.27	.49	.24
Speed scores:				
Initial test................	.29	.19	−.01	.15
Final test................	.27	.23	.18	.10

apparently reached the limit of his trainability. Although he was eager to read faster, all attempts to speed up resulted in hopeless inaccuracy and confusion. With the training he received, however, he was able to secure and to hold a fairly good job, even during depression years.

McCullough (43) questioned the assumption that students whose reading age was equal to their mental age could improve little in reading ability. In a ninth-grade class of 6 girls and 18 boys with I.Q.'s from 80 to 157, after nine weeks of instruction in reading, she found no relationship between intelligence and improvement in reading as measured by the Traxler Silent Reading Test. In a college class of 9 girls and 40 boys, also with a wide range of I.Q.'s, in which effective methods of instruction in reading were employed, no relation was found between gains in reading comprehension and intelligence scores. She concluded that methods that put a premium on intelligence have probably been responsible for reports of poor response to instruction on the part of less intelligent readers in remedial groups. Furthermore, since the reading ages assigned to reading-test scores have not been based upon ideally taught groups, it is conceivable that these age norms do not represent the upper limit of performance for students of a given mental age.

Spelling and Reading.—Spelling is likewise related to reading in a complex way. Usually students tend to be good or poor in both reading and spelling and to improve or deteriorate in both abilities as they go through the high-school grades. There is some evidence (19) that students in the grades from the seventh through the twelfth spell better the words that they have encountered in reading passages, and that pupils in the sixth grade (67) learn to spell more words as a result of wide reading and a great variety of learning activities in social-studies classes than they do from spending the same amount of time in history and geography classes of more traditional types. In both groups improvement in spelling was a by-product or concomitant learning, resulting from reading and study of other subjects without special instruction in spelling.

School Achievement and Reading.—Much of a student's success in school and college depends on the efficiency of his reading. Reading

TABLE 2.—COEFFICIENTS OF CORRELATION BETWEEN READING AND ACHIEVEMENT IN SUBJECTS

Subject	Comprehension in reading	Rate of reading
English..............	.67	.37
Social science.......	.53	.24
Biological science....	.49	.24
Physical science.....	.47	.16

comprehension is related to achievement in high-school subjects, especially in English and social science. Speed of reading, however, is not similarly related to achievement. In fact, a generally slow rate of reading is likely to accompany high achievement in science, mathematics, and Latin tests (7). The coefficients of correlation between the Iowa Silent Reading Tests and marks on comprehensive examinations given in the Chicago City junior colleges in June, 1936, reported by McCallister (41), are presented in Table 2.

Harvard freshmen, paired with respect to intelligence, who on the average made higher scores on the Nelson-Denny Reading Test, obtained higher college marks for all courses combined than did the group of poorer readers (3). In 1927, Book, without taking intelligence into consideration, found a marked relationship between efficiency in reading and credit points earned by college students. Reading abilities in different subject fields in college, as might be expected, may be only slightly related (51).

Personality and Reading.—Reading difficulty cannot be dissociated from the individual's total personality tendencies. A recent study of the personality organization of poor readers from the third through the sixth grade (18), using the Rorschach method as the main measure of personality organization, indicated that retarded readers are less stable and less well adjusted than are good readers, less adaptable socially, less secure in the face of challenges, less efficient in the use of their potential mental capacity, and more concerned with small detail. All this would indicate that retarded readers are, in general, less efficient in dealing with the complex challenge that reading offers.

The interaction between the child's personality and the environment must also be considered in this connection. Conditions in the home, the school, and the neighborhood—such as lack of parents' affection, parental preference for a younger brother or sister, repressed curiosity, intensification of a sense of guilt, sex conflicts, and repeated failure—may increase emotional instability and inner conflict. Parents' and teachers' anxiety over a child's not learning to read may be transferred to the child himself and thus interfere with his effort to learn. Resistance to learning to read may be the child's way of expressing hostility to some person in his environment, or it may indicate a lack of readiness for the reading experience as it is presented.

A plausible explanation of much reading inefficiency is that the individual uses up so much energy in his inner struggles that he is unable to put forth the effort that learning to read effectively requires. In these cases remedial reading is successful only when the worker is able to meet the emotional needs of the individual and thus free him to attack the reading problem. In other cases, despite unfavorable conditions, a child achieves proficiency in reading because of some more dominant motivation in his total personality and life.

In this respect also there are marked individual differences. Some pupils show marked improvement in behavior after they have learned to read more efficiently. Others show small change in behavior or none at all. This variation is quite understandable, for an individual's behavior arises from many complex sources. There are some cases where inability to read may be central to the maladjustment; there are others where success in reading may increase self-confidence in general. There are still other cases where the reading problem is relatively unimportant when compared with more serious anxieties and frustrations. For example, a student who has reading difficulty may develop an inferiority feeling that may cause him to withdraw from the activities of his class. Another individual may build up an intense hate for school, for the teacher, and for society in general, and express this hatred in aggressive acts. Still another may take a defeatist attitude; he feels beaten before he even begins a new task involving reading. This attitude has usually been reinforced by parents and teachers who have overemphasized his faults and found nothing in him to commend. Frequently students who cannot read adequately make up for this deficiency by trying to succeed in something else. But success in athletics or social leadership does not really compensate for lack of reading ability, because this ability is generally considered to be basic to success in many aspects of life.

The obvious aim, then, is to help every child acquire the kind of reading ability that is appropriate and functional for him, and to do this before his inability to read shall become a source of anxiety. It is equally important, at all ages, so far as possible to prevent emotional conflicts that may interfere with the learning process.

References

1. ADLER, MORTIMER J., *How to Read a Book:* The Art of Getting a Liberal Education, Simon and Schuster, Inc., New York, 1940, ix + 398 pp.
2. ANDERSON, IRVING H., "Studies in Eye-movements of Good and Poor Readers," Psychological Monographs, Vol. 48, No. 3, *Studies in Psychology of Reading*, Vol. 1, pp. 1–35, Psychological Review Company, Princeton, N. J., 1937.
3. ANDERSON, IRVING H., and WALTER F. DEARBORN, "Reading Ability as Related to College Achievement," *Journal of Psychology*, Vol. 11, pp. 387–396, April, 1941.
4. ANDERSON, IRVING H., and GRANT FAIRBANKS, "Common and Differential Factors in Reading Vocabulary and Hearing Vocabulary," *Journal of Educational Research*, Vol. 30, pp. 317–324, January, 1937.
5. BETTS, EMMETT A., "Factors in Readiness for Reading," *Educational Administration and Supervision*, Vol. 29, pp. 199–230, April, 1943.
6. BLOMMERS, PAUL, and E. F. LINDQUIST, "Rate of Comprehension of Reading: Its Measurement and Its Relation to Comprehension," *Journal of Educational Psychology*, Vol. 35, pp. 449–473, November, 1944.
7. BOND, EVA, *Reading and Ninth Grade Achievement*, Bureau of Publications, Teachers College, Columbia University, New York, 1938, x + 61 pp.
8. BROENING, ANGELA M., "Abilities Which Contribute to Effective Reading," *Education*, Vol. 62, pp. 11–17, September, 1941.
9. BUSWELL, GUY THOMAS, *Fundamental Reading Habits:* A Study of Their Development, Supplementary Educational Monographs, No. 21, University of Chicago Press, Chicago, 1922, xiv + 150 pp.

10. BUSWELL, GUY THOMAS, "The Improvement of Rate and Comprehension in Reading," in *Adapting Reading Programs to Wartime Needs* (William S. Gray, editor), pp. 248–252, Supplementary Educational Monographs, No. 57, University of Chicago Press, Chicago, December, 1943.

11. CANTRIL, HADLEY, and GORDON W. ALLPORT, *Psychology of Radio*, Chap. X, Harper & Brothers, New York, 1935, x + 276 pp.

12. DAVIS, FREDERICK B., "Fundamental Factors of Comprehension in Reading," *Psychometrika*, Vol. 9, pp. 185–197, September, 1944.

13. DEWEY, JOSEPH, "A Technique for Investigating Reading Comprehension," *School and Society*, Vol. 39, p. 276, Mar. 3, 1934.

14. DIETZE, ALFRED G., and GEORGE E. JONES, "Factual Memory of Secondary School Pupils for a Short Article Which They Read a Single Time," *Journal of Educational Psychology*, Vol. 22, pp. 586–598, November, 1931; pp. 667–676, December, 1931.

15. FADIMAN, CLIFTON, *Reading I've Liked*, Simon and Schuster, Inc., New York, 1941, lxiv + 908 pp.

16. FENDRICK, PAUL, "The Influence of Music Distraction upon Reading Efficiency," *Journal of Educational Research*, Vol. 31, pp. 264–271, December, 1937.

17. FLANAGAN, JOHN C., "A Study of the Effect on Comprehension of Varying Speeds of Reading," *Research in the Foundations of American Education*, pp. 47–50, Official Report of the American Educational Research Association, 1939.

18. GANN, EDITH, *Reading Difficulty and Personality Organization*, Kings Crown Press, New York, 1945, 149 pp.

19. GILBERT, LUTHER C., "Effect of Reading on Spelling in the Secondary School," *California Quarterly of Secondary Education*, Vol. 9, pp. 269–275, April, 1934.

20. GLICKSBERG, CHARLES I., "Semantics in the Classroom," *English Journal*, Vol. 33, pp. 408–414, October, 1944.

21. GOLDSTEIN, HARRY, *Reading and Listening Comprehension at Various Controlled Rates*, Bureau of Publications, Teachers College, Columbia University, New York, 1940, v + 69 pp.

22. GRAY, WILLIAM S., "Reading," in *Encyclopedia of Educational Research*, pp. 891–926, The Macmillan Company, New York, 1941, xxiii + 1344 pp.

23. GRAY, WILLIAM S. (chairman), *Reading in General Education*, pp. 1–17, American Council on Education, Washington, D.C., 1940, xiii + 464 pp.

24. GRAY, WILLIAM S., "Summary of Reading Investigations: July 1, 1942 to June 30, 1943," *Journal of Educational Research*, Vol. 37, pp. 401–440, February, 1944.

25. GRAY, WILLIAM S. (editor), "Theme of the Conference," in *Reading and Pupil Development*, p. 4, Supplementary Educational Monographs, No. 51, University of Chicago Press, Chicago, October, 1940, 355 pp.

26. GRAY, WILLIAM S., and BERNICE E. LEARY, *What Makes a Book Readable*, University of Chicago Press, Chicago, 1935, xviii + 358 pp.

27. GRAY, WILLIAM S., "Summary of Reading Investigations: July 1, 1943 to June 30, 1944," *Journal of Educational Research*, Vol. 38, pp. 401–429, February, 1945.

28. GREENE, EDWARD B., "Effectiveness of Various Rates of Silent Reading of College Students," *Journal of Applied Psychology*, Vol. 15, pp. 214–227, April, 1931.

29. HOGBEN, LANCELOT (editor), *The Loom of Language*, W. W. Norton & Company, Inc., New York, 1944, x + 692 pp.
30. HOLLINGWORTH, H. L., *Psychology, Its Facts and Principles*, D. Appleton-Century Company, Inc., New York, 1928, xviii + 539 pp.
31. HORN, ERNEST, *Methods of Instruction in the Social Studies*, Charles Scribner's Sons, New York, 1937, xix + 523 pp.
32. HUUS, HELEN, "Factors Associated with the Reading Achievement of Children from a Migratory Population, I-II," *Elementary School Journal*, Vol. 45, pp. 203–212, December, 1944; pp. 276–285, January, 1945.
33. IMUS, HENRY A., JOHN W. M. ROTHNEY, and ROBERT M. BEAR, *An Evaluation of Visual Factors in Reading*, Dartmouth College Publications, Hanover, N. H., 1938, 160 pp.
34. KERFOOT, JOHN B., *How to Read*, Houghton Mifflin Company, Boston, 1916, 297 pp.
35. KORZYBSKI, ALFRED, *Science and Sanity:* An Introduction to Non-Aristotelian Systems and General Semantics, 2d ed., with a new Introduction by the author, The Science Press Printing Company, Lancaster, Pa., 1941, lxxi + 806 pp.
36. LANGSAM, ROSALIND S., "A Factorial Analysis of Reading Ability," *Journal of Experimental Education*, Vol. 10, pp. 57–63, September, 1941.
37. LARSEN, ROBERT P., and D. D. FEDER, "Common and Differential Factors in Reading and Hearing Comprehension," *Journal of Educational Psychology*, Vol. 31, pp. 241–252, April, 1940.
38. LUCKIESH, MATTHEW, and FRANK K. MOSS, *Reading As a Visual Task*, D. Van Nostrand Company, Inc., New York, 1942, xvi + 428 pp.
39. LYMAN, R. L., *The Mind at Work in Studying, Thinking, and Reading*, Scott, Foresman and Company, Chicago, 1924, 349 pp.
40. MARCUM, DIXIE M., "Experiences, Concepts, and Reading," *Elementary School Journal*, Vol. 44, pp. 410–415, March, 1944.
41. McCALLISTER, JAMES M., "Reading Ability, II, In Relation to Survey Courses," *Chicago Schools Journal*, Vol. 18, pp. 79–82, November-December, 1936.
42. McCAUL, ROBERT L., "The Effect of Attitudes upon Reading Interpretation," *Journal of Educational Research*, Vol. 37, pp. 451–457, February, 1944.
43. McCULLOUGH, CONSTANCE M., "Relationship between Intelligence and Gains in Reading Ability," *Journal of Educational Psychology*, Vol. 30, pp. 688–692, December, 1939.
44. McNALLY, HAROLD J., *The Readability of Certain Type Sizes and Forms in Sight-saving Classes*, Bureau of Publications, Teachers College, Columbia University, New York, 1943, vi + 72 pp.
45. MERSAND, JOSEPH, "Radio Makes Readers," *English Journal*, Vol. 27, pp. 469–475, June, 1938.
46. MOORE, HERBERT, "Diagnosing and Caring for the Reading Difficulties of College Freshmen," *Journal of Psychology*, Vol. 1, pp. 139–143, 1936.
47. ORTON, SAMUEL T., *Reading, Writing, and Speech Problems in Children*, W. W. Norton & Company, Inc., New York, 1937, 215 pp.
48. PATERSON, DONALD G., and MILES A. TINKER, *How to Make Type Readable*, Harper & Brothers, New York, 1940, xx + 209 pp.
49. RICHARDS, I. A., "Certain Notions on the Theory of Interpretation and Reading," American Educational Research Association, *Official Report of*

1940 Meeting, pp. 10–14, American Educational Research Association, Washington, D.C., May, 1940, 192 pp.

50. ROBINSON, FRANCIS P., and PRUDENCE HALL, "Studies in Higher-level Reading Abilities," *Journal of Educational Psychology*, Vol. 32, pp. 241–252, April, 1941.

51. ROBINSON, FRANCIS P., and WILLIAM E. HALL, *Concerning Reading Readiness Tests*, Bulletin of the Ohio Conference on Reading, No. 3, Ohio State University Press, Columbus, Ohio, 1942, 16 pp.

52. ROGERS, MAURINE V., "Phonic Ability As Related to Certain Aspects of Reading at College Level," *Journal of Experimental Education*, Vol. 6, pp. 381–395, June, 1938.

53. SEARS, RICHARD, "Characteristics and Trainability of a Case of Special Reading Disability at the Moron Level," *Journal of Juvenile Research*, Vol. 19, pp. 135–145, July, 1935.

54. SEMMELMEYER, MADELINE, "Promoting Readiness for Reading and for Growth in the Interpretation of Meaning," in *Reading and Pupil Development* (William S. Gray, editor), pp. 56–62, Supplementary Educational Monographs, No. 51, University of Chicago Press, Chicago, October, 1940.

55. SIMPSON, RAY H., "Reading Disabilities among Teachers and Administrators," *Clearing House*, Vol. 17, pp. 11–13, September, 1942.

56. STRANG, RUTH, *Exploration in Reading Patterns*, University of Chicago Press, Chicago, 1942, ix + 172 pp.

57 STRANG, RUTH, "Relationships between Certain Aspects of Intelligence and Certain Aspects of Reading," *Educational and Psychological Measurement*, Vol. 3, pp. 355–359, Winter, 1943.

58. STRANG, RUTH, "Why Fifty Successful People Read," *Adult Education Bulletin*, Vol. 4, pp. 97–100, April, 1940.

59. STROUD, J. B., and MARGARET HENDERSON, "Rate of Reading and Learning by Reading," *Journal of Educational Psychology*, Vol. 34, pp. 193–205, April, 1943.

60. TEAD, ORDWAY, "Words and Deeds," *School and Society*, Vol. 58, pp. 225–228, Sept. 25, 1943.

61. THORNDIKE, EDWARD L., "Reading As Reasoning: A Study of Mistakes in Paragraph Reading," *Journal of Educational Psychology*, Vol. 8, pp. 323–332, June, 1917.

62. THORNDIKE, ROBERT L., *A Comparative Study of Children's Reading Interests*, Bureau of Publications, Teachers College, Columbia University, New York, 1941, vi + 48 pp.

63. TINKER, MILES A., "Eye-movements in Reading," *Journal of Educational Research*, Vol. 30, pp. 241–277, December, 1936.

64. TINKER, MILES A., "Speed versus Comprehension in Reading As Affected by Level of Difficulty," *Journal of Educational Psychology*, Vol. 30, pp. 81–94, February, 1939.

65. TRAXLER, ARTHUR E., "A Study of the California Test of Mental Maturity: Advanced Battery," *Journal of Educational Research*, Vol. 32, pp. 329–335, January, 1939.

66. TRAXLER, ARTHUR E., *Ten Years of Research in Reading:* Summary and Bibliography, Educational Records Bulletin 32, Educational Records Bureau, New York, March, 1941, vi + 196 pp.

67. TYLER, I. KEITH, *Spelling As a Secondary Learning*, Bureau of Publications, Teachers College, Columbia University, New York, 1939, ix + 116 pp.

68. U.S. Office of Education: *Communication Arts and the High School Victory Corps*, U.S. Government Printing Office, Washington, D.C., 1943, viii + 76 pp.

69. WAPLES, DOUGLAS, VERNARD BERELSON, and FRANKLYN R. BRADSHAW, *What Reading Does to People*, University of Chicago Press, Chicago, 1940, xii + 222 pp.

70. WAPLES, DOUGLAS, and RALPH W. TYLER, *What People Want to Read About*, A Study of Group Interests and a Survey of Problems in Adult Reading, American Library Association and University of Chicago Press, Chicago, 1931, xxx + 312 pp.

71. WOODWORTH, ROBERT S., and MARY R. SHEEHAN, *First Course in Psychology*, Henry Holt and Company, Inc., New York, 1944, 445 pp.

72. ZAHNER, LOUIS C. (chairman, Committee on the Function of English in General Education), *Language in General Education*, D. Appleton-Century Company, Inc., New York, 1940, xiii + 226 pp.

73. ZAHNER, LOUIS C., "The Testing of Comprehension," *Educational Record Supplement*, pp. 71–89, January, 1940.

CHAPTER III

THE READING PROCESS IN DIFFERENT SITUATIONS

If the poor readers were put into remedial reading classes would it be
necessary to teach reading in other subjects?

The many-sided aspects of reading presented in the previous chapter are not generally recognized. It is common to think of reading as
just *reading*, a single skill requiring a single adjustment on the part
of the reader. The prevalence of this opinion is partly due to the
fact that reading, for the adult, has become more or less automatic.
He does not have to labor consciously through all the processes of
word recognition and comprehension that baffle the beginner. He can
concentrate on the ideas of the author, oblivious to the routines through
which his developed skill is taking him.

Probably a further substantial source of the idea that reading is a
simple matter is the fact that many adults have developed one general
method of reading that they apply to everything. This is naturally
so, for in the schools where they were taught as children, reading was
merely reading. They learned a vocabulary and read stories and,
by the end of the third grade, became recognized readers with a
method of reading. It was not realized at the time that reading is a
many-sided occupation for which the reading of stories is an inadequate
preparation.

The truth of the matter is that superimposed upon the sheer,
basic mechanics of reading are certain conditions, which determine
how those mechanics may best be manipulated. One of these conditions is the kind of material to be read; the other, the purpose for
which it is read. Let us take a few types of material and discuss
briefly the kinds of adjustment that they require on the part of the
reader.

FROM SIMPLE SIGNS TO COMPLEX ARTICLES

Single Words.—The simplest reading material, the sign consisting
of a single word, such as "Stop" or "Exit," requires the quick recognition of the single form observed from left to right. For the adult who
is accustomed to such signs, as for the adult in the act of distinguishing
the name of the destination on a streetcar, the recognition is a matter
of a single glance at the general form of the word. When it is a

66

question of distinguishing "West" or "East," close attention to the first letter suffices. Consciously or unconsciously, the efficient adult makes adjustments to significant cues in order to achieve his purpose with the minimum of effort.

Phrases.—When the sign becomes a phrase—"To station," "To trains," "To street"—the reader must synthesize the two or more words into a meaningful whole; the directional word "to" and the name "street" combine into one thing, an index of destination. The skillful reader learns to synthesize these, taking in a short phrase at a glance and immediately appreciating the singleness of meaning in the combination of words.

Sentences.—A sign that consists of a sentence, such as "Drink Coca Cola" or "The wise man buys at Wiseman's," requires the reader to look at several words in several pauses made from left to right, and to determine as he reads the appropriate groupings of words into such associations as the author intended. The reader does this by means of his experience with natural language sequences, his familiarity with certain key or directional words (such as "to" suggesting the coming of a phrase, or "however," introducing an opposing idea), his consciousness of the import of punctuation within the sentence, and his appreciation of the way that words are arranged to form a sentence and of their relative importance within the sentence.

Consider what is required of a student when he reads the following sentence from a widely used high-school civics textbook: "The executive department of the government enforces the laws and administers the public work."

Obviously, the reader must focus his eyes on the sentence and move them along the line, pausing almost imperceptibly perhaps six or seven times before reaching the end. The images made on the retina, the photographic plate of the eye, must be transmitted to the brain, the printed symbols must be recognized, and their meaning must be comprehended. In addition to some words that are commonly used in everyday language, this sentence contains at least four terms that belong to the technical language of the social sciences—"executive," "government," "administers," and "public work." The meanings of the separate words must be fused into a sentence meaning that is more than the sum of the parts. Moreover, the sentence must be related to the context in which it appears. All this and more are involved in the reading of a sentence in the social-science field.

In the field of science, technical vocabulary may play a still more important part, as in the sentence, "One ampere of current delivered under a pressure of one volt will do one joule of work per second."

Although its structure is not difficult, this sentence as a whole is practically meaningless for anyone who does not understand the technical words that it contains.

Directions.—Directions for reaching a destination are usually tersely written; the reader must observe rather carefully the words and word groups and their relationships. Of special importance are the names of certain landmarks and directional words ("left," "right"). Words denoting position in time as well as in place, such as "before" and "after," also must be watched, since they make considerable difference in meaning. If in the course of the trip the reader forgets the name of a given landmark, he may skim the material until he reaches the area where it is mentioned. As he comes to each critical point of his trip, he perhaps skims and reads the succeeding portion. The skimming may take the form of looking in sequence at the names of the landmarks already passed, with a consciousness of the order in which they came.

Paragraphs.—Printed matter of paragraph length creates a larger problem than does any one of the foregoing. The reader must make the mechanical adjustment of passing the eyes from the end of a given line to the beginning of the next, a difficult step for children, though it is one that has become automatic for most adults. But further, the relationships of the sentences to one another and their combined relation to the whole idea that they concern are matters of importance in paragraph reading. A series of paragraphs raises the problem of seeing the relationship of the idea presented in one paragraph to the idea presented in the next, and the relationship of all these ideas to the whole meaning with which the author is concerned. Mental outlining and the retention of ideas, which makes such outlining possible, are characteristics of the efficient reader.

Life would be relatively simple if the foregoing problems were the only ones facing the reader, because these general types of adjustment might be mastered fairly readily. But the demands of reading are of many kinds. One does not simply have just a sign to read; one has to distinguish rapidly among many. One has not simply phrases or sentences or paragraphs to understand; one must master materials that are written in different styles, demanding more or less intensive reading and one or another type of approach.

Newspaper Articles.—The reader of newspaper articles is presented with a characteristic pattern, which he must recognize if he is to read them efficiently. The various headings and subheadings suggest the main concern of the article. The first sentence or paragraph usually gives the entire idea in a nutshell. Subsequent paragraphs elaborate upon the first, giving some details and implications.   If the article is longer, a third detailed reiteration of the whole matter is given, sometimes with various persons' reactions or predictions concerning it. For the reader who wishes to get at the truth of a situation, this third part is often the most fruitful, because it goes beyond the reporter's summary and the interpretation given in the headline, to supply the actual sources of generalization.   Hence, the reader who is on the lookout for propaganda will read the first two parts to sense the reporter's bias, and then the source material in the third part in order to compare the facts with the preceding summary and interpretation.[1]

A person who wants only the gist of the news confines himself to the headlines and possibly the first paragraphs.   "Yanks Have Enemy on Run" satisfies him, whether it means one enemy or an army; he is glad if the news is cheerful and does not care to know whether it is propaganda, intended to keep up his morale.   The person who has performed in a play the preceding night skims the article on the performance to find his name and the comment upon his acting.   The reader who has a pet theory and anticipates having an argumentative luncheon companion reads an article only to note facts that will support his side that noon, regardless of the presence of plenty of information on the other side.   So it can be seen that, while a given piece of material may have certain characteristics that determine to a degree how it may be read, the reading may still vary considerably according to the individual's purpose.

Topical Articles.—Articles or materials of a topical nature usually begin with an introductory portion setting forth the purpose of the discussion to follow.   In the last paragraph or so ordinarily, the argument is summarized or prediction is made of the dire consequences if the author's advice is not followed.   But the middle portion may follow any one of a number of forms, which the reader, to be efficient, must be ready to sense.   Perhaps the whole will be devoted to an explanation of the author's stand; or perhaps opposing ideas will be presented and made ridiculous, to assure a favorable reception of the author's proposal.   According to tradition, in well-written material the first sentences of many of the paragraphs will suggest to the reader the plan of presentation that the author is following.   A hurried reader may read only the first paragraph, to find out the author's purpose, and the last, to discover his conclusion.   If such a reader is curious to learn, besides, the reasons that the author has for his view or the details that compose or support this view, he may read certain portions of

---

[1] For a discussion of the ways in which newspaper material may be read, see "How to Read the News" (17).

the body of the article as well.   Anyone who wishes a record of the steps in the author's logic may take notes, outlining the main features. Another person, wishing to find the fallacy in the author's view, will read for the main steps of logic, constantly measuring them against his personal yardstick with such questions as: "Does this step follow logically?" or "Are there numerous exceptions to this?" until he finds the point of error, the leap in logic, the sly tangent, the flimsy analogy.

Reading two articles on the same subject may dispose the reader to make a comparison.   This comparison may concern form if the reader is interested in composition, mode of argument if he is concerned with forensics, or content if he wishes to note which points are selected for the reaching of different conclusions.   An author whose article had been condensed in *The Reader's Digest* was amazed to find he could not spot the points of omission.   To satisfy his curiosity, he reread the original, comparing it with the skillful condensation.

THE READING OF LITERATURE

The novel and the short story vary in several ways that affect the reader's purpose and ease in reading.   Given a simple plot, a story in which this plot is emphasized is easy to follow.   If the author confines most of the plot movement to the actions of his characters, the skillful reader who is interested primarily in plot will find himself watching for these passages of action.   If the author also uses conversation describing actions, or conversation in which characters decide upon actions to advance the plot, the reader will concern himself with this.   If a description of a place promotes the plot by setting the stage for coming action and assisting the reader to predict coming events, this then becomes the object of careful reading.   The reader not only is active in watching for developments in the plot, but is constantly making predictions based upon the development of the story as he has experienced it.   These conclusions as to what the next step will probably be are achieved by an analysis of the situation plus a comparison with life as the reader knows it.   A specialist in story structure is likely to make another mental calculation: the artistic necessity of a given thing's happening next.

When the story is largely concerned with character development or psychological changes, the plot may be relatively unimportant or almost nonexistent.   The author may create this character development through his own discussion of the psychological changes involved, through the comments of other characters about the person who is changing, or through the conversation or behavior or inner thoughts of the character himself. The well-oriented reader is aware of all these possibilities as he starts to read such a book, but quickly acquaints himself with the author's particular vehicles for the promotion of his special interest and notes these as he reads.

Some stories, particularly in recent times, have been written chiefly for the purpose of orienting the reader to the physical world. The author is a geographer or a scientist in novelist's clothing, so to speak. In such books, the story is there to create interest and to keep the reader interested all through the passages of description. But skillful young readers who have learned to avoid descriptive passages deftly skip over these, for passages with action or conversation. Thus they read the book quite rapidly and emerge unscathed by the environment of the Pueblo Indian or of Chilly, the Eskimo Boy. One effective way of realizing the author's purpose in such a book is to have the children read it to get information to be used in painting a mural depicting the country and its life. With this purpose in mind, the readers find descriptive passages becoming meaningful; the adjectives then are seen to be more than obstacles in the path to the names of things.

People who say that they read stories very rapidly are usually admitting to a selective type of reading. They read for plot, hurry to the romantic passages, or find the corpse in the first chapter and skip to the end to see "who done it." If as he reads the reader has a purpose in mind and learns to watch for the kinds of material useful to him, he is bound to achieve his purpose in shorter order than can the reader whose journey is aimless and undiscriminating. Rapid readers of novels are likely to be either of two kinds—people who have a limited appreciation of literature and read all books with the single purpose of seeking plot or love interest, and those sufficiently oriented to appreciate the particular emphasis that the author is making and to read especially for this.

It is perfectly true, however, that the quality of some literature is of such high order—the careful development of characters, the philosophy of the author, the vivid reflection of environment, the wealth of meaning in every sentence—that an adequate reading is necessarily slow. This statement is not intended to imply that a person may never legitimately read a great book in any other way. No one, to our knowledge, has condemned the authors of reference Bibles; yet surely in preparing their publications they combed the Bible for topics only, not for the implications, the interpretations, the character delineation, or the expression of philosophy for which the Bible is desirably and commonly read. The point to be made is only that certain works deserve a more considerate pace than habitual readers of lighter fiction are inclined to apply.

While poetry usually demands slow, intensive, or concentrated reading, it does vary in this respect. Some poetry appeals to the intellect, some to the emotions, and some—as W. Somerset Maugham suggests in the case of T. S. Eliot—to the unconscious. By tradition, poetry has been allowed to do a number of things to create difficulty for the reader. The capitalization of the first letter of the first word in every line is disconcerting. For the sake of a rhyme a sentence is often turned about in an unnatural manner, causing the reader to shuffle the parts of the sentence mentally until the relationships become clear. "To pass there was such scanty room, The gate descending grazed his plume," is scarcely the way one would tell the incident to a companion, even in poetic prose.

Frequently too the sentences are long and full of modifying phrases conveniently placed to throw the reader into confusion. The school of thought which holds that poetry should be couched in rare and elegant language has caused the reader further mystification. The use of analogy, of words chosen partly for their sound, and of figures of speech requiring interpretation of the meaning through symbolism, has been another distraction and reason for slow reading. Ballads and other poetry using the dialect of Scotland and other countries have been an additional hurdle. And the concentration of thought in a shorter space than is typical of prose—a feature common to most of the older poetry and some modern poetry—causes the reader to travel slowly to make certain of relationships and main intent.

Modern poetry whose metric pattern has become a flowing cadence rather than a predetermined form with an unchanging number and kind of feet in every line may present less of a problem. While the thought may still be so concentrated as to require careful reading, the cadence permits a continuity that reduces sentence distortion.

Narrative poetry is more easily read than most other kinds of poetry unless, of course, it presents special problems of dialect or some other incidental hazard. The form itself gives the reader the advantage of a thread of story to "hang on to." There is no problem, as in the sonnet, of discovering through the symbolism what the author has in mind. In "The Wreck of the Hesperus," to speak of a much overworked disaster, the title itself and the opening lines leave the reader in no doubt about there having been a wreck. On the other hand, in the sonnet beginning "Euclid alone has looked on Beauty bare," the reader's imagination is free to roam all the way from plane geometry to a burlesque.

The easiest of all narrative poetry, to many people, is the poetry of Stephen Vincent Benét. The length and rhythm of his lines change with the mood and tempo of the subject matter, so that in eye sweep and rhythm the reader is helped to grasp the idea the author has in mind. His sentences and phrases flow naturally and simply as in prose; yet in sound and flow and plane of thought they are poetically conceived. His figures of speech enrich rather than bewilder. He was the historian-philosopher of all the American people and used language in such a way that all could understand.

As with the novel, the purposes for which people read poetry vary partly according to literary taste. Edgar Guest is read for his homely sentiments; Vachel Lindsay is famous for his rhythms; Robert Service, for his characters and humor; Carl Sandburg, for his vigorous and unsparing forthrightness. It is usually the specialist who reads with an eye to technical perfection, a consciousness of figures of speech, and the appropriateness of rhythm and sound and length of line to the subject. But possibly the most common reason for turning to poetry is to experience encouragement or inspiration or kindred feeling through the author's response to something the reader, too, has experienced but has been unable to express so well. The reader is likely to study the poem with care, mentally comparing the author's situation with his own, and paying particular attention to the attitude with which the author has faced the situation.

THE READING OF MATHEMATICS

The intensity with which mathematics must be read is close to that required for poetry. It is commonly said that children fail in solving verbal problems in mathematics because they are poor readers. This, of course, is only half the story. Exercises couched wholly in mathematical symbols require for solution only the following of the technique, whereas verbal problems necessitate, besides reading skill, the ability to see in the particular situation the manner in which the generalization applies. "On what should the statement of equality be based?" "If x is to represent a fraction, how must the other values be translated?" These are problems of adjustment that call for the intelligence of adaptation.

As far as reading is concerned, problems of verbal mathematics present concise statements interspersed with figures, which break the continuity of phrases and slow the reading process. They contain a technical vocabulary of words, such as "product" and "quotient." One investigator found more than one thousand mathematical words used in more than half of the 24 textbooks that he analyzed. Cole (5) reduced her list of terms used in algebra to 151 essential words.   Verbal problems also contain characteristic patterns of expression (x is to y as . . .), which must be learned so well that mental translation of them into mathematical symbols becomes almost automatic.   "Is equal to" should immediately bring the symbol $=$ to mind; "the product of 3 and 4" should flash the multiplication sign $\times$; "x is to 4" should bring $x/4$, and so forth.   But some students assimilate these technicalities slowly unless much teacher help is given, and many readers go through mathematics curricula with only a slippery grasp of terms.   Occasionally a verbal problem will contain material unnecessary to the solution of the problem.   This imposes on the reader the task of selecting pertinent facts.

It is questionable whether any successful student of mathematics ever solves any but the simplest of verbal problems correctly in one reading.   In his first reading he notes the kind of situation involved and the technique applicable to it, the identity of the unknown, and the facts pertinent to the solution.   This reading is more rapid than succeeding readings but much slower than the usual pace for a popular novel.   A second reading probably centers attention separately upon pertinent words and groups of words, their meanings and their translation into mathematical symbols.   The third reading can focus upon the relationships among these words and groups and arrive at a determination of the statement of equality.   A fourth reading serves as a check upon interpretation and is punctuated with periodic reference to the symbols assigned to the words and groups.

In geometry the first reading will probably be a general one, in which the hypothesis and the conclusion are grasped.   A second reading of the hypothesis gives the details of the figure to be drawn.   After the reader has drawn and lettered his figure, a third reading with attention to the conclusion helps him to set up the symbolic statement that he must prove and to decide whether construction lines need to be added to his figure.   Another reading with reference to his figure and his statement checks upon his interpretation.   The proof of the statement involves the recall of previously learned theorems and axioms in response to the conditions of the problem.   This is translation in reverse, from the pictorial or symbolic to the verbal.

Successful students of mathematics adopt some such system of attack as those described above.   They approach a mathematics problem with confidence, not with the defeatist attitude expressed by one student: "I always think I'll get it wrong, so I do."   They give sufficient attention to each part of the problem; they do not stop at the superficial scanning described by one student in this way: "I never read the whole problem; just glance at the first few words and naturally I get it all wrong." A successful student thinks about what is given, what is to be found out, and what formula is involved; he does not "just look at the problem and pick out all the numbers and do something about them." He studies out the precise meaning of the words used and avoids misinterpretation of mathematical expressions. Difficulty in mathematics is cumulative; it is often due to failure to master preceding mathematical concepts and processes. Any difficulty that interferes with the interpretation of meaning may be considered a reading problem.

THE READING OF SCIENCE

Science textbooks contain some materials that are written with almost the conciseness of mathematics. There are statements of laws, definitions, formulas, lists of the characteristics of various groups, and lists of the names of members of various groups. Besides these, however, there are passages that are more descriptive and expanded and that have to do with steps to be taken in an experiment; with steps in the life story of a plant or an animal; or with processes that have produced inanimate forms, such as the conglomerate rock. The most modern texts often present facts on the basis of which the student must make his own generalizations and inferences. Sometimes the life and works of a famous scientist are developed much as one would find them in literary biography. Most science books are amply illustrated with diagrams or labeled drawings of certain forms or processes, or with pictures of stages in a life cycle or an experiment. All these types of material present a technical science vocabulary.

Junior high-school textbooks designed to orient students in a wide variety of science subjects present a particularly difficult reading problem, in that there is usually little carry-over in concepts from one area to another. A word is scarcely introduced before its subject is dropped, and that word is never heard of again. In this way a peculiar problem in memory is raised. There is no provision for repetition that would assist memory; so if the memorizing is a goal, these books certainly fail of their objective.

From the nature of the science textbook it can be seen that the student has to be prepared to vary his method of reading and the purposes for which he is reading when he turns to different kinds of material. Further, he must learn to recognize these types of material as he comes to them. He must sense that this is the biography of a great scientist and that the purpose of its being presented is probably to illustrate the arduous task of the pioneer, to demonstrate the scientific method, to make more memorable the scientific findings.   Or he must realize that this is a definition of a term that will recur and will cause him considerable trouble unless he becomes well acquainted with it; that this is a presentation of a life cycle, the steps of which he must remember in sequence; that this is the recounting of an experiment whose premises and steps are important; that this is the statement of a law whose verbal description will be more memorable if he studies also the diagram or series of pictures illustrating it; or that, because this topic has been allotted several pages by the author, it is probably something particularly important to remember.

Ideally in the use of science material the student does more than memorize the material on the page, more than sense the sequence of ideas and remember them in order.   As he reads he makes comparisons of one set of materials with another.   While reading about the life cycle of one creature he compares it mentally with a previously read life cycle of another, to see the likenesses and differences of the two. If the teacher is prone to ask such questions as, "What are the chief differences between vertebrates and invertebrates"? the student must be aware that it will be helpful to his preparation to make a mental comparison of vertebrates with invertebrates as he reads of one of these groups.   Thus the purpose for which a student reads science material is conditioned not only by the nature of the material as he finds it, but also by the types of thinking about the subject that the teacher is accustomed to require.

Perhaps the most important outcome of the study of science is proficiency in the problem-solving method.   At least four factors are involved in selecting and rejecting reading material with reference to its relevancy to a problem:

1. The ability to comprehend the problem
2. The ability to keep the problem in mind
3. The ability to comprehend the passage read
4. The ability to recognize the relevancy of facts in the passage to the problem

Too frequently students are required to read about problems far removed from their own interests and experiences and, without any planned orientation, are given books to read that are far too abstract and difficult.   Poor average reading ability and low interest in reading may often be traced to an unrealistic curriculum, poor teaching, and inadequate materials of instruction.

Maturity in science reading requires the ability to evaluate, verify, and judge the worth of the material; to define with precision words referring to specific substances or operations that can be observed; to describe relationships that can be observed; to select the facts related to a given topic; to picture an experiment from the written description; and to follow directions. Few high-school students are aware that these abilities are required in science reading. They do their assignments by reading and rereading and memorizing verbatim parts of the text, instead of attacking the reading assignment as a thought-getting process. In describing their methods of reading science material, high-school students frequently say something of this sort: "I read the lesson fairly rapidly but carefully, slowing up over difficult parts." "I read fairly slowly. If there is a complicated section, I read it over until I do understand it." One student who read, with excellent comprehension, a science article about the method of chromatographic adsorption, described his method as follows:

I read more slowly than usual because the material was not very familiar. I fixed in mind as well as possible the materials used in the method described and the facts about its invention and use. I tried to recall some of the work I had done in biochemistry and remembered using the method described in testing for vitamins. I tried to understand what the author had in mind, used my own background, and tried to get a picture of the whole sense of the article with the main ideas in the foreground. When I came to details I thought important, I stopped and tried to fix them in mind.

To help students in college read science material, Howland, Jarvie and Smith (8) prepared a manual describing the kind of thinking involved in reading technical material and providing practice in special skills.

The science vocabulary in textbooks of science for secondary schools was thoroughly studied by Curtis (6); and the vocabulary of college biology, by Stevenson (16). In the latter investigation 1,939 words were reported as "difficult" by 10 or more students.

THE READING OF SOCIAL SCIENCES

Geography.—Geography textbooks in the intermediate grades have been notorious for the difficulties that they have customarily presented to the pupil, and some of the difficulties have been unnecessary. Among these are an unduly difficult general vocabulary; definitions of technical words almost as difficult to understand as the words themselves; a style of writing that packs many facts into a small space and gives no clues as to the relative importance of ideas—and hence gives no indication of which ideas are most worth remembering; and an approach that assumes the reader to be an ardent geographer, who needs no motivation and no guidance in journeying from his known world into the strange territories dealt with in the textbook. Authors of more recent materials on this subject have tried to overcome some of these drawbacks.

Inherent in the very nature of geography, however, are a number of difficulties. As it is strange material, it necessarily presents the problem of a technical vocabulary and definitions. Association of the word with the definition is often aided by pictures, which it behooves the student to observe. In connection with this, sentences are frequently interrupted with reference symbols, such as "Fig. 8," indicating an adjoining picture that will be helpful. This interruption slows the reading process and, if the figure referred to is on another page, not only creates a long pause in the continuity of thought but sometimes even causes the reader to lose his place in the book. Another type of interruption is a parenthetical key to the pronunciation of a strange name.

Geography materials are largely descriptive. Sometimes the chief value of a paragraph is the main idea stated in the first sentence or so, but usually these materials deal in some systematic way with the physical conditions of a given region and the manner in which they affect the life of the people. One portion of a text may discuss physical features and climatic conditions and vegetation. Another may deal with the housing, clothing, food, and occupations of the people. Maps of the territory, pictures of the people and their land, charts of such matters as the relative production of various foods, and graphs of production or population changes and the like are provided to facilitate memory and understanding When maps or other helps are placed in an appendix to the book, it is necessary for the pupil to develop skill in locating the needed material and reading it while a marker or a finger holds the place in which he has been reading the main text.

On a low level of teaching geography, the teacher may require verbatim accounts or close approximations of the material as it is written in the textbook: she may require the students to prepare statements of main ideas accompanied by important details, to memorize the definitions, the complete lists of characteristics, the occupations, and the steps in sequence by which the natives produce certain goods or prepare the soil and plant and cultivate and harvest. As a rule this involves the student's memorizing statements with their supporting details, definitions, characteristics, and steps in sequence, just as the author presents them. It involves reading for certain main ideas and details and for a sense of sequence in the sequential type of material; plus, of course, the recognition of the different types of material as they come.

This is referred to as a low level of teaching geography because it has been so often proved that memorization is an unreliable index of true understanding. The teacher who wishes to make sure of her pupils' comprehension will cultivate answers to questions of definition that will incorporate the information in the pictures, maps, charts, and graphs, as well as the author's definition in the pupil's own words; if the author has dealt with the physical conditions apart from occupations or human adjustment to environment, the teacher may ask, "How can you tell the kind of country these people live in by the kind of houses they build?" Such a question causes the pupil to cut across the author's organization and make his own groupings of factual material for the purpose that the teacher has set. When asked, "What other people whom we have studied lived like these? Prove your point!" the pupil is led to make comparisons with previous material and is helped to retain earlier knowledge which but for repetition might easily be forgotten.

Thus in a course that requires a high quality of thinking in geography, the student must learn to profit by all the aids that enrich his idea of certain technical words, of certain regions, and the like; he must read to remember characteristics and lists that he will be able to recall only if he associates them with other information (To associate cheese and watches with Switzerland makes little sense unless one knows certain other things about the country). As he reads, too, he must make associations not only with material of comparable nature read much earlier and with observations of his own society and environment, but also with related or dependent material that occurs in the same set of lessons. He must know the symbols commonly used in reference aids in the text; the pronunciation symbols in the aids to pronunciation; the use of the key in maps; the explanatory labels in charts and graphs; and the use of the index, table of contents, and glossary. He must be a keen observer of chapter, sectional, and marginal headings and of the revealing details of the pictures provided; and he must understand the deceptive distortions in certain maps.

History.—Some specialists in reading find it very puzzling to determine exactly what the authors of many history textbooks expect the student to retain. Like geography books, histories are often packed so full of facts and afford so little guidance as to the relative importance of those facts that only a student with a photographic memory or a specialist in the subject could do full justice to the reading—and then at a pace much slower than that usually required if the material is to be "covered" within the time allotted in the syllabus. There is little doubt that, for many a poor reader, the subject is not only "covered," but well under the sod. Added to the fact-packing problem is the frequent use of a baffling general vocabulary and of specialized words that are defined either cryptically or not at all. In some books, the pictures illustrating the strange terms are actually the most deceptive of all. A Roman aqueduct, for instance, is represented by a group of people standing on a plain with some archways faintly outlined in the distance. Reluctance to provide definitions for certain broad historical terms, such as the French Revolution, and the tendency to leave the reader to gather a vague definition from lengthy discussions of facts and events are ascribed by one historian to a fear on the part of the author lest he be criticized by fellow historians for oversimplification. The preference seems to be to let the student flounder rather than to risk professional criticism. The authors of a few recent textbooks have done much to overcome these shortcomings.

History textbooks commonly contain about as great a variety of reading experience as one might hope to find within the covers of a single volume. Chapter headings, section headings, and marginal titles are helpful signposts. They must, however, be observed with concern for their relationships to one another; often the listing of headings with equal typographical stress is no warrant that the ideas in all cases are parallel or of equal importance. The chapter is sometimes begun with a question that is worth keeping in mind as the keynote of the entire chapter. Sometimes in the first paragraph or so the main idea of the chapter is suggested, while in a final paragraph or section all that has gone before is summarized. Some portions of the reading constitute a chain of events in a life or a period of history that requires a memory for details in sequence; others contain paragraphs setting forth a main idea that is important in itself, whether or not the details are retained; while in still other instances the main idea is useless without the supporting details that accompany it (as in a paragraph starting, "Many factors contributed to the downfall of this civilization."). In some kinds of material the author presents the characteristics of something or describes in detail conditions prevailing at a given time; these must be memorized if the student is to get the important contribution of that material. So the problem is an assemblage of reading material varying from rather expansive passages in which the main idea is the most memorable factor, to closely packed, detailed material that requires slow, careful reading. Meanwhile, the problem that presented itself in the case of geographical maps, pictures, charts, and graphs is manifest here, as well. Getting information from maps takes a specialized kind of reading. Just as a student has to master the vocabulary in a foreign language, so he has to learn the symbolic language of maps. Just as his impression of descriptive passages gains in vividness when he pictures the scenes described, so his reading of maps becomes more realistic if he visualizes the rivers, glaciers, and other features of the landscape portrayed by maps. He needs to be taught

1. To recognize that a map is a ground plan drawn to scale
2. To read a descriptive story from maps
3. To read different kinds of maps
4. To progress from the simplest to the more complex maps
5. To read maps in order to learn (12)

The student of history, then, must learn to make use of the chapter and section headings and the marginal notes for a general appreciation of the direction of the author's thought. He must be a good observer of maps, graphs, charts, and pictures, as well as an observer of footnotes, pronunciation clues, and other helps that the book may provide. He must know how to use the index, the table of contents, and the glossary to suit his purposes. Recognition of the kind of material he is reading and the kinds of items that are worth remembering for his purposes is necessary to efficient reading. As in many types of material, the chief problem is to select the more important and to discard the trivial. In paragraphs that simply expand the main idea, the student will try to retain only the main idea; in those whose main idea is vapid without facts, he will try to retain the most crucial; in those that relate a series of events, he will try to impress upon his memory the greater of these in sequence. The procedures used by an individual student, of course, will be conditioned by the purposes that are set by the teacher.

To all his reading in the social sciences the student needs to bring his background of experience. Comparisons between one situation and another, either read about or lived through, are valuable student responses to historical material. Whenever the author summarizes a period or a circumstance, the student should try, as he reads, to bring to mind the facts previously given that substantiate the author's generalization. Whenever the author fails to summarize, the student should himself be drawing conclusions and making helpful comparisons. And whenever the author has presented his material, for instance, as groupings of social, economic, political, and spiritual facts, the student should, as he reads, be putting these parts together in another relationship so that his reading will represent mastery of the material rather than a parroting performance.

The development of ability to understand common historical abbreviations and important words in the social-science field is aided by lists of words considered necessary. Lists of this kind have been compiled by several investigators (9, 13, 15).

Many students depend too much on sheer rereading. . They think in terms of time spent on pages covered instead of in terms of understanding gained. Others reread more selectively, as indicated in the following description:

> Reading for the first time from textbooks or magazines and newspapers, I read quietly and straight through. Then I go back and check up on things I am doubtful about and look up references in the encyclopedia or consult people. I like to read more than one textbook on the same subject, and I also like to read comparative material on similar subjects. In other words, when I read about the Monroe Doctrine, I also like to read about the Pan-American Union. In reading for review, I read quickly until I come to doubtful subjects, which I try to go over and analyze. In looking up a specific subject, I naturally use the index of the book and also other references.

Some students approach more closely the methods of reading described in this chapter; they describe their methods as follows:

> As to reading history, it depends on what I am reading. For instance, when looking for facts, I read the whole article, not skipping any of it, and pick out mentally the important points.

> When I am looking for an answer, I read until I find it. When I read social science I read for facts and when I have questions to answer I can learn more easily.

> The opening sentences of paragraphs are my best help in review. They usually bring to mind the important material included in the paragraph, and others are detour signs from unimportant material. In this way, the important matter of the review can be recalled or read again.

> I read according to some plan—*i.e.*, have some idea of what I am looking for.

> I read with anticipation of the outcome.

> I try to read with an open mind, with imagination, and with a thought of how the last sentence connects with previous passages.

CONCLUDING STATEMENTS

In this discussion of different types of reading material and different purposes for reading, it is hoped that a number of facts have been made clear. Each kind of material presents a different set of reading problems. Each author, through his use of vocabulary, organization of material, and tendency either to fact packing or to a more expansive type of writing, puts his unique stamp upon the material and its problems.   Each teacher, in the kinds of emphasis that she has in her course. further determines the kind of reading that the student must do.

Some skills recur in almost all kinds of school materials: reading for the main idea, for pertinent details, for inference, for drawing conclusions, for seeing relationships, and for a sense of sequence or outlining.   The understanding of various book aids—pictorial materials; indexes; tables of contents; footnotes; glossaries; chapter, section, and marginal headings; and questions—makes all the difference between a rich understanding of the material and a meager and vague exposure.   For all these materials the reader needs a quick recognition of different kinds of reading situations and a knowledge of what they demand of him as to the speed at which he reads and the things he looks for.

These facts suggest that the elementary school has a long but imperative task on its hands: to equip the reader with the varied reading experiences and to develop a consciousness of the way in which a particular piece of material may most efficiently be read.   They suggest that teachers need to help pupils set purposes for themselves before they read, since otherwise it is only a matter of chance that a pupil will hit upon the kinds of information that the teacher recognizes as important.   They imply also that no teacher should be so busy hurrying on to the next topic in the syllabus that she cannot stop to give the pupils a sound foundation in the use of books and book-reading aids or to allow them time to reflect on what they have already read.

That teachers' purposes are not always identical, that authors' styles are not uniform, that technical vocabularies may overlap but are not universal even within a given subject field, and that students are not equally skilled in reading at any one level in school progress— these facts suggest a further consideration.   It is that upper-grade, high-school, and college teachers should not assume that because reading has already been taught it need not be one of their concerns; they should not suppose that the English teacher alone is accountable for the reading readiness of students in every course in the curriculum. All teachers must take the responsibility for building concepts in their own classes, for exploring the abilities of the students to read text and reference books in the way the wise instructor believes they should and for searching their books to discover possible difficulties and reading hazards and then anticipating these obstacles before they break the confidence of the students.   Besides, the teachers should know specifically what their own purposes are and how these affect the selection of memorable materials; then they must show the students how to determine that selection and must give them exercise in this process, not in the spirit of impatience with youth's stupidity but in the realization that these precautions are necessary.

America will never be a safe country until its masses are raised from the level of meager and slow fact reading—which makes them easy prey to a dictator—to a level of ease and independence and continuous growth in reading. This level can be achieved, but only if one of its chief stumbling blocks is removed—the distaste for knowledge in general or for any of its various subjects that is created by the unsympathetic attitudes of teachers who fail to see that love of reading in their own fields can come only after this reading has been made possible and attractive.

References

1. ANDERSON, HOWARD C., FREDERICK G. MARCHAM, and SEYMOUR B. DUNN, "An Experiment in Teaching Certain Skills of Critical Thinking," *Journal of Educational Research*, Vol. 38, pp. 241–257, December, 1944.
2. ARTLEY, A. STERLING, "A Study of Certain Relationships between General Reading Comprehension and Reading Comprehension in a Specific Subject-matter Area," *Journal of Educational Research*, Vol. 37, pp. 464–473, February, 1944.
3. BOND, ELDEN A., *Tenth-grade Abilities and Achievements*, Teachers College Contributions to Education, No. 813, Bureau of Publications, Teachers College, Columbia University, New York, 1940, vi + 68 pp.
4. BRINK, WILLIAM G., *Directing Study Activities in Secondary Schools*, Doubleday, Doran & Company, Inc., New York, 1937, xiii + 738 pp.
5. COLE, LUELLA, *The Teacher's Handbook of Technical Vocabulary*, Public School Publishing Company, Bloomington, Ill., 1940, 119 pp.
6. CURTIS, FRANCIS D., *An Investigation of Vocabulary in Textbooks of Science for Secondary Schools*, Ginn and Company, Boston, 1938, viii + 127 pp.
7. DALE, EDGAR, *How to Read a Newspaper*, Scott, Foresman and Company, Chicago, 1941, xii + 178 pp.
8. HOWLAND, HAZEL POPE, LAWRENCE L. JARVIE, and LEO F. SMITH, *How to Read in Science and Technology*, Harper & Brothers, New York, 1943, xi + 264 pp.
9. KELTY, MARY G., "A Suggested Basic Vocabulary in American History for the Middle Grades," *Journal of Educational Research*, Vol. 24, pp. 335–349, December, 1931.
10. MCCALLISTER, JAMES M., "Determining the Types of Reading in Studying Content Subjects," *School Review*, Vol. 40, pp. 115–123, February, 1932.
11. MCKIM, MARGARET G., *The Reading of Verbal Material in Ninth Grade Algebra*, Teachers College Contributions to Education, No. 850, Bureau of Publications, Teachers College, Columbia University, New York, 1941, viii + 133 pp.
12. PARKER, EDITH P., "Learning to Read Maps," in *Adapting Reading Programs to Wartime Needs* (William S. Gray, editor), pp. 167–171, Supplementary

Educational Monographs, No. 57, University of Chicago Press, Chicago, 1943, 283 pp.

13. PRESSEY, L. C., and S. L. PRESSEY, "The Determination of a Minimal Vocabulary in American History," *Educational Method*, Vol. 12, pp. 205–211, January, 1933.

14. SCHNECK, JOHN W., and FRANCIS D. CURTIS, "The Important Scientific Terms in High-school Physics," *School Review*, Vol. 50, pp. 715–720, December, 1942.

15. STEPHENSON, ORLANDO W., and WILLIAM R. McGEHEE, "A Vocabulary Common to Citizenship and American History," *Journal of Educational Research*, Vol. 22, pp. 55–58, June, 1930.

16. STEVENSON, ELMO N., "An Investigation of the Vocabulary Problem in College Biology," *Journal of Educational Psychology*, Vol. 28, pp. 663–672, December, 1937.

17. U.S. Office of Education, "How to Read the News," Education and National Defense Series, *Pamphlet* 16, U.S. Government Printing Office, Washington, D.C., 1942, 27 pp.

CHAPTER IV

GROWTH IN READING

The dear people do not know how long it takes to learn to read. I
have been at it all my life and I cannot yet say I have reached the goal.

GOETHE

Learning to read is a lifetime process. From birth to old age, each
period of life makes its contribution to the development of reading
abilities, interests, and attitudes. Reading ability, as part of the
individual's total development, increases with his growth in interests
and general ability and with the challenge of increasingly complex
and difficult reading tasks at each successive educational level.
Although this is true, too few teachers from the fourth grade on realize
that they have a part in the tremendous responsibility for furthering
growth in reading. Nevertheless, the beginning should be made in
the first grade, when the simpler forms of the so-called "higher reading
abilities"—appreciation, organization of thought, critical thinking,
the making of inferences, and the applications of ideas—should be
developed within the range of the young child's interests and experience. This chapter sketches the general course of progress in reading,
beginning with preschool years, in order to give perspective on its
development during high-school and college years.

PREREADING EXPERIENCES IN PRESCHOOL YEARS

The infant takes his first step on the road to learning to read when
he distinguishes, out of the vague blur of light and darkness, his
mother's face and other objects that have interest and meaning for
him. Gradually he learns to see likenesses and differences in objects
and persons in his environment. At the same time he increases his
ability to communicate with others, using language as one means of
meeting the situations with which he is confronted.

Soon he begins to notice printed words in signs about the house
and on the street—"Hot" and "Cold" on the water faucets, "Bus
Stop" on the street corners. He notices the black-and-white marks
on his picture books and on the newspaper that his daddy is reading.
If he goes to nursery school, he may find his printed name above the
hook on which he is to hang his hat and coat. When he becomes aware

that printed words have meaning for him, he has taken a most important step in learning to read.

BEGINNING READING IN THE PRIMARY GRADES

By the time that the child enters the first grade, if he comes from a favorable home environment, he has acquired an oral vocabulary useful to him in his daily living. In school he needs experiences that develop him physically and socially and that make reading necessary and meaningful, for reading should grow out of activities of special interest to children. Before learning the printed words for animals, clothes, friends, houses and house furnishings, vegetables, fruits, flowers, and trees, children should have many different experiences with these objects. They should play with them, talk about them, notice similarities and differences among them, and cut out pictures showing many different varieties of each.

After these firsthand experiences, the child is ready to see the printed word pasted under the appropriate picture. For example, the word "rabbit" may be pasted on a page of pictures of many different kinds of rabbits in various poses. Experience comes first, labels next. Thus children begin to learn "to separate the symbol from the situation symbolized." As is now the practice in many schools, the child learns (10, page 395)

. . . to invoke single, limited images or notions in response to word stimuli. In his later reading this tendency leads to many misinterpretations. For words have multiple *values* and their *appropriate interpretation* for anyone at any given time and place must take into account their total context or setting.

In addition to these basic attitudes of seeking meaning in printed words and of realizing how many different varieties of object or situation a single word may represent, growth in specific reading skills may be expected during the primary grades. Here children should learn

1. To read from left to right across the printed page. This ability comes gradually and reversals of letters and words are common and natural in the first grades.
2. To recognize new words in context by identifying them with pictures, with their sounds, with familiar combinations of letters in them, or by other methods appropriate to the individual child
3. To recognize initial letter clues, and likenesses and differences in words that cause special difficulty
4. To find satisfaction and enjoyment in the reading of simple material dealing with their own background of firsthand experience

If learning to read could be made more natural, more like the process by which a child learns to talk, fewer reading difficulties would appear later. Reading, like talking, should be an intrinsic part of the child's living. If associating the printed word with the sound of the spoken word or with an object or action meets a real need in the child's life, it enlists his wholehearted attention and concentration. Moreover, the printed word is then learned with its meaningful associations.

Lack of incentive deters some children from gaining proficiency in reading during the early school years. Agnes Repplier did not learn to read until she was ten years old. Up to that time she had gained pleasure from books through hearing them read to her. She had not seen "any connection between the casual and meaningless things called letters and all the sweetness and delight that lay between the covers of books" (14, page 3). Then came an edict, "wise, harsh, and menacing." Her mother gave strict orders that no one should read her a line. The ten-year-old Agnes, after a few days of blank despair, sized up the situation and quickly, though not easily, learned to read.

CONSOLIDATION OF READING ABILITIES IN INTERMEDIATE GRADES

With a sound foundation of beginning-reading experiences, children make rapid improvement in the fourth, fifth, and sixth grades. They continue to participate in the meaningful affairs of everyday school life, many of which require reading. They learn to recognize unfamiliar polysyllables by dividing them into syllables. They perfect other basic skills acquired in the first three grades and integrate them into an efficient tool of learning. Thus children become able

1. To select and comprehend the main ideas in varied passages appropriate for them to read in any field
2. To comprehend pertinent details in order to relate them in proper sequence to main points
3. To make sound inferences and generalizations derived from their reading, within the range of their experience
4. To make application of their reading to the solution of practical problems

From their experience in "reading to learn" they should begin to build a variety of reading interests, to form the habit of evaluating the books and articles that they read, and to extend their experience through reading. By the time that pupils reach junior high school they should know that a skillful reader has a definite purpose or problem in mind, reads with an inquiring mind, pauses occasionally to summarize and see the relationships in what he has read (12).

Children who do not make the expected progress need special instruction. Too often these children have been neglected, and consequently their reading difficulties have accumulated. Students who do not improve may be the victims of a former teacher's inflexible application of a method of teaching reading that was inappropriate to them. If these retarded readers are to be helped, they should be given individual instruction and practice.

EXPANSION OF READING IN JUNIOR HIGH SCHOOL

When a child enters junior high school, he is usually confronted with new subject-matter fields and increased demands for wide reading. He not only has to comprehend assigned reading; he must also locate sources of information bearing on the topics or problems assigned. As in previous years, the incentive to acquire these reading skills will arise out of activities that seem important and interesting to the pupil.

More specifically, he should

1. Develop ability to find pertinent sources of information on a topic; to select from these sources the ideas that have a direct bearing on the topic or problem under consideration; to evaluate the material found with reference to its relevancy to the problem, its accuracy, and its adequacy; and to organize, in a unified way, ideas obtained from various sources.

2. Make progress in the subtle aspects of interpretation. As the pupils encounter sentences that present difficulties in interpretation, they should undertake an intensive word-by-word analysis, pooling possible meanings and determining the most exact. This process of "analytic rephrasing" requires an expansion of the original sentence. Sometimes a sentence or a paragraph is necessary in order to get back to the literal or plain sense meaning of a single word. Sometimes the reverse of this process is needed to condense an expansive passage into a simpler, more comprehensible unit.

3. Extend experience, appreciations, and interests through reading. During junior-high-school years, the child's world expands rapidly. Books make up for limitations in his physical environment, and he should learn to use them to take him out of his country, his times, and himself.

GAINING INDEPENDENCE IN READING IN SENIOR HIGH SCHOOL

During senior high school, students may be guided in taking more responsibility for their own improvement in reading—to study, under guidance, the results of reading tests; to set specific goals for themselves; and to plan their individual reading programs. This kind of initiative is highly desirable and represents real growth in self-direction.

Growth in interpretation of meaning should continue during senior-high-school years. Students should learn to "read between the lines," to determine the full and precise meaning of single sentences, paragraphs, and passages as a whole. This kind of interpretation requires understanding of the author's hidden intention, his tone, the setting in which he wrote, his attitude toward himself, his subject, the reader, and other people and things. Misinterpretations decrease as students analyze the mental processes that lead either to errors or to successful interpretations.

Students should also become increasingly appreciative of the personal values of reading. Through reading they can extend their experiences and become acquainted with new places and people. They can gain insight into how people may feel when they behave in certain ways. Thus the students can increase their understanding of themselves in their complex and often trying family and boy-girl relationships. These personal values of reading are not likely to be achieved, however, unless students and teacher recognize them.

If he has this personal point of view toward reading, the student thinks of each author as a person who has something to say to him. The experience of communication through reading should be almost as active and quickening as conversation with a friend. In marked contrast with this active communication between author and reader is the prevailing passivity of students who read aimlessly and unimaginatively. They have never learned that reading may have meaning in their lives.

Several phases of growth in reading may well be given special emphasis in the senior high school. The high-school student should

1. Acquire the methods of reading best suited to each of his high-school subjects.

2. Develop suitable reading interests and tastes during this flexible adolescent period. Investigations have shown that, under existing conditions, the amount of voluntary reading tends to decrease during high school and that, in general, the quality of the reading is poor. It has, however, been demonstrated (11) that, with proper guidance, interests become more mature and appreciations may be deepened. During these years, many students, when guided in their choice of books, outgrow the comic-book stage, find new reading interests, and read with increasing discrimination.

3. Develop ability to communicate ideas gleaned from printed material. Opportunities for growth in conversational ability through reading should be provided during high-school years. Too frequently only the intake side of communication is emphasized in the reading program. Students should be encouraged to discuss their reading and to use it appropriately in many social situations. Discussions in which each student gives his own spontaneous response to a book foster critical appreciation of responses to reading material, as well as appreciation of the material itself.

4. **Progress in the power of synthesis.** To every reading assignment students should bring previous experiences that have a bearing on the subject. For example, if they are reading about the conquest of tuberculosis, they may recall any cases of tuberculosis they have known; tuberculosis tests or X-ray examinations they have taken; and previous knowledge acquired from discussion, conversation, radio programs, films, books, or pamphlets. As they read, the new knowledge should take its place as part of their total pattern of understanding of the subject—should even be shaped into plans for the prevention of tuberculosis.

5. **Experience a growing pleasure in precision.** A desire to get the author's meaning, a discontent with vague generalizations, an unwillingness to abandon a passage that is only half understood, a rejection of inaccuracy—in short, a "reading conscience"—should be developed in many students who have acquired the wrong idea of the purpose and method of skimming and have emphasized speed without regard to comprehension. This "reading conscience" was developed early, but in a manner not to be generally recommended, in one of Ellen Glasgow's characters, Jenny Blair Archibald, who was reading *Little Women* "for the assured reward of a penny a page. . . . 'It isn't safe to skip,' she thought. 'Grandfather would be sure to find out.' " (6, page 3.) The pleasure in precision is not incompatible with the idea of skimming, for the reader who skims properly emerges with an accurate general impression or a few selected facts.

CREATIVE READING IN COLLEGE

During college years, students should not only improve in the abilities already mentioned, but also become increasingly aware of the different approaches needed in reading different kinds of material. Our language reflects our activities: our action is expressed in narration, our thinking in exposition, our feeling in lyricism. The student reads a book by Rachel Field, Thomas Mann, or Willa Cather differently from the way he reads a treatise on mathematics. These books, to be enjoyed, demand sensitivity to the sounds of words, the images that words evoke, and the subsurface meanings of metaphors. A book on mathematics demands a knowledge of the specific specialized meanings of words, an accurate understanding of their relationships, and the ability to translate words into quantitative symbols. In reading historical narration, students should focus their attention on the real events reported and reviewed. In reading imaginative narration, they will be interested in the psychological and literary qualities. In reading philosophy they will follow the author in his search for truth. In reading literature they may be interested in the construction of the plot, in the portrayal of characters and their relation to the events of the plot, in imaginative words and phrases, or in the work as a whole, reading it for the enjoyment that it gives. Obviously, the college student who does not recognize the need for a different mind-set for different kinds of material, and even for shifts from narration to exposition to lyricism within a single work, will not read with the greatest efficiency. Without this adaptability to the diverse demands of reading material, students are not likely to select judiciously, read critically, interpret cogently, appreciate fully, and adapt their reading rate and method flexibly to different kinds of material and to different purposes in reading.

Intelligent reading in college is essential to the development of a scholarly person—one who has the ability to speak and write effectively. Such a person should be able to draw upon a mind stocked with significant ideas—a mind precise, "poised in moderation against extremes," realistic, and richly human. College years, in fact all the years of formal schooling, offer unparalleled opportunities for employing the present in such a way as to build a useful past—a past stored with meaningful experiences and with success in using those experiences in meeting new situations.

When a student leaves college, he should be able

1. To find the reading material he needs
2. To adjust his rate of comprehension and method of reading to the material and to his purpose
3. To comprehend accurately what the author has said
4. To judge the soundness of the author's ideas and draw valid inferences and conclusions
5. To appreciate beauty of style and expression
6. To synthesize ideas gained from reading with his other experience
7. To "read between the lines"
8. To discriminate between facts and opinions, between acceptable evidence and propaganda
9. To remember and use ideas from his reading
10. To use reading as a stimulus to creative thinking and to the discovery of new problems for study

These reading abilities are likely to be the fruits of his growing conviction regarding the importance of reading to him personally, as well as in the world today, and of his growth in ability to plan and carry out an appropriate individual program of self-improvement in reading.

HIGHER LEVELS OF GRADUATE STUDY

For successful graduate study the reading abilities already described are a necessary foundation. Advanced students specializing in different fields will, however, show marked individuality in their reading methods (see pages 48–53). For example, Santayana describes a kind of reading that is quite different from the specific recall generally recommended (15, pp. 186–187).

. . . a particular alcove where there were philosophical books at hand, and foreign periodicals, soon became my regular place for reading. I could take my own books and notebooks there if necessary; but for the most part I browsed; and although my memory is not specific, and I hardly know what I read, except that I never missed *La Revue des Deux Mondes*, I don't think my time was wasted. A great deal stuck to me, without my knowing its source, and my mind became accustomed to large horizons and to cultivated judgments.

Occasionally Santayana learned great passages by heart. He makes an important distinction between a verbal comprehension and a much deeper kind of comprehension of philosophical writings (15, page 248):

Verbally I understood them well enough; they were not superficially obscure; but critically, as to their presuppositions, their categories and their place in history, I understood nothing.

Later Santayana found (15, page 248) that he was

. . . able to discount the language of a system and perceive from what direction it drew its inspiration.

These quotations call attention to the individual differences that must be allowed for in teaching "best" study and reading methods. The quotations also suggest that something more than verbal comprehension of the main ideas and supporting details is necessary for the highest levels of thoughtful, critical reading.

Every person has reading potentialities that can and should be developed for his personal satisfaction and social usefulness. Some are capable of comprehending difficult and abstract material, while others cannot attain so high an altitude of reading power, but are able to read widely in many fields within their range of comprehension. Some are also better adapted to one speed of reading than to other rates. This is to say that each person has a combined reading potentiality of altitude, breadth, and speed that should be discovered and developed.

At any age an individual's reading performance should be evaluated with reference to the reading potentialities toward which he is growing. Thus each student has his own reading norm, or standard, appropriate to his needs and ability. It is toward this developing individual reading pattern that instruction in reading is to be directed, to the end that the person's life may thereby be made more worth while.

References

1. "Better Reading Instruction," *Research Bulletin of the National Education Association*, Vol. 13, pp. 273–325, November, 1935.
2. BOND, GUY L., and EVA BOND, *Teaching the Child to Read*, The Macmillan Company, New York, 1943, x + 356 pp.
3. DURRELL, DONALD D., *Improvement of Basic Reading Abilities*, World Book Company, Yonkers-on-Hudson, N.Y., 1940, viii + 407 pp.
4. GANS, ROMA, *A Study of Critical Reading Comprehension in the Intermediate Grades*, Teachers College Contributions to Education, No. 811, Bureau of Publications, Teachers College, Columbia University, New York, 1940, vi + 135 pp.
5. GATES, ARTHUR I., *The Improvement of Reading*, rev. ed., The Macmillan Company, New York, 1935, xvi + 668 pp.
6. GLASGOW, ELLEN, *The Sheltered Life*, Doubleday, Doran & Company, Inc., New York, 1932. 395 pp.
7. HILDRETH, GERTRUDE, *Learning the Three R's*, Educational Publishers, Inc., Minneapolis, Minn., 1936, x + 824 pp.
8. KIRK, SAMUEL A., *Teaching Reading to Slow Learning Children*, Houghton Mifflin Company, Boston, 1940, 225 pp.
9. KNIGHT, PEARLE E., and ARTHUR E. TRAXLER, *Develop Your Reading*, Little, Brown & Company, Boston, 1941, ix + 376 pp.
10. KOPEL, DAVID, "General Semantics and Reading Instruction," in *Papers from the Second American Congress on General Semantics*, 1941 (M. Kendig, compiler and editor), pp. 392–399, Institute of General Semantics, Chicago, 1943, xxiv + 581, 12 pp.
11. LaBRANT, LOU L., and F. M. HELLER, *An Evaluation of the Free Reading in Grades Seven to Twelve Inclusive*, Ohio State University Press, Columbus, Ohio, 1939, ix + 158 pp.
12. LYMAN, ROLLO L., "The Teaching of Assimilative Reading in the Junior High School," *School Review*, Vol. 28, pp. 600–610, October, 1920.
13. OLSON, WILLARD C., and SARITA I. DAVIS, "The Adaptation of Instruction in Reading to the Growth of Children," *Educational Method*, Vol. 20, pp. 71–79, November, 1940.
14. REPPLIER, AGNES, *Eight Decades*, Houghton Mifflin Company, Boston, 1937, 304 pp.
15. SANTAYANA, GEORGE, *Persons and Places*, Charles Scribner's Sons, New York, 1944, 262 pp.
16. STANGER, MARGARET A., and ELLEN K. DONAHUE, *Prediction and Prevention of Reading Difficulties*, Oxford University Press, New York, 1937, ix + 191 pp.
17. THORNDIKE, EDWARD L., "Improving the Ability to Read," *Teachers College Record*, Vol. 36, pp. 1–19, October, 1934; pp. 123–144, November, 1934; pp. 229–241, December, 1934.
18. WITTY, PAUL, and DAVID KOPEL, *Reading and the Educative Process*, Ginn and Company, Boston, 1939, x + 374 pp.

CHAPTER V

FAULTS IN SCHOOL READING PROGRAMS PRODUCTIVE OF FAILURE IN READING

What common practices in the schools have contributed to our failure to teach everyman's children to read?

It is pleasant merely to talk constructively about the desirable features of a school reading program and to hope that as the result of such a discussion everyone will happily perceive the flaws to be avoided. Experience teaches, however, that we must be a little more specific than that if we are to be helpful or if we are to be helped. The truth is that there are several practices and sins of omission lying at the doors of administrators, supervisors, librarians, and teachers, the correction of which could do infinite good to our reading program. There are plenty of reasons why these practices have been indulged in, why the omissions have occurred. The following discussion is not designed to chastise the workers concerned. It is only to be hoped that, by calling attention to these factors and by pointing out their injuriousness to the reading program, we can provoke more cooperative effort directed toward their reduction or elimination.

LACK OF CONTINUITY FROM KINDERGARTEN TO COLLEGE

Even the best teacher, when limited by a shortsighted syllabus, supervisor, or administrator, cannot be responsible for the balanced and steady development of her students. The fact is that a peculiar carry-over from the origin of the American elementary school has distorted the reading program beyond any one teacher's ability to correct it. When the early elementary school took on the obligation to establish the foundations of higher learning, it naturally set the precedent of considering the reader below the age of twelve or fourteen as one kind of creature and the reader of greater age as quite another. Before high-school age one was expected to recognize words, to be able to analyze strange words, and to be able to read aloud acceptably. Any question about what had been read, whether silently or orally, was not one of opinion (except Did you like the story? to which only one answer could be given); nor was it a question requiring the application of original thought. Answering the question involved only the

95

catechismic process of finding the exact place in the book where the wording of the question left off and giving the remainder as the answer. (Where was Johnny? Johnny was in school.) This was considered adequate preparation for work in high school and college, where, suddenly, the student would be expected to use his head as he read.

This divorce of the elementary program from the secondary, and of the secondary from the collegiate, has had many manifestations; and it is a temptation to say that none of them has been good. The problems of the poor reader in high school and college are not unique, although they differ from those in elementary school in three important respects: (1) the poor reading habits of high-school and college students are more deeply established than the habits of elementary-school children and consequently are more difficult to revise; (2) their reading difficulty more frequently involves reasoning and interpretation and far less frequently the mechanics of word recognition; and (3) there is a dearth of suitable reading material of interest to adolescents who are seriously retarded in reading.

Research shows again and again that, while reading interests change, simple reading material on one level holds the same possibilities for the use of varied reading skills and purposes that are inherent in the more difficult materials on a higher level; that, in fact, there is no desirable and important reading skill whose beginnings cannot and should not be made with the very beginnings of learning to read. One of the most inexcusable and unfortunate errors of our time is the failure of the elementary, secondary, and college curriculum builders to unify their efforts along lines that are warranted by the findings of research.

CURRICULUM REVISION WITHOUT TEACHER EDUCATION

Another administrative or supervisory shortcoming is the revision of curriculum or method without the necessary teacher education. There is little that an administrator or a supervisor can do with a teacher who shows no capacity to learn and who has taught long enough to have life tenure; but it is not an infrequent occurrence to see a really fine reading syllabus wrecked in the hands of a short-sighted, uncomprehending teacher. If those in charge of schools would see to it that, in connection with every important curriculum revision, representatives from all groups of teachers either had the opportunity to assist in the work or were fully informed of its nature, the gap between the spirit of the syllabus and the use of it might be reduced.

Reading has probably been the most active field of research in the curriculum. Each year bibliographies appear containing many pieces of important research on the pedagogy of reading. Teachers and administrators alike are not sufficiently informed with regard to these findings. The finding by Gilbert, for instance, reported in 1940, that it is positively detrimental to the reading habits of children to have them follow in their books the oral reading of a classmate, may as well never have been reported as far as school practice is concerned. Yet unless the finding should be denied by further research, the children might better be out fishing than sitting in the classroom; from the standpoint of reading development, they would be making as great gain.

In a survey of reasons why school-wide reading improvement programs and remedial classes had not been set up in secondary schools, the most frequent reason was found to be the opposition of an uninformed principal and the next most frequent, lack of awareness of the problem on the part of teachers. Something needs to be done to keep research information flowing into the schools and reaching the ears and the eyes and the brains, not just the desks and the waste-baskets, of principal and teacher alike. It should not be left to the teacher to find the time and the money to take a graduate course at a university on the teaching of reading; learning about new trends and new truths should, rather, be as common and as dependable as the appearance of the new moon.

MISUSE OF TESTS

The findings of many a reading test are left to languish unseen on some dusty shelf in the principal's office. The children take the test, the median is calculated, the teachers sigh, "Now, thank the Lord, we can teach again," and the matter is finished. Or, superficially better but practically worse, the reading score is recorded in the student's cumulative record, but there is no education of teachers and administrators in the proper use of the test results for instructional and guidance purposes. Consequently, the score is too often used to reinforce a teacher's poor opinion of a student. When it is consulted one or two or three years later by, say, the chemistry teacher, it is taken to explain everything. Of course, anything may have happened in those years to affect the student's reading for better or for worse, and the general reading test given did not, in the first place, specifically measure ability to read chemistry. However, it is regarded as gospel, and the teacher feels absolved of all responsibility to try to find and understand the student's particular problem.

There must be greater general appreciation of the specific abilities that these standardized reading tests really measure. An administrator should refuse to purchase a test unless it is to be thoroughly understood before it is given and is to be used afterward by the teacher as well as put on the office record.   Furthermore, when a test in reading is given, the administrator should avoid using it in such a way that its effect will be to limit the teacher's conception of her job as a reading teacher; but that will be the effect if emphasis is placed on the appraisal of teaching ability rather than on the appraisal of the reading of individual students; if the stress is on general norms and competition rather than upon individual diagnosis; and if the test itself fails to yield a comprehensive picture of the reader's abilities.

TOO LITTLE UNDERSTANDING OF THE INDIVIDUAL

The teacher and the administrator have a combined responsibility for obtaining the knowledge of the individual child that is pertinent to his reading development.   The teacher is in a strategic position to make observations of language development and of habits of work and personal habits, to reach the parents, and to obtain the cooperation of the school nurse and the school physician on special problems. The principal can contribute to this fund of information by supplying test materials for measurement of intelligence and other phases of reading readiness, and by providing the time and assistance for administration of them.

One of the more absurd situations in our educational system is that, at the most crucial stages of school adjustment and of reading development, we provide the least opportunity for individualization and the poorest financial incentive to teachers.   There are classes of six, perhaps, in advanced seminars in college, while the freshman English classes bulge to include 35 or more.   Creative writing or advanced drama courses in high school are cozy tête-à-tête's in comparison with the groups of forty-odd seventh or ninth graders who are exposed for the first time to high-school requirements.   And while in many school systems the upper-grade classes are a comfortable 20 or 25, the kindergartens run to 50 and 60, and the first grades to 40, 50, and 70.

Any businessman would know better than to try to make 50 sales by approaching a group of 50 persons en masse.   Common sense would tell him that it would be physically impossible to make the proper psychological approach to each.   Yet the schoolteacher is expected to start 40 to 50 children at once upon the most difficult of all tasks— the translation of the auditory symbols of reality into equally curious visual symbols.   The situation is impossible; under these conditions, the accumulation of sufficient information about each child to suggest how his learning may best be promoted is beyond the capacity of the teacher, who can neither find out how the pupil may best learn nor

offer a sufficiently individual program for his best growth. It is true
that the experienced, gifted teacher, by dividing his large class into
smaller groups, by providing a wide variety of reading and practice
material, and by using every opportunity for observation and guidance
that offers itself during the school day, can give a certain amount of
attention to the needs of individual children even in a large class.
But under the present unreasonable conditions even the gifted
teachers, who are far and few, must expect a certain amount of
reading failure that is simply a matter of shortsighted and unsound
educational policy.

Adequate provision for the individual child is defeated also by the
lack of give-and-take among teachers working with the same children.
Often the teacher has just begun to grasp the comprehensive picture
of a child's reading problems and needs when that child is promoted to
another teacher; and, what with grade reports, charts, blanks, orange
crates, and hectographing, the two teachers never succeed in exchanging ideas until the second teacher also has begun to recognize the
problem, a semester or a year later. In some schools the situation
resembles a bucket brigade in which everyone passes the bucket so
quickly to the next that, as the last person prepares to heave the contents on the fire, he discovers there are no contents. This, of course,
is an extreme expression of the busyness against which a teacher must
constantly fight in order to achieve even a small portion of the amount
of individual work that he would like to do.

Not only lack of time, but lack of sensitivity to the needs of children,
retards progress in reading. The comments of teachers, classmates,
parents, and other persons in his environment go far toward determining a pupil's idea of himself; and this idea, in turn, influences the
effort that he expends in reading. If the report card, month after
month, tells the pupil that he is below average, he is likely to be convinced eventually that he is a failure. If the teacher says of a boy,
in the presence of his peers, "Oh, well, we couldn't expect anything
better of John," what incentive can he muster to read better the next
time? Many adolescents are impressionable and insecure and readily
accept other persons' evaluations of them. If a parent constantly
tells visitors that "John is slow, while his brother is eager and quick,"
John's slowness is likely to be intensified.

One teacher of reading tells of an interview with a student and the
student's mother. The teacher suggested that the boy tell him a
little about himself and his school. While the student was telling
about gymnasium and drawing classes, the medals that their teams
had won, and other (for him) positive features of school life, the mother

interrupted by saying, "Tell Mr.————that you haven't worked, you don't pay attention, you won't listen, and you won't study." Of course, the boy was embarrassed, but smiled and said nothing. The teacher encouraged him to continue his previous conversation and signaled to the mother not to interfere. Obviously it is important for all persons who come in contact with boys and girls to say things that build justified self-confidence—to make comments that have a favorable influence on the individual's development. Thus teachers will make their casual contacts count in the right direction.

Similar problems are created in the primary grades by lack of attention to individual differences in children's prereading experiences, in their readiness to read, in their mental ability to make progress in reading. A disregard for these individual differences frequently results in initial failure to read. This initial failure has psychological significance; it may lead the child to think of himself as "a child who cannot read"—an attitude that may persist into high-school and college years.

In the intermediate and upper grades, the continuation of mass methods and the application of grade averages that violate the principles of individual differences in reading interests, needs, and abilities not only intensify pupils' existing reading problems but create new ones. In these grades, teachers tend to spend a great amount of time with mentally retarded children, working intensively on reading materials that other members of the class grasp easily, in a vain effort to bring the lagging readers up to grade standards. These efforts are usually unavailing, not only because many children are incapable of comprehending the meaning of the reading material of their grade, but also because the methods used are not suitable for the slow-learning child. The teacher does not have appropriate objectives for each child.

Many children receive too little help in reading after the third grade. As a consequence, when they arrive in junior high school and are confronted with difficult subjects requiring much wider reading than they have been accustomed to, they lack the reading skills necessary to meet the new demands.

At every grade level, reading problems are rendered more acute by neglect of physical conditions, such as poor vision and hearing, glandular and nutritional disturbances; emotional instability; and tensions and pressures in the home or the school that have a detrimental influence on proficiency in reading. Many children come from an unstimulating and barren environment, in which there are no suitable books or other reading materials, and where older children and adults give no demonstration of obtaining pleasure and profit from reading.

Lack of clinical facilities also prevents rehabilitation of reading casualties. In the regions in which illiteracy is highest, reading clinics are practically nonexistent. The needs of most children who have reading disabilities are not being met (5). If our basic reading programs incorporated procedures learned in clinics and laboratories, much reading retardation could be prevented (12).

UNSOUND PROMOTION POLICIES

Schools in which promotion depends primarily upon a reading score also discriminate against good reading development; for a reading score is not a record of the child's psychological or social or emotional or experiential readiness for progressing or need for being held back. If children are to be promoted on the basis of their total developmental needs, general standards of achievement as well as promotion policy must be changed. For, if all pupils are required to meet rigid grade standards of achievement, the mentally retarded pupils and the poor readers will find themselves continually beyond their scholastic depth; they will feel constantly under pressure and will experience a hopeless sense of failure. Other related factors that create difficulty are lack of attention to the child who is "getting along all right," whether he is living up to his ability or not; lack of differentiated assignments and varied types of drill, to provide for differences in ability and needs; and lack of frequent informal tests to indicate stages of growth and evidences of the slightest retardation as soon as it occurs, rather than 6 months after it has struck root.

DISREGARD FOR READING READINESS

Reading readiness, originally a concept applying to the kindergarten and the first grade, is now recognized as a broad term applicable to the readiness of any person at any stage of development for reading and understanding the materials with which he is faced. It means that the kindergarten teacher must offer preparation for the types of experiences awaiting the child in first grade; that the first-grade teacher will teach reading to only those who are ready, and will plan suitable experiences for the unready child until he, too, can engage in beginning-reading activities; that subject-matter teachers at all levels will determine what their students need to learn in vocabulary or comprehension and will provide for that learning before they plunge the students into material too hard for them, or else will reduce the difficulty of material through the provision of easier books.

At all levels, it is true, provision for reading readiness is not a matter of letting students sit until the passing years have of themselves produced the necessary essentials for learning; it is rather a case of establishing a constructive program of activities designed to develop the ingredients that are deficient or lacking. Reading readiness, however, must not become a rigid goal. Some students cannot be improved sufficiently to become ready for an established level of work; the teacher and the administrator must try skillfully to help such students alter their expectations and set for themselves more realistic goals.

While for the past 20 years much has been written and spoken about the need of recognition of the readiness principle by the schools, much yet remains to be done in practice. "The boy over in the corner in the back seat is a slow learner who listens to our geography lessons and draws illustrations for us. He took the first grade over twice and still can't read above a preprimer." In a school system in which a sound readiness program is actually functioning, a history of that kind cannot exist.

LACK OF SUITABLE READING MATERIAL

The librarian, the teacher, and the administrator have a combined responsibility for providing suitable reading material for students and for assuring a balance of experience. One well-supported school system discovered, on giving a series of tests, that its children were below average in reading skills. The children were above average in mentality, experience, and the physical well-being that money can safeguard. The teachers had been conscientious in their work. They used several good sets of basal readers and the children became proficient in reading them; but no books other than these were used by the majority of the children in their schoolwork. The whole enigma was finally solved when a reading specialist pointed out the tremendous lack of supplementary reading in their school program. The specialist explained that the children failed on the reading tests, despite their proficiency in reading the basal readers, because the carefully developed vocabulary and the constant clues in pictures and context in the basal readers had become crutches for these bright children, who, never having been required to read independently, for the most part tended to lean heavily upon these aids and to fall down when, as in the test, their aids were removed. A balance in types of material must be offered if children are to become successful readers in all situations. We must ask ourselves, "What kinds of reading will children have to do as adults and what do they need now?" The answers to these questions should suggest our choice of materials and our emphases.

Suitable reading material for a class of 40 children really presents 40 different problems; not that there will not be some duplication in reading skills and tastes among the 40, but that the reading situation in the class cannot be suggested merely by a glance at the roster or at the faces of the children. The gayest looks of the extroverts will not reveal the truth of their reading retardation!

A wide variety of reading material is necessary, even for an individual pupil. At different times he will be reading at different levels, now selecting an easy book for recreation or because it happens to be on a subject that interests him, now choosing a much more difficult book that he will strive to comprehend—and by means of which he will grow.

OVEREMPHASIS OF CERTAIN SKILLS AND PRACTICES AND NEGLECT OF OTHERS

Among the avoidable faults in present-day reading practice are the kinds of things that teachers do or neglect to do for want of information on progress in the field or on the purposes that their work is to serve. Even when the teachers have been informed that a practice is detrimental to children's reading progress, they frequently continue it, for want of alternative procedures.

One of the chief sources of trouble in the teaching of reading has been overemphasis on certain skills or practices to the exclusion or neglect of others. An example of this is the tendency to stress one sense approach to the teaching of reading, usually the visual or the auditory. The picture-word method of teaching beginning reading attaches picture ideas to the printed symbols, gradually induces visual analysis of new words, and discriminates in favor of the child who senses differences best with his eyes. On the other hand, kindergarten ear training extended into the first grade leads children to attach auditory images to the appearance of the printed word and gradually to analyze new words by means of the sounds of initial letters, common endings, and common combinations of letters (ch, oi, ai, etc.).

A teacher who stresses the auditory approach over the visual develops in the child a slow method of word attack, which will be a help to him on only one out of every three words in the adult English vocabulary. A teacher who stresses the visual over the auditory establishes a quick method of word attack (inasmuch as it usually divides the word into fewer units and is not retarded by vocalization or subvocalization), which is nevertheless limited in application. Even when a teacher gives ample consideration to both of these, he may automatically produce poorer results, perhaps reading problems and cases of nonreaders, among those children who profit most by the method of tracing a word and getting a sense of its wholeness through feeling. Misinterpretations of this third method, such as that the child should spell the word letter by letter as he traces and that he should copy it elsewhere letter by letter instead of copying it from his memory of the whole, have probably been almost as detrimental as complete neglect of this method in the classroom. Nevertheless the fact remains that, whichever of the avenues the teacher ignores, be it visual, auditory, or kinoesthetic (muscular memory), a certain number of retarded readers or of nonreaders will result, who are deficient because the methods by which they learned lacked the comprehensive balance that would embrace their individual differences.

It is high time for school syllabuses, teachers' manuals, tests, work-books, and books on methods in reading to give the teacher concrete help in recognizing the learning idiosyncrasies of individual children and in planning a balanced and individualized word-recognition pro-gram. Failing this (be it to the shame of publishers and educators who should know better), it is time for the enterprising teacher to forge ahead for himself without benefit of these agencies.

Flash card drill is another technique in word recognition that is overdone by some teachers. The teacher whose program features this drill with great emphasis is proud to send the children on to the next grade equipped with a dazzling sight vocabulary. However, there are several drawbacks to this particular emphasis. In the first place, in order to hold the interest of the children in an overdose of flash drills, the teacher resorts to a wide variety of games involving the flash cards more or less. As he comes to the bottom of his barrel of tricks he has to indulge in such games as the fishing game, which is 99 per cent muscular coordination; or the train game, which exercises one child while the others squirm interminably; or the magic-circle game, in which one child reads cards arranged on the floor in a circle, and in the course of which he and many other children looking on are liable to observe the cards upside down. In the second place, the excess of practice with words on cards unhabituates the children to reading the words in context, so that a whole area—that of being able to keep the place on a page of print, of finding one's place on the line below the one on which one has finished reading, of learning to profit by the context in recognizing the word, of learning not only to phrase but to anticipate word patterns and emphases in the under-standing reading of a sentence—is reduced to an insufficient place in the child's practice experience. Reading becomes more a conditioned response than a comprehension of authors' ideas, and in such a program comprehension invariably suffers.

Overemphasis on phonic drill, as has been said before, can produce children who are handicapped because of ignorance of other methods of word attack that will work where phonics fail. It also tends to equip the children with forms that will be forgotten before ever any use for them occurs, or if through overlearning they should be remembered, no words may ever be found on which to apply them. A teacher can guard against the introduction of such fairly useless combinations by studying the frequency of their occurrence in the books that the children use. A further undesirable result of overemphasis upon phonics is that it makes children prone to analyze a word into very small units, rather than to observe more quickly the larger units that may be present—such as small words or familiar prefixes and suffixes—or to enlist the help of the context in ascertaining the meaning of the word and its identity. Persistent use of phonic analysis, in place of more efficient methods where these can be used, slows the reading process and defeats comprehension either because it entails long pauses between the analyses of words or because the heightened interest in words as words detracts from their meaning.

Many teachers have found it advantageous to discuss with the children the hard words that they are about to meet in a lesson. These teachers feel that it is psychologically more sound to have the children experience success in their reading and to create the opportunity for two observations of the strange new word rather than to risk one possibly unsuccessful encounter with it. This is a sound practice unless it dominates all the classroom reading experience. It is good sometimes to have children skim a new lesson for words that are new, to have the words put on the board and discussed from the points of view of their pronunciation and their particular meaning in the passage. The teacher can add to this list any words of common use that have a special, new meaning in the text. But constantly children must have the experience of reading independently, of coming upon strange word forms and using all their techniques to identify the word and to determine its meaning in the sentence. They must learn to look upon the methods of word attack that they have at their disposal as a kit of tools; they must learn to study the word from left to right for familiar parts, first trying to find larger units visually and then, if necessary, breaking the word into smaller units for the more laborious kind of analysis and reassembly.

They must also note the use of the word in the sentence and the suggestions of its meaning which may emanate from the surrounding words and sentences. For the life equipment of students, techniques for context analysis of this kind are as important as those for word-form analysis. For these reasons, teachers who give ample help in the analysis of strange words in new lessons must be sure to provide other free reading situations, in which children occasionally meet a problem in word form or word meaning that they must solve by themselves.

LACK OF BALANCE BETWEEN SILENT AND ORAL READING

Oral reading is one excellent means of diagnosing reading disabilities. It is also an impressive proof that the reader knows the names of all the words and how to put them together more or less expressively. Some people maintain that beginning reading cannot be taught without it, although Superintendent McDade of the Chicago Public Schools demonstrated otherwise. Recognizing the ill effects of teaching beginning reading by the oral method—with such results as lip movement, slow reading, thoughtless word calling—he proposed to circumvent these effects by a completely silent method, in which a discussion of the material to be read occupied a separate language period, while the reading period proper was devoted entirely to silent reading. The contribution of his experiment to the teaching of beginning reading is considerable, in that his method freed the imaginations of teachers to explore the possibilities of a completely visual approach. It introduced into the classroom many additions, such as pictures, charts, and actual objects, which could be referred to without the use of speech. When used as a supplement to the oral method, McDade's contribution is an enrichment of the beginning-reading program.

Some are of the belief that great stress should be laid upon oral reading throughout the educational system, although it is estimated that only about 1 per cent of the adult reader's reading life is spent in oral reading. Some feel that children should all look upon duplicate pages while one child reads aloud, although the listeners are not benefited, and the only person who gets the practice feels that he is reading for the sake of reading rather than reading for the sake of information, and so may become self-conscious and uncomprehending. It is time that overemphasis upon either oral or silent reading be tempered with a sane view of what the practice is good for and how much of it is good.

A beginning-reading program that ignores oral reading is depriving the child of one of the avenues through which he may learn words—the auditory. By hearing the teacher attach the spoken word to the written symbol as he looks at it, the child learns to associate the two until the symbol immediately evokes the word itself. For the development of this close association, the oral reading of the word in primary grades is important; but the earlier interpretation of this statement to mean that a child should do all of his reading orally, that he should always read sentences aloud, is an exaggeration.   Yet the fact that in some classrooms children sit with eyes fixed on the teacher instead of on their books when they are supposed to be "getting ready to read the next sentence" is suggestive of the impression that children may develop of the nature of reading through the guidance of some teachers.

Oral reading is a proof that the child can or cannot pronounce the words and group them meaningfully; but how much of the reading program should this testing constitute?   How often should we require proof of technical skill?   Word-recognition drills can prove that the child knows the word forms.   Dramatization with parts read from the book, the reading of favorite passages, and the reading of parts to prove a point that the child wishes to make to the class can constitute oral-reading exercises after the child has given the material a preliminary silent reading and an oral practice reading.   But oral reading without preparation and oral reading to the exclusion of silent, comprehending reading for a purpose can only result in the kinds of disability whose prevalence is testimony to present practice: slow silent reading, lip movements in silent reading, correct pronunciation without full comprehension of the meaning of what one is reading, and a low standard of oral-reading performance.

Sometime during the second grade the silent-reading speed of the average child outstrips his oral-reading speed and he develops into a rapid silent reader.   Unless preparation is laid for silent reading in the first experiences with reading, however, the child will assume that reading is reading, be it oral or silent, and will move his lips or form the words with his throat muscles in silent reading.   He will be so busy forming words that comprehension will take a secondary position. He will have a low standard for oral reading because his practice will be an impromptu performance or a repetition of someone else's reading. In the latter case, memory rather than reading is the large factor. The purpose will be to please the teacher, not to inform, to amuse, to delight, to motivate, to clarify, to transport his listeners into another world.   After repeated oral reading of a passage, any attempt that the teacher makes to capitalize also on the values of silent reading by asking comprehension questions is futile; the child has had ample opportunity to memorize the passage and can respond without reference to the page, even though he may go through the routine of staring at it a respectful length of time.

Reading is a meaningful process.   It is engaged in for the purpose of getting meanings.   It must be this from the beginning if the child is to appreciate what he is about.   But oral reading is a job in itself. The amateur can derive the full meaning of what he reads only by going over it silently before or after his oral rendition.   Therefore, even the teacher of beginners must see to it that some of his work is silent (see pages 153 and 238–246 for a fuller discussion of oral reading).

A teacher of beginning reading who realizes the scope of his responsibility will see to it that the child's word-recognition practice at times requires an oral response; at times a silent pantomime or picture selection; at times, in response to a picture or an act or a spoken word, the writing of the word without the finished forms being available for letter-by-letter copying.   Thus the word-form drills will require visual, auditory, and tactile responses and will not emphasize the mouthing of words to the exclusion of other kinds of proof that the child has connected the symbols with the meanings.   The approach to a new lesson will include the clinching of new words, and then silent reading in answer to motivated comprehension questions that are asked to determine the child's understanding of the passage, not to determine further his mastery of the new words.   In this way the teacher will test the child's recognition of new forms by word-form drills, and will devote silent reading to the sole purpose of reading—understanding the author's message.

If more word drill or phrase drill is desirable, the teacher can put the new words into a different setting, weave them into a different story for oral or silent reading, include them in a nonoral, following-directions game, or have the children themselves use them in a new way, as, for example, in dictation to the teacher or in tactile exercise. If the story deserves further consideration, the children can discuss puzzling or favorite parts, dramatize it, select parts to illustrate, read the conversational parts, and utilize oral reading when that is desirable.

Differentiated supplementary reading about a farm unit, for instance, can be the preparation for purposeful oral reading to the class on the kinds of animals on the farm, how the farmer takes care of his chickens, games farm children like to play, and so forth; each child then makes his contribution; each listener has his purpose for listening.   Pleasurable story reading in the classroom library and in library-club period not only can become a means of teaching, from the very beginning, such library skills and practices as the use of the alphabetized card catalogue, the signing in and out of books, the care of books, and the stimulation of interest in reading through the exchange of book experiences; but it can also provide a way of building standards for oral reading—expressive, enjoyable oral reading to an audience that has a reason for listening.

As the child advances in reading ability throughout the grades and high school, oral reading receives less and less time in the classroom, although, in order to maintain the skill and to allow it the attention that it deserves for its minor but significant place in adult life, the school must still give it time and consideration. But the functional approach to oral reading is as necessary to its development here as it is in the lower grades. To read orally without a real purpose, in the presence of an audience that is without a purpose, is destructive of the standards and skills that were developed in the earlier grades. Functional activities in oral reading common to the earlier program may be continued. Other means of keeping oral reading a fresh and vital tool in every subject field that requires reading are found in such activities as a classroom newspaper, for which children write and read their own compositions; debates, in which quotations are read; discussions of controversial material, in which opposing views are quoted; panel discussions, in which new material on a given topic is presented to inform the class; pseudo radio programs or assembly programs requiring good oral reading; choral reading, where the whole class is engaged in an exercise of good phrasing and interpretation of something that all have enjoyed; and the oral reading of difficult passages whose meanings are obscured by unaccustomed phrasing or a new use of a familiar word. Differentiated reading and the assignment of special topics for different members of a class mean that the retarded reader has not only the opportunity for silent reading on his own level, but the pleasure of reading new information to the class and gaining respect through his contribution.

In the uses of oral reading described here, however, the teacher should not see new reasons for letting oral reading monopolize her program. She should rather feel a new conviction that oral reading should be purposeful, and that it should be reasonably proportioned to its use in life and to the need for consideration of other language skills, such as silent reading and oral reporting without recourse to the printed page.

OVEREMPHASIS ON DETAILS AND VERBATIM ANSWERS

Another destructive emphasis in some teaching is that upon reading for details and verbatim answers. The teacher is not entirely to blame for this extreme, of course. While she may do it of her own volition, she has as precedent the lesson plans in teachers' manuals for current reader series and the questions on many widely used tests; but tests and manuals, although we should like to revere them, are man made and tend to make this apparent. Tests that emphasize detail questions, such as "Once there was a little girl named Red Riding Hood. What was the color of her hood?" very often test the human tendency to evasion rather than reading ability. A child seeing the word "color," which is commonly used and well known, can easily see that "red" is the only color mentioned in the sentence. The answer is inescapable. Again, in the case of "John and Mary went to school"—a completion-type multiple-choice item: "John and Mary went to school, to church, to play, to the dogs"—no sentence reading or even careful word discrimination is required. If the reader wishes or if he has no alternative because of his poor ability, he may simply compare the general shapes of the last word and the suggested answers.

Sometimes a somewhat more subtle question can be outmaneuvered. "The boys threw the bone to Fido and hurried off on their bicycles." To the question "To whom does 'their' refer?" the answer is obvious, since Fido is the only other participant in this little drama and can scarcely run competition to a plural. A prominent and widely used test for high-school students presents a paragraph followed by the question "About what country is this story? China, Japan, America, India." Since the only capitalized word in the paragraph is "China," it is no trick to read the question and skim for the lone capital without even reading the paragraph as a whole. Although these examples from existing tests show that the teacher who stresses reading for details is not alone in pursuing this practice, the fact remains that he is in bad company.

Reading for details is not an objective in itself; it is always and only important in relation to something else. Details are important sometimes to the substantiation of a main idea; again, to the presentation of a sequence of events or an outline or a formula for making something; again, to the drawing of conclusions, to the comparison of two objects of like and different characteristics. The kind of nest and the kind of tail have much to do with determining whether the animal in question is a ground squirrel or a tree squirrel; this is a case in which "details have it"; but the *comparison* is the feature of primary importance, while the *details* are the essential basis for it; a teacher who stresses the details and leaves out the comparison is making mountains out of squirrel holes. In general, it can be said that reading for details has its value and certainly should not be ignored; but if its value is to be appreciated, if children are to learn its use and to feel that the teacher's questions have a thought value as well as an exercise value, detail reading will always be functional, will always be presented in relation to something that gives it significance.

Some people thought that they had solved the problem of making details significant when they popularized the "prove" questions: "Prove that Johnny was a good boy." It can be easily seen, however, that this technique had two counts against it. In the first place, it is the reverse of the natural situation. Authors do not usually tell the reader that so and so is a good boy and then require the reader to find detailed proof. As soon as the author makes a flat statement of any kind, the reader is more likely to accept it as a necessary hypothesis to all that follows than to "sleuth" about, proving or disproving it. As preparation for the natural reading process, in which the reader gathers facts upon which he then bases conclusions, the "prove" technique is an utterly "through-the-looking glass" performance. In the second place, the teacher is featuring details rather than making them secondary and functioning. He has already drawn the conclusion, stolen from the child the stimulation of creative reading, and now is asking him for a post mortem—to find out how the teacher arrived at his own conclusion! Only Irvin Cobb or Will Rogers could have given adequate treatment to the pointlessness of this situation. As an occasional exercise in preparation for the curious demands of professors on examinations this may have some value, but as preparation for the natural reading situation it is entirely improper.

However, a slight alteration in teaching technique can transform this erroneous procedure into something of value. Instead of asking the child to prove that Johnny was a good boy, the teacher has merely to ask, "What do you think of Johnny?" or "What kind of boy was Johnny?" and then to append the request, "Tell why."

REQUIRED RESPONSES INAPPROPRIATE TO THE PASSAGE READ

Still one more common fault in the teaching of reading is the application of work-type study questions to all kinds of material regardless of its nature. Again a bad precedent has been set by the exhaustive, detailed examinations given after a child claims to have read a certain book, with the purpose of seeing whether he has read it and how much he knows. Story material usually has a few large values: perhaps the development of a character, the situation in which the story is laid, the story itself, or the implications of any or all of these—the purpose behind the book. It is, of course, desirable that we should not ask the child to read for a purpose that the author cannot have had in mind; we should rather determine what it is important to derive from the material and then design our questions with this as our objective. It is conceivable that one might ask fewer questions founded on a story of several pages than one would ask about a recipe for a cake, the instructions for making an airplane model, or the steps that led up to the American Revolution.

It is also possible that frequently one would ask questions involving the comparison of characters in a story, of characters in history, or of animal or plant forms in science. That is, so-called work-type or study-type questions and questions on material read for pleasure or for seeing life whole are not mutually exclusive. Appropriateness in questions is simply a matter of realizing the values to be derived from a given material and then keeping the questions of such nature and of such number as to bring out those values. A balanced program should give children at all levels both intensive and extensive study-type reading experience if they are to be prepared for the variety of their adult reading world.

Seatwork that keeps the child busy is not always good seatwork from the standpoint of reading development. One day a child was seen at his desk industriously pasting "yes" and "no" slips alternately after each hectographed statement. When the visitor noticed that one "yes" had been placed after a sentence like "Dogs learn at school," she asked the child what he was supposed to do. "Oh, just paste these words in these places." He thought his job was a cinch—and it was. Another waste of reading time is the laborious filling in of an adult drawing with a colored crayon, to prove that one knows the word form "red." It would be better education in muscular coordination for the child to draw an original something red, although even this exercise would lack the art value that it might have if the child were free to choose his own colors. A less attractive timesaver would be the simple drawing of a line of red.

Some seatwork is so arranged on the page that the systematic left-to-right movements essential to good reading habits are violated. This is true in certain types of matching question and of material presented in lists or patterns rather than in lines. Commercial seatwork correlated with a reader series is helpful to the busy teacher, but it contains some or all of these undesirable features along with lack of sufficient practice in each skill and of provision for the different avenues of learning. If they are used, these commercial practice materials should be supplemented with the teacher's own original exercises, which would compensate for these lacks.

In good seatwork for reading, the child does not spend an overwhelming amount of his time responding. Pasting, drawing lines, exhibiting colors—all these are simply means to an end; they should not outweigh the end. There are related art activities, however, which can assist the reading process and which are justified in the reading period for that reason.   After a child has read a story, the drawing of an original picture sequence, showing the development of the story in, say, four scenes, exercises the child's ability to recall the events in order and the details concerning them, makes him bring his own interpretation to the incidents, and shows the teacher whether his comprehension has been correct.   The making of an individual picture dictionary of words that the child knows at sight will supply practice in alphabetizing, in writing the word, and perhaps in giving a definition and a sentence in which the word is used.   The original drawing enhances the whole.   The process of drawing the illustration is one of intense concentration on the meaning of the word and assists in the association of the meaning with the symbol.

In the same way, sentence meanings can be reinforced through original illustration of them.   In class after class one hears the child say, "If we get done early, may we draw a picture on the other side?" Filling in dictated colors is something to "get done"; original drawing is a desired reward.   Here is ample motivation that can be utilized by the wise teacher; filling in is a filler-in that may well be omitted.

Completion sentences give the child an opportunity to use the tactile sense in writing the omitted word while keeping it in the proper habitat—in a sentence where it is meaningful.   In exercises matching words, phrases, or sentences, the violations of left-to-right eye movements can be avoided by grouping the duplicate words, phrases, or sentences at the bottom of the page, to be cut out and pasted next to the matching items, or by having the items arranged across the page, with multiple choices following each other along the line.

Another characteristic of good seatwork is that it does not always simply reinforce what has already been learned; it should frequently teach something new or give practice of an individual nature that cannot easily be provided in the regular group reading period.   This means that making the assignment in seatwork must be a longer, more careful process, and that it will take more ingenuity on the part of the teacher to introduce the new work so that the children will not encounter difficulty.   But with the increasing size of classes and the need for more grouping within the class, each child has less time in the reading group and more time at his seat.   Increasingly his progress must be effected in the seatwork.

OVERPRODDING THE SLOW READER

Another extreme in method is often witnessed in the case of the slow-progress pupil.   The teacher, feeling that it is going to take this pupil forever to get anywhere, is eager to get him there a little faster.

Conscientiously the teacher spends extra time with the boy and gives him extra drills to do when others are reading books. Anxious to keep a close check on his progress, the teacher has him read aloud a great deal. Systematically and in all earnestness this teacher produces a child who is sick of reading the same baby stuff over all the time, who has, indeed, memorized it; who dislikes the drill and the sheer work of reading. As his program includes none of the joys of free, easy book reading, the boy begins to think of reading as anything but his objective in life; he continues to be a word reader because of the excess of word drill; he continues to read slowly because of the excess of oral reading. A slow reader of normal proportions becomes molasses in January and a book hater at that.

It is too bad that a slow reader cannot be just that. Why should he have to go through all this sulphur-and-molasses treatment before learning that it is good to be alive and in the same chair with a book? There are many ways in which slow readers can learn the joy of reading without shame or boredom. A group of four boys with ten-year-old interests were still reading in preprimers. They wanted to write an original, red-blooded story and illustrate it themselves. The teacher took dictation, simplified their version of the story, which was a cross between *Dick Tracy* and *Terry and the Pirates*, and gave them a sentence a day to illustrate. In the end, each boy had his own book and read it proudly. They were started on their way. In another case, a teacher told some retarded readers in high school that the second-grade teacher wanted some stories for her classroom library; she asked their help in looking through old second-grade readers for stories that they thought good enough. The boys, as they found stories that they liked, discussed these until their suitability had been agreed upon, then removed them from the discarded books, bound them, and made a proud presentation of them to the lower grade. This experience in easy reading resulted in a fluency that these boys could never have gained in laborious word drills or in the uphill work of their own grade.

High-school teachers also may make reading distasteful to students in a variety of ways. One way is to treat reading merely as a means of getting school credit in the form of a mark. Another is to give assignments for which students feel no real need or for which they have inadequate background or reading ability. Forcing reading on a student who is not ready for it is not likely to increase his reading proficiency. If students repeatedly experience failure in getting meaning from the reading material assigned, they are likely to say, "Oh, what's the use?" and to give up the attempt to make reading an avenue of learning. Too often there is an absence of reading instruction at critical points for the group or for the individual. These conditions lead students to think of reading as a tool to be used only when they are required to wade through a certain number of pages of history or science in order to regurgitate a reputable array of facts for a teacher. It has not occurred to these students that reading is pertinent to life itself. For them reading is synonymous with required homework.

WANTED: A WELL-ROUNDED, INDIVIDUALIZED DEVELOPMENTAL PROGRAM

In this discussion of the various ways in which a teacher may go to extremes, "overemphasis" has not been defined.   There is danger in failure to define it, for a teacher who is presenting a perfectly balanced program may feel, after reading these suggestions, that he should do more of this or that. The prime requisite for avoiding overemphasis on anything is that no important and necessary skill or groundwork for a skill be omitted from the program in order to fatten the offering in some other skill. Everything of importance should be represented. The second requisite is that these skills be given an amount of time proportionate to the present need for them and to their future importance. The third requisite is that the teacher shall watch the effects of his teaching on the class and on individual progress, and, as he notes deficiencies, shall determine the cause of them in his program and adjust his emphasis to remove the cause. The reading deficiencies for which we have said that the teacher's methods are responsible are matters of emphasis; a balance means good reading, while a lack of balance means an overdose and the compensatory retardation. However, proper balance for one child may not be proper balance for another. For this reason, it is necessary for the teacher to keep a close check on individual reactions as well as on the variety of his offering.

People are wont to ask, "If the first-grade teacher really did a good job, wouldn't that put an end to all the difficulty in reading in the higher grades?" If every first-grade teacher were given a small enough class and sufficient materials to do a really good job and then did it—though it appears that we shall not see this in our time, so uninformed are the mighty and so slowly does the earth turn—there would still be plenty of grief in the higher grades. People who ask such questions forget the many factors involved in a child's success and the fact that reading is a continuous growing process, not a gift from one's first-grade teacher. A first-grade teacher may present the most admirable of programs and suit it as well as he can to a particular child; yet the child may not learn.   There are health factors, physical factors other than health, psychological factors, social and emotional factors, and home-background factors that can defeat the best work that a teacher can do.   For this reason alone, the person who says that the retarded reader is all a matter of poor teaching displays his remarkable ignorance of the subject.   Any of us can put up a screen and fool ourselves into thinking that in our school such things do not happen; the fact remains that even the best of schools includes a few children—if it keeps them—who in spite of the teacher's best efforts and wisest procedure are cases of retardation.   It is amazing that, after all our years of experience with the concept of the "normal curve," we should be surprised that 50 per cent of a seventh-grade class is necessarily below average in reading.

Above the first grade, and through college, there are skills to be learned and perfected.   Someone is always needing to learn some stage of word analysis or context analysis which he is only then ready to appreciate.   There are new words, old words with new meanings, and characteristic expressions in every subject.   Each author presents his unique problem in organization, vocabulary, and sentence structure. Each book presents its contents and study aids in a special manner that must be understood and appreciated.   Each teacher has particular objectives that require certain kinds of reading of the text or texts.

Teachers who make assignments in which the purpose of the student's reading is not clear, who fail to give practice in the skills necessary to the reading of their subject, who ignore the student's need for help in the use of book aids and reference materials, whose idea of oral reading is something that will take up time until the bell rings, who do not acquaint the student with the pleasures of reading easy, current materials in their fields or related fields that will broaden the student's conception of the subject and may establish a life interest, are more responsible for the meagerness of the average American's reading ability and for the cases of retardation than is the first-grade teacher.   After all, it was the latter's duty merely to establish a basic sight vocabulary of 100 words; to guide children into the beginnings of word analysis, which, in most cases, could not, in the first year, be more than the recognition of certain initial consonants and three or four common endings; to give them the experience of reading meaningful materials for well-motivated and varied purposes; and to instill a delight in reading guaranteed to last them to the threshold of the next teacher's room.   "What's done is done" is a completely erroneous statement of the reading process. "What's done can be undone" is nearer the truth; and it is well to add the statement that no teacher can assume that he knows beforehand where his work is to begin or where it is to end. Every teacher can be sure that he must teach reading if he is to maintain or to continue the good work that has gone before.

References

1. DOLCH, E. W., "Sight Syllabus versus Letter Phonics," *Elementary School Journal*, Vol. 41, pp. 38–42, September, 1940.
2. GILBERT, L. C., "Effect on Silent Reading of Attempting to Follow Oral Reading," *Elementary School Journal*, Vol. 40, pp. 614–621, April, 1940.
3. HYATT, ADA V., *The Place of Oral Reading in the School Program*, Its History and Development from 1880–1941, Teachers College Contributions to Education, No. 872, Bureau of Publications, Teachers College, Columbia University, New York, 1943, vii + 140 pp.
4. KOPEL, DAVID, "Reading Textbooks and the Reading Program," *English Journal*, Vol. 32, pp. 420–428, October, 1943.
5. KOPEL, DAVID, and JOHN J. DeBOER, "Reading Problems of Pressing Importance," *Review of Educational Research*, Vol. 13, pp. 69–87, April, 1943.
6. LaBRANT, LOU L., *An Evaluation of the Free Reading in Grades Ten, Eleven, and Twelve for the Class of 1935*, Ohio State University Studies, No. 2, Ohio State University Press, Columbus, Ohio, 1936, ix + 158 pp.
7. McCULLOUGH, CONSTANCE M., "Learning to Use Context Clues," *Elementary English Review*, Vol. 20, pp. 140–143, April, 1943.
8. SMITH, DORA V., "Adolescent Literature Syllabus," University of Minnesota Press, Minneapolis (mimeographed).
9. TRIGGS, FRANCES O., "Current Problems in Remedial Reading for College Students," *School and Society*, Vol. 53, pp. 376–379, Mar. 22, 1941.
10. WITTY, PAUL, and ANNE COMMER, "Reading the Comics in Grades IX–XII," *Educational Administration and Supervision*, Vol. 28, pp. 344–353, 1942.
11. WITTY, PAUL A., and HARVEY C. LEHMAN, "The Reading and Reading Interests of Gifted Children," *Pedagogical Seminary and Journal of Genetic Psychology*, Vol. 45, pp. 466–481, December, 1934.
12. YOAKUM, GERALD A., "An Ounce of Prevention in Reading," *Journal of Educational Research*, Vol. 37, pp. 100–109, October, 1943.
13. ZELLAR, DALE, *The Relative Importance of Factors of Interest in Reading Materials for Junior High School Pupils*, Teachers College Contributions to Education, No. 841, Bureau of Publications, Teachers College, Columbia University, New York, 1941, viii + 90 pp.

CHAPTER VI

IMPROVEMENT OF READING IN THE SCHOOL AS A WHOLE

What can people who are not reading specialists do to raise the general level of student achievement in reading?

In every type of school there are many students who are not realizing their reading potentialities. Some students are nonreaders, and some have very poor reading ability. Others are reading as well as can be expected, but their reading interests and tastes could be improved. Still others, although they are superior to the average reader, are not using reading to their own fullest capacity. Inability to read often pervades the student's attitude toward school as a whole. One high-school boy said, "I seldom read for pleasure; it takes me too long to do my homework. If I could only read my homework and remember it, I think I'd like school." Some students are so anxious about themselves and their poor reading that they are resistant to instruction; others seem not to have any anxiety, in the first place, or to care how deficient in reading they may be. In any class there are innumerable patterns of reading attitudes, interests, tastes, and abilities, all of which may be improved. Every student can be helped to read more effectively in accordance with his needs now and later.

In attempting to meet these reading needs, many schools are handicapped by the following circumstances:

1. Lack of specialists in reading to serve as consultants and to do intensive work with seriously retarded readers
2. Lack of special training in reading on the part of teachers
3. Heavy teaching schedules and large classes
4. Lack of diagnostic testing
5. Lack of sufficient suitable reading materials for students of diverse interests and abilities
6. Lack of facilities for correcting physical defects
7. Poor cultural backgrounds and environments that do not stimulate students to desire to learn by reading

Despite these handicaps and the conditions more fully described in the preceding chapter, the problem of improving reading in junior and senior high schools and in colleges, universities, and trade and professional schools can be attacked more vigorously. This chapter will suggest steps that can be taken in the school as a whole.

PROVIDING FAVORABLE PHYSICAL CONDITIONS

Physical conditions, those conducive to good health in general and to proper illumination in particular, need immediate attention as part of the whole school program. It may be that some students do not read so well as they might because of physical discomfort. Their efficiency and pleasure in reading may be unfavorably influenced by poor illumination. In visiting college libraries, one is impressed by the marked differences in reading comfort. Some are dark and dingy, with uncomfortable chairs and varnished tables that reflect the light into the reader's eyes, thus causing glare in the gloom. Others have indirect lighting that approaches fine daylight conditions of illumination, without glare or other discomfort. One basic contribution that administrators can make to the improvement of reading is to provide optimum conditions of lighting.

One of Tinker's most recent contributions to this field was "to determine the critical level of light intensity for reading (7-point) newspaper type" (16). He found the critical level of intensity of illumination to be approximately 7 foot-candles; below this intensity, speed of reading was retarded. At 7 foot-candles and above, the rate of reading was not significantly influenced by changes in light intensity. He concluded that students should not read at the critical level of intensity, but he provided with an intensity between 15 and 20 candle power, which would provide a margin of safety.

Luckiesh and Moss (12, pages 370–384) recommended the following "specifications for optimum readability":

1. A type size of at least 12 point, held about 14 in. from the eyes
2. A level of illumination or brightness of "somewhere between 100 and 250 foot-candles." The minimum of 100 foot-candles presupposes freedom from preventable glare and "surroundings of appropriate brightness." This is a much higher intensity than that usually recommended, for example, by Tinker (16), who suggested 15 to 20 foot-candles for reading newspapers.
3. White paper to ensure the best brightness contrast
4. Nonglossy paper and ink
5. Rest periods, or relaxation from reading, of 10 minutes after 1 hour of reading, or more frequent briefer rest periods, such as viewing a distant object.

CREATING CONDITIONS THAT MAKE READING NECESSARY AND MEANINGFUL

Obviously the next step in a school-wide program is to examine the curriculum to see whether the reading required is meaningful—whether it is recognized by the students as meeting some need in their lives, and whether it is identified with some aspect of their growth. It is essential that they experience some satisfaction from reading, out of which grows the conviction that reading is not a meaningless, difficult, and therefore disagreeable task. Then students will read for the continuous satisfaction reading gives and not because the teacher has assigned a certain number of pages.

When reading is conceived as a means of self-realization and social usefulness, courses will be modernized, books simplified. Under ideal conditions, curricular modification should be even more basic than this. School experiences should have such meaning and purpose to the student that he will feel the need for reading and the understanding that can be gained from books. Among the motives that appeal to students are reading to prepare themselves to take part in short plays and in class discussion or conversation, or to make an interesting report to the class, or to get as much as possible from excursions or trips to places of historic or vocational interest.

In order to make desirable changes in the curriculum, teachers should know more about what their boys and girls now want and what they should want to do, to make, to learn, to become. The next step is to ascertain their present level of reading proficiency. Having gathered this information, the school should make every effort to provide a wide variety of suitable reading material and to guide students in their choices. As students become really interested, they will welcome specific help in improving their reading.

LEARNING THE STUDENTS' READING NEEDS AND INTERESTS

Students can do for themselves a great part of the study and planning that teachers ordinarily do for them. They can suggest reading projects, assist in the appraisal of their own reading, and keep records of their progress. The teacher's part is to obtain an understanding of the student that will check and supplement the student's appraisal of his own reading ability and progress.

Even in large classes in a departmentalized school, the teachers can gain some understanding of their students' interests and needs for reading. Teachers have made use of all the following means:

1. Observation in class—appearance and manner, interest or lack of interest in different topics discussed in class and in assignments, choice of books or articles in free reading periods and for book reviews, remarks made during class discussion. Observations in the library may supply a great deal of information about students' favorite books, attitude toward reading, and apparent concentration while reading different kinds of material.

2. Compositions—subjects chosen when students are free to write on any

subject, or compositions on special subjects, such as "If I had three wishes," "My reading autobiography," "Report of interviews with persons in different kinds of work about their reading."

3. Casual conversational contacts with individual students in which they may express their interests and needs.

4. Class discussions of books and reading, and of the part that reading plays in their daily lives.

5. Comparative study of students' interest in different kinds of reading material. The teacher gives the students a selection to read, and notes their interest and attention and the questions asked while they are reading, as well as their comments on the article or the story after they have read it. In this way the particular reading interests of a group may be discovered.

6. Study of home backgrounds. One teacher took the names and addresses of students with him, as he rode around the town in his car, and located the house and neighborhood in which each student lived. Another teacher went over his list of students with the school nurse, who had valuable information from her home visits. Teachers who visit the homes themselves find these visits very rewarding. This understanding of the individual student's interests, needs, opportunities and facilities for reading, and of the encouragement he receives in reading, is part of the total guidance work. The teacher's appraisal of students' reading will be facilitated, of course, by an adequate cumulative record system to which all members of the staff contribute and which is available to all who will use the information for the good of the student (see pages 330–333 on reading records).

APPRAISING STUDENTS' READING ABILITY

Observation, Casual Conversation, and Analysis of Their Work.— The teacher, by observing the individual student, talking with him, and studying his written compositions and examinations, can find out considerable about his reading ability, his interests, and his need for reading. When he reads orally, the teacher can immediately detect mispronunciations, substitutions, insertions, omissions, additions, repetitions, and reversals of letters, syllables, words, and phrases. He can note the student's fluency and phrasing, his embarrassment in reading before a class, or his apparent self-confidence. By asking him to summarize what he has read or to answer questions on it, the teacher can obtain valuable information on the pupil's comprehension.

Informal Tests in Each Subject.—By assigning a passage from a textbook or a reference book, timing the reading, and testing the comprehension, the teacher will learn much about how well the students read the text or reference books used in his subject. An example of this kind of test,[1] used with senior-high-school and college students, follows:

[1] Reprinted from *Science Education*, Vol. 29, pp. 83–86, February, 1944.

READING A SCIENCE ARTICLE

Directions: Read the following article in the way in which you would naturally read similar scientific material. As soon as you have finished reading, write on the blank "Time" the figure you see on the board. Then turn over the article and write the answers to the questions from memory.

CHEMICAL ANALYSIS BY COLOR

Simple Method Makes "Spectrum" of a Complex Mixture

By means of bands of color, adsorbed by columns of alumina, magnesia, precipitated chalk, or even powdered sugar, chemists can now readily separate the constituents of complex chemical mixtures that not long ago defied division. By the same simple technique they can also purify chemicals; determine the structure of molecules; concentrate such substances as vitamins, hormones, and pigments from extremely dilute solutions; identify and compare drugs, dyes, and food products almost instantly. Although still employed chiefly as a tool in the research laboratory, experiments are being conducted to adapt the method to the isolation, purification, and testing of materials in the chemical and drug industries.

This "new" technique, named chromatographic-adsorption analysis by the inventor, was first developed back in 1906 by the Russian botanist M. Tswett, who was investigating the pigments in plant leaves. In his pioneer experiment, duplicated in principle in the photographs above, a chemist's dream was realized: the ingredients of a complex mixture were spread out for investigation like the colors of light in a spectrum. Still more amazing, they could be cut apart with a knife!

The reason for the separation of mixtures into distinct bands on an adsorption column is now considered to be this: molecules of different substances travel down a column of adsorptive material at different rates, depending upon their individual affinity to the adsorbent. Substances that have a strong affinity for the adsorbent travel down slowly. Substances that have less affinity travel down faster. Tswett's simple but revolutionary method of chemical separation was little noticed for twenty-five years. In 1931 it came suddenly into prominence when Kuhn and Lederer passed carotene through an adsorption column and found that, instead of being a simple substance, it was made up of a number of substances.

From the separation of plant pigments, it was only a step to the isolation and purification of vitamins. Some of the first pure specimens of Vitamin A, for instance, were made by chromatography. Vitamins D, E, K, B_1, B_2, and C were separated and purified by this method.

Means were soon found to isolate bands of chemical substances that were colorless or very faintly colored. By using quartz tubes in place of glass, and viewing the column by ultraviolet light, many ordinary colorless chemicals were found to fluoresce with different colors.

Colorless Vitamin D_3 was isolated from fish-liver oils by means of an indicating pigment. Vitamin A, in a column, was detected by painting a streak down the column with the Carr-Price reagent, which turns dark blue in the presence of the vitamin.

(Answer Sheet)

Name_____Grade_____Age_____

Time_____

PART I

What did the author say?

PART II

A. It is important to understand the main ideas of what you read. In each exercise below check the best, most complete, most accurate statement of the main idea.

1. By means of bands of color
   ____(1) drugs may be detected
   ____(2) chemicals may be identified and purified
   ____(3) scientific experiments can be performed
   ____(4) new elements can be created

2. The principle that underlies this color method is
   ____(1) that substances have an affinity for the adsorbent
   ____(2) that colors of light rays spread out in a spectrum
   ____(3) that molecules of different substances travel down a column of adsorptive material at different rates
   ____(4) that molecules have the same degree of affinity to the adsorbent

3. One of the most important applications of this color method is
   ____(1) in the isolation and purification of vitamins
   ____(2) in the separation of carotene into a number of substances
   ____(3) in the manufacture of ultraviolet lamps with quartz bulbs
   ____(4) in the improvement of human life

B. It is desirable to understand the important details you have read. Below are statements of important details in the passage. If the statement is true, according to the passage, put a plus (+) on the line at the right of that statement. If the statement is false, according to the passage, put a zero (0) on the line at the right of that statement.

1. The technique described in this article was first developed in 1906.   ____
2. The new discovery immediately caused revolutionary changes in chemistry.   ____
3. Carotene was found to be a single substance.   ____
4. Bands of chemical substances that were colorless could be distinguished.____
5. Vitamin D_3 was isolated by means of a certain pigment.   ____
6. In using the ultraviolet-light method, quartz must be used.   ____
7. Substances that have a strong affinity for the adsorbent travel down slowly.   ____

C. It is important to be able to answer questions about what you have read. Write the answers to the following questions using *only* those facts which are discussed in the passage and which help to answer the questions.

1. What is the name of the technique described in this passage?_____
2. Who invented this technique?_____
3. What does the technique enable chemists to do?_____
4. How was the technique used in the study of vitamins?_____

D. It is important to be able to draw conclusions from what you have read. If you think a conclusion below is probably true, considering the facts in the passage, put a circle around PT. If you think a conclusion is false, put a circle around PF. If you think the facts given in the passage are insufficient to allow you to make a decision, put a circle around the (?).
1. Chemical analysis by color has produced revolutionary changes in chemical methods. PT PF ?
2. Vitamins would not have been so rapidly isolated in pure form if the method described had not been invented. PT PF ?
3. The application of Tswett's invention was delayed by lack of funds. PT PF ?
4. The method will be used in research laboratories only. PT PF ?

E. It is important to know the exact meaning of words in a passage. In the exercises below check the word or phrase which means most nearly the same as the italicized word in the sentence.
1. By means of bands of color, *adsorbed* by means alumina, magnesia . . .
   _____process of adhesion of molecules to the surface of solids
   _____assimilated
   _____molecules dissolved in a liquid
   _____adopted
2. . . . who investigated the *pigments* in plant leaves . . .
   _____paints and enamels
   _____colorless substance
   _____coloring matter
   _____segments
3. *Molecules* of different substances travel down a column . . .
   _____a compound of elements
   _____a kind of mould
   _____a small particle of dust
   _____a unit of matter

PART III

A. Now think back and try to describe the process you used in reading this article.
B. Answer thoughtfully and accurately.
1. Just how did you get the main ideas?
2. Just how did you find and remember details?
3. What do you do when you read that makes it possible for you to answer questions?
4. What do you do when you read that makes it possible for you to draw conclusions?
5. How do you figure out the meanings of unfamiliar words?

Informal tests of this kind supply valuable information about the way each student organizes his ideas as he reads, the adequacy with which he can express them, and the accuracy with which he can comprehend the main points and important details and can draw inferences. If questions on reading method are included in the test, the teacher and the class gain specific suggestions as to effective methods of reading the kind of material tested.

Standardized Silent-reading Tests. *Choice of Tests.*—By means of a suitable standardized reading test, the teacher can obtain additional information about his students' reading ability and can compare the reading skill of his pupils with that of pupils in the same grade in the country as a whole. A considerable number of reading tests is available for use in the elementary school, in the junior and senior high school, and in college.

The following tests are among those most widely used in elementary schools.

The Gates Reading Tests (28), which have been used in the elementary school grades for about 20 years, have recently been revised and restandardized. The Gates Primary Reading Tests for grade 1 and the first half of grade 2 include three types of tests: word recognition, sentence meaning, and paragraph reading. There are three forms of each type. The total working time is 50 minutes.

The Gates Advanced Primary Reading Tests are designed for the second half of grade 2 and for grade 3.   They consist of separate booklets for two types of reading: word recognition and paragraph reading. The working time is 15 minutes for the first type and 25 minutes for the second type. Forms 1, 2, and 3 are available in each type.

The Gates Basic Reading Tests are intended for use from the second half of grade 3 through grade 8.   There are separate booklets for four types of reading, as follows: Type A, Reading to Appreciate General Significance; Type B, Reading to Predict Outcome of Given Events; Type C, Reading to Understand Precise Directions; and Type D, Reading to Note Details.   The total working time for the four types is approximately 35 minutes.   Reliabilities reported in the manual of directions for the Basic Reading Tests vary from .76 to .94.   The intercorrelations of the four types are rather high, ranging from .72 to .92.

The Chicago Reading Tests (27) by Max D. Engelhart and Thelma Gwinn Thurstone include four booklets: Test A, for grades 1 and 2; Test B, for grades 2, 3, and 4; Test C, for grades 4, 5, and 6; and Test D, for grades 6, 7, and 8.   Each test exists in three forms.   Test A is designed to measure comprehension of words, phrases, sentences, directions, and paragraphs.   Test B yields separate scores for comprehension of words, comprehension of sentences, comprehension of story directions and paragraphs, and rate of reading.   Test C provides scores for comprehension of words; comprehension of sentences;

comprehension of stories, maps, and paragraphs; and for rate of reading. Test D is similar to Test C, but it includes the reading of graphs in the part on comprehension of stories, maps, and paragraphs. The total working time is as follows: Test A, 31 minutes; Test B, 42 minutes; Test C, 45 minutes; and Test D, 42 minutes.

According to data reported by the authors of the tests, the reliability coefficients for the total comprehension scores range from .85 to .99. No reliability data are given for the part scores.

The Sangren-Woody Reading Test (36), which has been used for more than 15 years, is planned to yield a more detailed diagnosis of reading achievement than is secured in most other reading tests. It contains seven parts, as follows: Word Meaning, Rate, Fact Material, Total Meaning, Central Thought, Following Directions, and Organization. It is designed for use in grades 4 through 8 and is available in two forms, A and B. The total working time for the test is 27 minutes. The short time allowed for the parts causes speed to be an important factor in all the scores. The manual of directions reports reliability coefficients for the parts ranging from .777 for fact material to .919 for organization on the basis of the scores of seventh-grade pupils, but certain other studies have shown somewhat lower reliability coefficients. There are public-school grade norms for each part and for the total score. The Educational Records Bureau has very reliable independent school norms for grades 4 and 5 on this test.

The Iowa Silent Reading Tests, New Edition, Elementary Test (29), published in 1939 and revised in 1943, are a revision of the older form published in 1933. The test booklet contains the following subtests: Rate, Comprehension, Directed Reading, Word Meaning, Paragraph Comprehension, Sentence Meaning, Alphabetizing, and Use of the Index. There are four forms, Am, Bm, Cm, Dm, all of which are adapted for machine scoring. The total working time of each form is 49 minutes. The raw scores on the different subtests are converted into standard scores, which are intended to be equivalent and thus to provide a diagnostic profile showing strengths and weaknesses. Data in the files of the Educational Records Bureau suggest that these standard scores may not be entirely comparable and that they should be used with a certain degree of caution. The manual of directions reports Spearman-Brown reliabilities for the subtests ranging from .605 for sentence meaning to .939 for alphabetizing, and a study by Townsend (17) in general verifies these reliabilities. The reliability of the median standard score is reported as .93. It should be kept in mind that, because of the speed factor, the reliabilities may be spuriously high. Public-school norms for grades 4 to 9 are given in the manual of directions for this test, and the Educational Records Bureau has independent school percentile norms for grades 4 to 8, inclusive.

The Iowa Every-pupil Tests of Basic Skills (33)—Test A, Silent Reading Comprehension, and Test B, Work Study Skills— are available on two levels: an elementary battery for grades 3, 4, and 5, and an advanced battery for grades 6, 7, and 8. In each battery there are four forms, known as L, M, N, and O. The elementary battery of Test A measures reading comprehension and vocabulary, while the advanced battery provides separate scores for paragraph comprehension, details, organization, total meaning, and vocabulary. The elementary battery, Test B, contains five parts: Map Reading, Use of References, Use of Index, Use of Dictionary, and Alphabetization. The advanced battery of this test consists of five parts, known as Comprehension of Maps; References; Use of Index; Use of Dictionary; and Reading Graphs, Charts, and Tables. The working time is as follows: for Test A, Elementary Battery, 44 minutes; Advanced Battery, 67 minutes; for Test B, Elementary Battery, 44 minutes; Advanced Battery, 78 minutes. Grade norms are available for these tests, and there is a diagnostic profile chart on which the results for an individual pupil may be plotted in terms of T scores or public-school percentile ratings. These tests have been carefully constructed, and they are probably comparatively high in reliability and validity, but no data relative to validity or reliability are given in the manual of directions.

The Metropolitan Reading Tests (24) are a part of the Metropolitan Achievement Tests, but they are also published in separate booklets. There are three batteries—a primary battery for use in grade 3 and the first half of grade 4; an intermediate battery for grades 4 to 6 inclusive; and an advanced battery for grades 7 and 8. There are three forms of each battery. These tests measure reading comprehension and vocabulary. The administering time is 30 minutes for the primary battery and 45 minutes each for the intermediate and advanced batteries.

The Stanford Reading Tests (34), like the Metropolitan tests, are a part of a longer battery. There is a primary test for grades 2 and 3, an intermediate test for grades 4 through 6, and an advanced test for grades 7 to 9. There are three forms of the primary test and five forms of the advanced test. These tests cover reading comprehension and word meaning. The working time is 25 minutes for the primary battery and 30 minutes, each, for the intermediate and advanced batteries.

The Durrell-Sullivan Reading Capacity and Achievement Tests (26) provide a somewhat different type of diagnostic measurement from that obtained from the other elementary school reading tests. These tests are designed to determine whether or not the reading achievement of a pupil is up to his reading capacity. There are two levels, an intermediate test for grades 3 to 6 and a primary test for grades 2 to 4. There are two sections at each level—one for reading capacity and one for reading achievement. The reading-capacity test consists of a word-meaning part and a paragraph-meaning part. This test is administered by means of dictation and picture identification. The pupils do no reading in this test. The main portion of the reading-achievement test also contains a section on word meaning and one on paragraph meaning. In addition, there are a spelling test and a written recall test, which may be given at the option of the teacher. The reading-capacity test requires about 30 to 40 minutes of administering time; the required tests in the reading-achievement test call for a total working time of 30 minutes. According to data provided by the authors of the tests, the reliability of the total score on the reading capacity test is .89 to .94 and the reliability of the reading achievement total score is .94 to .96. Reliability data are not given for the subtests. The value of the Durrell-Sullivan tests probably depends, in considerable measure, upon the skill of the examiner in administering the reading-capacity test.

The Haggerty Reading Examination, Sigma I (32) is one of the simpler and easier tests to use in grades 1 to 3. It consists of two parts. The first part contains 25 items requiring the pupils to follow directions, and the second part is a sentence-meaning test consisting of 20 questions to be answered by "yes" or "no." Twenty minutes of working time are allowed for Part I and 2 minutes for Part II. There is only one form of this test. According to the manual of directions, the test-retest reliability of the total score for 200 pupils in grades 1 to 3 is .84, which is fairly satisfactory for a test designed for young children. Age and grade norms are given in the manual of directions. The Educational Records Bureau has reliable independent-school percentile norms for grades 2 and 3.

The following are among the most frequently used tests in junior and senior high schools.

The Cooperative Reading Comprehension Tests (25) are a part of the Cooperative English Test, forms Q, R, S, and T; but they may be used separately, since they are available in separate booklets as well as in a single-booklet edition. These reading tests are published on two levels. The lower level, C1, is intended for junior and senior high schools; and the upper level, $C2$, is planned for the upper high-school grades and for college students.   Each level contains two parts, vocabulary and reading, and yields scores for vocabulary, speed of comprehension, and level of comprehension, as well as a total score. The level score is obtained through a repeating-scales technique, by means of which speed of reading is eliminated so that the score tends to be one of power of comprehension.   The total working time for the test is 40 minutes—15 minutes for vocabulary and 25 minutes for reading.   The publisher's data indicate that the reliability of the total reading score is .94 or .95, and that the reliabilities of the parts vary from .75 to .92, when the range is confined to a single grade level. The median of the intercorrelations among the three scores yielded by the test is .671, according to a study made at the Educational Records Bureau.   There are both public-school and independent-school percentile norms for this test.

The Iowa Silent Reading Tests, New Edition, Advanced Test (30), are closely similar to the elementary tests already described.   There are nine subtests: Rate, Comprehension, Directed Reading, Poetry Comprehension, Word Meaning, Sentence Meaning, Paragraph Comprehension, Use of Index, and Selection of Key Words.   The tests exist in four forms—Am, Bm, Cm, and Dm—which may be scored on the International test-scoring machine.   The raw scores of the nine parts are translated into standard scores.   The score for the whole test is the median score or the middle one of the nine scores when they are arranged in order of magnitude.   In setting up the standard scores, the authors of the test first established standard scores for the elementary battery on the performance of twelve-year-old pupils.   The scale was devised with a median of 150 and a standard deviation of 20.   Standard scores were developed for the advanced test, which were intended to be comparable to those on the elementary test. These scores were based on a median of 166 and a standard deviation of 20 and were derived from the performance of pupils at the age of sixteen.   Results obtained at the Educational Records Bureau raise doubts concerning the actual comparability of the standard scores on the parts of each battery and concerning the comparability between the elementary and advanced batteries, although the standard scores are unquestionably much more nearly comparable than raw scores would be (17).

The manual of directions for the test indicates that the Spearman-Brown reliabilities of the parts range from .683 for poetry comprehension to .871 for word meaning.   The reliability of the median standard score is given at .918.   A study by Townsend (17) tends to support these results. The Iowa test is designed for use in grades 9 to 12 and in college. The working time is 45 minutes.

The Nelson-Denny Reading Test (35) is designed to measure vocabulary and paragraph reading. It is suitable for use with pupils in the senior high school and students in college. There are two forms, A and B, each of which requires 30 minutes of working time. The responses of the students are recorded on a separate answer sheet, which is scored by means of the Clapp-Young self-marking carbon-paper device. Both public-school and independent-school norms are available for this test. The author reports a reliability coefficient of .91, found by correlating scores made on forms A and B by college ·freshmen.

The Traxler Reading Tests (39) consist of the Silent Reading Test for grades 7 to 10 and the High School Reading Test for grades 9 to 12. The Silent Reading Test measures reading rate, story comprehension, word meaning, and paragraph comprehension, and yields a total comprehension score and a total score. There are four forms of this test, the last two of which are adapted for machine scoring. The High School Reading Test measures reading rate, story comprehension, and understanding of main ideas in paragraphs; and it also provides a total score. There are two forms, which may be machine scored. The working time is 45 minutes. Public-school percentiles for part scores and total scores are available for both tests. There are independent-school percentile norms on the Silent Reading Test for grades 6 to 9, inclusive. The average reliability of the Silent Reading Test, based on correlations of two forms of the test administered to pupils at a single grade level, is .80. The reliability of the total score is .92. The average reliability of the part scores in the High School Reading Test is .81; the estimated reliability of the total score is .93.

The Van Wagenen Reading Scales (41) are designed to measure comprehension of the reading of material in different fields. There are four separate booklets entitled Reading Scales in Science, Reading Scales in Biology, Reading Scales in History, and Reading Scales in Literature. There are two forms of each scale. The grade range is 7 to 12. The tests are not timed. The results are expressed in terms of derived measures known as C scores. Data on reliability or validity are not available.

The United States Armed Forces Institute Tests of General Educational Development (40) likewise include tests designed to measure reading ability in different subject fields. Among these tests there are booklets for the measurement of the Interpretation of Reading

Materials in the Social Studies, the Interpretation of Reading Materials in the Natural Sciences, and the Interpretation of Literary Materials.   There are a high-school level and a college level of these tests.   In each test the student is required to interpret and to evaluate reading selections representative of schoolwork in that particular field. The working time for each test is 2 hours.   The results are expressed in terms of standard scores based on a mean of 50 and a standard deviation of 10.   High-school and college percentile norms have been established for these tests.   Information concerning the reliability, validity, and intercorrelation of the tests of general educational development is not at present available.   It should be made clear that the reading tests are only part of the general educational development tests.   These tests also include a test of correctness and effectiveness of expression at both high-school and college levels and a test of general mathematical ability designed for the high school.   All the tests of general educational development in the high-school series are planned for use near the end of the senior year of high school, although they could, no doubt, be used in lower years, particularly in schools enrolling pupils of high ability.

The following reading tests are useful for both elementary schools and high schools.

The Progressive Reading Tests (38) consist of overlapping batteries, which cover the entire range of grades from the first grade through the junior college.   The grade level of each battery is as follows: primary battery, grades 1 to 3; elementary battery, grades 3 to 6; intermediate battery, grades 7 to 9; and advanced battery, grades 9 to 13.   These reading tests are printed in the corresponding batteries of the Progressive Achievement Tests, as well as separately. The three lower batteries consist of three forms and the advanced battery has two forms.   The Progressive Reading Tests have two main divisions, reading vocabulary and reading comprehension, and each division yields several subtest scores.   There are no exact time limits for the Progressive Reading Tests, but about 50 minutes of working time are required.   According to the manual of directions, the reliabilities of the two main parts are approximately .90.   Reliabilities are not reported for the subdivisions, but in view of their brevity, these subdivisions are probably not very high in reliability. The public-school norms on the Progressive Reading Tests may be supplemented by fall independent-school norms obtained at the Educational Records Bureau.

The Shank Tests of Reading Comprehension (37) consist of tests at three levels: Test I for grades 3 to 6, Test II for grades 7 to 9, and Test III for grades 10 to 12.   Three forms are available for each test.   These tests yield directly only a single total score, although the questions are so arranged that it is possible to tabulate the results according to six or seven types of questions.   The working time is only 20 minutes, which is considerably less than the time required by most of the other reading tests.   According to the author's data, the reliability of the total score of the test on each level is approximately .90.   End-of-semester public-school norms, based on testing in the Educational Records Bureau program several years ago, have also been prepared.

The Van Wagenen-Dvorak Diagnostic Examination of Silent Reading Abilities (42) is one of the longest available reading tests and is intended mainly for diagnostic purposes.   The test is published on three levels: an intermediate division for grades 4 to 5, a junior division for grades 6 to 9, and a senior division for grades 10 to 12 and for college.   Each division has two booklets, a small booklet designed to measure rate of comprehension and a large booklet including tests of vocabulary and different aspects of comprehension.   The entire examination is planned to measure rate of comprehension, ability to perceive relationships, vocabulary (words in context), vocabulary (isolated words), range of general information, grasp of central thought, retention of clearly stated details, interpretation of content, integration of dispersed ideas, and ability to draw inferences from content. The manual of directions does not contain information concerning reliability or validity, but a study made at the Educational Records Bureau indicates that the reliability of some of the parts is comparatively low and that the intercorrelations among several of the subtests are high (19).   The scores of the different parts can be plotted on a profile chart.   The test also provides a reading-level score and a reading index somewhat analogous to the I.Q.

The following are reading tests recommended for use in college:

Several of the reading tests already listed may be used in college as well as in high school.   These tests include the Cooperative Reading Comprehension Test C2; the Iowa Silent Reading Tests, New Edition, Advanced Test; the Nelson-Denny Reading Test; the Progressive Reading Tests; the Van Wagenen-Dvorak Diagnostic Examination of Silent Reading Abilities; and the United States Armed Forces Institute Tests of General Educational Development.

The Minnesota Reading Examination for College Students (31) is a test designed to measure vocabulary and paragraph comprehension at the college level.   There are two forms, A and B.   The working time is 6 minutes for the vocabulary part and 40 minutes for the paragraph-reading part.   According to data reported by the authors, the reliability of the total score is .865, based on the repetition of Form A with 216 college juniors.

There is also an unpublished college reading test by Ivan A. Booker, which has been used in a number of research studies.

Speed-of-reading tests are relatively unreliable and difficult to interpret.   An apparent deficiency in rate of reading may result from the student's effort to gain a far more complete comprehension of the passage than the author of the test intended.   A high score, on the other hand, may merely represent skill in reading just enough to answer the questions.

There has yet to be constructed an entirely satisfactory silent-reading test, and it is quite possible that when such a test does appear, no one will buy it except for use in clinical situations.   A truly adequate test would have to be too long, with too many parts to score and too many kinds of material, for any school to find time to use it on a school-wide basis.   From among the tests now available, the choice of test for a particular group depends upon the school's objectives in reading; the time, money, and personnel available for testing; and the use to be made of the test results.   The following are questions suggestive of the criteria that a prospective buyer should consider in selecting a silent-reading test:

1. Does it deal with the vocabulary and the subject matter in which you are interested?   If you are a science teacher, you want a test containing science material as well as general reading material.   You want the vocabulary to compare favorably with that which you expect the students to acquire in your course or to bring to your course.

2. Does it cover amply the levels of difficulty that interest you?   You want a test that is easy enough so that the poorest reader will have some success and hard enough so that the best reader will not make a perfect score. If the poor reader can get no item right, you have no idea how poor he is. If the good reader is 100 per cent right, you have no idea how good he is.

3. Are the reading tasks typical of your demands in the classroom?   A social-studies teacher said, "I should like to use such and such a test in my class, but it asks all questions of detail, while, in my teaching, details are secondary to questions of relationship and inference."

4. Are the reading tasks eminently suited to the materials presented? A good way to find this out is to see whether a specialist in the field (science, social studies, etc.) feels that the questions asked are the questions; that he would be likely to ask on such a passage.

5. Do the tests actually test what they claim to test?   Sometimes the vocabulary test is really an analogy test, which puts a premium on intelligence, instead of a test involving simpler synonyms, which would probably

reflect better the true status of the students' knowledge of the words. Sometimes the comprehension test is so full of hard words that it tests vocabulary more than it does understanding of the relationships of the words and the thought pattern created by them. Sometimes the speed test is a test of speed of reading and answering questions, as well as a test of speed of reading; and sometimes a speed test has no check on comprehension to show whether the student has understood as he read at that speed.

6. Is the print comparable to that of the book? Some tests are printed on such poor paper in such small type that they are an ocular as well as a reading hurdle.

7. Are the directions clear? Imagine that you are your dullest student and see what you would do with the directions.

8. Are many adjustments required in answering the questions, so that intelligence and emotional stress become prominent in the test score? Certain vocabulary tests require many subtle mental adjustments. As definition for "hasten" there may be "hurry"; these are synonyms. For "flora" there may be "roses"; these are a general term and a specific. For "emu" there may be "animal"; these are a specific term and a general. For "bowl" there may be "dish"; these are two specifics for the general term "pottery." Experience for yourself the mental discomfort of the twists of thought required in finding the right answers. See also whether the multiple-choice answers are harder words than the word that is being tested.

9. Are the examples typical, misleading, or a dead giveaway?

10. Are some of the multiple-choice answers debatable?

11. Do the incorrect multiple-choice responses represent plausible errors? If the wrong responses are not plausible, the student who does not know the correct response is likely to get the item right by a process of elimination.

12. Are the factors that you are most interested in well isolated, so that you may easily determine a student's mastery of them? Ideally, there should be separate parts for the kinds of reading ability that you want to know about. Sometimes by analysis of the test you can pick out the items that deal with the skill you are interested in; but, of course, this is more work.

13. Are enough time and space given to each skill to make the parts reliable? The more parts you have in a 40-minute test, or a test of any given length, the more you sacrifice in reliability, the less sure you can be that each part of the test gives a good picture of the student's achievement in the aspect of reading covered by that part.

14. May the test be used for diagnostic purposes? As long as you are buying a test, you may as well get one that can be used either for survey or for diagnosis purposes.

15. Is the scoring simple without confounding the purpose of the test? A test that yields a single score can do little to show the nature of the student's retardation.

16. Are the norms, according to the manual of directions, based upon a population of a size and character compared with your class? Are they based upon rural or city, private or public schools?

17. Do specific directions as to the manner in which a passage is to be read precede the test paragraphs? Unless the student knows what is expected of his reading, he cannot apply an efficient technique. Neither can he demonstrate his ability to read for different purposes. The directions and the example should make clear to him the kind of comprehension expected, just as in life or in the classroom a purpose is set for the kind of reading to be done.

At best, the existing standardized tests show the students' present status in the kind of reading that is measured by these tests. They may show merely temporary gains in certain reading abilities. They are limited in their application because they represent somewhat artificial, rather than natural, reading situations. They measure a specialized ability to match words with suggested meanings, or phrases with proposed statements. None of the standardized tests now available measures adequately the high levels of reading ability—the abilities to comprehend relationships in a long passage that calls for sustained attention, to organize content, to draw inferences, to grasp metaphors and shifts of meaning, and to apply what is read. In short, they do not adequately measure all aspects of the growth in reading to be expected during high-school and college years. Objective-type tests represent a misleading oversimplication of the reading process. Most of them neglect the ability to interpret the subtle meanings of difficult passages. Standardized reading tests should not be used without recognition of their limitations.

Administration and Scoring of Tests.—After the test is chosen, plans for its correct administration should be made. If the results are to be compared with the norms, the test must be administered strictly according to directions. More specifically, attention should be given to the following details:

1. The students should be seated in such a way as to ensure comfort and avoid the stimulus to copy; lighting should be as good as possible; and unnecessary distractions should be avoided.

2. The test should be introduced in such a manner as to arouse interest but not anxiety.

3. All questions should be asked and answered before it begins, not while it is in progress.

4. Timing should be accurate. The signals indicating when to begin and when to stop should be emphatic.

5. The examiner should watch the class to see that they turn pages at the proper time and follow directions accurately.

6. Observations may be made of individual students' methods of work. For example, the following observation was made of a college student taking the Nelson-Denny reading test:

On the vocabulary test he worked in a very tense fashion—feet pushed way back under chair, shoulders hunched. When the time was up, he said he had done very poorly. He changed seven out of thirty-seven responses. He asked whether anyone ever finished the test and I told him rarely, that the test was made so most people didn't finish. He worked with less tension on the paragraph-reading test.

Needless to say, the scoring should be done according to directions and checked to ensure accuracy. The scores may be entered in various ways on alphabetical lists. Tables 3, 4, 5, and 6 illustrate several

TABLE 3.—APRIL SCORES OF 9B PUPILS ON IOWA SILENT READING TEST, ADVANCED FORM Am

Pupil	Total comprehension score	Grade level, based on national public-school norms	Percentile rank, based on this school's scores
Frick, David.................	187	13.0+	93
Smith, Betty.................	173	12.7	66
Englewood, Bob..............	171	12.1	61
Thomas, John................	168	11.3	50
Young, Peter.................	165	10.6	43
Mann, Luke..................	159	9.4	29
Heart, John..................	154	8.5	18
Hayes, Alma.................	152	8.2	14
Albert, Pearl.................	144	7.0	5
Karl, Elmer..................	128	5.1	1

ways of presenting students' scores, interpreted in terms of appropriate norms.[1] In interpreting scores, it must be remembered that norms of reading tests are based on reading as it is now taught, not as it might ideally be taught.

Interpretation of Test Results.—When a test is administered and scored, only to be shelved in the cumulative record files, it is an extravagant use of school funds. If the time and money involved are to be justified, certain simple observations should be made on silent-reading-test results. The following observations of the student's responses on the test are helpful:

1. *The Speed Score.*—*a.* Notice whether the comprehension of the material on which a speed score was given was perfect, nearly perfect, mediocre, poor.

[1] In each table except Table 6, only a few names from the class list are given to illustrate the form of record.

b. Note whether the student is apparently a *rapid-careful* reader, one who reads rapidly and understands completely; a *rapid-careless* reader, one who reads rapidly but does not remember much about

TABLE 4.—FEBRUARY SCORES BY PUPILS IN GRADE 10 ON IOWA SILENT READING TEST, ADVANCED FORM *C*m (REVISED)

Number representing pupil's name	1 Rate	1 Comprehension	2 Directed reading	3 Poetry comprehension	4 Word meaning	5 Sentence meaning	6 Paragraph comprehension	7A Use of index	7B Key words	Median standard score
1	163*	154	182	135	180	198	166	150	173	166
	43†	26	79	7	77	95	50	21	65	51
2	202*	193	188	163	208	183	194	164	166	188
	96†	91	87	44	99	81	91	45	49	92
3	134*	130	154	135	129	131	129	135	146	134
	6†	3	26	7	2	4	3	5	14	1
4	181*	151	169	163	171	131	166	150	128	163
	75†	21	55	44	61	4	50	21	3	42
5	137*	161	164	141	172	169	153	175	176	164
	8†	38	45	12	63	57	26	67	70	45

* Standard score.
† Percentile rank based upon author's norms for 10.8.

TABLE 5.—RESULTS OF NELSON-DENNY READING TEST, GRADUATE STUDENTS

Number representing pupil's name	Vocabulary			Paragraph meaning			Total		
	Raw score	College senior percentile	Local group percentile	Raw score	College senior percentile	Local group percentile	Raw score	College senior percentile	Local group percentile
1	76	92	70	64	92	80	140	95	76
2	70	88	50	44	50	22	114	80	35
8	49	49	10	36	25	8	85	36	8
15	86	94	88	40	30	14	126	87	54
20	52	51	20	52	70	44	104	64	25
25	47	46	5	26	9	0	73	22	1

what he reads; a *slow-careful* reader, one whose speed is poor but whose comprehension is so good that he may as well read more rapidly; or a *slow-inaccurate* reader, one who reads slowly and does not know much about what he reads.

TABLE 6.—TRAXLER SILENT READING TEST FOR GRADES 7 TO 10, FORM 3, GRADE 10
(Distributions of rate, word meaning, total comprehension, and total scores in one high school)

Score	Rate	Score	Word meaning	Score	Total comprehension	Score	Total score
60	5	46	1	96–97	4	156–158	1
59	2	45	1	94–95	3	153–155	
58	2	44		92–93	5	150–152	1
57	1	43	4	90–91..	...2 ..13	147–149	1
56	2	42		88–89	5	144–146	1
55	1	41	2 *	86–87	2	141–143	
54	3	40	5	84–85	7	138–140	3
53	2	39	5	82–83..	...7 ..12	135–137	7
52		38	5	80–81	10	132–134	4
51	2	37	1	78–79	8	129–131	4
50	9	36	1	76–77	7	126–128	9
49	6	35	7	74–75	10	123–125	9
48	3	34	5	72–73..	...7 ..11	120–122	13
47	6	33	7	70–71	21	117–119	9
46	8	32	11	68–69	15	114–116	13
45	6	31	5	66–67	8	111–113	13
44	5	30	10	64–65..	...15 ..10	108–110	13
43	14	29	9	62–63	18	105–107	15
42	14	28	9	60–61	16	102–104	12
41	4	27	7	58–59	12	99–101..	...15 ..10
40	15	26	16	56–57..	...14 ...9	96–98	18
39	6	25	13	54–55	17	93–95	26
38	4	24....	..14 ..10	52–53	12	90–92..	...10 ...9
37	13	23	16	50–51..	...10 ...8	87–89	16
36	9	22	15	48–49	14	84–86	17
35	23	21	21	46–47	14	81–83..	...20 ...8
34....	..24 ..10	20....	..10 ...9	44–45	11	78–80	14
33....	..15 ...9	19	9	42–43..	...4 ...7	75–77	10
32	17	18....	...7 ...8	40–41	8	72–74..	...8 ...7
31....	..13 ...8	17	10	38–39	8	69–71	8
30	5	16	15	36–37..	...5 ...6	66–68	7
29....	..20 ...7	15	13	34–35	8	63–65	6
28	13	14	15	32–33	2	60–62	5
27	5	13....	...9....7	30–31	5	57–59	5
26	11	12	11	28–29	5	54–56	1
25	1	11	4	26–27	2	51–53	3
24	10	10	7	24–25		48–50	1
23	3	9	6	22–23	1	45–47	
22	6	8	1	20–21..	...2....4	42–44	
21	4	7	6	18–19		39–41	
20	2	6	2	16–17		36–38	
19	2	5	1	14–15		33–35	1
18	1	4		12–13		30–32	
17		3	1	10–11		27–29	
16	1	2	2	8–9		24–26	
15	1	1	1	6–7		21–23	
Total......	319		319		319		319
Median....	34.7		22.1		60.8		95.8

... Public-school medians, for indicated grades.

    c. Relate this evidence to what you know of the student's experience, background, and intelligence and of the natural tempo of other members of his family; to the student's explanation for his errors; and to his opinion of his own reading.

2. *The Vocabulary Score.*—*a.* Notice the student's relative position on the norms. Is he where he should be for his grade, intelligence, background?

    b. Notice the types of words missed. Do they suggest lacks in certain fields, or difficulty with abstract versus concrete ideas? Do they suggest ignorance of the meanings of certain roots, prefixes, and suffixes important to further vocabulary growth?

    c. Notice the level of difficulty of the words missed. If the words are arranged in the test in order of difficulty or rarity, it is easy to see whether the student's errors are in the higher, rarer, harder regions, or whether he has a uniformly bankrupt vocabulary. This indicates a difference in the kinds of words to be used in giving him special help.

    d. Relate this evidence to the student's reasons for errors (sometimes the error was not due to ignorance of the word meaning), and to his explanation of his method of building his vocabulary, if there is any; to his classroom experiences and his outside reading experiences.

3. *The Comprehension Score.*—*a.* Notice the student's relative position on the norms. Is he where he should be for his grade, intelligence, background? What does this position mean in terms of competition in his class, length of assignments, time required for preparation, reading material to be provided?

    b. Notice the proportion of items of a given kind that are missed. In which areas has he missed more questions: in grasping details, making inferences, drawing conclusions, following directions, outlining, getting sequences? What are the kinds of comprehension in which he apparently needs the most help?

    c. Notice the number of items covered. If there is no other speed score, this observation can yield an evaluation of the student's speed. The items wrong at this speed, especially if they are scattered through a test that grows progressively hard, suggest the accuracy of the student at the speed he used.

    d. Notice the difficulty of the items missed. Does this suggest something about the student's maturity of comprehension?

    e. Notice the subject matter of the items missed. Does the student show greater facility with science, social studies, fiction, or some other kind of material?

    f. In order to discover the student's power as divorced from speed, have him finish items that he did not complete in the first testing. This will suggest what his possibilities are if he can increase his speed or if he is given ample time for assignments.

Private preparatory schools will usually find the norms for independent schools[1] much more useful than public-school norms, owing to the fact that, at the secondary-school level, the average independent-school student is at least two grades ahead of the average public-school pupil in reading achievement. Consequently, a student in a private school whose reading score falls as low as the public-school norm is retarded in terms of independent-school standards and may require corrective measures.

In Table 6, which presents a picture of the reading achievement of students in a senior high school, it will be noted that the median total score made by the group of 319 tenth-grade pupils on the Traxler Silent Reading Test for grades 7 to 10 was 95.8, which is a little below the norm for public-school pupils in the tenth grade. In word meaning and total comprehension the medians are between the public-school norms for grades 9 and 10. The median score in rate of reading is slightly above the public-school tenth-grade median.

In all aspects of reading achievement shown in the table, the distributions of scores are very wide. The rate score of the fastest reader is four times that of the slowest reader. For the total comprehension scores, medians for the grades above and below those for which the test is designed have been extrapolated. The prediction of grade norms in this way is subject to a certain amount of error, but the medians are useful as indexes of the approximate range of the scores in terms of grade equivalents. One observes from Table 6 that the range of scores is more than 10 grades, and that even the middle 50 per cent of the scores covers a range of three grades. Obviously, in this one school system, the pupils classified in grade 10 and presumably expected to cover similar amounts of work show startling differences in reading achievement.

The general conclusions drawn from a study of this distribution of scores are (1) that the students in the tenth grade of this high school are, on the average, somewhat below the public-school norm for their grade in reading, and (2) that the individual students vary so widely in reading achievement that they cannot possibly be expected to do the same quality of schoolwork.

Results of standardized tests may be used to group students according to their level of reading achievement, to supply information to the teacher about the reading achievement of her class as a whole and the individual students in it, and to inform the student about his reading and stimulate him to improve it.

[1] Independent-school norms for a number of reading tests are available at the Educational Records Bureau, New York City.

Use of Tests in Grouping for More Effective Instruction.—Students may be grouped in various ways for more effective instruction. In schools having (1) small classes, (2) teachers skilled in reading methods, and (3) adequate reading material, attention may be given within the regular classes to the reading needs of individuals and groups. The teacher's judgment as to grouping within the class may be aided by his study of the score of each student on each part of the test, as well as by his study of the total scores. Thus he will make sure that students who are extremely low in some important aspect of reading, such as paragraph comprehension, are scheduled for special help, even though they may be up to average on the test as a whole. Thus in schools whose equipment is favorable for instruction in reading and whose students' reading difficulties respond to classroom methods of improving reading, no grouping other than that within the class itself is necessary. In schools where the students' reading deficiency is so great that they cannot profit by the kind of class instruction offered, special classes are necessary. These are remedial in nature and are offered for students who are so seriously handicapped in the basic reading skills that they require special materials, instruction, practice, and guidance in overcoming their deficiencies. These special reading groups will be described in Chap. VIII.

There is much to be said for flexible and voluntary grouping. If a pupil is arbitrarily placed in a group of poor readers, he may feel resentful or discouraged and stop trying. If, on the other hand, the possibility of joining a group that is working on some special aspect of reading is presented to a pupil as an opportunity for him to get help that he, too, needs, he is likely to want to join. Thus grouping becomes social and voluntary. The teacher and the specialist in guidance must constantly guard against stigmatizing children who need help. Referral to a reading class or for clinical study can be handled as a privilege, and the individual can be made to feel more important because of the extra attention he is getting. His attitude may then be, "I'm worth spending extra time on. I'm not a hopelessly poor reader."

Although scores on tests are an important criterion for determining grouping of students for special instruction, they are far from being the sole index of reading ability. They should be supplemented by informal tests, records of books and articles he has read in his directed and free reading, and samples of his responses to long passages. The student's attitude toward grouping and his own evaluation of his progress in reading should also be taken into consideration in grouping.

Use of Tests in Appraising Individual Reading Ability.[1]—When using the part scores on silent-reading tests for the analysis of the reading achievement of individual pupils with respect to certain broad categories, the teacher will find it helpful to employ whatever tables are provided by the authors of the various tests for use in changing the row scores to standard scores or percentile ratings or some other type of derived score, so that the scores on the parts can be compared directly. The manuals of directions for some reading tests contain tables of percentile equivalents for all scores, from the lowest to the highest. Some teachers insist that they do not understand percentile ranks, but the interpretation of percentiles is really very simple. An illustration will perhaps be helpful in explaining the use of percentiles in analyzing the scores made by pupils on the parts of a reading test. The following percentile ratings correspond to the rate scores, word-meaning scores, total-comprehension scores, and total scores made by six tenth-grade pupils on the Traxler Silent Reading Test for grades 7 to 10:

Pupil	Rate	Word meaning	Total comprehension	Total
Davis, Mary	50	3	3	8
Hill, William	92	10	6	30
Jones, Earle	17	77	77	58
Long, Alice	59	55	52	54
Martin, Phyllis	95	99	97	98
Sullivan, Joseph	5	1	3	2

A percentile rank shows the proportion of the pupils in a group whose scores are equaled or exceeded by the score of a given pupil. For example, the percentile for Mary Davis's total reading score is 8, which means that this pupil is up to or above only 8 per cent of the tenth-grade pupils whose scores were used in setting up the norms. On rate of reading, Mary has a percentile rating of 50, which is exactly at the median or average for the tenth grade, but in word meaning and total comprehension she is in the lowest 3 per cent of the tenth-grade group. It appears that she does not need to increase her rate of reading, but that she needs to improve in vocabulary and power of comprehension.

William Hill's percentile ratings provide an even more marked contrast between rate of reading, on the one hand, and word meaning

[1] See also pp. 234–246.

and total comprehension, on the other hand. This boy is in the highest 10 per cent of the tenth-grade pupils in reading rate, but in the lowest 10 per cent in vocabulary and comprehension. Probably he needs to learn to read study-type material more slowly, as well as to develop in knowledge of words and in ability to understand reading materials.

The reading-test percentiles of Earle Jones form a contrast to those of the first two pupils. He is a very slow reader, but he understands the meanings of words and comprehends reading material better than do three-fourths of the pupils in the tenth grade. Because of his relatively high word-meaning and comprehension scores, probably it is safe to put considerable pressure on this boy to get him gradually to increase his reading speed through practice.

Alice Long is consistently close to average for her grade. Her scores give no indication of either marked strength or unusual weakness in reading.

Phyllis Martin seems to be outstanding in all phases of reading measured by this test. In total reading score she has a percentile rating of 98, which means that in general reading skill she is in the highest 3 per cent of the tenth-grade pupils, as measured by this test. She should probably have great freedom in planning her own reading activities, but frequent checks on the status of her skills are necessary if she is not to develop bad habits through lack of supervision.

Joseph Sullivan, on the other hand, is much retarded in rate, word meaning, and comprehension. His total score is in the lowest 2 per cent of the scores of the tenth-grade pupils. He may require individual remedial teaching. Further diagnosis is necessary.

It is obvious that an analysis of this kind does not carry the diagnosis very far, but it is a useful beginning and one that can be made rather quickly.

In the interpretation of all such test results, one should, of course, keep in mind the fact that there is nothing final in the scores on a single test of this kind. While considerable confidence may be placed in the results, as far as groups are concerned, the scores of an individual pupil may fail to indicate his true reading ability because of lack of reliability in the test itself, unfavorable conditions of administration of the test, lack of correspondence between the material in the test and the material in the courses the pupil is studying, and other factors.

From a study of the results of the tests, students should understand better, as measured by the test, not only their general level of reading ability, but also some of their specific strengths and weaknesses. For the majority of students this knowledge supplies real motivation and paves the way to independence in planning their own reading programs. For example, the Nelson-Denny test may furnish high-school juniors and seniors and college students with valuable information, individually or in groups, about their vocabulary and methods of paragraph reading. The following information about a tenth-grade student's knowledge of vocabulary was brought out in a discussion of his performance on the vocabulary section:

When we went over the words, we found that he had associated "idolatry" with "idols," and knew what "felon" meant, although he had marked the wrong response on the paper. He said "decrepit" means "firm." When I asked him why he marked "firm," he said, "I couldn't pronounce the word, so I guessed." "Conflagration" was confused with "congregation." He knew what "penitent" meant and thought he had marked it right, but he had confused it with the idea of "mourner" rather than "sinner." He knew "omnipotent" from the line in the hymn that includes "omnipotent hand." In fact, he seemed to know more about the Bible and hymns and church than most young people. "Allayed," he thought, meant "allied."

The Iowa Silent Reading Test shows a student's rate of comprehension; comprehension of poetry; comprehension of words, sentences, and paragraphs; and ability to locate information. Unfortunately there is little or no variety in difficulty of material within each section of this test, so that for any one section the examiner cannot determine by the score how poor or how skillful the reader is in terms of easier and harder material. The following is typical of the kind of information that may be obtained from a reading test with subtests, such as the Iowa:

B——— is in the tenth grade and his reading ability tends to be above the average. His comprehension score of 168 is at the 54th percentile. All his other scores are considerably above the median for his grade, with the exception of those for poetry comprehension and use of the index. His standard score in poetry comprehension, 152, corresponds to a tenth-grade percentile of 25. In the use of the index he has a standard score of 143, which is equivalent to a percentile of 12. The results of the test indicate that, although the pupil's reading achievement is in general satisfactory for his grade level, special attention could appropriately be directed toward increasing his comprehension of poetry and improving his facility in using the index of a book. In the interpretation of the scores, however, one should remember that the parts of the test are rather short and therefore not highly reliable, and that it is desirable to check low scores by observation and further testing of the pupil.

In these ways—through observation and class contacts, informal tests, and standardized group reading tests—it is possible to appraise students' reading ability in groups, with a minimum of interference with the regular school organization and schedule of classes. A more thorough diagnosis, through individual oral reading tests and other diagnostic procedures, will be described in Chap. IX.

PROVIDING SUITABLE READING MATERIAL[1]

In a rural school in one impoverished county the only reading material was the Sears Roebuck catalogue. In some communities raising money to buy books is a serious problem. In many communities, on the other hand, there is a wealth of reading material that has not been utilized. After students have decided upon the kind of books and magazines they need, they can sometimes ferret out a great amount of material. They may know persons in the community who can help them obtain many books, pamphlets, and magazines of a recreational nature, besides other reading material that will help them solve their problems.

In low-income regions the raising of money for books is particularly difficult. Some schools have supplemented the totally inadequate amounts allotted for the purchase of books in the following ways: by asking each family to contribute a certain small amount; by enlisting the help of the Parent-Teacher Association and social and civic clubs; by holding fairs and box suppers, giving plays, staging rallies, and by other money-raising projects that are of educational value to children and adults. For instance, one school had a music festival for which the students in the art department decorated the outdoor court, and the music department prepared the program as part of its regular music work. The evening was an inspiration to all who attended and brought in a goodly sum for the purchase of new books. High-school students themselves have each earned money to buy a 10-cent book or a 25-cent pocket classic, which they donated to the class library after they had finished reading it.

The books sent to soldiers and made available in USO and other centers may be distributed to the schools after the war. In the meantime, many valuable pamphlets are supplied without charge to schools by the Metropolitan Life Insurance Company, the National Tuberculosis Association, the National Dairy Council, and other organizations. State or federal funds should be available to supply less fortunate communities with reading material that will make possible the improvement of reading.

After the money has been raised, the next problem is that of selecting the books. To make a successful choice, two kinds of knowledge

[1] See pp. 102–103, Chap. V and Appendix A.

are necessary—(1) knowledge of the students' reading needs, interests, and abilities; and (2) knowledge of books and the approximate level of difficulty of each.

Students' interest in different kinds of material can be ascertained fairly well by close observation of them while they are reading. For example, Helen Carpenter reported her observation of a group of sixth-grade children, who had I.Q.'s between 75 and 90, while they were reading two short passages. The first story was about ghosts. When the pupils began to read, their faces were noncommittal, but as they proceeded, their expressions became animated and eager. No one raised his hand for help on vocabulary, although there were words that the teacher knew were unfamiliar: "rooted," "stunned," "evil," "whimper," and "stuttered." The pupils seemed to be able to get the meaning of these words from the context. They were eager to discuss "Who was the ghost?" Each pupil who gave an opinion read the part of the story that supported his point of view. Throughout the period there were spontaneous comments such as, "This is a good story." "When do we get the next chapter?" "May we keep this story?" The most frequently mentioned reasons for liking the story were, "It is interesting." "It is exciting." "Spooky." "Fun to read." "Could happen." With evidence of this kind, the teacher had no doubt but that this story was interesting to this group and well within their ability to comprehend.

Quite different was the response to another selection, "Cultured Pearls," given to the same pupils to read, a week later. They remembered the ghost story and approached the reading period with eagerness. The interest, however, soon died down. They began to raise questions about the meaning of the title and of some of the hardest words—"scientist," "oyster," "artificial," "cultivated," "experiment." They were not able to get the meaning of these words from the context, and their attempts to illustrate parts of the story showed lack of comprehension. Although the pupils gave some explanations for liking the story—"Won't throw away pearls now when eating oysters," "Tells you things," "New idea"—there were no spontaneous expressions of interest as there had been about the previous story. The following week, instead of asking, "Do we have another story?" they said, "Is it another test again?"

The observation of pupils while they were reading and their spontaneous comments about the two selections left no doubt as to the greater appeal of the first story. Several weeks later it was still remembered vividly and named immediately as the selection that they liked best. This procedure is suggested as a method of discovering reading material that makes the strongest appeal to different groups of adolescents and the difficulties encountered in their reading of less appealing material.

In selecting books the librarian is an invaluable asset, for he knows books and keeps in touch with new books and with book lists of various kinds. If the aim is to provide suitable reading material for all students, everything from the comics to the classics should be available.

A teacher may anticipate a span of at least six grades in reading ability in a class above the third. He needs to remember this in selecting materials for his class. A subject-matter textbook, if it is used, must be readable for as large a percentage of the class as possible and should be supplemented by other books suitable for the other children. If the span of reading ability is very great, it is better to have many reference books of varied difficulty and differentiated assignments than to concentrate on the mastery of one textbook. With selections of passages and vocabulary from the books proposed, the teacher should devise a test to determine the suitability of the books for the children. All the difficulties inherent in a book, including the table of contents, illustrations, questions, glossary, index, footnotes, picture captions, vocabulary, sentence structure, and organization, should be considered before attention is given to the format, the name of the author, or any other prestige consideration.

Interest in reading for its own sake is rarely a lasting motive for reading. But many children find enduring pleasure in reading about the things that interest them. For many years the unpsychological approach of the required book list—"These are good for you; let the chips fall where they may."—failed to recognize the importance of children's interests for establishing the reading habit. A chasm resulted between what the children read outside the school and what they read perforce in school—a chasm of literary quality and content.

When reading-interest surveys showed the nature of children's reading tastes, schools began gradually to consider these in their selection of material for class study. Still, many teachers failed to survey the tastes in their own classes and tended to take the general reading-interest survey findings as completely applicable to the students in those classes.

There is need for a wider practice of some of the good developments in the field of reading interests: (1) the use of book ladders, such as those developed by Dora V. Smith at the University of Minnesota, which start with titles of low literary quality that children commonly read and lead up through successive levels of books that have similar interest appeals but are of higher literary quality; (2) surveys of interests and abilities in the class, and individual guidance in book selection; (3) the compilation of school-wide reading-test scores and records of children's reactions to books, to determine the reading-ability range within which given books can be enjoyed; (4) the use of such book lists as *Reading for Fun* on the elementary level, *Leisure Reading* on the junior-high-school level, *Home Reading* on the senior-high-school level, and *Good Reading* on the college level, to broaden the area in which children may feel free to browse; the use of such lists as *Gateways to Readable Books* and *Gateways to American History* with high-school students of low reading ability; and (5) permanent records of children' voluntary reading, to be used as an index of development and to show the neglected areas into which certain students need to be steered.

As the Second World War developed, a number of industrial cities experienced an influx of children, many of junior- and senior-high-school age, completely illiterate or substantially so. This put a serious burden on the public schools. None of the reading materials that are available for use in elementary reading classes on the high-school level seemed suitable to these students. Most of those materials assume at least second- or third-grade reading ability. These newcomers had none at all. Much of the available material was too immature in subject matter. Materials that were illustrated showed little boys and little girls assuming childish postures and engaging in childish activities, producing a horse laugh from these denizens of the city, who were fourteen years old or more. If these boys had been old enough for the Army, they would doubtless have been put into reading classes and would have enjoyed the thrill of learning to read the Army Reader, which soundly deals with the Army environment and Army words. Those junior-high-school teachers who had to think up something fast to do for 40 minutes a day with these students found it impossible to locate materials at once easy enough and mature enough. They found that it was very difficult to create a reading program that would duplicate the effectiveness of the Army reader. Such a situation, although it may be only temporary in some parts of the country, nevertheless illustrates the need for really mature subject matter that will appeal to such students as worthy of the dignity of their age and will present a group of ideas familiar enough and challenging enough for them to learn and to want to learn.

From the reading material available, the teacher, with the help of the librarian and the students, may select the areas in which the group is most interested and choose as many books for purchase as the budget allows. Occasionally, when publishers are willing to send sample copies for inspection, committees of students read all the books sent on approval and select for purchase those most suitable for the group. This highly motivated reviewing is excellent practice in reading for those who serve on the committee.

ACQUAINTING STUDENTS WITH BOOKS AVAILABLE

After the books have become available, there are many effective ways of introducing them to students. In the classroom a bulletin board on which book reviews and the gay covers of new books are posted attracts attention. One teacher made effective use of the bulletin board by pasting pictures about the war, sports, important persons, and other topics, and by placing on a table below each section, books, bright little booklets, and magazine articles relating to the same topic. This material could be read in the library or checked out to be read in study hall or at home. The retarded readers were attracted by the pictures on the bulletin board and by the bright, illustrated pamphlets and magazine articles relating to the pictures. A reading corner in the classroom where books are attractively displayed, and where there are comfortable chairs and gay hangings and potted plants, invites recreational reading.

Book reviews written by the students, sometimes on a country-wide basis and published in the Sunday edition of the local newspaper, disseminate students' recommendations for reading. One ninth-grade group made bibliography cards with headings such as "Books about Real Girls," "These Will Make You Chuckle," "Adventure Ahead," and "Mystery Stories." The cards were 8 by 14 in. in size, with three columns giving author, title, and a brief comment signed by the student who wrote it. These cards were placed conveniently on a table and students added items to them of their own volition whenever they read a book that they particularly liked. Tenth-grade students made similar cards on some specific subject of interest to them, using all the library facilities they could find. Among the topics chosen were "Aviation," "Horses," "Daniel Boone," "Snakes," "Quacks and Quackery in Medicine." Grading another student's book review is a stimulus to see whether a second critic also "felt that way" about a book. This also helps each student to become sensitive to good and poor features of book reviews.

From time to time the teacher may read to the class exciting, dramatic, or humorous parts of books or magazine articles in which he wishes to stimulate interest and, after their interest has been aroused, invite the students to get the book or the article from the library or to read it in their free periods. Informal class discussion of books read, similar to the conversation of an intelligent group of adults, is an effective way of stimulating interest and, frequently, of elevating reading tastes. Reading charts for individual students not only give the student himself a sense of accomplishment and direction in his reading but, if posted, interest his fellow students.

Interest in newspapers and magazines was aroused in one school by creating enthusiasm for crossword puzzles and "quiz" questions. As a result of this interest, the use of the dictionary increased and the students read other material in the newspapers and magazines more widely. One ninth grade studied a few representative magazines of different types—family, science, travel, and fiction. These they evaluated as to types of articles or stories, types of illustrations, types of advertising, interest appeal, quality of writing, and reading difficulty. A tenth grade spent two periods on how to read newspapers. In the first period the students learned how a newspaper is constructed, how to get the most important news quickly, and how to evaluate a newspaper. In the second period as many different newspapers as possible for the same day were compared and evaluated by means of certain specific questions, such as "How does each of the headlines make you feel about Russia?" "Which words in the heading carry the most feeling overtones?" "What is the editor's purpose in each case?"

Books may be advertised by posters that are of value both to the art student who reads them in order to select a subject for his poster and to students who become interested by seeing them displayed in all parts of the school building. Students in any class may be encouraged to design and draw jackets for the books that they have read. On these covers they try to portray some feature of a book that will make others want to read it. More extensive art work depicting dramatic scenes from stories about aviators, cowboys, dogs, and other subjects is another way of introducing available books more widely.

A special class in reading for enjoyment may be offered as an elective. This class not only is a means of introducing students to new and better books, but also provides time for recreational reading within the school program. This is especially valuable in times when many high-school students are engaged in three or four hours of remunerative work after school hours. In one junior high school there is a reading-seeing-listening room that combines the qualities of browsing room, lounging room, music-appreciation room, and art center. Deep-cushioned furniture is used, the lights are pleasant, records of classical music are played at intervals during the day, and a small but well-selected group of pictures, frequently changed, is on display. The students enjoy this room and like to spend their time there; of their own volition, they read some of the good books available. Colleges might well include a room of this kind in their dormitories and student-union buildings.

Book clubs have social and voluntary features that appeal to many students. These groups, sometimes scheduled during the school day, sometimes after school, are devoted to discussion of books, to exploration of new books, to reading short plays, and to special projects, such as setting up exhibits, giving an assembly program on books, and raising money to buy new books. One group, which had been making a study of communication by sound in a science class, did a great amount of reading to discover the right play for their broadcast. The speech department at a college near by cooperated by supplying a microphone amplifier and loud-speaker. A small room was used as the "studio" and an adjoining classroom as the auditorium. Whenever situations like this can be created, in which students feel a real need for reading, interest is high and effort is put forth. The reading club may do much toward associating reading with enjoyment and pleasure.

When a difficult book has to be taught, the skillful teacher tries to provide a background of experience that will make it more interesting and easier to read. For example, a teacher in the sixth grade, who was expected to teach Hawthorne's story, *The Great Stone Face*, spent a period in which he and the children who had seen the mountain told the others about it. Several more periods were spent in looking at pictures of the region and in reading simple, illustrated books about American life in those times. Then the teacher read the first part of the story aloud, to familiarize the class with Hawthorne's vocabulary and sentence structure and to interest them in the story. After they had finished reading the story themselves, they made a frieze depicting scenes in the story, to decorate their room. This required further reading to be sure the costumes and scenery were authentic.

Highly interesting assembly programs may introduce new or especially valuable books through book "sales talks," dramatizations of scenes from books, lively panel discussions of reading, or a "guess-who" program presenting characters from books. Similar publicity for new books may be obtained through the school newspaper.

Interest in other kinds of reading may be aroused by asking students to record all the reading that they do outside of books—street names, signs, menus, advertisements, and other "environmental reading." If, in addition, they make a quiz of the material that "stumped" them, the class will discover many unrecognized reading needs in their environment.

A community survey of reading practices conducted by high-school students interests them in the availability of reading material and in the quality of the books and magazines that are read by people in their community. The investigators are often shocked by the poor reading habits that they find, and this concern is reflected in an improvement in their own reading interests and tastes.

GUIDING INDIVIDUAL STUDENTS IN THEIR CHOICE OF BOOKS

The teacher's task is not to condemn the students' reading, but to guide them to better reading. This objective may be best reached by letting them read what they wish at first, regardless of its literary value. Nothing is gained by prohibitions. The teacher will make most rapid progress by providing activities in which the students discover for themselves that ability to read is of value to them and that they have the capacity to read better. This is the first step in assuring the use of the books available.

Most guidance in reading will be done casually. When a student expresses an interest, the teacher may suggest a book along the line indicated. If the interest is genuine and the book suitable, connection between the book and the pupil will be made. But the gap between where he is and where the teacher would like him to be cannot be bridged all at once; he cannot be expected to desert *Terry and the Pirates* for *Ivanhoe*. In the case of retarded readers, it is very important that the book or the article recommended be not too difficult; for if the student attempts to read material quite beyond him his impression of the futility of reading is confirmed.

More systematic guidance of the reading program of individual students is desirable. Through guidance in their individual reading programs, students can be encouraged to broaden their reading interests and include more reading of biography and social-science material as they progress through junior and senior high school. In a private school a class period each week is set aside for individual conferences. On "parallel day," which is held in lieu of the class period on Friday, the boys remain in study hall until they are sent for. They come to the office of the English teacher singly. In the average class, from 5 to 8 minutes can be allotted to each interview. If this does not prove long enough, additional time is made by appointment during study hour that evening.

During the first parallel session of the month the boy is asked what type of book he wishes to read that month. Often he himself suggests the title of a book that he has chosen to read. If it is not approved by the teacher, or if the boy has no choice, certain book titles are suggested and the boy is sent to the library to browse, later reporting back to the teacher. The only hard and fast rule that the teacher makes regarding the choice of books is that half of the books for a given semester must be nonfiction. Subsequent sessions are devoted to discussing informally the progress that has been made in reading the book.

Finally from the older boys a short, written book review of not more than 1,000 words, fewer if possible, is required—a real review, not an old-fashioned book report. The book reviews are judged for their literary merit, not simply as evidence that the book has been read.

PLACE OF ORAL READING IN THE SCHOOL-WIDE PROGRAM[1]

In a group of below-average readers, some oral reading by the students as a group may be helpful. If each student has practiced the oral reading of his section beforehand and has learned how to pronounce new words, the group oral reading has the effect of improving phrasing and of providing an immediate stimulus to more efficient reading in the case of those whose silent reading lags behind the ordinary rate of oral reading. These desirable results will not be obtained, however, if the students stumble through passages too difficult for them and the poor readers feel embarrassed while the good readers feel bored.

Occasional reading aloud by the teacher is also a legitimate part of the total reading program. In addition to furnishing enjoyment, reading aloud by the teacher sets standards of good oral reading and is a means of introducing new books. It is sometimes the best means of giving retarded readers contact with literature that they could not otherwise enjoy. Oral reading of the beginning of a new book makes subsequent silent reading of it easier by acquainting the students with the author's vocabulary and style.

AROUSING TEACHERS' INTEREST IN THE IMPROVEMENT OF STUDENTS' READING

Teachers, in general, are aware of the need for the improvement of reading. They feel that they cannot teach if the students cannot read. The results of a standardized test make the degree and extent of reading deficiency more concrete and also personalize the problem. A vocabulary test on the words that each teacher expects students to know and tests of the comprehension of selected representative para-

[1] See pp. 106–109, Chap. V, for discussion of oral reading.

graphs from their texts and reference books show still more clearly the way in which students read the books assigned.

Students who have left school write frequently, in no uncertain terms, of their reading difficulties and of the help that they wish their high-school teachers had given them. These comments show teachers the kind of reading that their students do later on in life. Follow-up information of this kind is stimulating to both teachers and students.

Another aspect that interests teachers is the relation between reading and school achievement, which has already been discussed. When a teacher realizes that a student may read well in one subject and poorly in another, she is more convinced of the necessity of teaching reading in her own class and the futility of depending entirely upon the English teacher or on a remedial reading class. Time is another element in the situation. One teacher realizes that unless some of her fifteen-, sixteen-, and seventeen-year-old boys improve their reading before they leave school, they will probably remain nonreaders for the rest of their lives. Yet she has no free time for working with individual students or for developing new methods and materials for helping them. Her chief problem, as she sees it, is lack of time. Time is obviously a factor. Under similar conditions, however, some teachers have made the improvement of reading an intrinsic part of their teaching, and have found time for work with individuals during periods of free reading or independent study. In a sense, unless the teacher takes time for reading, all the time pupils spend in study is lost.

When teachers begin to ask "How?", they are ready for books, pamphlets, and practical discussion of ways of improving students' reading. Particularly helpful to teachers are demonstrations of individual methods of diagnosis and remedial work and group methods of providing practice and instruction. As their knowledge and interest grow, they may be encouraged to experiment in their own clasess. If they discover an effective procedure, they will be glad to tell other teachers about what they have done that works.

CONTRIBUTION OF THE PRINCIPAL TO THE IMPROVEMENT OF READING

The principal must first recognize the need for improving reading. The principal of a school that offers work from the first through the eleventh grade described the problem as follows:

Somewhere we have failed to give our children what is needed. The reading difficulties, the reading problems in our school are alarming. A test given by the County Board last spring showed that our ninth-grade students were, in general, two or three grades below the average reading level of the county as a whole.

The evidence from test results, plus studies of the part played in individual failures in content subjects by inability to read and of improvement after instruction in reading, are effective means of increasing both the principal's and the teachers' awareness of the importance of reading.

Recognition of the need should be followed by the sort of vision expressed by the same principal in the following words:

I should like to see the children, each according to his capacity, develop through the varying stages and levels of reading, writing, and speaking, to the fullest, with the intelligent guidance of their teachers.   I should like to note improvement from absolute inability to read to the stage of recognizing, comprehending, and using words and statements from the printed page of ordinary books, magazines, and papers.   I have the duty to help my teachers find out the causes of reading difficulties, learn the remedial steps that can be taken, and acquire sound methods of instruction in reading.

If the principal invites teachers to cooperate with him in developing the reading program, they are much more likely to become aware of their need for continued study and to welcome any effective plan of in-service education in reading methods that he can make available to them.

It is also the principal's responsibility to provide time for special instruction in reading, if such instruction is needed.   Time has been provided in the following ways:

1. A daily 30-minute period for reading obtained by shortening the other periods by about 5 minutes

2. Thirty minutes in the daily home-room period, when any necessary attention may be given to reading

3. Reading classes a full period in length twice a week in the eighth, ninth, and tenth grades.   If a special reading teacher is employed, he makes a written report on reading deficiencies and the results of reading tests, so that each classroom teacher may give attention to the weaknesses that are evident in his groups.

The following is a summary of procedures that may be used by a principal in order to initiate and develop an interest in the improvement of reading in his school.

1. Administration of a standardized reading test and analysis of the results.   This is a useful procedure in showing the teachers the level of reading in the school and the wide range of reading ability in each grade.   Unless the teachers feel the need for help in their reading problems, however, the test may simply be viewed as more work and

as a target for their condemnation. Skillful use of the test will involve a discussion of the results with the teachers and decisions on classroom emphases to remove deficiencies in certain areas.

2. Development of a reading program, which gradually grows out of the interest and experimentation of those teachers who are especially interested in this type of program. The best features of this program can ultimately be spread throughout the school.

3. Rotation of remedial reading responsibilities in the school from year to year, so that ultimately every teacher becomes a teacher of reading. This is an arbitrary method of bringing the entire faculty into the program. A chief drawback is that the personality and background of many teachers are not conducive to successful work in a reading program. The attitude of some teachers is also unfavorable, but their initial attitude will usually be somewhat altered when they become informed in the field.

4. The scheduling of a series of faculty meetings centered around talks by specialists and discussions of their suggestions; reports by various faculty committees; and mimeographed materials on the problems of reading, on the psychology and physiology of the reading process, on particular kinds of reading skill demanded by different subjects, on the specific skills needed for each subject and the specific ways in which a teacher of a given subject can help her pupils develop and use the skills necessary for the reading course. Case references concerning bright pupils who are doing well in some subjects but who are not developing the reading skills required in other subjects are enlightening, provided that care is taken in the selection of such cases to prevent the personal element from defeating all the good arguments that the use of objective information has built up.

5. Follow-up of study-hall difficulties and complaints from teachers that certain pupils come to class unprepared because of inadequate reading achievement. This procedure is an especially helpful way to enlist cooperation, because it grows out of the teacher's own realization that individual pupils need special help in reading.

6. Use of questionnaires to graduates and extracts from letters by former students on their college or life reading problems and concerning the advantages and limitations of the training in reading that they received in high school. If individual letters are discussed with the faculty, one should be sure that they are from graduates whose opinions are respected by the teachers opposed to changes in method or emphasis on reading.

7. Calculation of correlation coefficients between reading ability and marks in courses or scores on tests. These results can be used to

show that in the subjects requiring reading there is a substantial relationship between success and reading ability.   Unless the explanation of the correlation coefficients is very clearly presented by a respected faculty member and is accompanied by additional illustrative data, the nonmathematical faculty members are liable to go home mystified and unimpressed.   On the other hand, the statistical-minded faculty members will probably be unimpressed by the raw correlations, because they realize the influence of intelligence on both reading achievement and scores or marks.   For this reason it is desirable to present correlations obtained by procedures under which intelligence is held constant.

8. Local construction of reading tests in each teacher's field.   The teachers may be asked to select representative paragraphs from their textbooks and to make tests on words that they think important and questions that they would ordinarily ask on such material.   The reading should be timed to see how long it takes the pupils to read the different kinds of material.   A supplementary value in this procedure is that it helps to indicate the texts that are difficult for certain pupils and the specific nature of the difficulties.

9. Analysis of textbooks in order to discover the kinds of difficulty they present to the student.   An objective analysis of the texts with respect to anticipated student difficulties may be supplemented by evidence obtained from the study of the results of informal tests and observations of classroom difficulties by the teachers of each subject.   This analysis can be the beginning of an appreciation of the need for additional references to enlarge on meanings that are difficult for students or that are too briefly discussed in the basic book.   It can also help teachers see the need for varying and enlarging upon the background information presented to classes that include pupils with serious reading difficulties.   A variety of texts also makes possible differentiated assignments according to individual reading deficiencies.

10. A study of pupils' interests reported by the librarian, which should check the carry-over of interests from classes to library and should increase the teacher's appreciation of the differences in ability among students that require adjustment of teaching methods and textbooks.

CONTRIBUTION OF THE LIBRARIAN TO THE IMPROVEMENT OF READING

Librarians have a large share in providing experiences that help young people to become interested in books, to enjoy them, and to interpret what they read.   Among the activities sponsored by libraries are dramatizations and little-theater groups, community "sings," "nationality nights" with programs of folk songs and folk dances of different countries, exhibits of local handicrafts and colonial household tools, exhibits of pictures from public and private sources, games and walks for various purposes, garden clubs, handcraft groups, the making of Christmas wreaths, hobby groups, stamp clubs, radio programs, and motion pictures. In ways like this the librarian supplements reading with firsthand experience and creates situations in which reading seems desirable and necessary.

Many libraries, however, do not make this approach to reading and do little to attract and encourage readers. Reasons given by young people for not using the library service in their communities include the following: other ways of using leisure time that are more appealing, difficulty with library rules and fines, books that are out of date, the bother of getting to the library at the times when it is open, and other explanations. One dissatisfied girl is quoted as saying, "I don't like their books. They are either fairy tales or too deep for me." Too often the librarian has not made sufficient effort to supply individuals with reading material about things that are of vital concern to them.

By visiting classes at the invitation of teachers, one town librarian encouraged many school children to come to the public library. He brought new books with him that he thought would be particularly interesting to the group to whom he was speaking. He showed them some of the pictures, read appealing incidents, and made comments relating the book to their background and experience. The teachers with whom he cooperated were enthusiastic about this service.

The librarian should be aware of the different purposes for which people read, so that he can supply the books they want and can suggest reading methods appropriate to their individual purposes. Starting from where people are in interests, tastes, and experience, he can gradually encourage them to extend their experience through reading. Knowing the reading needs and abilities of his public, through his contacts with them, he may be able to influence publishers to print more books that are suitable for these readers.

The library should provide progressive reading experiences. Very small children can early become familiar with books through looking at them and handling them. First-grade children may have library cards as soon as they can write their names. Their exploration of books for pleasure should continue during elementary school years. In junior high school they should read eagerly and begin to do considerable reference work. In senior high school required reading and other interests tend to crowd out recreational reading. Young married people tend to come back to the library, either to resume reading where they left off in high school or to find help on their present problems.

One group of sixth-grade children, who were not reading up to capacity, discussed with the librarian in their first library period how they wanted to use library time. Someone suggested that they could help other students by becoming "specialists" in some field. Each child chose a field and built up a reference file on the subject. These files were to be a permanent part of the library and available for all who wanted to use them. Thus books in the library reinforced interests that had been created elsewhere. When the school was asked to give a broadcast, this group was chosen to prepare it. They selected some of their "specialists" to report on books that they had read. Many favorable comments on the broadcast reached the students and pleased them greatly. This project was a significant experience for them. The slow readers obtained excellent practice by reading rapidly many books below their level of reading ability in order to canvass the field. Old interests were strengthened and new interests were discovered. It was an excellent opportunity for the librarian to become better acquainted with individuals; it had all the values of a worth-while, cooperative enterprise.

The school librarian works with teachers, parents, and students. He is a resource to teachers, helping them to find references on the topics that they are studying in class, suggesting new books for students' recreational reading, and supplying books for classroom libraries. He also cooperates with teachers in helping students to acquire the best methods of locating information. To the teachers' professional growth he may contribute by keeping them informed concerning new curricular content, textbooks, courses of study, reference books on teaching, and visual aids. In a college the librarian may supply dormitory as well as classroom libraries. In one college, rotating collections of 250 books were placed in residence halls. Thus, during the year, students in a single residence had immediate access to 1,000 different books.

The library should be the reading center of the school. A well-equipped library is the student's most important laboratory. There students will find books and articles that will illumine and heighten their interest in required reading, increase their sympathetic understanding of and curiosity about a subject, and make it real and imaginatively stimulating. Thus the librarian helps to make study a delight, instead of drudgery.

The librarian supplies whatever books or magazines students are interested in; he is alert to opportunities to guide them to something better in the same field and, eventually, to extend their interests to other fields. This he does in many ways. For example, one school librarian arranged books of different literary quality according to specific subjects so that he could say to a student who had been enjoying a book of poor literary quality, "You'll find other stories like this on the same shelf."

Both librarians and teachers may stimulate and guide students' reading by attractive and well-planned displays and exhibits, informal talks about books, a favorite-book poll, and mimeographed or printed bibliographies on special subjects. A mimeographed book-review magazine, written by young persons who use the library, may be the responsibility of a library club.

Whereas teachers are likely not to know books, librarians are likely not to know students. Knowledge of both is necessary. One librarian recognized this need when he said:

I think a librarian should know more about the reading problems of young people in order to guide them better in selecting their books. Too often we know our books, but for various reasons do not get them across to the young-sters. I hope to learn how to help the boys and girls read more and more in an ever-broadening field, taking them from their present level to higher ones.

As the librarian serves at the desk of a high-school or a college library, she has a chance to study the reading trends in her school as well as to discuss reading interests and problems with individual students. Thus she performs a valuable readers' advisory service.

The librarian supplements the teachers' instruction in the location of material. After students have discussed their reading programs individually with their teacher or, as a group, have formulated a problem for study, they may have a conference with the librarian, to learn how to locate materials and otherwise use the resources of the library for a specific purpose. A quick way of orienting students to the library, at the beginning of the year, is to have them fill in a mimeographed chart of the reading room, indicating where different types of books are located, such as travel, aviation, biography, science.

In one school, from the seventh to the twelfth grade, every student becomes acquainted with the location of books on the library shelves, the card catalogue, and the use of the *Readers' Guide* and other indexes. Teachers take older students to the public library, where the librarian helps to acquaint them with the ways of finding material in a public library. Then they are given an assignment to find material relating to a topic in one of their courses.   They make out cards and compile a bibliography, for which they receive credit in that course, as well as in English.   The film, "Found in a Book," available through the Bell and Howell Company, Chicago, is a useful aid to instruction in the location and use of reference material.

Even graduate students need expert help in locating books that they need.   For example, a student, Mr. G, studying for his master's degree in history, received a great deal of help from a librarian interested in the field of reading.   Mr. G admitted that he was finding it increasingly difficult to keep up with extensive reading.   He was swamped by a mass of detail.   Moreover, he was distressed by his inefficiency in finding material for papers that required bibliographical research.   His difficulties were specific and his needs were simple to diagnose.   Obviously, his work and study habits were inefficient.   A rearrangement of his daily schedule for study and exercise helped. Demonstration of how to examine a book for important features before reading it—*i.e.*, considering the table of contents, preface or introduction, and introductory and summary chapters—showed him how an author selects and organizes material.   By examining the author's clues for each chapter and making a preliminary reading of each section before beginning to take notes, he learned something about selecting and organizing central ideas.   These exercises were supplemented by specific directions in the location of material for his special field of history:

1. Careful explanation of the card catalogue as the index of all material on a specific subject available in a given collection and as the starting point for a bibliography.

2. Description of special indexes to periodicals, such as the *Readers' Guide*, and of selective bibliographies of history, especially, Channing, Hart, and Turner, *Guide to the Study and Reading of American History;* Larned, *Literature of American History;* and Griffin, *Writings on American History*, 1906 *to Date;* discussion of the value of bibliographies in encyclopedias of history and dictionaries of biography, as short cuts to the key books in special fields.

3. Explanation of guides to special libraries and special collections, especially Green and Morris, *Guide to the Principal Sources for Early American History* (1600–1800) *in the City of New York*, an invaluable timesaver for the historian in search of primary sources.

4. Description of Dutcher, *Directions and Suggestions for the Writing of Essays and Theses in History*, as an aid in the selection and organization, as well as in the location of material.

These aids were all unknown to Mr. G.   Introduction to the knowledge and use of them saved him untold time and energy.

In a teachers college or school of education the librarian may offer a course on library science to equip teachers to perform some of the services of librarian in a small school.   Subjects such as How to Use Reference Books and Book Selection are stressed.   The student may be tested by being required to compile a suitable bibliography on some special subject.

A brief summary of common library practices in a developmental reading program is offered below.   It is arranged according to the amount of cooperation the librarian has achieved or may expect from students and teachers.   A librarian may easily skim through for suggestions that she may not as yet have tried.

Level I.   Activities requiring little or no cooperation from faculty:

1. Become acquainted with lists of books for retarded readers.   Remember that library association lists are likely to be based on the choices of good readers rather than on the abilities and maturity of interests of retarded readers.
2. Develop your own lists of easier books on the more mature levels of interest; for students' use, list by interest, not by grade level of difficulty.
3. As this list is made and used, add comments on the sex, age, personality, and interests of the persons who like the books.
4. Have students make comparisons of the books as to difficulty so that you can get a sense of the relative difficulty of books dealing with a certain interest.
5. Make ladder lists from easier to harder books on a given subject.
6. Gradually buy the books that would interest your poorer readers (14).
7. Have bookmarks listing good books in different centers of interest, starting with easier books.
8. Form a library club.
9. Print a book-popularity table in the school newspaper.

Level II.   Activities requiring some faculty and student cooperation:

1. Draw attention of the faculty to newer books that would appeal to their classes and suit the poorer readers.
2. Agitate for reading scores on pupils—to have tests administered if they have not been given and to have access to the scores if they have been given.
3. Have the students help you make an interest-centered card file or a one-interest poster or book display by writing brief annotations, signed as endorsements.
4. Have assembly programs introducing new books.   One idea might be to flash various exciting pages on the screen, thus proving to the poorer readers that they can read some of your books.   Talks or plays based on the books could also be a part of the program.

5. Help teachers to secure books on the various units in their subjects which will be easy enough for the poorer readers.

Level III.   Activities requiring considerable cooperation:

1. Procure data from the lower school on the interests of the incoming class and prepare for them by displays in the library—bulletin-board blurbs, showcases of book jackets with comments relating to a given center of interest, books of high interest and easy reading open to a sample page.

2. Arrange with teachers for visits of their classes to the library for orientation, special reference work, book talks, or leisure reading.

3. Visit certain classes, showing new books and holding discussions on the value or appeal of each.

4. Have the English teachers give you the reading scores on their students and notes from the students to you indicating the kinds of books they particularly like or feel that they need; then arrange to have small groups come to you to look over the materials you think that they might like.   This is fine for English composition and a good introduction to the librarian as a friend.

5. Plan programs of summer and leisure reading or reading in connection with classwork for individuals with given difficulties.

6. Enlist the cooperation of library- or writing-club groups to write and illustrate materials on a given topic that is highly appealing to poor readers but for which there are no easy books.   These original materials can be bound and used as introductory reading to establish concepts through pictures, careful definitions, and simple explanations of the topic.   This project may be, for instance, a cooperative effort on the part of a science teacher, an art teacher, an English teacher, and their classes and the librarian.

CONTRIBUTION OF THE GUIDANCE WORKER
TO THE IMPROVEMENT OF READING

Guidance and the improvement of reading are inseparable.   The principal frequently asks the director of guidance to assist in developing the school-wide program of reading.   The largest percentage of problems referred to deans and counselors are educational-guidance problems, many of which involve reading and study habits.   One dean of girls in a junior-senior high school, who has responsibility for developing the guidance program in the school and also teaches two classes, is fully cognizant of the relation between reading and guidance:

In my classes I come up against reading problems; likewise in my work as dean and guidance director of the school I find a great many educational-guidance problems that seem to originate with reading problems.   I have problems of students not knowing how to read and not knowing how to study, and this often is the real cause of their not getting along better in their school-work.   As guidance director I also have conferences with the elementary-grade teachers and find that many of our high-school problems can be traced to reading problems there.   Consequently, I feel that much can be done to help solve this problem in our school.

If the guidance worker has had preparation in methods of teaching reading, he can assume leadership among teachers in this respect, passing on to them suggestions, materials, and devices useful to them in their classes.   He may be asked to plan and conduct classes in the improvement of reading.   Certainly, in his counseling, he will meet many seriously retarded readers who need the intensive study and treatment described in Chap. XI.

CONTRIBUTION OF THE TEACHER OF EACH SUBJECT TO THE IMPROVEMENT OF READING

As we noted in discussing the contribution of the principal, the teacher's first step is to become aware of the reading problem and to have a vision of the improvement in reading that is possible for his group.   One teacher in a junior high school stated his goals as follows:

I expect my eighth-grade students to read orally with some degree of appreciation, and to read silently or orally with comprehension of the material. I expect them to further that understanding by increasing their knowledge of vocabulary and by analyzing (along lines necessarily not too complicated) the structure of certain types of literature and the behavior of the people met through reading.   I always hope to develop at least the first step toward critical analysis of literary matter.   My aims along these latter lines, how-ever, are realized only in a very few cases, owing to a peculiar problem facing our junior high.   Most of the students are unable to understand eighth-grade literature; a few cannot pronounce a printed word as simple as "majority."

Another teacher, who has spent much time directing plays in school, has attempted to correlate the communication arts in his regular classroom teaching.   One of his classes has organized an English-class radio program, another has compiled a book of short stories, a third edits a class magazine.   The successful operation of these programs depended upon a real desire on the part of the students to communicate to each other information that they had read or had written themselves.   He says:

My hope in teaching reading in junior high school has always been to broaden the reading interests of my students.   I attempt to "expose" them to types of literature with which they are either unfamiliar, or in which they have had no interest, and, through class reading and discussion, to incorporate these into their already established interests.   It is my hope that students will recognize certain standards in readings of their own choice, and that their selections in reading will be based on sound criteria.   I have never used comic books as illustrations of poor reading matter, but have rather tried to suggest, through discussion of other types of reading which the student can readily associate with comics, the value of better types of reading.

On the other hand, teachers have been known to stimulate genuine interest in the folk heroes of America by starting with Superman and leading to Paul Bunyan, Davy Crockett, and Daniel Boone.

Teachers in every subject have opportunities, through reading, to teach students to think.   They ask such questions as What is your evidence for that statement?   May new facts have been discovered since that book was written?   How do you know that is a true story? What has been said on the other side of the question?   Questions like these help students to learn to be more precise and accurate in their statements, to distinguish the true from the not true, to seek and evaluate evidence.   Teaching students to read in order to think straight is one of the teacher's most important tasks.

Each teacher should accept the student where he finds him and guide him as far as he can go.   Whether he is teaching a heterogeneous class or a group selected because of reading difficulties, individualized instruction is necessary.   This can be achieved in part through the use of a wide variety of recreational and practice material with individuals.   The class as a whole may be divided into smaller, more homogeneous groups, and instruction may be given to one group while the others are engaged in doing practice exercises or free reading. Individual assignments, home-study programs, and teachers' comments on individual students' work are other ways of adapting instruction to individual needs.   Encouraging students to work out programs for the improvement of their own reading is one of the best ways of helping each student to develop his reading potentialities.

Cooperation among teachers on the reading problem is essential. In one consolidated school, for example,

. . . teacher cooperation was very good, and each of us tried to aid the others. We tried to make the pupils see that certain words and certain readings as well as certain skills could be used in many classes, and not just in the one in which these were assigned.   For example, the English teacher would accept books on history for reports, and pupils were encouraged to give, as oral reports, material which they had learned in science or agriculture or some other subject.   This lessened, somewhat, the reading burden, and fostered interest in what was read.

Various departments may work out projects together, in that way giving the student more time to do his work thoroughly and to read more widely on one subject of special interest to him than would otherwise be possible.   There is a prevalent tendency for each department to consider its own work so important that it makes disproportionate demands on the student's time.   As a result, the total accumulation of required work prevents the student from doing wide and intensive reading in any field.   By conferring about their reading requirements and combining projects, teachers may avoid giving rise to the idea that reading is an intolerable burden.

Teachers should realize more fully that helping students to read more efficiently is part of their professional job, not something in addition to it.   There is real danger that a "reading program" will be viewed by teachers as an extra task, over and above their teaching of the subject.   However, if teachers conceive of their job as the development of the best potentialities of every student, if they possess the personal qualities of patience, breadth of interest, ability to inspire confidence, considerateness, and understanding and appreciation of young people, the success of the school-wide reading program is assured.

References

1. BOND, GUY L., and EVA BOND, *Developmental Reading in High School*, The Macmillan Company, New York, 1941, xi + 363 pp.
2. CARPENTER, HELEN, *Gateways to American History*, The H. W. Wilson Company, New York, 1943, 255 pp.
3. CARPENTER, HELEN M., and DOROTHY J. WHITTED, "Readable Books for Slow Learners," *Social Education*, Vol. 7, pp. 167–170, April, 1943.
4. CONANT, MARGARET M., *The Construction of a Diagnostic Reading Test for Senior High School Students and College Freshman*, Teachers College Contributions to Education, No. 861, Bureau of Publications, Teachers College, Columbia University, New York, 1942, viii + 156 pp.
5. DAVIS, FREDERICK B., "What Do Reading Tests *Really* Measure?" *English Journal*, Vol. 33, pp. 180–187, April, 1944.
6. GORMAN, FRANK H., "Teaching Upper-elementary and High-school Pupils to Read," *School Review*, Vol. 51, pp. 423–427, September, 1943.
7. GRAY, WILLIAM S. (compiler and editor), *Co-operative Effort in Schools to Improve Reading*, Proceedings of the Conference on Reading held at the University of Chicago, Vol. 4, Supplementary Educational Monographs, No. 56, University of Chicago Press, Chicago, 1942, xii + 338 pp.
8. GRAY, WILLIAM S. (compiler and editor), *Reading in Relation to Experience and Language*, Proceedings of the Conference on Reading held at the University of Chicago, Vol. 6, Supplementary Educational Monographs, No. 58, University of Chicago Press, Chicago, 1944, 226 pp.
9. "A High School Reading Program," *Maryland High School Bulletin*, Maryland State Department of Education, Baltimore, 1941, 127 pp.

10. HILDRETH, GERTRUDE, and JOSEPHINE L. WRIGHT, *Helping Children to Read*, Bureau of Publications, Teachers College, Columbia University, New York, 1940, vi + 90 pp.

11. "How Libraries May Serve," Educational and National Defense Series, *Pamphlet* No. 17, U.S. Government Printing Office, Washington, D.C., 1941, 20 pp.

12. LUCKIESH, MATTHEW, and FRANK K. MOSS, *Reading as a Visual Task*, D. Van Nostrand Company, Inc., New York, 1942, xv + 428 pp.

13. McCAUL, R. L., "Economic Training in Reading at the Secondary School Level," *High School Journal*, Vol. 21, pp. 117–125, April, 1938.

14. STRANG, RUTH, ALICE CHECOVITZ, CHRISTINE GILBERT, and MARGARET SCOGGIN, *Gateways to Readable Books*, The H. W. Wilson Company, New York, 1944, 104 pp.

15. THORNDIKE, EDWARD L., and IRVING LORGE, *The Teachers' Word Book of 30,000 Words*, Bureau of Publications, Teachers College, Columbia University, New York, 1944, xii + 274 pp.

16. TINKER, MILES A., "Illumination Intensities for Reading Newspaper Type," *Journal of Educational Psychology*, Vol. 34, pp. 247–250, April, 1943.

17. TOWNSEND, AGATHA, "A Study of the Revised New Edition of the Iowa Silent Reading Tests," 1944 Fall Testing Program in Independent Schools and Supplementary Studies, pp. 31–39, *Educational Records Bulletin*, No. 42, Educational Records Bureau, New York, January, 1945.

18. TRAXLER, ARTHUR E., "The Nature and Use of Reading Tests," *Educational Records Bulletin*, No. 34, Educational Records Bureau (in cooperation with Science Research Associates), New York, October, 1941, 64 pp.

19. TRAXLER, ARTHUR E., "A Study of the Van Wagenen-Dvorak Diagnostic Examination of Silent Reading Abilities," 1940 Fall Testing Program in Independent Schools and Supplementary Studies, *Educational Records Bulletin* 31, pp. 33–41, Educational Records Bureau, New York, January, 1941.

20. TRAXLER, ARTHUR E., *Techniques of Guidance*, Chaps. VIII and X, Harper & Brothers, New York, 1945.

21. WILKING, S. VINCENT, "Do Our Reading Tests Test the Right Words?" *Journal of Educational Research*, Vol. 36, pp. 35–39, September, 1942.

22. WOODRING, MAXIE N., and CECILE WHITE FLEMMING, *Directing Study of High School Pupils*, rev. ed., Bureau of Publications, Teachers College, Columbia University, New York, 1935, vi + 254 pp.

23. ZAHNER, LOUIS C., "The Testing of Comprehension," *Educational Record*, Vol. 21, Supplement No. 13, pp. 71–89, January, 1940.

Reading Tests

24. ALLEN, RICHARD D., HAROLD H. BIXLER, WILLIAM L. CONNOR, FREDERICK B. GRAHAM, and GERTRUDE HILDRETH, *Metropolitan Reading Tests*, World Book Company, Yonkers-on-Hudson, N.Y., 1932–1940.

25. DAVIS, FREDERICK B., and others, *Cooperative Reading Comprehension Tests*, Cooperative Test Service, New York, 1940–1943.

26. DURRELL, DONALD D., and HELEN BLAIR SULLIVAN, *Durrell-Sullivan Reading Capacity and Achievement Tests*, World Book Company, Yonkers-on-Hudson, N.Y., 1938.

27. ENGELHART, MAX D., and THELMA GWINN THURSTONE, *Chicago Reading Tests*, E. M. Hale and Company, Publishers, Milwaukee, 1939.

28. GATES, ARTHUR I., *Gates Reading Tests*, Bureau of Publications, Teachers College, Columbia University, New York, 1942.

29. GREENE, H. A., and V. H. KELLEY, *Iowa Silent Reading Tests*, New Edition, rev., Elementary Test, World Book Company, Yonkers-on-Hudson, N.Y., 1943.

30. GREENE, H. A., A. N. JORGENSEN, and V. H. KELLEY, *Iowa Silent Reading Tests*, New Edition, rev., Advanced Test, World Book Company, Yonkers-on-Hudson, N.Y., 1943.

31. HAGGERTY, MELVIN E., and ALVIN C. EURICH, *Minnesota Reading Examinations for College Students*, University of Minnesota Press, Minneapolis, 1930.

32. HAGGERTY, MELVIN E., and MARGARET E. NOONAN, *Haggerty Reading Examination*, Sigma 1, World Book Company, Yonkers-on-Hudson, N.Y. 1920.

33. HORN, ERNEST, MAUDE McBROOM, H. A. GREENE, E. F. LINDQUIST, and H. L. SPITZER, *Iowa Every-pupil Tests of Basic Skills*, Test A, Reading Comprehension, and Test B, Work Study Skills, Houghton Mifflin Company, Boston, 1940–1941.

34. KELLEY, TRUMAN L., GILES M. RUCH, and LEWIS M. TERMAN, *Stanford Reading Tests*, World Book Company, Yonkers-on-Hudson, N.Y., 1941,

35. NELSON, M. J., and E. C. DENNY, *Nelson-Denny Reading Test*, Houghton Mifflin Company, Boston, 1929.

36. SANGREN, PAUL V., and CLIFFORD WOODY, *Sangren-Woody Reading Test*, World Book Company, Yonkers-on-Hudson, N.Y., 1927.

37. SHANK, SPENCER, *Shank Tests of Reading Comprehension*, C. A. Gregory Company, Cincinnati, Ohio, 1929.

38. TIEGS, ERNEST W., and WILLIS W. CLARK, *Progressive Reading Tests*, California Test Bureau, Los Angeles, 1937.

39. TRAXLER, ARTHUR E., *Traxler Reading Tests*, Public School Publishing Company, Bloomington, Ill., 1934–1942.

40. *U. S. Armed Forces Institute Tests of General Educational Development*, Cooperative Test Service, New York, 1944 (also distributed by Science Research Associates, Chicago). Interpretation of Reading Materials in the Social Studies, Interpretation of Reading Materials in the Natural Sciences, Interpretation of Literary Materials.

41. VAN WAGENEN, M. J., *Van Wagenen Reading Scales*, Educational Test Bureau, Minneapolis, 1938.

42. VAN WAGENEN, M. J., and AUGUST DVORAK, *Van Wagenen-Dvorak Diagnostic Examination of Silent Reading Abilities*, Educational Test Bureau, Minneapolis, 1939.

CHAPTER VII

READING IN THE SUBJECT FIELDS

Many teachers of such subjects as geography, history, mathematics, science, and English would do something about the reading problem in their fields if they knew what to do.   Some of them try to make a careful selection of a textbook, so that the one chosen will be easy enough for almost every student to read.   Others, realizing that no one textbook fits all the students, go to a great deal of trouble to differentiate assignments and books according to their guesses about student ability.

Most of them know that their students range in reading ability six or more grades, not because they are of different chronological ages, but because their abilities, opportunities, and application to studies have varied.   These teachers know that some read faster and comprehend better than others.   A few know also that their particular subject requires a special kind of reading or several special kinds, and that students who have not yet learned how to read in these different ways must be taught, if they are ever to become well acquainted with the subject.

Reading instruction in each of the different content fields is more effective than instruction in one subject only.   Under present conditions, reading ability is not always successfully transferred from one field to another.   Better results can be expected if students are made more aware of the processes by which they read effectively in each subject.

Certain reading procedures, however, are common to many subjects.   In reading a textbook or any other key book in a field the following steps are necessary:

1. Read the preface and the chapter headings and glance through the book to get a sense of direction and perspective—an idea of what the author is trying to do and of how this book or article fits in with one's previous knowledge and present need.

2. Read to grasp the main idea of each paragraph, noting the relation of one idea to another and the important details that support the main idea.   As the student reads, he should form the ideas into a pattern based on his previous background of experience and knowledge in the field.

169

3. Make the main ideas vivid and memorable by looking at illustrations; collecting anecdotes and other material that support the main ideas; making charts, pictures, and graphs; reading supplementary material on the subject; summarizing the facts in an outline or a précis or in a "quiz" program, and comparing different views on the subject.

4. Read creatively, anticipating the author's ideas, guessing, and supporting the guesses with fact and logic, jotting down tangential ideas and questions, measuring facts against one another and against personal experience. When reading a book or an article from a personal slant, two persons may derive entirely different ideas. However, these flights into one's own personal realm of meanings must be based on a clear understanding of what the author is trying to say.

5. Relate this book to other books and articles in the field.

These steps cannot be followed unless the books are within the individual's range of comprehension. No advantage is gained by requiring a student to read a book he cannot comprehend. Only confusion and dislike of reading result because of insufficient command of language, reading ability, low mentality, or lack of experience, if he cannot grasp the author's meaning. He would gain more, for example, from Frank Beal's simple story of Kit Carson than from Shakespeare's *Julius Caesar*.

Common reading abilities may be developed by one teacher who assumes basic responsibility for the improvement of reading, while all subject-matter teachers reinforce these learnings in their own classrooms and teach the reading methods peculiar to their own subjects.

There is obviously considerable overlapping among reading abilities in different subjects. Artley (2) obtained a coefficient of correlation of .79 between the scores of 242 eleventh-grade pupils on a general reading comprehension test (Cooperative English Test C, Reading Comprehension, Form Q, measuring speed of comprehension and level of comprehension) and measures of reading comprehension in the social studies. If the same relationship holds in the actual reading situation, the work in reading that the English teacher does should improve students' reading in the social studies, and the social-studies teacher who develops skills in comprehension will contribute to improvement in reading in other fields.

Swenson (18) studied the relationship between 217 eighth-grade pupils' scores on a general reading test (the Traxler Silent Reading Test, grades 7 to 10) and on tests in science that he constructed. The latter contained passages like those in the texts and references in use in science classes and were similar in form to the Traxler test in their methods of measuring speed of reading, vocabulary, and comprehension. It was found that pupils rating high in vocabulary and comprehension in the reading of science material, as a group, also rated high in the general reading test, and those who rated low in science were similarly low in general reading material. Swenson's study adds another bit of support to the impression that a good reader, as measured by one type of reading test, is likely to be a good reader of other kinds of material. In individual cases, however, this is not necessarily so; nor does it follow that a science reading test is a good prediction of one's ability to read *Ivanhoe*.

Going a step further, Corrigan (5) tried to measure the extent to which 24 weeks of special drill in reading carried over into other subjects. The differences between the mean scores of the control group and those of the reading group in the history test, the biology test, and the Carroll Prose Appreciation Test were all statistically significant. These results led to the conclusion that instruction in reading is likely to produce some improvement in other subjects. However, statistical significance does not answer for the individual case; and certainly it is unreasonable to conclude that a general reading exercise program can substitute perfectly for the teaching of special reading techniques in each class as they are needed.

ENGLISH IN A READING CLASS

Examples of Instruction in Reading in Different Subjects.—In the senior year of a traditional public high school, the English teacher made an effort to follow a difficult prescribed course of study in English literature, which required the students to read books by Pepys and Lamb, Shakespeare's *Richard the Third*, modern one-act plays, short stories, and works of the chief romantic, Victorian, and later nineteenth-century poets. The teacher first discussed with the students the great variety of material included in the course, the time and interest and effort they were willing to expend on it, and their present methods of reading and study. Out of the discussion grew an appreciation of the need for reading widely different material in different ways. For example, they learned that a whimsical essay such as Lamb's *Dream Children* must be approached differently from Macaulay's *Essay on Warren Hastings*. They also discussed the personal nature of literary experience and the values they could expect to get in return for the time and energy expended.

This preliminary discussion was followed by daily laboratory periods in the reading of literature. The teacher was interested in the way the students approached each assignment, tried to understand their difficulties, and gave instruction and practice in overcoming them. If the author's vocabulary presented a difficulty, he spent some time in illustrating and discussing unfamiliar words, and teaching the efficient use of the dictionary. If students were failing to get the main ideas of paragraphs in a particular essay, he helped them to study the way in which that author builds his paragraphs, and gave them practice exercises—based on paragraphs in the essay—in selecting the main ideas, choosing the best title for a paragraph, and answering questions designed to bring out the relation between a main idea and supporting details. Throughout the year part of each period was spent in overcoming reading difficulties encountered in this unsuitable but required English literature course.

Class Procedures in Teaching the Reading of Poetry.—The poetry required in many English courses in the eleventh and twelfth grades does not appeal to students of this age, boys especially. They say, "Poetry is sissy, and I don't like it." They do, however, like a good story. Knowing this, a teacher introduced poetry with some lively narratives, having as few difficult idioms and as little poetic reversion as possible. He usually read the poem aloud to the students while they read it silently, and then asked them to tell the story as well as they could in their own words. When they compared their account with the original poem and tried to analyze the difference, they usually could see how much vividness and beauty their version had lost.

In other selections they watched for the flashing phrase and the words that suggest far more than they say. Then one student read aloud a part that he particularly liked; another student wanted to read his choice, and a beginning in shared appreciation was made. This appreciation took more definite form as they discussed some of the methods by which a poet gets the effects that he wants—how he often omits words that are essential in prose, how he sometimes inverts the usual prose order, how he uses unusual or "peculiar" words to create a certain feeling. Browning's "How They Brought the Good News from Ghent to Aix" appealed to almost all the boys. The swing of its lines is contagious—"quite jazzy," one boy said. It helped to make them realize that they feel poetry when they read it properly. After reading and enjoying poetry in this way, one science major, who had previously thought poetry "silly stuff," was discovered by his mother one day alone on the porch reading her volume of Robert Frost.

Various forms of exercise may increase the students' ability to concentrate upon and to appreciate poetry. But teachers should be sure that any questions they ask are helping students to concentrate in a sensible direction. "Practice is art" only when the practice contributes to the realization of sound objectives. The wrong kind of exercise would befog or hamper a young mind more effectively than a more casual reading of the original passage. Consider the relative value of these two exercises in appreciation of Matthew Arnold's lines:

> Oh, love, let us be true
> To one another! for the world, which seems
> To lie before us like a land of dreams,
> So various, so beautiful, so new
> Hath really neither joy, nor love, nor light,
> Nor certitude, nor peace, nor help for pain;
> And we are here as on a darkling plain
> Swept with confused alarms of struggle and flight
> Where ignorant armies clash by night.

1. The alarms are confused because of . . . darkness—shouting—flight—pain.
2. The poet believes that in this world he can rely only on . . . truth—justice —love—hope.

In the first of these exercises the statement itself is unimportant and confused, and the qualifying words from which choice is to be made are irrelevant and undifferentiated. The second exercise is better, in that it is importantly concerned with the selection quoted and tests the subject's comprehension of the one element of security presented in the passage. However, even this kind of intellectual appreciation is not a substitute for the organic reverberation that Housman says is the test of real poetry.

Improving Reading in Social Science.—In one large city system the following procedure was used with heterogeneous classes in the social studies. On the basis of the results of informal tests (see pages 188–199), three or four groups were formed, according to levels of reading ability. Pictures, maps, pictograms, charts, books, and magazines from many sources were collected for the class library. The students' interest in the library was so keen that they contributed much relevant reading material on different levels of difficulty. As different kinds of pictorial material were brought in, the class spent some time in learning to get information from each of these sources. For the retarded readers, the teacher selected the most suitable books in the Unit Study Series (20) and the Poughkeepsie Writers' Guild Series. From the Gateways to American History Series (4) she selected books on topics in American history at appropriate levels of difficulty. For individuals who needed practice in certain skills she provided workbooks or practice exercises in skimming, interpreting paragraphs, finding the central thought of a passage, indexing, locating pertinent information, disregarding unessential data, and interpreting maps and diagrams.

Each group had a leader who could work with its members, if necessary, while the teacher was engaged in instructing another group that was in greater need of his help.   The students entered into the planning of the work in their groups and made suggestions as to better ways to carry it on.   Subgroups of four or five were formed as students felt the need for drill on some special skill or for some other particular experience.

With seriously retarded readers the teacher found some time to work individually, having them read aloud from selected sources, and giving them special diagnostic and remedial aid along the lines suggested on pages 229–273.   With some of these students he made a special effort to build the self-confidence and security essential to success.

The unit organization in the following plan provided opportunity for individual initiative and for instruction in reading:

In our world history classes we use the unit method.   During each unit the student is expected to work on either an individual or a group activity. He is usually permitted to select the type of activity he prefers.   Many suggestions are given, but if the student has a personal interest or can suggest an original activity on the topic we are studying, he is encouraged to follow it. He is given a card, on which he writes his name and the activity on which he has decided to work.

Before the students go to the library to work on their activity, the librarian and I take the cards and jot down one reference on each.   We consider the student's ability as well as the topic on which he is working.

In this way, the student is not overwhelmed by a long list of books, and he has something with which to start.   After he has read the information from the one book, he can use the card catalogue, the *Readers' Guide*, or other sources to find additional information.

The librarian has found this card system a great help, because he knows, in advance, the topics on which the students are working and can frequently arrange special exhibits.   It also gives him an opportunity to talk with individual students regarding their problems.

In these times, articles on current affairs has high interest value. Students should be encouraged to read news magazines and current books, to listen to news broadcasts and commentators, and to interpret modern events in the light of historical perspective.   In one class, the students chose to spend about 30 minutes a day on discussion of current problems.   The boys were particularly interested in airplanes, submarines, and new methods of transportation. *Popular Science* and *Life* were their favorite magazines. Sometimes they shared stories with one another.

Singing, too, has a place in the social-science class. Many songs written about historical events, legends, and people arouse interest in and supply background for the reading of history. For example, an eighth-grade group that had been studying the Civil War chose as a project "Songs of the North and the South." The students asked whether they would be permitted to sing in class the songs they had found. The teacher said that they might if they would take responsibility for the program. It was the best student-conducted class of the year. Even the poor readers enjoyed reading about John Howard Payne and Stephen Foster. Singing gave them new words and word sounds in an entertaining way.

A group of seventh-grade students became interested in Erie Canal ballads. Although the music for these was not readily obtainable, they got the "feel" of the songs by reading in rhythm. Even the dialect did not bother them. They liked "Low Bridge, Everybody Down" best. If the teacher makes reading live, the students will enjoy and remember it.

Oral reports likewise stimulate reading. Individuals or small groups responsible for presenting special topics to the class learn to use various indexes to find sources of information. They also acquire a conception of reading as communication and realize that knowledge gained through reading should be used to help others and not merely be filed away in one's mind or in a notebook.

Building their own reference file is another valuable reading experience for students. It has been described as follows by a high-school teacher.

In my social-studies classroom I have two files, one legal size, the other 5 by 8 in. The materials in each are arranged according to the units we are studying.

The legal-sized file is used for clippings, pictures, and magazine articles. Whenever I or any student comes across an article or picture that we think would be suitable for a particular unit, we clip it out and give it to the committee in charge of the file for that unit. Since we have a limited space in the file, at the end of the unit the committee goes over the material brought in and decides what is worth filing for future use.

In the 5- by 8-in. we file suggested activities and references. Frequently a student comes across a book, suitable for a particular unit, for which I have no card. He makes out a card giving the following information: author, title, city, publisher, and copyright date; and notes whether it is in the school or the public library. If a student comes across an article in a magazine that cannot be cut for the legal-sized file, he is asked to list the article on a card for the 5- by 8-in. file.

While the student is working on his activity, he may think of original projects; if so, he writes his suggestions and gives them to me. If I think they are suitable, I add them to my file.

Of four techniques of studying history—repetitive reading, marginal note making, outlining, and précis writing—Arnold (1) found no one technique, as used by 242 college students, consistently superior to another. Marginal note making and underscoring seemed to be superior to outlining, but students did apparently as well using one technique as another. The efficiency with which any technique is used probably depends to a great extent on the student's habits of study. More intensive research is needed to determine which methods are best.

Certain new tests in the social studies purport to measure abilities in line with sound objectives. The Progressive Education Association Test of Application of Principles in the Social Studies is an attempt to measure ability to see logical relations and ability to evaluate arguments. The Cooperative Test Service's Test of Social Studies Abilities, Experimental Form Q, purports to appraise knowledge of sources, ability to organize, ability to interpret, and ability to apply generalizations. Independent-school norms, as well as those for public schools, are available for this test. The Cooperative Test Service's Survey Test in Social Studies was constructed to measure "achievement of a topical content nature in the several social studies areas."

Improving the Reading of Science.—To provide a rich background of experience in science, in addition to laboratory work, some teachers make use of motion pictures on scientific subjects and of excursions to industries and health and welfare agencies. Both motion pictures and excursions are preceded and followed by discussions in which pertinent questions are raised. Still more varied experiences are obtained by members of the science club, or the Junior Academy of Science, which includes in its program reports by members, speakers of note, demonstrations, and motion pictures.

To encourage wide reading in science, one teacher calls for volunteers to look up additional information whenever the text does not give sufficient information on a subject or leaves some of their questions unanswered. When it is necessary, he suggests sources of information. He leaves new popular-science magazines, pamphlets, and books where students can read them in their spare time.

To encourage thoughtful reading of science material, a teacher may give students passages of different kinds: a news article, a literary description, and a science article—all of the same length (17). After they have read all three articles and answered questions on them, a discussion of the time required and of the methods used for successful reading of each brings out clearly the need for slower reading of science material; for precise comprehension of each scientific term and formula; and for deriving sound scientific generalizations from the experiments, demonstrations, and descriptions presented.

Certain words often present difficulty because of shifts of meaning and because of special scientific meaning. "Source," used in connection with the study of water supply, is a hard word for many students, in spite of the fact that it is short and apparently simple. In biology, "to cross" may mean to hybridize; and "expose" has a special meaning when it is used in connection with bacterial plates. One girl, when asked to *draw* conclusions from an experiment, made a labeled diagram. In a biology textbook for high-school students such words as "altimeter," "anemometer," "atmosphere," "barometer," "elevation," "gauge," and "precipitation" occurred. The teacher, anticipating difficulty, made a list of technical words in each chapter and prepared a vocabulary test of the following type:

> Directions: Place in the space the word from the list on the board that best suits the meaning of the word or sentence listed:
> _____The layers of air that are around the earth
> _____Instrument for measuring the amount of moisture in the air

This he introduced as a diagnostic test to gauge some of the difficulties.

In a college class in chemistry, the students, approximately sixteen to eighteen years of age, varied greatly in school background. Academically, most of them were not ready for college. They did not know how to study and their reading of chemistry, to which they felt completely alien, was quite uncritical. The first step in improving their reading was to find out how they read their text and references in chemistry. To do this, a test such as that described on pages 122–124 was given. The results showed clearly their inability to get the pattern of thought in a passage, to select the main points, to remember important details accurately, to draw inferences, to make generalizations, and to understand technical words. The few students whose comprehension was high were asked to describe their method of reading the passage.

A great part of the responsibility for self-analysis and self-guidance was placed on the students. They were encouraged to analyze their errors on weekly quizzes and to try to think through why they were doing poorly and how they could do better.   This attempt frequently led to conferences with the teacher and a more systematic exploration of strengths and weaknesses in their science and mathematics background, their reading methods, and their vocabulary.   As the students felt the need for practice in certain skills, the teacher tried to provide suitable practice exercises, using passages in science books as practice material.   He frequently used 10 or 15 minutes of the class period for practice in a particular science-reading skill with which the class as a whole was having difficulty.   Sometimes there was a work period in which the best readers served as tutors to individuals or to small groups who were having difficulty.   At the end of the period, all spent a few minutes discussing the best method of reading the assignment for the next day.

The laboratory work provided opportunity for practice in reading and interpreting directions.   The accuracy or inaccuracy of a student's reading was apparent as soon as he began to set up an experiment. Errors in performing the experiment were traced back to errors in reading, and ways of avoiding this kind of error were discussed with the individual.

An effort was made to arouse the students' interest in wide reading in the field of science.   For this purpose, popular-science articles and books were made available and credit was given for voluntary reading. Among the materials provided were *Popular Science Magazine*, *Popular Mechanics*, *The Science Digest*, and *Amazing Stories Magazine*. The improvement of reading in chemistry proved to be important, not only for success in that field, but also for the pervasive feeling of self-confidence that results from mastery of a difficult subject.

Reading in Mathematics.—In a mathematics class conducted as a laboratory, practice and instruction in reading may be given whenever the need for them is indicated.   Common words with special mathematical meanings and technical terms that may be recognized but not invested with accurate and precise meaning should be studied.   If mathematical words are read, written, and used, as well as explained, they will become a part of each student's scholastic equipment.   It is obviously an important part of the mathematics teacher's job to teach the meaning of the technical words in his field.

Instruction and practice are also needed in the reading of problems. Frequently the sentence structure of a problem needs to be analyzed. Exercises in stating what is given, what is to be found, what relationships are involved, what contribution is made by each word and phrase, and what clues there are to the understanding of the problem as a whole are needed to focus attention on the reading of the problem. During this kind of practice, computation of the problem should be omitted, especially with students whose approach to problems is to begin juggling figures in the hope that the right answer will slip into place, much as one can sometimes solve mechanical puzzles by assiduous manipulation. Practice in reading mathematical material may be carried on with the class as a whole, with smaller groups having common difficulties, or with individuals.

Although recreational reading in mathematics is not so readily available as in other subjects, there is a recreational aspect that should not be neglected. There are interesting books of riddles and "catchy" exercises that students enjoy repeating to their friends. Hogben (9) has clarified mathematical concepts for many persons. The biographies of mathematicians and the early history of mathematics make interesting reading.

The following practices are designed to compensate for the difficulty of a mathematics text.

1. Help students to become familiar with mathematical concepts through

   a. Having them read comparable lessons in an easier text first
   b. Using the approaches of an easier text in preparatory lessons
   c. Having better students write a verbal problem in their own words, using shorter sentences instead of one long, involved sentence; and hectograph these simplified versions for all students to read

2. Help students understand the nature of a problem by having individuals

   a. Invent verbal problems that reflect a common life problem that can be solved by the method under study
   b. Insert nonessential facts in problems of a known type, and have the class find the essentials for solution
   c. Compare similar problems differently worded to see that different words may have the same meaning

3. Aid students in reading the problems in their regular texts by

   a. Encouraging the prereading of lessons, with questions at points of difficulty
   b. Having a student committee look ahead for trouble spots and clarify the difficulty
   c. Having better students help poorer students and report to the teacher what their difficulties are and how they are overcoming them
   d. Having students for whom a difficulty has been clarified explain it to the class at a subsequent meeting

  e. Cultivating in the students the habit of looking back for helpful information, using the index or page-number references in their notebooks

  f. Eliminating or changing verbal problems whose wording presents an ambiguity

  g. Having students do as much as they can toward the solution of a problem, before reading the textbook explanation, until they meet a difficulty and feel the need of explanation

  h. Writing in notebooks simple explanations of processes that are poorly explained in the text

4. Give effective instruction through having better students tell how they have unraveled a puzzling problem; having them illustrate

  a. Reading for a general impression
  b. Reading to identify the unknown
  c. Reading details to convert specific words and phrases into symbols
  d. Reading to relate these words and phrases to one another
  e. Reading for the statement of equality

5. Help students build a mathematical vocabulary by

  a. Having them write in their notebooks a list of new words, illustrating each, if possible, and using them in phrases or sentences

  b. Having students make a list of words or phrases that have caused difficulty, converted into mathematical terms

  c. Listing a few new or troublesome words on the board, each accompanied by an illustration or a definition, and encouraging their use informally in class

  d. Giving frequent tests and exercises involving new or difficult words

  e. Using the first few minutes of each class in dramatizations, pantomimes, quiz programs, or experiments involving new and troublesome words

  f. Giving practice in visualizing the meanings of certain words and phrases by having students bring in illustrations, make their own illustrations, match words with proper pictures

  g. Having the students contribute their illustrations and original work to a file of helps for future classes

  h. Giving practice in deriving meanings of new words through all the means provided by the text: context clues, definitions, illustrations, experiments.

ANALYSIS OF BOOK AND STUDENT PRETEST

  The first opportunity a teacher has to do something about reading is in selecting texts and references for the course. There are certain features that make a book difficult and baffling or easy and usable. It is important that as many students as possible find the book, and hence the subject, easy and enjoyable. The book can make all the difference in the establishment of favorable or unfavorable attitudes. Hence, if the teacher is free to choose his own texts and references, he should certainly view the possible books from the standpoint of readability.

If a teacher is assigned a text instead of being given a choice, he still has an opportunity and an obligation to do something about reading. In this case, it is not a matter of whether to accept the book or not; the book is there and must be fitted to the students somehow. Both those who can choose and those who cannot are faced with the same problem: what are the reading assets and liabilities of this book?

Another problem is added to this. Suppose that a book is analyzed and found to have many points in its favor. Suppose that it provides many student helps. Can all the students use them? A wonderfully organized, easily worded, well-illustrated, highly usable textbook can be a delight in the hands of a skillful reader but a thorn in the side of a poor reader, just as a fine motorcar can fly like a dream in the hands of a skillful driver and stall like a mule for an amateur.

The job of the teacher is, then, twofold: (1) he must analyze the textbook for its reading hazards and helps, and (2) he must test the students to see which of them can use the textbook skillfully and which still have a variety of things to learn about reading in this subject or reading this particular book. The analysis of the textbook would be hard without some guidance, such as that in the outline given below. The appraisal of students' abilities to use the book would require guidance in making the test, and time to give it. The needed guidance is given below in a column parallel to that on the analysis of the textbook. With regard to time, it may be said that this test need not be given all at once. In fact, in some cases, that is not feasible. The test need not steal time from regular assignments, either. It may, instead, be embodied in the first several assignments given in the course. Desirably, these assignments would be carried out in a supervised-study situation so that each student would surely do his own work.

FORM OF ANALYSIS AND PRETEST

Textbook Analysis	*Pretest for Students—to Measure Ability to Use Text*
Table of contents	
Is it meaningful or cryptic and couched in technical terms?	Read the table of contents and write a sentence describing the scope of the author's study. What is the meaning of item_____?

Can the student use it?

> In what chapter will you find item
> _____? (Use the exact wording of
> the author.)
> In what chapter will you find item
> _____? (Paraphrase the author's
> wording or mention a topic which
> might logically be expected under a
> certain chapter heading.)

Is the organization clear?

> How did the author determine the
> order in which he put his chapters?
> How can you tell?

Chapter headings, subheadings, marginal headings

Are the headings suitable titles for the contents?

> (If so:) Read a section and give it a title.
> See if your title corresponds in thought
> to the author's.
> (If not:) Summarize the contents of the
> various parts of the chapter in sen-
> tences or headings of your own.

Can the student use them as a guide to effective reading?

> Read the chapter headings, subheadings,
> and marginal headings and tell what
> you think the chapter is about. Give
> the gist of the chapter without repeat-
> ing the author's headings or making
> it too long. Jot down a few things
> you know about this topic from your
> own previous experience. (This indi-
> cates the student's real understanding
> of the headings.)

Is the organization clear? (Sometimes subheadings or marginal headings, not parallel in importance or thought, are printed as parallel. Students should realize this.)

> Make an outline showing the relation-
> ships of the marginal headings and
> subheadings to each other and to the
> topic of the chapter.

Introduction and summary

Does the chapter have an introduction and a summary?

> (If not:) Looking at the title of the
> chapter, write a sentence suggesting
> how the topic concerns you.
> After reading the chapter, write a
> sentence expressing the main points
> the author seems to be trying to make.
> (If so:) Read the introduction and the
> summary and write in a sentence the
> main idea the author is trying to set
> forth in this chapter.
> What might make another good title
> for this chapter?

What points do you think the author will take up in this chapter, considering what he has implied in his introduction and summary?

Illustrations

Pictures: Are the points the author wishes to make clearly brought out in the picture?

(If not:) Try to get supplementary illustrative material to compensate for and clear up misconceptions.

(If so:) Look at the picture on page _____ and list the things it tells you about_____.

Are the captions helpful?

(If not:) Write a better caption for the picture.

(If so:) What does the caption help you to notice in the picture?

Are the pictures placed in a convenient location in reference to the printed matter? Or do they require much turning of pages and losing of the place?

Where is the picture illustrating what the author says on page_____paragraph_____?

Tables, graphs, and charts

Are the relationships clearly indicated by the labeling, the organization, and the representation?

(If not: clarify these things for the student as he comes to these illustrations in the text.) Does such and such a fact as pictured in the illustration seem reasonable, and why or why not?

(If so:) Answer the question that requires the reading of the chart or graph.

Are the captions helpful?

(If not:) What would be a better caption?

(If so:) What does the caption mean?

Maps

Are there any distortions, such as a rough edge indicating a break or omission in the map, an inset enlarging a portion of the map, or a global perspective showing the outer curve of the earth and reducing the size of the outer countries and oceans?

(If so: draw attention to them and ask what they mean.)

Does the key amply provide the information needed for interpretation?

(If not: give assistance where it is needed.)

(If so:) Locate_____.

What is the distance between_____ and_____?

Give the latitude and longitude of
_____?

Look at the map and tell why the
_____were able to maintain peace
while others warred.

Look at the map and tell what
kinds of work the people of_____
probably do. How can you tell?

Are the captions helpful?

(If not:) Study the map on page_____
and give it another title.

(If so:) Put the meaning of the caption
into your own words.

Questions

Are there questions at the beginnings
of the chapters?

(If not:) Looking over the chapter
headings, subheadings, and marginal
headings and illustrations, what question do you think you should have
in mind as you read? What do you
want to find out in this chapter?

(If so:) What facts does the question at
the beginning of Chapter_____lead
you to expect to find in the chapter?
Read the chapter to answer the
question.

Are there questions at the ends of the
chapters?

(If not:) After you have read Chapter
_____, make a list of_____impor-
tant questions you think the chapter
answers best. Write down your
answers briefly.

(If so:) Read the questions at the end
of Chapter_____. List the kinds of
information you must look for in the
chapter in order to answer these
questions. Read the chapter and
answer them.

Do the questions suit the teacher's purpose?

(If not: substitute others and see whether
the student can answer them.)

Suggested activities

Are there activities suggested at the
ends of the chapters?

(If not: make up your own activities.)
How can you prove the facts presented in this chapter (especially
for science or mathematics)? How
can you use the facts, etc.?

Are they activities that the student can
do independently or in groups, with
or without elaborate equipment, with
or without teacher help?

Do they help the student understand the text better (tie up with his life, provide concrete examples, cut across the organization of the material in a new way, require thinking versus sheer memory) and provide for repetition and hence retention of important ideas?

Vocabulary lists

Is there a vocabulary list at the close of the chapter?

(If not:) As you read Chapter_____, check the new words you think important to know. List these and write a definition of each in your own words.
(If so:) After you have read Chapter _____, write down the meanings of the words listed on page_____.

Are these crucial words or are there others equally important for the students to remember? A hard word of only passing utility to the student will not be remembered anyway; hence, effort may better be directed toward other things.

Bibliography

Is there a bibliography at the close of the chapter?

(If so:) Look at the list of books on page_____.
In which ones may you find more information on the following:_____?
Which volume will probably give the latest information about_____ (student should note date of publication here)?

Are the titles in the bibliography annotated?

Italics, capitalization, or boldface type

Are the important ideas capitalized, put in italics, or printed in boldface type?

(If not:) What idea in section_____, page_____, do you think the most worth remembering?
(If so:) Which idea on page_____does the author think the most important? Give this same idea in your own words.

Index

Are the items in the index well chosen for the needs of the student? Can the student use the index?

Write the numbers of the pages on which you may expect to find information on the following:_____

Put some of these into the exact words of the author.

Put some in other words, which the student must translate to those of the author.

Use some items that are subheads under items in the index, to show whether the student knows how to use these subheads.

Glossary

Can the student use the glossary?

Indicate by phonetic spelling how you would pronounce the following words:

———

Paragraph structure

What kinds of paragraph structure does the book present?
1. Paragraph in which the main idea is of prime importance:
   a. Main idea stated first
   b. Main idea stated last
   c. Main idea not stated in so many words but to be gathered by the reader from the cumulative effect of the ideas presented
   d. Complex main idea, with a subordinate idea given first
2. Paragraph that enumerates characters, qualities, or elements in a group or situation
3. Paragraph that enumerates a sequence of events or points in a logical progression
4. Paragraph that compares or relates two sets of data

Are the paragraphs well constructed for unity and emphasis?

Write in a sentence the idea you must remember above all in the first paragraph on page———. (Other paragraphs indicated)

What is important to remember in this paragraph?

What is important to remember in this paragraph?

What is important to remember in this paragraph?

(If not:) how can you help the student to read the text?)

Sentence structure

What kinds of sentence structure does the book present?
1. Easy sentence structure
   a. Short
   b. Simple, presenting subject first, then verb and object.
2. Difficult sentence structure
   a. Complex
   b. Compound

c. Inverted (beginning with "there are" or a prepositional phrase, subject coming last of all)

d. Long, full of qualifying phrases and clauses

e. Compact, giving the essence of the idea instead of illustrating it, or containing only one idea per sentence. It is easier to read several sentences, each contributing to a whole picture, than to read one sentence with all these ideas packed into it in concentrated form.

Give an illustration of the point the author is making in sentence_____, page_____.

General vocabulary

Are there few rare words?

Give the meanings of the following words:_____, page_____, etc.

Are the meanings of the rare words revealed by the context?

Give the meanings of the words that are left out of the following passages. (Here, lift sentences from the text containing hard words with context clues to their meanings. Leave blanks in place of the hard words to see whether the student can benefit from the context.)

Technical vocabulary

Are there pronunciation helps?

Give the pronunciation of the following words. (Same technique can be used here as for glossary.)

Are there definitions to make the meaning clear?

Give the definitions of the following words in your own words.

Are there context clues?

Read paragraph_____, page_____, and write in your own words all you know about_____from this reading.

Are there concrete examples?

(If not:) What examples of_____have you met in your experience?

(If so:) What examples does the author give of_____?

Speed and comprehension

If the above analysis and test do not take account of the kinds of questions the teacher usually asks in assignments and class discussions, he should incorporate in the test a set of his typical questions, which the student should read first before he reads the chapter to answer them. The teacher should classify these questions for himself according to the reading skill involved, such as reading for the main idea, reading for a few important details, reading for a sense of sequence or outlining, and reading to draw conclusions or to infer. Thus he can learn what skill the student lacks. The students should be timed when reading to answer such questions so that the teacher will have some idea of the length of assignment appropriate to the abilities of the different readers in his class.   A good technique is to have the students mark in their books the places in which they are reading after they have read for 10 minutes.   Another method is for each to raise his hand when he has finished so that the teacher can note the length of time taken.

Marking the Pretest.—On a pretest of this kind, the object is not to see how much the student can do, how high a score he can make, but rather to find out what kinds of things he can or cannot do.   Thus the marking of the pretest is rather simple.   A total score of items correct would be of no value.   The assignment of values to each item— five points here and two points there—would be equally futile.   The only important consideration is whether the student gave a satisfactory answer or not.   If he did, his success may be indicated by a plus (+); if he did not, his failure may be indicated by a minus (−).

Sample Test on Junior-high-school Level.—In a reading-methods course at Brigham Young University in the summer of 1944, Mr. G. Grant Gardner, principal of the junior high school in Payson, Utah, analyzed the textbook he expected to use in his civics course for ninth-grade students.   His plan for and discussion of the resulting pretest follow:

The following list of reading abilities represents a beginning approach for a group of students who have had little of this type of direction since they left the elementary reading program.   How much they had there is in some question.   As they become more able to read effectively under these types of situations, other more refined abilities may be added.

Most of the abilities listed will be tested in the survey of reading abilities, and all will be developed in exercises forming a purposeful study in units to follow.   The reason why not all of the abilities are tested in the survey is that this type of test does not lend itself readily to a few of the skills that follow.

The following skills in reading[1] are thought to be necessary to the study of citizenship, and will be developed further in this paper:

1. Locating information

   a. Use tables of contents and indexes
   b. Use materials alphabetically arranged
   c. Use the dictionary effectively
   d. Locate information in maps and graphs
   e. Skim for answers to questions
   f. Locate information in pictures

[1] Many of these were obtained from H. K. Bennett's *A Plan for Directed Study Through Work-type Reading*, Klipto Loose Leaf Co., Mason City, Iowa, 1939, 120 pp.

2. Comprehending or interpreting what is read

    a. Find answers to direct questions
    b. Answer questions from memory after reading an assignment
    c. Use related words in getting the meaning
    d. Prove a point by citing words or phrases from a text
    e. Select items from the text as references
    f. Follow directions
    g. Define words or phrases from the context
    h. Recognize similar ideas
    i. Paraphrase sentences and paragraphs
    j. Read rather extensively to find answers to involved thought questions

3. Organizing, summarizing, outlining, and evaluating what is read

    a. Find the key word in a sentence
    b. Select the main thought or idea in a paragraph
    c. Rearrange material into groups
    d. Summarize a paragraph, topic, or section of material from an assignment
    e. Select from an assignment the important points
    f. Organize material around a definite problem
    g. Supplement ideas read with personal experience
    h. Make a simple outline of facts

4. Ability to remember what is read

    a. Analyze what it is necessary to remember
    b. Organize material as an aid to memory

Survey Test of Fundamental Reading Abilities Necessary for Reading a Ninth-grade Citizenship Test.—Though it lacks the objectivity of standardized tests in reading, which determine specific abilities of students to use their text effectively, this brief test attempts to give some indication of specific skills possessed by students in doing the type of work they will be called upon to do during their study of the problems of citizenship. The purpose of such a test, of course, is to determine as nearly as possible just what assistance students will need in developing skills for specific situations such as those listed above.

The questions or problems are based on the first chapter of the text (6, pages 1–18), Wings over America, and are keyed back into the specific abilities referred to above. The test does not deal directly with the problem of rate in reading, but it is planned that at intervals during the course short test exercises will be administered that will measure rate of reading as well as comprehension.

1. Look over the title of the chapter and the topic headings quickly and then write in one sentence what you think the chapter will be about (3-*d*).[1]

2. Look over the following questions before you read the chapter *Wings over America*. See if you can find the answers to the questions as you read. If you fail to find all of the answers this way, skim through the story again and find what you missed. Then answer each question briefly in writing (1-*a*, 1-*e*, 2-*a*, 2-*b*).

Questions
  a. In what way is every farmstead a kingdom in itself?
  b. How may highways be compared with rivers?
  c. Name several networks that link communities together.
  d. List reasons for believing that farmers and city folk depend on one another.
  e. Why is farm land near the city more valuable than farm land many miles away from it?
  f. Explain why suburbs grow up at the edges of cities.
  g. Why is a great city sometimes compared with the hub of a great wheel?
  h. List several sections into which an average town or city is divided.
  i. What is meant by a civic center?

3. See if, after your reading, you can answer these questions. You may find help in the following books besides your text (1-e, 2-b, 2-j, 3-d):

> ARNOLD, JOSEPH I., and DOROTHY J. BANKS, *Building Our Life Together*, Row, Peterson and Company, New York, 1941, 744 pp.
> EDMONSON, JAMES B., and ARTHUR DONDINEAU, *Civics in American Life*, The Macmillan Company, New York, 1941, xiii + 702 pp.

Questions:
  a. Compare houses in "Millionaires' Row" with those in the slum section of Huntington.
  b. Mention ways in which the smallest village and the largest city are alike; then name several differences between the two communities.
  c. How is your community different from the small communities Bob saw from the airplane?

4. See if you can discover the meanings of the following words and phrases without the use of a dictionary, by studying each in its relationship to the rest of the sentence.

Arrange the words in alphabetical order at the left-hand margin of your page. When you have decided on the meaning of a word, write that meaning as briefly as you can opposite the word—in one word or phrase, if possible (1-b, 2-c, 2-g):

	Page	Paragraph
marred	4	2
approached	5	8
aqueduct	8	2
suburbs	8	3
teeming	9	2
kimonos	11	3
tenements	13	3

[1] The number and letter refer to an objective stated in the preceding outline of skills to be achieved.

Skills Tested											
Table of contents											
Alphabetical arrangement											
Use of dictionary											
Maps and graphs											
Skimming											
Information in pictures											
Answers to direct questions											
Memory questions											
Citing from the text											
Selecting text references											
Follow directions											
Define words from context											
Recognize similar ideas											
Thought questions											
Key words in sentences											
Main idea in paragraph											
Summarize materials											
Select important points											
Add personal experience											
Make a simple outline											
Analyze to remember											
Organize to remember											
Organize materials around a problem											
Relate to your life today											

5. Turn now to page 5 of your story. Read again the first paragraph of the topic, Towns from the Air, and then see if you can summarize the paragraph in one clear-cut sentence (3-b, 3-d).

6. Read again the beginning of the story down to the topic, The World Below. Now see if you can summarize this part of your story in one sentence (3-B, 3-D).

7. You will note that the story is divided into subdivisions called topics. Beginning with the sentence you have just written in question 6, and using that as sentence number one in your outline, enlarge each of the nine topics into a sentence that as nearly as possible suggests the part of the story appearing under that topic. On completion of this problem, you will have a sentence outline of the chapter (2-H, 3-H).

8. We are told in this story that Bob and his mother are just returning from Japan. See if you can find anything about Japan in your text outside this chapter. When you have found the information, state it briefly in your own words and give the reference as to where you found it. Also state what means you used in locating the information (1-A, 3-B, 3-D).

9. List other chapter titles in the Table of Contents that sound as if they might tell us more about farmers (1-A).

10. What changes have come about in American life since 1700 as represented by the picture graphs on pages 14-15 (1-D)?

11. Name two ways shown in the picture on page seven in which space is saved in the building of railroad tracks (1-F).

Note for students: If you come across any hard words in the reading necessary to answer any of the questions of the test, write the word down below your answer to the question. Remember that one very important skill in reading is that of reading directions to do something. This skill is involved in every one of your questions. Be sure you know just what to do before you begin. If the directions are not clear to you at first reading, go over the problem. Following directions requires slow, careful reading.

Sample Test on College Level.—A slightly different approach was used at Western Reserve University in the construction of two tests, one in science and the other in history, for first-semester guidance of freshmen in those courses. In the case of the science test, an interested professor asked his students to compile the questions that he asked in class and on the periodic and final examinations. An analysis of these questions showed that the professor was interested in having the student know statements of biological law, sequences in biological histories, the elements or characteristics or members of a biological group, the definitions and functions of biological terms, and the identification of scientists. These were the facts for which students were to be held responsible. If they could not read the test for these facts, they would obviously fail the course. Therefore, a pretest had to be constructed on this basis.

The textbook used in the course was studied for passages containing the types of information in which the science professor had shown interest, and five passages varying in length from one to five paragraphs were selected for the pretest.   One of these passages contained a table and another a graph.   Desirably, of course, there would also have been a picture to be interpreted or reproduced, but none was included. Each passage contained one or more of the kinds of information the students would have to notice and memorize in order to pass the course.

On the college level there are three main questions that must be answered before a student can be given specific help in studying in a given course.   They are (1) What does the student freely select to remember in the material he must read?   (2) Can he read for the kinds of information the professor wants him to get, and if not, why not?   (3) Can the student remember the information that he intends to remember?

To obtain the answer to the first question, the entering freshmen were given the five passages and some fresh sheets of paper.   They were told to read these passages as though they were parts of an assignment in the subject.   After reading each, they were to jot down the notes they would normally take, in order to remember as much as they could expect to remember in an assignment of that length.   In other words, they were given a free situation in which to demonstrate the kind of preparation they would consider adequate.   The results showed whether they were able to pick out the points that the professor would be interested in or whether they missed them, whether they tried to remember too much, whether their note taking was systematic and meaningful.   As the students finished this exercise, they took their papers to the examiner's desk, and a record of the time they had taken suggested whether the students would be spending too much time or too little on such an assignment.   An alternative exercise would have been to have the students underline important points rather than take notes, but the note taking was considered a valuable feature.

For the answer to the second question, the examiner gave each student, as he finished the first task, sheets containing questions that the professor would normally expect the student to be able to answer. Blanks were left for the student's answers.   In addition to these questions, the sheets contained words in the passage that were expected to cause difficulty in comprehension.   The student was to indicate the meanings suitable to the context.   The student was directed to reread the passages to answer these questions and to assign appropriate meanings to the hard words.

If the student could answer the questions in this second task but had failed in the first, it would be apparent that his was a problem of selection of important points, of tuning himself to the professor's special interests and watching for them. If the student could not answer the questions and also failed to assign the correct meanings to the hard words, he would obviously have to do something about mastering the vocabulary of the textbook. If he assigned the correct meanings to the hard words but could not answer the questions, careful questioning on the meaning of each sentence might reveal the nature of his difficulty: the ignoring of punctuation clues to sentence structure, confusion in determining the word referred to by a pronoun, or lack of confidence for seeing a long sentence through.

For the third part of the examination, the student exchanged all his previous sheets of paper for a fresh sheet, on which some of the same questions previously asked were reiterated. The student was to answer these without aid, the passages and his previous notes and answers having been taken by the examiner. Success on this part of the pretest would indicate that the student could recall the information he was trying to remember. This, of course, was immediate recall after two readings, note taking, and the answering of questions—a rather full study procedure.

A similar test was constructed for the history course commonly taken by the entering students, but the method of construction was somewhat different. Freshmen who had taken the course were asked the kinds of questions the professor usually put. The professor was also asked. Then the students themselves looked through the text for passages containing the kinds of information that the professor chose to stress. They then analyzed these passages for the types of reading they required. Some of these, they found, were reading for a main idea in a paragraph containing nothing else important; reading about a given country, time, or person, in order to classify the knowledge gained under such headings as political, social, or economic; and reading to remember the enumeration of causes, effects, or characteristics. The students then built a test to be given to the incoming freshmen. They included passages illustrative of these three types and added a map to be memorized and reproduced. Happily, the textbook in history contained no really difficult words as had the science text, but the students found a few that they thought might cause trouble (see Appendix C).

Obviously, the tests described leave much to be desired. Hand hewn, they are not of standard caliber; but they have the validity of the professors' examinations and the students' vivid memories, the validity of being designed for and from the textbook the student must actually use. And, although they are by no means a complete picture of the difficulties the texts present or of the extent of the student's reading skill, they nevertheless give the counselor an indication of the student's status and needs, the trouble he is going to encounter unless he is warned of his difficulty and shown how to overcome it. There is an intimacy with the real local problems of college reading in a test of this sort that the infinitely more comprehensive and reliable standardized test cannot rival.

Tabulation of Test Results.—If, as in the case of the college test described above, nothing is to be done about the reading difficulties of the student beyond discussing them in an interview, it is probably unnecessary to tabulate the results of the test for the whole class. Certainly in most cases, however, a single interview is not sufficient guidance for the student on any level. He should be given practice in the skills he needs to develop and sufficient understanding of each skill to practice it intelligently.

The teacher who has tabulated the pretest results for his class can readily see what kind of exercise the class as a whole needs and what he can expect of students. He can also note indvidual deficiencies that must, therefore, be handled as an individual problem and made the basis of special reports and study assignments by that student.

TABLE 7.—SUGGESTED TABULATION SHEET FOR PRETEST RESULTS

Pupil's name	Table of contents	Headings	Introduction and summary	Illustrations	Others	Individual scores on test items
1.						
2.						
3.						
4.						
5.						
Etc.						

On the accompanying tabulation sheet (Table 7), a plus or a minus in the appropriate blanks after each student's name can indicate the

success or failure of each student on each item listed.   Then a quick
glance at the entire chart, down any column, will show the success of
the class in a given type of task.   If most of the class is already capable
of certain tasks, it becomes a matter of helping a few, showing them
the rudiments and then seeing to it that they have ample opportunity
to practice each skill.   If most of the class is deficient in one type of
skill or another, the teacher must take class time to develop that skill
with the majority.

Table 8 is an example of another type of tabulation sheet, which
may be needed under certain conditions.   Some teachers in designing
a pretest of the skills they think important find that they have tested
a certain skill in more than one item.   In that case, there needs to be
a summary at the foot of the chart, showing the frequency of a type
of error.

TABLE 8.—SUGGESTED TABULATION SHEET WITH SUMMARY OF PRETEST RESULTS

Pupil's name	Individual scores on test items					
	1	2	3	4	5	Etc.
1						
2						
3						
4						
Etc.						
Skills tested:						
Using an index		17			15	
Reading main idea				20		25
Reading details	38			42		
Reading maps			12			9
Etc.						

The numbers 17 and 15 indicate the number of students who successfully completed tasks 2 and 5 in using an index.   In a class of,
say, 45 students, this proportion of the group—roughly, one-third—

gives promise of being able to handle an assignment requiring the use of an index. Two-thirds of the class needs training in that skill. In reading details, 38 and 42 of the 45 pupils showed ability. The few students who were unable to cope with the task of reading details should be given special help. Sometimes, if the reason for their failure is the same for all, they can be handled as a group.

Individual Interview.—Many teachers are so loaded with work and deal with so many students during a day that they feel it impossible to interview any students with regard to their deficiencies. There is no question but that energies are drained by the end of a day of working with 200 or more students, 40 or more at a time. However, whenever it is at all possible, the desirable course is to see individually the students whose performance on the pretest suggests marked retardation. Sometimes such an interview must be relegated to time after school or during the "activity period" when everyone else is supposedly enjoying himself. Frequently, however, it can be sandwiched into a period of supervised study or free reading or reference work in the course concerned, when the teacher can control the room with his physical presence and one eagle eye, the while he devotes a friendly and helpful eye to the inefficient reader. If by this process he does not develop schizophrenia in himself, he may develop something more desirable in the needy student!

One technique to be used in the interview is to ask the student to repeat the task in which he has failed, giving him the same material but not his own erroneous paper. If he fails again, it is a good plan to have him tell just what he did to arrive at his answer. Sometimes by this method it is discovered that the difficulty lay not in the task itself but in some incidental factor, such as a vocabulary obstacle. This may be especially true in reading for details, which is the most elementary of reading tasks. Given the needed vocabulary and sufficient attention and intelligence, any reader should be able to read for details. If, however, the vocabulary is difficult and the sentence structure involved, a student may appear unable to read for details. He needs to be referred to an easier text, if such there be.

A follow-up technique is to ask the student what suggestions he has for ways to overcome his difficulty. His own suggestions may be more functional, in the long run, than any that the teacher may offer. His own ideas have the further advantage of bearing his trademark and, hence, his affectionate devotion. In any event, the interview should conclude with a constructive plan for improvement and an agreement on the time of the next meeting or on the time when the student will give proof of the effect of the proposed practice.

Provision of Class Practice.—Meanwhile, the teacher should not leave all practice and all improvement to the student himself. Through a number of means the teacher can give the individual and the class as a whole the opportunity of keeping a skill fresh or of improving it.

Mr. Gardner followed up his pretest and analysis with a series of exercises based upon the first two units that he was to undertake with the class. Each exercise was designed to give practice in one of the skills represented in the pretest, and in both units several exercises of each kind were planned. Thus when a student was found on the pretest to be deficient in a given skill, he was immediately scheduled to be responsible for certain types of assignment in the two units, types that would give him practice in the skill he lacked.

Hence by exercises and questions in an assignment, a teacher can give a whole class a certain kind of practice. By assigning special tasks on an individual basis, a teacher who is able to find the time that this extra planning requires can make class discussions more interesting, besides designing those special tasks to fit special needs. Furthermore, by exercises and questions in class he can not only provide the needed experience in the required skills but give group practice in approaching each skill. It is often valuable to have a successful student tell how he achieved his answer, to have the one who did the job most rapidly and correctly reveal his technique, to have the whole class then try his method and see the difference in accuracy and speed.

In order to facilitate the teacher's work of providing guidance and practice in the skills important to his subject, a list of reading and study activities has been compiled (see Appendix D). It is based upon the kind of textbook analysis proposed earlier in this chapter and is organized so that a teacher of English, for example, need only read down the left-hand margins of the pages for a capital E in order to find the types of exercise appropriate to his subject. The suggestions are addressed to the student rather than to the teacher, so that no translation is necessary except for an immature student who requires simpler wording. In this list a large number of suggestions are given from which the teacher may choose those that are applicable to a particular reading situation.

The purpose of the procedures, analyses, and exercises described in this chapter is to make it easy for teachers in the subject fields, under present conditions, to do something intelligent and constructive about reading. By analyzing textbooks and reference books and providing pretests and exercises based on students' assignments, they should achieve improvement in students' reading with the least loss of time to themselves and with an actual gain in time for the student.

References

1. ARNOLD, HENRY F., "The Comparative Effectiveness of Certain Study Techniques in the Field of History," *Journal of Educational Psychology*, Vol. 33, pp. 449–457, September, 1942.

2. ARTLEY, A. STERLING, "A Study of Certain Relationships Existing between General Reading Comprehension and Reading Comprehension in a Specific Subject Matter Area," *Journal of Educational Research*, Vol. 37, pp. 464–473, February, 1944.

3. BENNETT, H. K., *A Plan for Directed Study through Work-type Reading*, Klipto Loose Leaf Co., Mason City, Iowa, 1939, 120 pp.

4. CARPENTER, HELEN, *Gateways to American History*, The H. W. Wilson Company, New York, 1943, 255 pp.

5. CORRIGAN, MARIE, "Reading Studies Go to Work, *English Journal*, Vol. 31, pp. 31–36, January, 1942.

6. FINCHER, E. B., R. E. FRASER, and W. G. KIMMEL, *Democracy at Work*, John C. Winston Company, Philadelphia, 1941, vii + 566 pp.

7. FLESCH, RUDOLF, *Marks of a Readable Style*, Bureau of Publications, Teachers College, Columbia University, New York, 1943, 70 pp.

8. GRAY, WILLIAM S. (editor), *Adapting Reading Programs to Wartime Needs*, Supplementary Educational Monographs, No. 57, The University of Chicago Press, Chicago, December, 1943, viii + 283 pp.

9. HOGBEN, LANCELOT, *Mathematics for the Million*, W. W. Norton & Company, Inc., New York, 1937, xiii + 647 pp.

10. HOVIOUS, CAROL, "Reading in a Language Program," *English Journal*, Vol. 27, pp. 831–839, December, 1938.

11. McINTIRE, ALTA, "Written Exercises to Improve Reading and Thinking in the Social Studies Field," *Elementary School Journal*, Vol. 45, pp. 270–275, January, 1945.

12. RICHARDS, I. A., *Basic English and Its Uses*, W. W. Norton & Company, Inc., New York, 1943, xxi + 143 pp.

13. RICHARDS, I. A., *How to Read a Page, A Course in Effective Reading with an Introduction to 100 Great Words*, W. W. Norton & Company, Inc., New York, 1942, 246 pp.

14. RUSSELL, DAVID, and others, *Reading Aids through the Grades*, Bureau of Publications, Teachers College, Columbia University, New York, 1938, vi + 90 pp.

15. SHORES, J. HARLAN, "Skills Related to the Ability to Read History and Science," *Journal of Educational Research*, Vol. 36, pp. 584–593, April, 1943.

16. SHORES, LOUIS, "The School Librarian as a Reading Teacher," *Wilson Library Bulletin*, Vol. 15, pp. 117–121, October, 1940.

17. STRANG, RUTH, *Exploration in Reading Patterns*, University of Chicago Press, Chicago, 1942, ix + 172 pp.

18. SWENSON, ESTHER J., "A Study of the Relationships among Various Types of Reading Scores on General and Science Material," *Journal of Educational Research*, Vol. 36, pp. 81–90, October, 1942.

19. THORNDIKE, E. L., *The Teaching of English Suffixes*, Bureau of Publications, Teachers College, Columbia University, New York, 1941, 82 pp.

20. *Unit Study Series*, American Education Press, Inc., Columbus, Ohio, 1932–1933.

21. WHITE, VERNA, and J. B. ENOCHS, "Testing the Reading and Interpretation of Literature," *English Journal*, Vol. 33, pp. 171–177, April, 1944.

22. YOUNG, WILLIAM E., "Recent Research on Reading in the Social Studies," *Education*, Vol. 62, pp. 18–26, September, 1941.

23. ZAHNER, LOUIS C., "Basic English and Language Study," *Education*, Vol. 64, pp. 319–325, January, 1944.

CHAPTER VIII

SPECIAL READING GROUPS

According to some reputable calculations (32), about one-seventh of our adults are unable to read a newspaper intelligently. Yet with an average of 8 weeks' intensive instruction in the special training units of the armed forces, around 90 per cent of these men were brought up to fourth-grade level in reading. Encouraging results of remedial programs have also been reported for high-school and college students whose reading ability is "regrettably inadequate."

Remedial programs should, however, be viewed not in isolation but in relation to the basic program of reading experiences and instruction. If the whole-school program is conducted in small classes and with adequate attention to the correction of physical defects and the provision of suitable reading material, and if the reading experiences each student needs are provided at each stage of his development, a minimum of special "remedial" instruction in reading will be needed. Of course, there will always be individuals who, for various reasons, have difficulty in reading; but, if these students can be helped with their reading problems within the regular class groups, without interfering with their work in each subject, they are likely to make a better total adjustment.

Remedial programs were the way of solving the problem of reading deficiency reported by 201 out of the 334 liberal-arts colleges, teachers' colleges, and normal schools surveyed by the University of Minnesota Press in 1942. Seventy-four additional institutions said that they were planning to offer such programs the next year.

McCaul (13) studied the cost of remedial reading programs in 18 colleges that were known to have "seasoned" reading programs. The median cost, including salaries, materials, and equipment, was $851 for the program as a whole and $6.27 per student served. The range in cost was from $200 to $3,400. Salaries were the largest item. Expenses for materials covered a range from $0 to $400. The remedial-reading teachers were most frequently recruited from departments of education, English, psychology, teacher training, and personnel work and testing. Eight of the colleges that were studied charged a fee, usually $1 or $2; the highest fee charged was $10. The number of students served varied from 1.2 per cent of the students enrolled at the levels at which remedial reading was offered to 100 per cent of the freshmen. One type of program is described here (13, pages 363–364).

Judging from the responses, one type of inexpensive, yet effective, program would be the following: A member of the faculty would train a number of graduate students or education majors in the theory and practice of remedial reading. These students would then help freshmen and upperclassmen who needed or desired to develop their reading ability. More seriously retarded readers would be referred to the faculty member for individualized or small-group instruction. In this way a large number of students could be served at small cost, and at the same time graduate students and education majors would secure experience in teaching, would be made conscious of the prevalence of reading problems, and would become skilled in solving reading difficulties. Equipment would not be necessary, for satisfactory diagnosis and remediation could be undertaken without machines. As for teaching materials, the texts used by the remedial-reading students in their courses could be employed with all except the most deficient readers. Under these circumstances the students would be improving their reading upon materials which it is essential that they be able to read better, and the question of accomplishing a transfer of improvement in reading from remedial to course materials would not exist.

If the seriously retarded readers on any educational level cannot be given in their regular classes the stimulation, instruction, and practice that they need, special groups should be formed. Provision is commonly made for students unusually low in reading ability through special sections of English and through special classes in remedial reading. If this is done, care must be taken not to attach any stigma to membership in the special class. The academic morale of the poor reader is usually low enough already, without increasing his sense of inferiority by segregating him in a class labeled "remedial reading." For this reason, terms like "reading home room," "special English," or "reading laboratory" should be used to designate the special class for retarded readers; and the class should live up to its name. Care should be taken not to make the special reading class a dumping ground for the school's unwanted disciplinary problems.

Teachers, administrators, and personnel officers are repeatedly confronted with situations like the following, and are asking the same questions.

In a ninth-grade English class (1) where the students range from the well-read to the absolute nonreader who cannot recognize one- and two-syllable words, (2) where the subject matter is already more extensive than can be covered, (3) where much of the material in the textbooks is beyond the group unless there is overparticipation by the teacher, what would be your step-by-step procedure in setting up an efficient remedial reading program?

. Would you set aside time once a week during the term or would you work intensively for 2 or 3 weeks to launch the program?

What materials would you use if teaching in such a situation?

It is questions of this kind that this chapter and Appendix A will attempt to answer.

ADMINISTRATIVE CONSIDERATIONS

Bases for Selection.—Many bases for the selection of students for special reading classes have been reported, the most common of which are results of a reading test. Some schools refer all students whose total reading score, according to the norms, is more than one grade below their actual grade placement. This procedure, however, does not take account of the capacities and needs of the students, or of the level of reading achievement in their own classes. If some schools that enroll students who tend to be below average in mental ability were to follow this plan, they would have in special classes more than half of their students, many of whom are reading up to their capacity. Other schools that attract students above average in mental ability might have no students more than one grade retarded in reading on the basis of the norms; yet there would undoubtedly be some who were in need of special instruction to help them realize their reading potentialities.

Because of these objections to selecting students for special instruction by measuring them against a general reading standard, many schools prefer to assign to the remedial groups students who are in the lowest fourth of their class in total reading score. The advantage of this basis of selection is that the reading ability in the local school is likely to determine the level of reading skill a student will have to reach in order to do acceptable work there.

It is frequently advocated that intelligence as well as reading ability be considered in grouping. Of two students, one high and one low on an intelligence test, the one with more mental alertness might be expected to make the more rapid progress in reading and, therefore, to show the greater return for a given expenditure of the teacher's time. However, there is some evidence to indicate that high-school and college students whose intelligence and reading ability both measure low (see pages 58–59) will show improvement in reading under proper instruction and guidance.

Evidence of need of special instruction is obtained most realistically from observation of the way that students' reading actually functions in their classwork.   On this basis alone, some schools refer students to special reading classes.

Some students in senior high school and college recognize their inefficient reading habits and voluntarily apply for help. These students should be admitted to special reading groups for several reasons: their motivation is initially strong; they serve as a stimulus to other students; they may be helped to increase their total reading and study efficiency.

From the foregoing discussion it is evident that referral to special-reading classes should be made on the basis of many factors: evidence of poor classwork, judgment of teachers, results of reading tests considered with reference to the local group as well as to the national norms, intelligence-test results, other personal data, and the expressed desire of the individual student.   Only when various factors are considered with reference to the individual can placement in the most appropriate group be made.

Tact is involved in referring students to the class.   In an interview or group discussion, the special class can be described as an opportunity to get the most out of high-school and college years.   In these days of speed and efficiency, students do not want to lag behind in the horse-and-buggy stage of reading.   The special group will help them to attack their immediate study and reading problems more effectively and thus to gain time for other activities.

Size of Class.—There is seldom a dearth of students who need reading assistance.   The work of rehabilitation of the retarded reader, however, is highly individual; hence, the organization of the class, if that is the administrative choice, should be done with this fact in mind.   Successful group work with retarded readers has been accomplished in groups varying in size up to 25.   Larger classes appear to mean the forfeiture of some, if not all, of the gains that can be made in smaller groups.

Attendance.—Present practice is divided between making attendance in the special reading class compulsory, and putting attendance on a voluntary basis.   If enrollment is voluntary, regular attendance is usually required after the initial decision is made.   In both high school and college the best plan seems to be to provide regularly scheduled time in the freshman program for improvement in reading. Those who need special instruction and practice may spend this time in the remedial reading classes.   Those who are already proficient readers may use the time for voluntary reading in new fields or more intensive exploration of familiar fields.   Having this regularly scheduled time for all students has several advantages; it relieves pressure on students for whom a period of reading instruction, added to a program that is already proving too heavy for them, would be a last straw; it makes attention to the improvement of reading a requirement for all students; it gives status to reading among both students and faculty. Far less satisfactory is the practice of offering special sections in English, in addition to regular English classes, as electives to students who have previously failed in English.

A quite different kind of provision for special instruction in reading is the helping, or guidance, period scheduled for 1 hour, 3 days a week, directly after the last regular class period. Students come voluntarily, individually, or in small groups, to see the teacher who in their estimation can help them most. One teacher reported that her "help period" often lasts from two to five o'clock, for the boys and girls voluntarily stay, to chat about books and exchange ideas, after their specific reading problems have been considered. Obviously, the use made of this kind of period depends largely on the teacher and on the attitude that she creates.

Time Devoted to Special Instruction.—The length of period varies from 30 minutes to 1 hour. When the reading instruction is substituted for a regular class, the group meets three to five times a week for the entire semester. When a special class is introduced, the time is frequently limited to one period a week, sometimes with an additional individual-conference period. Under conditions of individualized instruction, the length of time spent in the special reading group may best be regulated by the proficiency acquired. The student may drop out of the class when he has achieved his goal of reading ability.

Under a more common form of organization, in which various reading skills are practiced systematically with the group, an individual may be proficient in the reading skill emphasized one week, but deficient in that to be taught the next week. Thus he must remain in the class until the skills he needs have been covered. The advantages of the truly individualized procedure are obvious but difficult to realize in a large, heterogeneous group. One way out of this dilemma is to summarize the diagnostic information for the group and then provide first the practice and instruction needed by all, later working with small groups and individuals on their special reading problems. Another procedure that has been found useful is to give an informal pretest when each skill is introduced, and to permit the individuals who are proficient in that particular skill to do free reading while the other members of the group are working on the skill in which they are deficient.

Credit in Special Reading Classes.—If credit is given, the reading work acquires status in the eyes of faculty and students. Credit may be given as part of, or in place of, English credit. However, when the class is organized on an informal basis, credit is not usually given. Compulsory attendance, a regularly scheduled class in lieu of an English class, and credit for the work accomplished go together as part of one pattern.

Personnel.—Russell (19) has mentioned three methods of providing instructors to do the remedial teaching:

1. The school employs one or more full-time remedial teachers who do no regular classroom work.
2. One or more teachers are released from certain duties to do part-time remedial work.
3. All the teachers of the school system are expected to have some training in diagnostic and remedial procedures and to make use of them.

The first of these plans is feasible in a large school, a city system, or a rural area in which the expert serves a number of schools. In this way essential leadership and practical help are made available for the teachers who will do the actual classwork. Like the reading specialist, the teacher assigned to do remedial reading work part time will assist in developing the school-wide reading program and will work with retarded readers individually and in small groups. The third plan represents an ultimate goal that is far from realized at present. To accomplish it will require leadership of the kind mentioned in (1) and (2). By working with individual teachers on their reading problems, by conducting faculty meetings or study groups on reading, and by recommending books and articles and summer and extension courses in reading, the specialist will gradually help every teacher to become an effective teacher of reading.

PROCEDURES

Before considering specific remedial programs and procedures, let us first summarize certain features that should be incorporated in all special reading classes.

The General Atmosphere Should Be Optimistic.—The general atmosphere of the class should be pleasant and optimistic. Students can share in making their reading room attractive with paint, pictures, travel posters, book covers, plants, gay curtains, cushions, reading games, and bookshelves filled with multicolored books. More important than these physical features is the psychological atmosphere created by positive expectancy that improvement is possible, faith in each student, freedom from unnecessary failure, belief in reading as a source of pleasure and personal satisfaction, recognition of social goals that can be achieved through reading, encouragement of genuine effort—a general atmosphere of accomplishment, enthusiasm, belongingness. Most of all, this atmosphere depends upon a friendly relationship between teacher and students and upon a recognition by the teacher that poor reading is only one of many factors that enter into each student's total adjustment. The teacher's attitude should be similar to that of one rural teacher who, when asked to list her gifted children, wrote, "All my children are gifted." She recognized that every one of her students had certain special talents that could be developed.

Activities and Materials Should Stimulate Reading.—The activities of the group must be interesting and conducive to reading. The emphasis is on learning through reading. Suitable books are easily available. If students are stimulated to choose and if they feel free to do so, they are more likely to approach books with interest and enthusiasm. It should be borne in mind that many a student who belongs to a special reading class has never read a book voluntarily or with enjoyment and thinks of reading as a difficult, disagreeable task. The first and most important accomplishment of the reading teacher is to help such students acquire a favorable attitude toward reading.

In one group the teacher let the students talk about their interests—hobbies, spare-time activities, adjustment to the new school, and vocational plans—until they themselves became tired of this rather aimless use of time and began to say, "I thought this was a reading class. When do we begin to read?" Thus the demand for reading came from the group. They then began to talk about "why people read" and "what reading means to me." They thought it would be a good idea to take a test and to grade it themselves so that they could find out what their reading problems were. Thus, the teacher helped this class to develop their own program and to view it as an experiment that would be of help to other schools.

Another teacher set aside 10 or 15 minutes of each period for free reading. Magazine articles and short stories that could be finished in the time allotted were available. The pleasure in this reading was not shadowed by a test of comprehension. Instead, they felt free to read as they pleased and to share with others, in a period of informal conversation, any vivid impressions or ideas that they had gained. Another class spent part of the reading period in the library, where they could look around and find books that they would like to read.

Both librarian and teacher were ready to guide the individual in his choice, sometimes getting clues by asking him to tell about any books he had liked or about his immediate interests. Later the students were helped to find other books that represented a progression of reading experience for them. Units on radio, motion pictures, airplanes, and other topics of current interest stimulated wide reading. As a result, they began to think of reading as something that they liked to do, rather than as something that they had to do.

The writing of their own newspaper, of stories about the most exciting thing that ever happened to them, and of "tall stories" has two values. It gives appreciation of sentence and paragraph structure and supplies excellent reading material for other students who find the experiences of their contemporaries interesting and their vocabulary and sentence structure familiar and easy to read.

Individual contract cards suggesting reading for different purposes and practice material for improving specific reading skills enable students to carry out an appropriate reading program with a minimum of supervision from the teacher.

Difficulties Should Be Recognized.—As students begin to enjoy the free-reading period and to read the books assigned in other subjects, they encounter difficulties. Close observation gives the teacher many clues about these. With help, the students can recognize these difficulties and make plans for overcoming them. It is essential that the student obtain early a sound and accurate understanding of his reading difficulties, as a basis for improvement that he recognizes as possible (see Chaps. VII, IX, and X).

Instruction Is Necessary.—Too frequently the activities of the special reading class consist mainly of practice and testing. Instruction is neglected. Continued practice of poor reading methods does not improve reading. Students need help in reading directions effectively, in grasping the main ideas, in recognizing important details, and in all the other reading skills that are required in college and secondary school. Time for discussion of the specific reading methods appropriate to the passage should be provided before and after each period of practice. For example, words that have been selected for study by the students may be related to previous experience, and new experiences may be introduced to make the words still more meaningful. Instruction should be given in ways of attacking unfamiliar words, and students should experiment with methods of guessing the meaning of a word from its context, learn to sound out a word by syllables, and become adept in using the dictionary (see detailed discussion of vocabulary on pages 276–285).

Practice Should Be Provided.—In the remedial reading class there is a place for drill, but this is not the exalted place that it once held. The class should be divided on the basis of specific difficulties, and practice material for each group should be provided. Parts of the many workbooks now on the market may be used to good advantage, and additional practice material may be prepared to meet special needs and interests. For example, practice in reading directions may be obtained through real directions to be read and followed. Instead of telling the students what to do at the beginning of each period, the teacher may hand out typed or mimeographed direction sheets or may write the directions on the blackboard. This kind of written directions may be illustrated by the following paragraph:

The reading selection for today, "The Law of Club and Fang," starts on page 401. The selection has four parts, which fit together like links in a chain. First read the story from beginning to end. Then go over it again to try to decide what the four parts are. Make a brief note about each part, to aid you in the discussion that we shall have when the entire class has finished reading. Find the place and begin to read now.

Practice in getting the main idea may be obtained through writing headings for articles posted on the bulletin board, headlines for the school newspaper, and similar projects. For many suggestions for practice exercises see pages 290–291 and 365–367.

Progression Should Be Evident.—The student should see that he is making progress; otherwise he will ask, "Why attend the class?" In order to prevent a sense of failure, reading should begin at or a little below the student's initial level of fluency. In order to give a sense of progress, reading material should increase in scope and difficulty as rapidly as the individual is ready for it. Thus he may move on to proficiency in many reading skills, move ahead to greater speed and accuracy in each skill, and move outward from exclusive reading of comics and fiction to biography, popular science, and other types of reading material. A balanced program of reading should include some books that challenge the student's skill and some easier books on his previous level to promote fluency. To stimulate interest in one class, each student recorded and posted daily the number of questions he answered correctly and the number of seconds required to read passages of the same length and similar content. The students' aim was to increase the first figure and make the second smaller from week to week.

Application Should Be Made to Regular Classes.—Linking the reading in the special class with the activities of regular classes has several advantages: it ensures further practice in the reading methods taught; it appeals to the students as practical and timesaving; it gives them the satisfaction of success in subjects in which they have previously felt inferior. For example, the students in one reading class that had made a study of the dictionary and its uses, for the first time assumed leadership in their regular English class when this topic was introduced.

TYPES OF GROUPS

In addition to the regularly scheduled reading classes, units on reading may be introduced in various courses, and reading clubs may be formed, to meet during school hours or after school.

Short Units on Reading.—The introduction, in an English or a home-room period or in an orientation course, of a relatively short practice period in reading may have a marked influence on the reading ability of the students. This seemed to be the case in a *Reader's Digest* reading-improvement program. Landry (9) set up a carefully controlled experiment involving 7,556 pupils in grades 7 to 12 in 12 representative cities. The control classes pursued the regular course of instruction in English; the experimental groups, matched with the control groups with respect to intelligence test scores and initial scores on the Cooperative Reading Comprehension Test and the Traxler Silent Reading Test, devoted 226 minutes per month to systematic practice and testing on selected articles from current issues of *The Reader's Digest*. At the end of the experimental period, the average reading gain on the reading tests for all the experimental classes was 13.2 months; for all control classes, it was 6.2 months. It seems that a program of this kind under the proper guidance of an average teacher can produce real reading improvement in junior and senior high school over and above that produced by the usual class instruction. It should be added, however, that the effectiveness of such a program is due partly to the appropriateness of the material selected. Some very heterogeneous classes would require not one exercise book, but several at different levels of difficulty.

Reading Clubs.—Reading clubs have been formed, both within remedial reading groups and as voluntary organizations. The president conducts the meetings; the secretary and a committee or a series of rotating committees take charge of the program. The secretary in one club posted the dates on the bulletin board; and volunteers, including the teacher, signed up when they had something that they wanted to read to the group.

In one club the reading was oral and the purpose was enjoyment of the story, the article, or the play. Sometimes the students read; sometimes the sponsor. The meetings were social in nature and were held twice a week. The members did considerable silent reading outside the club period, to find selections to present and to finish stories that were not completed in the period.

Somewhat more serious in its purpose was a college international-relations club, which met every 2 weeks. Membership in the club was voluntary and open to all. The members were either majoring in social science or keenly interested in that field. Six or eight books on current events were donated for reading during the year and were later presented to the library.

A book club composed of about 50 college freshmen and sophomores, all interested in books, met once every 2 weeks in the home of the English professor and his wife. At each meeting, members reported on three or four books, usually of current interest. Occasionally the professor or an invited faculty member or some other guest brought several books to the attention of the group. The reports were followed by a social period, during which light refreshments were served. The students greatly enjoyed the friendly home atmosphere and the opportunity to become better acquainted with the faculty. The club created an interest in reading for pleasure and for information. It also helped the professor to know his students better.

EXAMPLES OF SPECIAL READING CLASSES

Improvement in Reading in a Slow-learning Group (16). *Description of Students.*—Ages 12 to 16; I.Q. from 67 to 102; from Illinois Soldiers' and Sailors' Children's School. Reading levels, grades 2-2 to 6-5.

Method of Selection.—Initial reading levels were determined by the Monroe Diagnostic Reading Examination, Chicago, Institute of Juvenile Research, 1932. Gray's Oral Reading Check Test and the Stanford Silent Reading Test were given. Graphs of test scores were given to the students and, in preparation for the next 6 weeks' work, each discussed the errors he had made.

Organization.—Two 35-minute periods were scheduled each week. The children attended alone or in pairs. No two children followed the same plan, although the procedure for all was basically similar.

Procedures.—Word study was emphasized. For those whose reading level was below grade 3, fifth month, vocabulary drill was given: the first 500 words of the Gates word list were printed on separate cards for flash-card drills.   Words missed were studied; examined for clues; read in short, prepared sentences until mastered.   Ten words were studied at a time; the flash-card drill for each lesson ended when the child had mastered 10 words.

For children who had mastered 500 words, and for those who had a reading level of grade 3, phonetic drills were begun, in which the method used was that described by Thorlief F. Hegge, Samuel A. Kirk, and Winifred Kirk in *Remedial Reading Drills*, George Wahr, Ann Arbor, Michigan, 1941.   For this group, silent reading was on the third-grade level.

Those who had reading ability above grade 3 used remedial exercises recommended by Brueckner and Lewis in *Diagnostic and Remedial Exercises in Reading*, John C. Winston Company, Philadelphia, 1935. These were supplemented by word analyses and the learning of prefixes, suffixes, and other word elements.   Books at least one grade below the child's reading level were chosen for oral reading.   After a child had read orally, other children asked questions and made comments. Each child kept a record of his own mistakes.   The word study and oral reading were correlated.

Comments.—This program represents the approach to reading through specific drill.   The underlying theory is that distaste for reading may be caused by lack of word knowledge and by inability to comprehend.   If, by working for accuracy and complete mastery in some of the basic reading skills, the pupil is brought to the point where he can succeed, he is started on the road to reading proficiency. These pupils, ranging in I.Q. from 67 to 102, may have enjoyed the simple routine exercises and gained a sense of achievement.   Among the features that may account for the success reported for this program are

1. The individual's level of reading ability and interest is accurately ascertained.

2. Practice in improving his reading is begun at, or a little below, his present level, where he can succeed.

3. From that point he is helped to move ahead as fast as he is able and is kept aware of his progress.

4. He feels that the teacher is genuinely interested in him and expects improvement.

Special Reading Classes in a Junior High School (18).   *Description of Pupils.*—Two hundred junior-high-school pupils, with chronological ages of 11.5 to 15.4 and I.Q.'s of 52 to 144.

Methods of Appraisal.—Initial tests given: Terman-McNemar Group Test of Mental Ability, Iowa Silent Reading Test, New Stanford Reading Test; later, Traxler Silent Reading Test; final test, Form B of the Iowa Silent Reading Test. Observation of the reading ability of each pupil. Constant evaluation was made as an intelligent basis for guiding the procedure.

Procedures.—Wide reading was encouraged by an attractive environment. Many books covering a wide range of interest and difficulty were put within easy reach of all pupils—on shelves, tables, and desks in a bright, cheerful, sunny browsing room—books of all colors and sizes, difficult and easy, humorous and serious, fact and fiction. In short, there was a book for every taste. Pupils were urged to pick them up, turn the pages, browse through them. Gay book covers with a hint as to the books' content were put on the bulletin board. On a wall chart there was a miniature shelf for each pupil, on which he pasted colorful little books bearing the titles of those that he had read.

Classes met for 45 minutes each day. No lengthy book reports were required—only a card giving the name of the book and its author and stating the student's honest opinion. In class, the teacher sometimes supplemented this written report with a few questions about the book.

Intensive work was given to each pupil according to his need, some being allowed 30 minutes, some 10 minutes, others less time. Teacher-made tests were frequently used. Each pupil watched his progress by referring to wall graphs bearing his number.

Results.—The results of this program are shown by the following figures:

Class	Initial test, October		Final test, January	
	Score	Grade	Score	Grade
Seventh grade.................	49.1	5.6	61	7.2
Eighth grade.................	54.4	6.3	65	7.8

Comments.—This program emphasized enjoyment in reading and, first of all, the developing of a favorable attitude toward reading. The application of the following principles probably accounts for the increase in reading ability reported.

1. Start with reading material that brings satisfaction, in order to develop a love for reading, rather than a distaste for it.

2. Detect any spark of interest and nourish it carefully and gradually, being careful not to smother it with a heavy "must" diet.

3. Forget the required reading lists.

4. Show consideration of the feelings of those who are seriously retarded in reading.

5. Guide each pupil from his present level into deeper and more worthwhile channels.

6. Take no chance of killing the interest of the brightest by giving them books too easy to challenge their best efforts.

Corrective Reading in Seventh and Ninth Grades of a University School (25, pages 121–136).—A reading program carried out with substantial gains in rate and comprehension included emphasis on specific reading skills and habits of regular, independent reading.

Procedures.   The procedures in this case were as follows:

1. Learning to read and follow directions

   a. Printed directions preceding the reading
   b. Directions written on the blackboard

2. Learning to find facts in a paragraph

   a. Reading to find certain definite facts
   b. Reading and then answering fact questions from memory of the paragraph

3. Learning to find main ideas

   a. In single paragraphs
   b. In a series of paragraphs organized about a central idea
   c. In a whole selection

4. Learning to find details that support main ideas in paragraphs and to recognize them as supporting material when found

   a. Near the beginning of a paragraph
   b. Near the end of a paragraph
   c. Throughout a paragraph
   d. In succeeding paragraphs

5. Learning to find certain definite points through rapid reading of a selection covering several pages

   a. Words, such as names of animals, games, or inventions
   b. Ideas, expressed in phrases, sentences, or paragraphs (At this point attention was directed toward rate of reading)

6. Learning to identify the large, general divisions, or links, in longer selections

   a. Narrative reading
   b. Descriptive reading
   c. Expository reading

7. Building up the power to grasp and interpret meaning through

   a. Reading literature orally in small groups and later telling stories to the rest of the class
   b. Silent reading to answer thought questions
   c. Silent reading with discussion of questions that require interpretation of what has been read
   d. Reading under the pressure of test conditions
   e. Studying new words

Comments.—This approach to the improvement of reading combines systematic practice in essential reading skills with activities that are inherently interesting. Its success was probably due to the following practices:

1. Instruction and practice were given in specific reading abilities for which students felt a need in their schoolwork.
2. These selected reading skills were really taught, not merely superficially touched on, as in some programs.
3. Instruction progressed logically from the simpler to the more complex reading skills.
4. The social stimulation of the group experience reinforced individual practice.

A Modified Ninth-grade English Class (7). *Description of Students and Setting.*—A gifted young teacher was discouraged by her first experience of teaching English to a group of ninth-grade students who were totally unable to comprehend the books required by the state course of study. They were in a fog that showed no sign of lifting. These students were from homes where there was little opportunity for reading or interest in it. Most of them had never in their lives read a book voluntarily and their attitude toward reading was poor. With the permission of the principal, this teacher undertook to make their English work more profitable to them.

Procedures.—After a period spent in talking with the students about their interests, she learned that they liked to read about the adventures of persons like themselves. Why not, then, begin reading about their own experiences? The next day they were to come to class prepared to tell the most exciting and interesting experiences that they had had during the summer. These were taken down in shorthand by a senior commercial student, typed, and returned to the ninth-grade youngsters. After editing their stories, they had them retyped and bound into a little booklet, which served as very good reading material.

Their next interest was in making books of travel. Each one decided upon some place that he would like to visit and obtained pictures and information from a great many sources, including library books, copies of *The National Geographic Magazine*, etc. Each of these travel "diaries" served as reading material for the other youngsters, as well. This kind of material aroused great interest in reading and led to practice in the reading of assignments for other classes. By use of the information gained through their work in the reading class, the students were enabled to discuss questions in their other classes with a success that they had never before experienced.

Comments.—This program was psychologically sound. Its success may be explained in terms of these fundamental principles:

1. The lack of reading interest and ability in the group was recognized and accepted.

2. Their other interests were ascertained and tied up with reading, and suitable reading material was obtained.

3. After interest in recreational reading was developed, a transition was made to reading in other school subjects.

A Ninth-grade Remedial Reading Class (31). *Description of Students.*—From an entering ninth-grade class of 250 students, 21 were chosen on the basis of having reading ages 2 or more years lower than the averages of their educational and mental ages.

Procedures.—The following tests were used as part of the diagnostic procedure.

> Measures of physical growth and health
> Stanford Revision of the Binet-Simon Tests
> Porteus Maze Tests
> New Stanford Achievement Test, Form V
> Gray's Standardized Oral Reading Paragraphs   ·
> Gates Silent Reading Tests
> Pintner-Patterson Performance Scales
> Informal class tests and observation.

Thus information was obtained about each student's reading difficulties and their causes.

In this 13-week reading program, the teacher first of all convinced the students that they were much more capable than the reading tests indicated and that improvement was possible. The next step was to give them the experience of pleasure in reading. For this purpose a book was chosen that was interesting and easy for them to read (14). In each class period they read about 15 pages and made a game of finding and reporting as many word pictures as possible. They drew on their past experience and discovered that their backgrounds of experience might be extended by reading. At this stage no work-type responses were called for. At the end of 2 weeks, when the reading of the book had been completed, the students felt that they had improved in their ability to read for details and were beginning to think of reading as a pleasant task. They were now ready to choose a book to read at home.

The next step involved cooperation with the social-studies teacher in helping the students to learn to read their assignments more effectively. The social-studies passages that were used in the reading class as practice material one day were discussed the next day in the social-studies class; thus the students were convinced that better reading was profitable.

The reading skills acquired were then applied to a long narrative— Stevenson's *Kidnapped*. The first assignments were short and carefully tested. As the students began to show proficiency in this type of reading, they read longer assignments, increasing their speed as they were spurred on by interest. To the ability to note details, react to sensory images, and follow the narrative as a whole was added the new skill of drawing inferences, such as that required by the following question: "Stevenson tells you a great many things that Alan did, but does not tell you outright what kind of man he is. What do you know besides what Stevenson says?"

A volume of short stories was next used, to correlate all the skills that had been developed thus far. Students chose selections that they might teach to the class. The last unit consisted of reading *The Canterbury Pilgrims*, which was so interesting to the students that they finished it in advance of assignments.

Throughout the course, emphasis was put on discovering the meaning of words from the context, and "only a limited use was made of the dictionary."

Results.—With this group of retarded readers, the procedures employed resulted in an increase in reading skills of from 1 to $2\frac{9}{10}$ grade years, in wider voluntary reading and in a changed attitude toward reading.

Comments.—This skillfully planned program illustrates the development of a remedial reading course based on carefully selected material. Instead of starting with activities in which the students were interested, this program assumed an intrinsic interest in certain kinds of reading material, which were used to develop reading skills. Some of the features of this program that account for its success are

1. The initial diagnostic procedure supplied accurate information about the reading status of each student.

2. On the basis of this knowledge of the students it was possible to select suitable reading material for them.

3. Although this material was read chiefly for pleasure, it was also used to give practice in the reading skills in which students were particularly weak.

4. Interest aroused in class led to voluntary outside reading.

5. The students' concern for their success in other classes was capitalized by having them use social-studies assignments as practice material and then giving them opportunities in the social-studies class to demonstrate their newly acquired reading proficiency.

A Controlled Experiment in the Tenth Grade (8). *Description of Students.*—Seventy-seven pairs of tenth-grade pupils, selected on the basis of the Iowa Silent Reading Test, Form A, Advanced.

Organization.—Experimental group—remedial reading for one period a week for a semester, organized on an individualized group-instruction basis, the units being self-administered as far as possible. A control group, matched on the basis of the reading test scores, carried on their regular school program.

Procedures.—Students were given 36 reading units specially prepared for pupils in grades 9 and 10. The passages were selected on the basis of their interest to students, their social significance, and the difficulty of their content. The exercises were designed to improve pupils in six aspects of reading comprehension: (1) word meaning, (2) total meaning, (3) central thought, (4) detailed meaning, (5) organization, and (6) summarization. The reading units were organized in such a way as to enable each pupil to get practice on phases in which he was weak.

Results.—"The average improvement made by the experimental group was greater than that made by the control group."

Comments.—This senior-high-school remedial program was of the formal type. Its main feature was carefully prepared practice exercises, designed to be intrinsically interesting and valuable and to give practice in six important reading skills.

A Remedial Program for College Freshmen at the University of Cincinnati (23). *Description of Students.*—All freshmen whose scores on the Nelson-Denny test placed them below the 30th percentile were organized into required reading classes. These classes were divided into groups on the basis of their major field, *i.e.*, all engineering students were in one group.

Organization.—Students met 2 days a week in 50-minute periods for 8 weeks.

Procedures.—The Iowa Silent Reading Test was used for ascertaining the specific areas of weakness indicated by that test.

The second form of the Nelson-Denny test was used, at the end of the 8 weeks, to ascertain improvement in the reading skills measured by this test.

The first 10 minutes of every period were devoted to speed and comprehension exercises (each time, one exercise from Strang's *Study Type of Reading Exercises*). The remainder of each class period early in the course was devoted to techniques for improving sentence and paragraph comprehension. At first workbooks were used, to provide practice in the specific skills. After the students understood what was expected, they were given mimeographed exercises in the same skills, based on materials from books that they were reading in their courses. These lessons were concerned with comprehension of large sections and chapters rather than single paragraphs. "In every instance each student's assignment for a remedial reading period was all or part of an assignment that would be studied by him for a regular University class in the near future." Because of the homogeneity of the groups, it was possible to work with students' actual assignments in this way.

Comments.—In this program, the remedial work was closely allied with the actual reading jobs that students had to do—with "the complex mental activity inherent in meaningful reading." There were differentiation for individual needs, and emphasis on helping students develop skill in formulating their own purposes in reading. Using passages from their college books as practice material was more practical than using workbooks, most of which consist of material unlike the assignments that the student has to read.

Remedial Reading at Yale University (28). *Description of Students.*—Students whose predicted score was below 2.0 were invited to attend the preliminary meetings of the classes in remedial reading and efficient study methods. Those who came to the preliminary meeting (approximately 80) were given the Traxler High School Reading Test. According to their scores on this test, a number of the students did not need remedial reading. Thirty decided to join the class.

Organization.—These students met twice weekly over a period of 7 weeks. They were divided into three subgroups on the basis of reading ability. No effort was made to compel attendance. Classes were conducted informally and no outside assignments were given.

Procedures.—Approximately one-third of the time was spent in discussion of study methods—preparing for and taking examinations, note taking, vocabulary, and spelling.

Corrective procedures were used to overcome mechanical defects, such as regressions and moving of lips, tongue, or head.

Early in the term each student filled out a personal-information sheet and a time schedule. All personal data were collected in the files of the clinical psychologist, and specific personal problems were worked out in individual conferences.

A supplementary feature, designed to facilitate the transfer of skills and attitudes learned in class to materials and situations met outside the class, consisted of selecting and reading a book for 20 or 25 minutes a day, according to the most approved method. The gains of students who cooperated in this exercise were greater than those of the ones who did not.

Comments.—This college viewed reading problems in their setting of study habits and personal problems. The success of the program may be attributed largely to these features:

1. The total adjustment of the student to his college program was considered of importance.
2. Common academic problems were brought up for discussion.
3. Reading skills practiced in class were used in outside-class reading.

Adult Reading Clinic at the University of Chicago (4).—The adult reading clinic offers a diagnostic examination and "a series of corrective exercises organized usually into a unit of 20 1-hour periods. The corrective work is done individually rather than in classes" (4, page 248).

Description of Students.—Of 62 cases, all but 8 were college students, the majority of whom said that they wanted to improve their rate of reading.

Procedures.—Initial and final tests were given. These were modified forms of the Diagnostic Examination of Silent Reading Abilities prepared by Van Wagenen and Dvorak.

The chief technique employed for improving rate was a gradual but persistent pressure, using in part a projection mechanism and in part a reading-rate controller. The amount of pressure exerted ranged from 80 to 100 words per minute faster than normal reading as long as comprehension did not fall below 70 per cent as measured by the McCallister test (11).

By this method the average rate of reading for the 62 subjects was increased from 197 words per minute to 315 words per minute—a gain of 60 per cent. This gain in rate was achieved without loss in the initial percentage of comprehension, which was 67 per cent.

Comments.—The procedure used in this clinic is particularly appropriate to one type of reader—the reader who comprehends what he reads but has acquired unnecessarily slow perceptual habits and rate of reading. In the case of students like these, the pressures of college life themselves often increase reading efficiency. If to these demands is added that of remunerative work, the student's need for increasing his reading and study efficiency becomes imperative. Under these conditions, some students, without special instruction, have learned to read faster and still maintain the necessary comprehension. Others, however, need the immediate stimulus of mechanical devices like those used in the Chicago Reading Clinic.

This so-called "pressure method" would not be appropriate for an individual whose experience has been limited and who needs "a broad education, with stimulating ideas to motivate interest in reading" (4, page 252). Nor would it be appropriate for a student whose basic difficulty is in comprehension and critical thinking and whose slow rate of reading is merely a symptom of some underlying difficulty. It is, therefore, important to distinguish between (4, page 252)

. . . those individuals whose techniques of reading are so poor that even within their own range of understanding they cannot read effectively, and those individuals who can read effectively within their own range of understanding, but who do not read widely and have not learned to apply the techniques of critical thinking needed in a liberal education.

A Reading Program with a Professional Emphasis. *Description of Students and Organization of Course.*—Students in the New Jersey State Teachers College at Glassboro took a course on the teaching of reading that met three times a week during the first semester of their junior year. The course was in three sections—for primary, intermediate, and upper elementary grades. Students needing additional aid with their own reading were referred by the faculty for special instruction, usually twice a week.

Procedures.—In this course the students first study their own reading. They analyze their scores on the Nelson-Denny Reading Test and learn procedures for improving their rate, vocabulary, and comprehension.

They observe frequently in the demonstration school, in order to study the development of reading readiness, the conduct of a variety of reading lessons, and the kinds of materials used. Each student works with one or more children in the development and reading of a story. He administers a standardized reading test in the public school, scores it, and analyzes the scores. All juniors take part in making a large reading exhibit of books that they have classified and evaluated. The librarian sets up attractive exhibits and tells students of various books that they might enjoy.

Comment.—In this program, personal and professional interests in the improvement of reading are fused. The study of their own reading gives prospective teachers a realistic approach to the teaching of reading that they will have to do later.

The Army's Training Program (30). *Description of Subjects.*— Illiterate, non-English speaking, and educationally retarded men had to be taught quickly so that they might be made available for war service.

Organization.—The program of instruction was organized in special training units 8 to 12 weeks in length; 18 hours a week were given to reading, language, arithmetic; the remainder, to military subjects. The class size was 15 to 18, so that individual work could be done. Reassignments were made when individuals were able to do the basic-training work.

Procedures.—The program was kept flexible to meet individual needs. Each man's past school attendance, occupational history, avocational interests, and intellectual abilities were studied. He was given an initial literacy test, a unit test in reading, and an examination in arithmetic. Four unit reading tests were built around the *Army Reader*, and progress charts were made from the test results.

The subject matter used was highly functional, dealing with Army life. A basic sight vocabulary list of 48 words, all associated with *A Day with Private Pete*, was built up. Each word had a rich association of meanings and was taught with the aid of film strips showing the printed word and a picture representing it. After these basic words had become familiar, *The Army Reader*, also based on *A Day with Private Pete*, was introduced. This was divided into four parts, roughly corresponding to first-, second-, third-, and fourth-grade level of difficulty. The *Reader* was supplemented by a weekly paper or magazines, which gave opportunity for applying newly acquired reading skills. The men read for details, for central thought, and to follow directions.

A guide to instructional materials was prepared for teachers. This manual gave inexperienced teachers suggestions for diagnosis and remedial measures, such as helping men to analyze words in order to see their common elements.

Comments.—The Army reading program incorporated many of the features of the best reading programs that have been developed in public schools and in colleges. Its success was probably due to these main features:

1. Instruction was given in relatively small classes under conditions where close attention was expected.

2. Learning to read was highly motivated.

3. The present reading status of each man was accurately determined.

4. The material was based on familiar experience and carefully graded according to difficulty.

5. As much practice as each man needed for mastery of a basic vocabulary was provided by means of the film strip and other devices.

6. Supplementary reading material helped the men to make the transition from the basic reading text to newspaper and magazine reading.

7. Help was given in overcoming specific reading difficulties.

Reading Class in an Adult-education Program (3). *Description of Students.*—Adults representing many educational levels, from elementary grades to college graduates, and many types of occupations and interests.

Selection.—Any adult interested in improving his reading ability could enroll in the course at one of several off-campus centers established under the auspices of the University of Florida. The only provision was that he carry out the requirements faithfully.

Organization.—Courses were held 4 hours a day, 1 day a week, for a period of 12 weeks. The first 2 hours were devoted to lectures, discussions, assigned readings, and quizzes. Then there was an hour's intermission, followed by 2 hours of demonstrations, laboratory work, and exercises. The size of the classes ranged from 20 to 35. Of the 180 adults who registered for the course, 175 completed it.

Procedures.—One form of the Iowa Silent Reading Test was given at the beginning and a comparable form at the end of the 8-week practice period.

Facts about reading were presented. Students' objections to reading were raised and discussed. For example, a student said, "I just don't have time to read." The instructor read aloud Rupert Hughes's "So You Haven't Time to Read."

Another student said, "That's all very well, but you can't teach an old dog new tricks." The instructor briefly summarized Thorndike's research in adult learning.

Attitudes toward reading crystallized in expressions such as "bookworm," "brain trust," and "walking encyclopedia" were modified through discussion of the use of reading by successful persons in all walks of life.

Laboratory Work.—Each student was asked to pair off with a friend, one holding the other responsible, under time pressure, for quick comprehension of the daily column, "The Washington Merry-Go-Round," and other current material. They urged each other to read with a purpose and not to loaf mentally, and to ask questions such as, "Do I agree with this? What does the article attempt to prove?"

Physical Aspects.—Visual difficulties were checked with the use of the telebinocular, and photographic records of eye movements were made. Subsequent examinations by an oculist showed a real need for checks on visual efficiency.

Materials.—Factual and informational content on contemporary topics, well written in highly emotional, romantic, or dramatic style, that lend themselves to objective-type testing.

Results.—At the beginning, 71.4 per cent were reading below college or adult level.

After 8 weeks, 49.7 per cent were reading below college or adult level.

Comments.—The unique features of this adult reading program were

1. The individual's resistances to reading were brought out into the open and faced frankly.
2. The laboratory work in pairs provided personal interest and stimulation.
3. Suitable current articles of interest to the group were used as practice material.

ERRORS TO AVOID

Some of the common faults in remedial reading groups should be avoided in the future.

1. The mechanical aspects of reading should be subordinate to the central emphasis on comprehension and interpretation of meaning. A few machines for photographing eye movements, recognizing visual defects, and stimulating phrase reading do not constitute a reading program.
2. Complete reliance on drills should be replaced by the purposeful use of drills, as specific need for them is recognized by the students.
3. The practice material should resemble the kind of reading the individual needs to do in his school and out-of-school life, and should emphasize the importance of differentiated reading, so that the student will develop flexibility and adaptability in shifting from one type of material and purpose to another requiring a markedly different rate and/or method of reading.
4. The reading done in the special class should grow out of interests and activities with which the student is vitally concerned.

RECOMMENDATIONS FOR SPECIAL READING PROGRAMS

Those descriptions given in this chapter are only a few examples of the many unique programs that have been developed in different situations. There is no one best program; each is necessarily somewhat different, as it is adapted to the needs of the students, the facilities available, and the type of person who must assume responsibility for it. However, we would recommend the following basic features:

1. Select students for special reading classes who are in the lowest fourth of their class on a standardized reading test, have given other evidence of reading difficulty, and want to improve their reading efficiency.

2. Provide time for the class in the student's regular program—preferably, two class periods a week and an additional conference period for individual help.

3. Give students as much responsibility as possible for planning and carrying out a realistic program, suitable to their abilities and their present and future needs for reading.

4. Administer additional silent and oral reading tests, both standardized and informal, for further diagnostic information.

5. Create an atmosphere of optimism reinforced by experiences of success in reading.

6. Use on-going activities and already established interests as natural incentives to read.

7. In the beginning, supply reading material of intrinsic interest that is at, or slightly below, the student's present reading ability.

8. Use assignments in other subjects as practice material and as a basis for specific instruction.

9. Give drill whenever necessary in individual cases or in the group as a whole to overcome a specific reading difficulty.

10. Help each student to keep a record of his progress in reading.

11. Help students to make the transition from the reading class to reading in other classes and to voluntary reading.

12. Evaluate changes in reading ability made during the special class.

VALUES TO BE ATTAINED

The values that may be gained from special instruction and practice in reading are well summarized by Simpson (20), as follows:

1. Consciousness of the fact that reading methods can be improved. One student wrote: "When I first started to practice in the workbook to improve speed, grasp the central idea and the meaning of the whole, I was inclined to think that the whole procedure was rather silly, but when I am confronted with my own results, I must admit I was quite wrong. . . . "

2. Learning to use different methods with varying kinds of material.

3. Improved concentration.

4. Valuable information.

5. Tools with which to work. One student said: "I feel that the class practice was most beneficial because it showed us how to go about improving our reading skill. Once we know how, we can practice ourselves. . . . "

6. Learning to grasp the central thought.
7. Improvement in vocabulary.
8. Improvement in outlining and drawing conclusions.
9. Increased confidence in one's ability to read efficiently.
10. Transference of principles learned in class to daily reading.

These are important outcomes toward which to work in any reading program. They can be measured to some extent. Changes in attitude toward reading, increased confidence, and greater ability to concentrate can be observed in the student's conduct and are indicated by his written or oral comments as to how he feels about reading. His approach to a reading assignment can be ascertained in an interview, as suggested on page 197. Increase in knowledge may be indicated by his marks in various subjects. Improvement in rate of comprehension, vocabulary, sentence and paragraph reading, and ability to draw conclusions and make applications from his reading can be ascertained by standardized tests and by informal tests based on the kind of material that he is required to read. Too frequently evaluation of a remedial reading program has been made solely on the results of a standardized test, which may completely fail to measure the particular reading skills on which the student has been working and in which he has gained a real proficiency that the test cannot reveal. In order to prevent discouragement on the part of the student and of the instructor of the special reading class, if for no other reason, this broad type of evaluation, in which observation and introspective reports play an important part, should be made.

References

1. BLAIR, GLENN MYERS, "The One Hundred Books Most Enjoyed by Retarded Readers in Senior High Schools," *English Journal*, Vol. 30, pp. 42–47, January, 1941.
2. BLAIR, GLENN MYERS, "Remedial-reading Programs in Senior High Schools," *School Review*, Vol. 49, pp. 32–41, January, 1941.
3. BROXSON, JOHN A., "Improving Reading," *Adult Education*, Vol. 2, pp. 95–100, April, 1943.
4. BUSWELL, G. T., "The Improvement of Rate and Comprehension in Reading," in *Adapting Reading Programs to Wartime Needs* (William S. Gray, editor), pp. 248–252, Supplementary Educational Monographs, No. 57, University of Chicago Press, Chicago, December, 1943, 283 pp.
5. CHARTERS, W. W., "Remedial Reading in College," *Journal of Higher Education*, Vol. 12, pp. 117–121, March, 1941.
6. COLE, LUELLA, *The Improvement of Reading with Special Reference to Remedial Instruction*, Farrar & Rinehart, Inc., New York, 1938, xii + 338 pp.
7. COLLYER, M. ARLENE, "Improving Reading in the Ninth Grade," *English Journal*, Vol. 29, pp. 37–43, January, 1940.

8 GUILER, W. S., EMILY MURPHY, and J. H. COLEMAN, "Improving the Reading Ability of High School Students," *Journal of Educational Research*, Vol. 36, pp. 445–456, February, 1943.

9. LANDRY, HERBERT A., "Teaching Reading with the Reader's Digest," *English Journal*, Vol. 32, pp. 320–324, June, 1943.

10. LAZAR, MAY, "The Place of Reading in the Elementary School Program," *Educational Research Bulletin* 7, Bureau of Reference, Research and Statistics, Board of Education of the City of New York, New York, May, 1944, iv + 43 pp.

11. McCALLISTER, JAMES M., *Purposeful Reading in College*, D. Appleton-Century Company, Inc., New York, 1942, 170 pp.

12. McCALLISTER, JAMES M., *Remedial and Corrective Instruction in Reading*, D. Appleton-Century Company, Inc., New York, 1936, vii + 300 pp.

13. McCAUL, ROBERT L., "The Cost of Remedial-reading Programs in 18 Colleges," *School and Society*, Vol. 56, pp. 361–364, Oct. 17, 1942.

14. MILLS, ENOS A., *The Story of a Thousand Year Pine and Other Tales of Wild Life*, Houghton Mifflin Company, Boston, 1913, 119 pp.

15. MONROE, MARION, and BERTIE BACKUS, *Remedial Reading: A Monograph in Character Education*, Houghton Mifflin Company, Boston, 1937, xii + 172 pp.

16. PEDIGO, LOUISE, "Junior High School Children Learn to Read," *English Journal*, Vol. 33, pp. 187–190, April, 1944.

17. RIEFLING, ADELINE ALDRICH, "Report of Two Reading-English Classes," *School Review*, Vol. 50, pp. 587–595, October, 1942.

18. RUDDY, ISABELLE, "A Reading Program for Junior High School," *English Journal*, Vol. 33, pp. 325–327, June, 1944.

19. RUSSELL, DAVID H., "Ways of Preventing Reading Failures in Elementary and Secondary Schools of Different Sizes," *Secondary Education*, Vol. 28, pp. 485–489, January–February, 1940.

20. SIMPSON, RAY H., "Improving Reading and Related Study Skills of College Women," *College English*, Vol. 1, pp. 322–332, January, 1940.

21. SIMPSON, RAY H., "Reading Problems of Teachers and Administrators and Books Found Most Valuable in Meeting These Problems," *Educational Administration and Supervision*, Vol. 28, pp. 520–527, October, 1942.

22. SMITH, NILA B., "Reorienting Remedial Reading in a Natural Setting—the Library," *Educational Method*, Vol. 19, pp. 156–162, December, 1939.

23. STEWART, JAMES R., "A Remedial-reading Program," *Journal of Higher Education*, Vol. 15, pp. 83–86, February, 1944.

24. STRANG, RUTH, "Scientific Method in Reading Science," *Science Education*, Vol. 29, pp. 72–77, March, 1945.

25. TRAXLER, ARTHUR E., "Corrective Reading," *English Instruction in the University High School*, Publication No. 4, the Laboratory Schools of the University of Chicago, 1933.

26. TRIGGS, FRANCES ORALIND, "Remedial Reading Programs: Evidence of Their Development," *Journal of Educational Psychology*, Vol. 33, pp. 678–685, December, 1942.

27. WHIPPLE, GERTRUDE, "Remedial Programs in Relation to Basic Programs of Reading," *Elementary School Journal*, Vol. 44, pp. 525–535, May, 1944.

28. WITTENBORN, JOHN, "Classes in Remedial Reading and Study Habits," *Journal of Educational Research*, Vol. 37, pp. 571–586, April, 1944.

29. WITTY, PAUL A., "Practices in Corrective Reading in Colleges and Universities," *School and Society*, Vol. 52, pp. 564–568, Nov. 30, 1940.
30. WITTY, PAUL, and SAMUEL GOLDBERG, "The Army's Training Program for Illiterate, Non-English Speaking, and Educationally Retarded Men," *Elementary English Review*, Vol. 20, pp. 306–311, December, 1943.
31. WITTY, PAUL A., and LOU L. LABRANT, "Some Results of Remedial Instruction in Reading," *Educational Trends*, Vol. 2, pp. 7–13, January, 1933.
32. WITTY, PAUL A., and GOLDA VAN BUSKIRK, "Beam in the Eye," *Childhood Education*, Vol. 21, pp. 80–85, October, 1944.
33. ZEHRER, FREDERICK A., "Methods of Remedial Reading Instruction at the High School Level," *Harvard Teacher's Record*, Vol. 6, pp. 154–162, June, 1936.

CHAPTER IX

SPECIFIC READING DIFFICULTIES

In the previous chapters emphasis has been placed on achieving individual reading goals, on the developmental nature of reading, and on conditions that prevent or promote effective reading. Although this positive treatment is sound, it is not adequate to meet present conditions of piled-up reading difficulties in the upper grades. There is a place for the analysis of specific reading deficiencies. In every subject, as well as in special reading classes, it is essential to discover these difficulties, to describe as completely and accurately as possible the conditions that seem to have given rise to them, and to provide practice, instruction, and treatment to correct them. This process is commonly called appraisal, or diagnosis, and remediation.

READING DIFFICULTIES

Among the reading difficulties frequently recurring among high-school and college students are the following:

1. Slow rate in silent reading
2. Incorrect or inadequate interpretation of passages read
3. Failure to note and remember important points and related details
4. Inability to understand without rereading
5. Inadequate vocabulary
6. Word-by-word reading
7. Passive reading that lacks any sense of a specific purpose
8. Inability to draw inferences and conclusions, to evaluate and see relations
9. Inability to apply reading to the solution of practical problems
10. Lack of appreciation of literary quality
11. Lack of flexibility in adapting method of reading to the material and to the purpose for which it is read

Faulty eye movements, poor attack on unfamiliar words, lack of interest, and meager background of experience are symptoms or causes of some of the difficulties already mentioned.

FACTORS IN READING DIFFICULTY

Many factors may be involved in any of the above difficulties. These range from specific causes—such as lack of sufficient visual

229

acuity to perceive the printed words—to general, obscurely related personality factors. The conditions most likely to be related to reading will be briefly reviewed. They are treated at length elsewhere (23, pages 307–422).

Defective Vision and Other Physiological Factors.—Defective vision may enter into the complex of causes of reading difficulty. However, not every student who has errors of refraction and muscular imbalance will necessarily be retarded in reading. Dearborn and Anderson pointed out (16, pages 576–577) that

A slight nearsightedness may make it easier for a person to read because he is already focused for near work. Farsightedness is the more grave defect because it requires an exercise of the accommodation for near work which may produce ocular fatigue. The eye defects which most seriously affect the ability to read are those which result in fusion inadequacies.

Aniseikonia (*ana*—a negative; *iso*—equal; *eikon*—image) is a condition of the eyes in which the ocular images are unequal. This condition causes disturbed "interpretation of the positioning of planes and surfaces" and difficulties in fusion, and may be manifested in headaches and other signs of visual discomfort. It may affect reading by producing either ocular or general fatigue, or both, and thereby reducing the student's desire to read and his ability to concentrate. This defect may also interfere with the visual processes during reading, especially with the "peripheral view of the line of print, which is so requisite for the proper spacing of the fixation pauses." Relative size differences of less than 1 per cent are considered negligible, whereas differences of more than 5 per cent may prevent fusion entirely. However, individuals differ widely with respect to the effect of different degrees of aniseikonia on reading (16, page 562).

Dearborn and Anderson concluded from their controlled experiment that there was "a significant relationship between disability in reading and aniseikonia"—a more significant relationship than prevails with other eye defects studied. They believe that "it is a factor to be taken into account in approximately 50 per cent of extreme cases of reading disability," but remind the reader that "severe disability in reading almost always occurs as a consequence of the accumulative influence of many factors, not on the basis of the effect of one alone" (16, page 575).

At present a quantitative relationship between the degree of aniseikonia and the amount of reading disability has not been established. The diagnosis presents difficulty, for special apparatus and highly skilled examiners are required and changes must frequently be made in the size correction of glasses, owing either to difficulty in obtaining accurate measurement or to changes that occur after testing. A great many persons with a size difference may have no symptoms of eye difficulty, while others with a relatively small difference may complain of fatigue while reading, inability to concentrate, headaches, and photophobia. It is probably true that a large percentage of the latter have a psychological or functional rather than a physical or structural basis for their complaints. Individuals strive in a variety of ways to attain their goals. Thus they respond differently to visual defects, some compensating successfully for a defect serious enough to cause marked reading difficulty in a less highly motivated person.

Although we have little evidence that any single physiological factor is positively related to reading ability, it is quite possible that defective vision, hearing loss, and poor motor coordination affect learning in general and help to create conditions out of which reading difficulties arise. For example, even though by dint of effort a student with a visual defect may achieve high scores on a reading test, he may do so with a feeling of strain and discomfort that makes sustained reading distasteful to him—a condition to be avoided whenever possible. In individual cases visual, auditory, and motor defects have been shown to be clearly related to reading efficiency.

Defective hearing may be a factor in reading difficulty in certain cases. However, unless the hearing loss is great or unless the individual has been taught chiefly by phonetic methods, his reading ability may be only slightly affected.

Reading ability is likely to be affected, however, when hearing and visual defects are both present, when either is especially severe, when the child is not able to compensate for them, when the teacher makes no effort to modify instruction so as to minimize these initial handicaps, or when these defects occur in combination with other home and school conditions that interfere with a child's learning to read.

Speech defects and difficulties in pronunciation and enunciation are often associated with reading difficulty. This is to be expected, in view of the close relation among the language arts and the carry-over of self-consciousness, embarrassment, and other concomitants of poor speech to reading situations.

Still less is known of the relation of the endocrine glands to reading development. Mateer (29, pages 80–81) reported a much higher incidence of pituitary deficiencies among a group of poor readers than among a control group. It is probable that certain glandular deficiencies would affect reading, as well as other avenues of learning.

Environmental Conditions.—A number of factors in the home may account for a student's attitude toward and proficiency in reading. If another language is spoken in the home, the child has the problem of mastering two avenues of communication; one is complex enough for the child of average or below-average ability. Suitable, readily accessible books and periodicals and parental attitude toward reading afford a stimulus that may influence reading development. Even more important is the parents' relationship with the child and their interest in his reading. Overconcern on the part of anxious parents has been an important cause of resistance to reading in some cases. In other cases, the child has used his inability to read as a means of expressing his hostility to his parents.

The individual's daily schedule should also be considered. Home duties or remunerative work or social activities may crowd out reading. A student's use of leisure time suggests interests to which reading may contribute. The nature and extent of his voluntary reading comprise an important bit of diagnostic information.

His school history likewise contains clues as to conditions that may have contributed to reading difficulties. Frequent changes of school in the early years, a serious illness that has resulted in loss of reading instruction, and ups and downs in marks from subject to subject and from year to year—all these may be significantly related to reading difficulty in junior or senior high school. Knowledge of the methods of instruction and remedial measures employed in each grade likewise helps to explain subsequent reading problems (22).

Emotional Factors.—It is difficult to distinguish between emotional factors that result from inability to read and those that cause reading difficulty (see pages 60–61). Improvement in reading is not a cure-all for manifold behavior problems. This overemphasis has too often led teachers to refer to reading clinics or remedial reading classes, disciplinary and emotional problems in which the reading deficiency was a minor factor. On the other hand, a neurotic constitution may be a direct cause of reading disability, inasmuch as it makes impossible the sustained effort and cooperation required in learning to read.

Baker and Leland (5) describe certain symptomatic behavior that may indicate emotional disturbance: takes a negativistic attitude toward school, is indifferent, has poor social relations, makes long pauses before words, resists reading. These kinds of behavior are frequently associated with serious retardation in reading. Other writers have presented case studies of poor readers whose emotional tensions seemed to be alleviated when their reading difficulties were partially corrected (9, 12, 25).

Recently there has been perhaps too strong a tendency to assume that emotional factors are causative and to neglect technical analysis of the specific reading disability. Care must be taken not to identify a symptom as the cause of the learning difficulty.

NATURE OF DIAGNOSIS

It is a generally accepted principle that the process of helping a student to reach the reading level appropriate to him should start where the student is. This implies finding out where he is—the process of appraisal, or diagnosis.

Diagnosis is a continuous process, the purpose of which is to guide the individual in his best reading development. It involves a systematic plan for observing the student's growth in all the kinds of reading that he needs to do and for acquiring knowledge of the factors that may be related to his reading ability. His own analysis of his needs and difficulties is an important part of the process.

Different levels of diagnosis should be recognized. These range from the casual observation that a student appears to be nearsighted to the clinical detection of aniseikonia; from a vague realization that a student is having difficulty in reading to an astute analysis of the process by which he gains meaning, enjoyment, and value from printed sources. The procedures outlined in this chapter cover a range from the least to the most technical.

As the causes of reading difficulty are frequently far removed from the symptoms as manifested, all the areas mentioned may need to be explored. This exploration should be a unified, dynamic process rather than a mechanical piecing together of unrelated information. The reading case study should develop in the same way that an artist paints a picture. First he has a vague impression; then he gradually fills in relevant details until the entire picture is clear, complete, and in proper focus.

This process goes on simultaneously with practice and instruction. Some of the most valuable diagnostic information can be obtained by talking casually with the student, observing him at work on practice material, analyzing his responses, and discussing his method with him. Moreover, when diagnosis and remediation are thus fused, the student feels that he is making progress from the beginning, not wasting 3 or 4 hours in purely diagnostic procedure. With this method in mind, the reader will consider the following suggestions not as steps to be taken in chronological order (although in many cases this would be done), but as procedures to use as indicated by the needs of the individual and the resources of the situation.

DIAGNOSTIC PROCEDURES[1]

1. Collecting and interpreting information already available in cumulative personnel records, or other records and reports. Results of standardized tests previously taken should, of course, be obtained (see pages 136–140). By means of standardized tests, fairly reliable measurements of rate, vocabulary, and comprehension can be obtained. Thus students who are low in one or more of these areas can be identified and initial corrective work can be planned before one begins the more detailed diagnosis based on careful observation and further testing during the teaching process.

Results of one or more intelligence tests will frequently be available. For purposes of reading diagnosis, intelligence tests vary in value. Group tests that yield both a linguistic and a quantitative score (2, 11, 13, 18, 34) are of obvious value in differentiating students who have a language handicap from those who are generally low in mental alertness. The Kuhlmann-Anderson Intelligence Tests (28) have been frequently used with reading cases because this series employs less verbal material than do some of the other intelligence tests. It is preferable, however, to use an individual intelligence test, such as the Stanford-Binet for children up to senior high school, and the Wechsler-Bellevue Test for adolescents and adults.

2. Interviewing the student to establish a friendly relation and to give him an idea of the kind of service being offered and of his responsibility for analyzing and improving his present reading ability. In interviews, insight is gained concerning factors important in the particular case as the student talks about symptoms of eyestrain, his inability to recognize words accurately, his interests and experiences, his need for reading, his reading habits, and his reading problem as he sees it. Typical of the reading problem, as many college students see it, is the following statement:

I have to read 100 pages of history a week. I can only read 12 to 15 pages an hour and should read 20. The text is closely packed with facts; the facts are required in order to answer composition-type questions. My reading in English, French, and science is of the same concentrated type.

During the interview equally valuable information may be obtained about the student's attitude toward reading, his speech, his oral vocabulary, and the way his mind works. If interviewing time is limited, or if the student prefers writing to talking, he may be asked

---

[1] For more details see case studies, pp. 310–334.

to write a reading autobiography, tracing his reading development as he remembers it, up to and including the present need for improvement.

3. Referring the student to an approved oculist. Visual defects are indicated by the Snellen test, the Massachusetts Vision Test, the Eames Eye Test, or the Betts tests of visual ability, as well as by observation.

4. Giving an audiometer test, if hearing loss is indicated by observation, and informal hearing tests, such as having the student listen to controlled whispers or the ticking of a watch.

5. Giving an oral reading test.

6. Giving and interpreting additional silent reading tests, as the need is indicated. Informal tests, such as described on pages 121–125 and 180–197, based on a variety of material of the kinds that the student is reading, supply especially valuable diagnostic information and, at the same time, can be used for practice and instruction.

7. Using reading laboratory periods for continuous observation and study of the student's methods of attacking unfamiliar words and of his ability to apply what he has to read to the solution of real problems, to communicate ideas obtained from reading, to sense the author's intent, mood, and purpose, and to use other reading skills that he needs.

EYE-MOVEMENT RECORDS

When a person reads, his eyes move along the line of print in a succession of stops and starts. The stops are called *fixations*. It is during the fixations that the printed word is seen. If the reader is unable to grasp the thought or is puzzled about a particular word, or if his eyes have raced ahead of his thought, his eyes tend to move back over the line. These movements are called *regressions*. The three main considerations, then, in eye movements are the number of pauses, the length or duration of pauses, and the number of regressions. These vary with the ability of the reader, his purpose in reading, and the nature of the material read (35)—in other words, with the "central adaptations required in meeting the demands of various reading situations."

We usually think of eye movements of the poor reader as having a larger number of fixations per line and more regressions than those of the good reader, although a good reader encountering difficult material will manifest these characteristics. The eye movements of the average high-school or college student are excellent when he is reading "The Little Red Hen"; they are good when he is reading an absorbing story; they are fair when he is reading a chapter in a social-studies textbook; and they are very bad when he is reading an article by

Einstein, unless he relinquishes all effort to understand the article, in which case the eye movements are likely to become good again.

Comprehension is the determining factor in the process. If one fails to understand a sentence in a paragraph, it is perfectly natural for him to have regressive movements in an attempt to pick up the thread of the thought. If one encounters a word about which he is in doubt, a confusion period while the word is analyzed is entirely normal. If the reader went blithely ahead, regardless of understanding, he would maintain creditable habits of eye movement but he would also practice indefensible habits of comprehension. Anderson (4), in an excellent summary of this problem, showed that "with increased difficulty of reading material the eye movements approach a pattern peculiar to more immature stages of reading development." Good readers are distinguished by a greater flexibility in eye movements when reading for different purposes.

Photographic records of eye movements have long been used in research laboratories in the diagnostic study of reading ability. Under carefully controlled conditions, the study of eye movements is probably the most precise and scientific of all diagnostic techniques in the field of reading. A record of the number and duration of fixations and the number of regressive movements, when projected on the material read by the student at the time his eye movements were photographed, can be extremely revealing.

Within the last few years, a small portable device for photographing eye movements, known as the Ophthalm-o-graph, has been developed for distribution to schools on a commercial basis (38). It is now being used in diagnosis by a considerable number of schools. It may be a valuable aid to the reading program if the following reservations are kept in mind.

1. It lacks the precision of the laboratory eye-movement camera that has been used for years with much success by such experts as Dearborn, Judd, Buswell, and Gray.

2. There is evidence that each pupil should read at least 250 words while his eye movements are being photographed, instead of just 50 words, the number in the standard exercises for the Ophthalm-o-graph (26).

3. The interpretation of eye-movement records requires technical skill and should be done by one who has had special training and experience in photographing eye movements and using the results.

In general, it is advisable for a school whose budget for reading is limited to spend its money first of all on personnel and on reading materials. The purchase of mechanical equipment should usually be deferred until these more fundamental requirements have been met.

A rough idea of the eye movements of different pupils, which may be sufficient for the purposes of most classroom teachers of reading, can be obtained by using the Pressey Diagnostic Tests in Fundamental Reading Habits.[1] The only materials needed for this work are a small mirror, the appropriate folder of reading selections, a book against which to hold the mirror and the folder, and the pupil's record card. The analysis includes three simple measurements of eye movements, one of vocalization, and one of certain elements in the acquisition of vocabulary. Or one may use a simple, homemade device that has been described by Miles and Segel. This consists of three or four paragraphs of reading material mounted on a cardboard holder with a peephole, $\frac{3}{16}$ inch square, in the center of the cardboard. The observer holds the material close to his eye and watches, through the small hole, the movement of the child's eyes as he reads. It should be admitted, however, that the examiner's eye will miss a number of eye movements that a photographic record would show.

If more precise information about the eye movements of certain very retarded pupils is desired, and if an eye-movement camera is not available at the local school, it would be advisable to consider the possibility of utilizing the services of research centers, clinics, or laboratories in universities. This would not only relieve a person who might be relatively untrained for this type of diagnosis from the necessity of securing reliable records, but would also make it possible for the teacher to obtain expert advice in interpreting the record.

The realization that poor readers have inferior eye-movement habits had led some workers in this field to try to correct reading difficulties by striving to produce regular eye movements. In some instances, inefficient eye movements may contribute to reading difficulty. Occasionally a pupil may reach high school without learning how to move his eyes along the line from left to right or how to make accurate return sweeps to the beginning of the next line. In these cases, mechanical training of eye movements is likely to be of some value.

There can be no real doubt, however, that faulty eye movements are more often a result of inadequate comprehension instead of a cause of poor reading. Expensive machines, such as the metronoscope,[2] when they are used indiscriminately to increase speed of

[1] Public School Publishing Company, Bloomington, Ill.

[2] A rather elaborate mechanical device—a kind of triple-action, synchronized tachistoscope costing about $300, in which a roll of printed material is exposed phrase by phrase until the story is completed and test questions are presented. When the speed is not adjusted to the individual, as in the use of the machine in a

reading, do not cure reading difficulties that are really due to meager vocabulary, inability to recognize words, and to poor comprehension and interpretation.   Some of the simpler tachistoscopic methods, such as flash cards and the flashmeter, are helpful in calling attention to phrase reading and in shaking students out of unnecessarily slow habits of reading.

The reading films made at the University of Chicago and at Harvard University represent the present high point of development of the tachistoscopic method.   Like the metronoscope, the films motivate the student to grasp phrases more quickly than he otherwise would.   When used in a group, they are subject to the same criticism as the metronoscope.   The films, however, permit more flexible and natural phrasing, and the tests of comprehension seem much superior to those prepared for the rolls of the metronoscope.

It is axiomatic in all therapeutic work that one cannot cure a disability by treating a symptom.   When eye movements are symptomatic of reading disability, one cannot improve the reading by applying direct mechanical treatment to the eye movements.   A much better procedure is to make every effort to improve comprehension.   There is much evidence that when comprehension is built up to a satisfactory level for the reading material in question, the eye movements usually take care of themselves.

This is not to say that the metronoscope or the Harvard motion-picture variation of the tachistoscopic method are valueless in corrective reading.   Either one may be a useful device, provided that it is used mainly for training in comprehension and only incidentally for training of motor eye-movement habits.   It has not been established on the basis of research, however, that any of the mechanical devices for presenting material are more effective in a corrective program than are good classroom methods of teaching of reading.

ORAL READING TESTS

The oral reading examination is indispensable to a thorough exploration of a student's reading abilities.   For this reason, it is essential that materials for such an examination should be easily available to the teacher and that methods of administering it and noting students' errors should be made clear to him.

---

group, there is danger of interfering with the established eye movements of students whose rate of reading is faster and whose eye span is wider than the phrases presented in the machine.   Moreover, the phrasing is not always natural, the shutters that go up and down are distracting, and the tests of comprehension are inadequate.

Ideally, an oral reading examination is a series of paragraphs graduated in difficulty from something certainly easy for the student to something certainly hard for him, chosen from the subject matter in which his reading difficulty has arisen. Because of the complex nature of reading, a student may have difficulty in one kind of subject matter and not in another.   Therefore, if it is the history teacher who is concerned about his reading of history, he should be tested in historical material.   Only in this way can his scope of historical vocabulary, his equipment in the general vocabulary of the authors concerned, his grasp of historical sequence, his memory for historical facts, and his ability to understand historical relationships and to generalize from historical data be determined.   Ideally, too, the oral reading examination deals not only with the subject matter in which the reader appears to have difficulty, but also with the kinds of comprehension problem that commonly arise in it.

A homemade test of this kind is likely to be crude; mistakes in gradation of materials are made; teachers may overestimate abilities and have a test actually too hard for the retarded readers in whom they are interested.   Nevertheless, such a test is likely to be closer to the true difficulties and capacities of the students in the subject concerned than any general, commercial test would be.

For the convenience of teachers who find it impossible to give time and study for the construction of their own tests, there are several oral reading tests on the market.   A number of them are suitable for extremely retarded junior-high-school students; but, because of their omission of very difficult passages, these would probably be an improper measure of the more capable students' difficulties or of the more mature students' reading needs.   Among such tests are the Gray Oral Reading Check Tests,[1] which come in four levels of difficulty representative of the reading material in the elementary school.   They have the advantage of coming in five different forms, so that for any one level a teacher might test a student five different times, at intervals during the remedial program, to note his progress.   They have the disadvantage of having been produced before all that is now known of vocabulary control was available to the author for the construction of equivalent forms.   The method for scoring is very comprehensive in its consideration of the reading problem and is easily adapted.

The Jenkins Oral Reading Test[2] contains paragraphs that are more gradual than those in the Gray test, but it is not so difficult in the upper levels and has a scoring method which to those who have used

[1] Public School Publishing Company, Bloomington, Ill.
[2] C. A. Gregory Company, Cincinnati, Ohio.

the Gray test seems very limited. The Gray scoring method, of course, can be used on any material, including the Jenkins test.

The Durrell Oral Reading Test[1] also consists of a series of paragraphs in duplicate form, like the Gray Oral Reading Check Tests, and is accompanied by a very comprehensive diagnostic sheet on which to record the different types of error noted.

The Gray Oral Reading Paragraphs[2] is a series of 10 passages of increasing difficulty. The easiest passages are of elementary-school difficulty, while the hardest are a fair challenge to the retarded reader in college. The scoring is the same as for the Gray Oral Reading Check Tests. It comes in only one form.

When an oral reading test is given, a record should be kept of the number and the nature of the errors. The pupil may read from one copy of a selection while the teacher marks the errors on a duplicate copy. Any uniform method of indicating the errors will suffice. The accompanying code is somewhat similar to the one employed in the Gray test.

Errors	Marking
1. Failure to recognize a whole word	Underline the word
2. Failure to recognize part of a word	Underline the part mispronounced
3. Omissions	Encircle the word or part of the word omitted
4. Insertions	Write in the word or phrase inserted
5. Substitutions	Write the word above the one for which it was substituted
6. Repetitions	Make a wavy line under the part repeated

An application of this plan of indicating errors is given in the following paragraph:

Vancouver

Vancouver is Canada's western port(al) It lies in a sheltered bay at the foot of the high evergreen mountains. It is a modern, progressive city, named in honor of the young naval officer who was the (first) European to visit the landlocked harbor

places   never

where merchant ships from all parts of the world now discharge their cargoes.

The examiner, who sits preferably facing the student, asks him to read the passage aloud. Some examiners preface the reading with the suggestion that the subject read as he ordinarily would; others,

[1] World Book Company, Yonkers-on-Hudson, N.Y.
[2] Public School Publishing Company, Bloomington, Ill.

with the frank remark that they wish to see how well he can read orally. Some students have a preconceived notion that they are to read very rapidly; hence, some examiners warn the subject to read as fast or as slowly as is necessary in order to read his best. The reader's attitude toward the test, and consequently the validity of the score, depend to a great extent upon the examiner's success in putting him at his ease. Preliminary remarks are useful only if they make the reader less nervous and more sure of what he is to do. Each examiner adapts his method to the personalities he encounters.

One certain aid in putting the reader at his ease is to start with material that he is surely able to read. This requires some knowledge of his previous schooling or inquiry into the types of materials he is now accustomed to reading. After the reading of each paragraph or set of material of given difficulty, the student advances to a more difficult piece until, as Gray suggests, his errors exceed eight to a piece. This is an arbitrary number indicating a degree of difficulty beyond which the reading becomes incomprehensible. When a student has trouble with one out of every five or ten words, he is liable to miss the point of almost every sentence. If the student makes as many as eight errors in a given passage, the examiner has considerable evidence of the nature of his reading difficulty.

At the conclusion of the reading of each paragraph or set of material, the examiner asks the student to lay the piece aside and to tell in his own words what he has read. The purpose of this part of the test is to ascertain the extent of his recall and the scope of his comprehension. The difficulty is that, again, the matter of personality intervenes: some students are by nature voluble, while others are taciturn like Calvin Coolidge, who, when asked what the preacher's sermon was about, answered, "Sin." Further questioning evoked the information, "He was agin' it." Questions designed to reveal nothing, but to elicit the ideas that the student remembers, are in order in case of laconic replies. The examiner should then, on his copy of the material in question, make a notation regarding the apparent ability of the student to comprehend and recall. This memorandum should be sufficient to remind the examiner whether the student did or did not give evidence of having grasped the main idea; whether or not he remembered a few important details, only the unimportant ones, or all of them; whether he remembered the last few ideas only, the first few only, or ideas scattered here and there throughout the passage; whether he retained or lost an important sense of sequence; and whether or not he seemed to appreciate the implications of a situation or the facts given.

Some examiners, in asking for recall on the first passage read, intend to let the student know what is to be expected of him in succeeding passages rather than to pass judgment on his comprehension from a first reading, which, because it is first, is perhaps less representative of his natural recall in a natural situation; they take more seriously the recall on the second passage and on subsequent passages, up to the last; recall on the last passage can be so difficult for the student and add so little to what the examiner already knows about the student's ability that some examiners dispense with it. All this seems to be a matter of what an examiner is looking for; if his intention is to see whether the emotional stress of reading difficulty on the last passage will have its effect upon the student's memory of his incorrect reading, recall on the last passage will be useful to him.

The examiner's copies of the passages read should also bear notations with regard to the fluency of the reading. Some people prefer to time the reading and to write the number of seconds that it requires. In the case of a class made up of a mixture of Southern drawl, Maine deliberateness, and the brisk urgency of Eastern cities, one is reluctant to time any student's reading and measure it against norms that have been established by the authors of the test. Even aside from locality, there is so much difference in the rates at which people naturally speak that a time score is scarcely a clear evidence of reading skill. Obviously, someone who stumbles over every other word, repeats words, and pauses before difficult words, has taken more time to read a passage than one who reads it perfectly. Thus the errors record is an indirect record of time consumed. Much more significant than a time score, in the opinion of some examiners, is a note on the page concerning fluency. It may simply say "Word-by-word reading" or "Good phrasing" or "Ignores punctuation," although this last-mentioned item is clear from the record of errors, if the examiner has simply circled the marks of punctuation ignored. Again, this type of notation seems to be more significant in its application to passages read with fair ease than to the last and most difficult passage, which, because of its difficulty, may cause the reader to lapse into a reader's natural response to unusual words—word-by-word reading.

Following the reading and the recall, the examiner sometimes finds it fruitful to ask certain questions about the points of difficulty. Some students make no attempt upon a word which, if put to it, they really can comprehend. Some make substitutions for words which, on second look, they can recognize. It is worth while to know whether the student is really incapable of the kind of analysis that the word requires, whether he is dependent upon leading questions for its solution, whether an omitted word is really well established in his sight vocabulary but has been omitted by reason of carelessness. The leads which the examiner derives from this kind of analysis are invaluable to the subsequent tutoring, for they suggest areas of further investigation as well as remedial procedures.

If the student fails to solve a word beginning with *sh*, for instance, one thing that needs investigation is whether he can recognize other words beginning with *sh*. If he does recognize these words and can solve other unknown words beginning with the same pattern, it is evident that his problem is not *sh*, but something else in the word. If there is trouble with *sh*, perhaps other phonic combinations that are usually taught during the same period of reading development are troublesome. The examiner then looks for such evidence in the oral-reading-test results. He may even find it desirable to take an inventory of the student's ability to produce the correct sound for the commonly occurring and troublesome phonic combinations, or he may wait to take his cues from errors that will reveal themselves later in the remedial work. For another example, suppose that the student has failed to recognize a word because he has not discerned a smaller word in the larger one. There are at least three possibilities: (1) he may not be acquainted with this smaller word, even though it is quite common; (2) he may know it but fail to recognize it when it is embedded in another word or when it takes a particular position, such as the middle of the word; or (3) he may have a general deficiency in respect to noting small words in larger ones and need practice in it.

To discover whether the first possibility is true, the examiner needs only to present the small word in isolation or in a sentence by itself and then to ask its identity. If the second supposition is correct, the student will be able to recognize this word in the first test but will fail to recognize it when it is incorporated in larger words. Presented with a paragraph containing many words composed of small words within larger ones, some of which contain the small word he failed to recognize in the oral test, the student, if his difficulty is with that particular small word in a larger setting, will fail to note that word within the larger ones. Suppose that the word is "some." In the words "something," "winsome," and "handsomely"—words in which "some" occurs in various positions—he may fail to note the small word. If he fails to note the word in only one or two of these, we have a clue to the possibility that he does not attend to the small word when it occurs in a certain position within the larger word. If he generally fails to note the small words in the larger words in the entire paragraph, while he is able to recognize them in isolation following perusal of the paragraph, the suggestion is that his entire method is faulty and that he needs help in this type of word analysis.

Some students find an oral examination very trying and may be hindered in making their response simply by the stress of the moment. A student, asked directly to define a word with which he has had difficulty, may suffer embarrassment that crowds pertinent thinking from his mind. In dealing with such a student it is well for the examiner to remember that he is investigating, not scoring. His attitude may be one of interested inquiry and his questions indirectly productive of the information that he needs. Instead of saying, "Now, let's make sure that you know some of these words," or "Give me this word again," he may, through a fact question, have the student reread the word that he miscalled in the first reading by asking "Will you find and read the sentence that tells what the wolf ate?" If the reading is again "grahamcrackers" instead of "grandmother," the examiner's work is cut out for him. Meanwhile, a deserved compliment, if occasion for it can be found, is reassuring to the insecure and anxious student.

The oral reading test serves also as a situation in which general information can be gained about a student's pursuits and interests: activities that he prefers in his leisure time; motion pictures and radio programs that he likes; his occupational goal (an incidental argument for reading can be inserted here in relation to his chosen field); the parts of the newspaper that he always reads; magazines that he likes and what he likes about them; favorite subjects of study, hobbies, methods of study, and hours for study; his method of remembering something (clue to his preference for a particular avenue of learning —visual, auditory, or motor); the leisure activities of his family and friends (this to determine the incentive to read generated by his environment); his analysis of his reading difficulties, what he thinks may have caused them, and in what kinds of materials they seem to occur most frequently. These pieces of information, casual and subjective, are yet valuable and may be fitted into the general picture of the case as the examiner has derived it from many sources. Participation in the diagnosis, particularly with regard to his self-analysis, will also make the reader feel more like a consultant, less like Queer Duck No. 999.

A similar procedure has been developed with a series of more difficult paragraphs for use with high-school and college students (37). The first and second paragraphs are of about fifth- or sixth-grade level of difficulty, the third paragraph is of about twelfth-grade difficulty, and the fourth paragraph is from John Dewey's *Human Nature and*

Conduct. This range of difficulty and content enables the examiner to see how the student attacks unfamiliar words and how his mind works when confronted with both simple and complex reading.

In addition to the analysis of errors already described and in addition to acute observation of the subject's attitude toward reading, his oral vocabulary, conversational ability, etc., these oral tests afford the examiner a chance to learn much about the subject's thought process in reading. When, after reading the first paragraph, the subjects are asked "What did the author say?" their answers may reveal reading processes ranging from most inadequate to most adequate, which may be summarized as follows:

1. Pronounces words with no attempt to get their meaning, *e.g.*, "I never know what I read aloud."

2. Responds with a vague generalization, *e.g.*, "The flow of the digestive juices."

3. Shows inaccurate comprehension, *e.g.*, "He was guilty, if the rice got wet."

4. Goes off at a tangent, *e.g.*, "The author says you can use the amount of saliva flow to tell whether you are telling the truth."

5. Mistakes an illustration for the main idea, or gives overpotency to a minor point, *e.g.*, "India has a test for guilt."

6. Comprehends an illustration accurately, but does not grasp the main idea that the anecdote illustrates, *e.g.*, "He said you can tell when a man is guilty of a crime by putting rice in his mouth. If the rice gets wet, he isn't guilty, and if it stays dry, he is guilty because he is afraid."

7. Recognizes the main idea of the passage and expresses it in his own words; also reports the illustration accurately, but does not make implicit the connection between the main idea and the illustration, *e.g.*, "The emotions influence the flow of the digestive juices. The test of India is to give a prisoner a handful of dry rice. If he is not afraid, the rice becomes wet from saliva."

8. Recognizes the main idea and shows how it is related to the illustration, *e.g.*, "The author discusses the reaction of fear on digestion. He said that fear can stop the flow of digestive juices. As an example, he described the old custom in India of putting rice in the mouth of a criminal to see whether or not the rice remained dry or became wet. If the rice remained dry, he was judged guilty."

By means of this one simple question the examiner can learn a great deal about the student's methods of reading. He notes whether the student merely snatches unconnected words and phrases as he reads, or whether he grasps relationships; whether he merely memorizes and repeats the author's words, or whether he translates the author's words into his own vocabulary and interprets what the author said accurately and creatively.   The examiner also notes whether the subject fails to report the author's thought because he has been carried away by his own interests or emotions or prejudices, or whether he is using the passage merely as a stimulus to new ideas.   Introspective reports made by the subject immediately following the oral testing throw further light on the subject's reading and thinking process. This is the most important part of the diagnostic procedure, because it helps to answer the question "Why?"   It calls attention to verbalism, defined as mere word calling without real comprehension of meaning; to lack of experience essential for interest and correct interpretation; to unfamiliarity with key words and inability to tease their meaning from the context.

The values of an oral reading test are thus seen to be many: it provides a situation that is better than a formal interview, in that the student's attention is centered on the test and his incidental revelations of personality are less studied; it offers a beginning in diagnosis of reading difficulties and suggests the information about comprehension and vocabulary that must be obtained in a silent reading test; it indicates the attitude that the student has developed toward reading. Evidence on this latter point is meaningful, even though it is as slight as complete refusal to attempt an unknown word or a reckless stab at it, careful repetition of phrases and sentences of which he is unsure, or rushing through material without regard for correctness or meaning. In as short a time as 15 or 20 minutes, in some cases, the examiner will have a wealth of useful suggestions that he could not have obtained in the equivalent time by any other method.   The person who fails to follow the clues of the test and to search for causes of the various errors is forfeiting a valuable means of insight into the student's reading problem.

THE LEARNER'S DIFFICULTIES WITH WORD FORMS

A Psychological Explanation.—Some years ago in his *Passing Parade* series, John Nesbitt offered a movie short entitled *Willie and the Mouse*, in which he gave a remarkably clear, if perhaps misleadingly simple, explanation of children's learning difficulties.   Willie was the school child everybody knows, the one who couldn't learn, and the mouse was Willie's counterpart in white-rat experiments in psychology.

The mouse and a rival mouse were put through a maze in which the cheese goal was clearly visible.   While Mouse No. 1 wandered pleasantly from dead end to dead end, Mouse No. 2 nimbly followed the trails in the direction of the cheese and early gained his reward. Mouse No. 1 was never clear as to what that race had been about.

In the second competition, the cheese was not to be seen, but a warning gong rang every time that the mouse took the wrong path. Again a rival mouse was pitted against Mouse No. 1. The latter ignored the warning sounds and wound up in the most unlikely places, arriving at the goal only to see the last bit of cheese disappear among his rival's whiskers.

By this time, according to this Hollywood production, our hero was a thoroughly disintegrated personality. He moped about with his fur unkempt and his head in his paws. What did life hold for him? Certainly not cheese. Like the child in the classroom who experiences defeat through alien methods of learning, this mouse was manifesting antisocial attitudes; the world was against him.

The third maze was one in which the cheese could be neither seen nor approached by the aid of auditory signals. Its correct paths and blind alleys were to be distinguished by the difference in floor texture, the one type being rough, the other smooth. And Mouse No. 1, like Willie, happened to be a largely kinesthetic learner; his sense of touch told him more than the sight or the sound of anything could. While the rival mouse listened in vain for a warning gong and searched the pathways for the sight of the cheese, Mouse No. 1 followed his feet on the paths of one texture and achieved his golden glory. Likewise Willie, through classroom methods suited to his particular preference in learning apparatus, benefited at last from the teacher's efforts.

John Nesbitt's *Willie and the Mouse* may be too pat an explanation of the avenues through which a child may learn. Only in extreme cases of physical handicap, perhaps, would we find a child devoid of two sense avenues through which he might learn. At the same time, we appreciate the fact that the more senses through which a child may be made aware of the unknown, the more likely he is to become well acquainted with it. We know, for instance, that a child who learns the word "butter" through making butter, tasting butter, feeling butter, seeing it, and saying it, is more likely to retain his impression of the word "butter" in association with the idea of butter than a child who meets it through only one of the possible sense avenues. If John Nesbitt's explanation does oversimplify Willie, it nevertheless makes for deeper appreciation of the fact that the teacher of reading must utilize all the avenues within his power to make associations between ideas and symbols impressive and permanent.

The instruments by which we can determine a child's ability to make his different sense avenues work for him in learning how to read are relatively few. The Monroe Reading Aptitude Tests, which are used to determine the readiness of children for first-grade reading, contain several tests of visual, motor, and auditory skill and discrimination. The author of these tests does not claim that the test results will yield a score to indicate exactly what a child's native ability in the different senses is. Since visual, auditory, and motor discrimination is improvable to a certain extent through practice, it is quite possible that lack of experience of a certain kind would make a child appear on the tests to be inferior in a certain sensory discrimination, which later might be developed beyond the others. But this is beside the point. The point for teachers of reading is that they must utilize the best abilities in a child and all abilities in the child, in order to promote the teaching of reading. It is stupid that a teacher should stress in his teaching a visual approach, for instance, to the exclusion or neglect of an auditory or a motor approach, or even a taste or a smell approach, if children in his class have meager visual discrimination and, at their particular stage of development, cannot profit so well by his use of this method. For this reason it is desirable that a teacher know, within the limits of the test instruments available, just what the status of the child's abilities in sensory discrimination is.

The use of the Monroe Reading Aptitude Tests prior to entrance to first grade often yields interesting information with regard to the teacher's first-grade reading methods. In a heterogeneous class of 40 first-grade children, it has been found by one of the authors that the Monroe Reading Aptitude Tests and the semester-end reading achievement of these children show the stress of the teacher upon the auditory approach to reading. The children who had achieved well by the end of the semester were children who had scored high in the auditory tests, in comparison with the visual and the motor tests. The children who were high on the visual tests, in comparison with the auditory and the motor tests, fared less well; and the children who were high in the motor tests, in comparison with the visual and the auditory tests, fared still less well. This situation has suggested to the author the importance of a teacher's knowing more about the abilities of his children and recognizing those abilities in his teaching, or, at least, if not knowing the abilities of the children, recognizing the importance of many sense avenues in all possible details of his work.

We know that children who have failed by the look-and-say and hear-and-see beginning methods, now learn to read by the kinesthetic method. It is true that some of them might have failed by the kinesthetic method, as well as by the other methods, if this one had been used first; but the uniform tendency throughout the United

States for teachers to stress the look-and-say and hear-and-see methods, to the exclusion of the kinesthetic method, suggests that some of these failures are due to that omission and could have been avoided. Without seeming to throw caution to the winds with regard to the causes of such failure, it is still possible to take precautions in teaching and to avoid casualities while we await the pronouncements by research.

Types of Recognition.—The errors in word recognition observable in an oral reading test reflect the kind of word analysis of which the student is ignorant or which he has failed to apply. If the examiner is unfamiliar with the ways in which a child normally develops methods of work attack, he is likely to generalize regarding word difficulties rather than to see in them individual patterns of reading deficiency. For this reason, it is important for us to preface our discussion of word-form disabilities with a consideration of the way in which a child deals with the forms of words.

The Chinese read vertically down the page; Jewish prayer books are numbered from the back; there is no very good reason for the way most of us do things except that we have started that way and may as well continue. To children, who are new to our world, the fact that one must read across a page from left to right, starting systematically in the upper lefthand corner and proceeding to the bottom of the page, is utterly strange. Yet, because this is the primary fact of reading by our method, it must be mastered if the reader is not to become hopelessly entangled in reversals. Observation of individual words from left to right should be established early as a reading habit.

The first thing that a child is likely to observe about a word is its general shape, the kind of observation we make when the streetcar is still a block away and we can see only the hazy shapes of the words stating its destination. When an adult mistakes a word like "patter" for a word like "yellow," he is probably relying on the first method he ever employed to distinguish words: observation of their general contours, their hills, valleys, and plateaus. An adult has difficulty understanding why a child may be able to learn words of greater length like "telephone" before he can distinguish "bear" from "deer." The fact is that one does what one has to do in this world. A child does not observe a word systematically letter by letter or syllable by syllable until he finds it necessary. He depends upon the length and shape of a word to suggest its identity until he finds that this method is no longer feasible in all cases. He retains this first method all his life, even as a commuter and headline reader, but he supplements it with other more elaborate techniques of word analysis as he finds the need.

Early, as a rule, the new reader finds that the initial letter of a word often suggests its identity. This method of attack may be partially dependent upon another—guessing from context, from the association of other words with the strange one. When in the story the puppy is only one month old and someone says, "See the l_____ puppy!" it is fairly obvious to the child who recognizes the consonant and knows the sound it makes that the puppy is little. So the word "little" is guessed from its initial consonant sound and from the meaning that the situation suggests. Similarly, words with like endings but different initial letters, like "fear," "dear," "tear," are easily dealt with by knowledge of the beginning letter sound. A person who reaches maturity still reading "bent" for "bald" shows dependence upon initial consonant sounds, word length, and perhaps context, for getting the identity of words; incidentally, he demonstrates the inefficiency of the technique. Children who are so intent upon attacking words that they ignore meanings, and other readers who are reading beyond their depth of understanding, will make substitutions of this kind that are utterly meaningless in the context.

When a child encounters such difficulties as the above, he begins to appreciate the importance of noting the endings of words. He enters a world of "word endings"—a rather orderly world, be it gratefully said, in which one does not have to know a thousand different endings to recognize a thousand different words, but may benefit by the common occurrence of suffixes such as *s*, *es*, *ed*, *ing*, *ly*, and the frequency of such a form as *and:* "sand," "band," "land," "demand." In the smaller word forms, knowledge of initial consonant sounds and certain simple word endings serves the young reader well and is, in fact, completely adequate.

But another trouble soon appears in the distinction between "want" and "went," "silver" and "sliver," and other words whose middles make all the difference between sense and nonsense. The reader's new chore is to note the middles as well as the beginnings and endings of words, noting them on his way from left to right across the new territory. Perhaps because this attention to middles comes relatively late in the reader's analytical development, perhaps because the middle of a word is not so frequently distinctive, even adults sometimes manifest a disregard for this type of analysis.

Ultimately the child has a repertory of words and parts of words that he readily recognizes, forms that he does not have to puzzle over but can recognize on sight. This he uses when he encounters strange words. Just as a person in a strange city meets and passes people who remind him in one way or another of some that he knows at home, so the reader, with his treasure of word friends, is reminded of one or another as he meets the stranger. In the word "something" he is likely to see his old friends "some" and "thing"; in the word "breakable," the common verb "break" and the familiar ending "able"; in "aileron," the ending of "fail" and "sail" and "pail" and "mail," combined with the common suffix er and the preposition or adverb "on." These analyses are not always according to Webster, but the important fact is that this method can compass the larger units of a word without dissecting it into single letters that are difficult to reassemble. An adult who has not mastered this technique will be found laboring over a strange word's phonetic parts or spelling the word out, in spite of the presence of larger units that he knows in isolation or in different association.

Phonic observation of a strange word is analyzing it by recognizing and sounding certain familiar units, usually small. It begins with a child's noting that "ball" and "boy" and "big" not only begin with the same letter but start with the same sound; the sight of the letter b evokes the sound that b has when in combination with other letters in a word. It has its antecedents in the kindergarten when rhymes loved and learned draw attention to rhyme endings; and when, in beginning reading, the child learns to know the printed words "Jill" and "hill," and the connection between "ill," the sound, and "ill," the printed form, becomes established.

There are three kinds of trouble for which the phonic approach to word analysis is chiefly criticized: (1) Its emphasis upon units smaller than a syllable tends to slow the reading process so that the reader becomes a word tackler rather than a thinker; the meaning intended by the author through the association of words in the sentence is lost in the vast emptiness between difficult words slowly analyzed. Hence, any teaching of the phonic method has to be offset by other more rapid techniques of word analysis and by much practice in reading easy materials for meaning, unhampered by encounters with difficult words. (2) Logical, adult minds find phonic analysis so attractive in its orderliness that certain school systems have tended to emphasize phonics to the exclusion of other methods. In such systems the expression "word analysis" conveys only one meaning to the teacher of reading—phonic analysis. The result has been the presence in reading clinics throughout the country of children retarded in reading because of their ability to make only one kind of attack on a strange word. The fact is that only about one-third of the words in the common English vocabulary are capable of phonetic analysis, and some of these are not entirely like their appearance in sound but demand a partly visual analysis for familiar parts as well.   (3) In its attention to small units the analysis of the sound of a word may leave the amateur word sleuth with a lot of little parts, which he finds himself incapable of reassembling into a meaningful whole.   In other words, this method requires the blending of isolated sounds to form the syllables it has broken—something like cutting oneself while trying to open a first-aid kit.   The word "slake" can become a monster with "sluh" for a head and an "ake" in its back, if dealt with from a purely phonic standpoint; whereas, if treated to a combination of phonic and visual analysis, it will become the easily sounded letter *s* with the familiar "lake" attached.   This latter attack, heresy to the phonic diehards, is the sensible approach for the retarded reader whom the pure phonic method has left years behind himself in reading achievement.

Syllabication, a method auxiliary to the methods previously described, consists of the temporary division of the strange word into its syllables.   The word "unchangeable," if divided into its pronounceable parts, "un-change-a-ble," is readily recognized as a welding of a common prefix, a common word, and a common suffix.   Children are commonly taught syllabication, often in connection with dictionary study, in the third grade and those above it.   Help in this kind of approach is often needed by students in the subsequent years of schooling.   A student untutored in this respect often reads "active" for "attractive" and writes "iniative" for "initiative."

One looks in vain in the literature on the pedagogy of reading for a word in defense of the spelling method of analyzing a word.   It seems to be the child's effort to attack words systematically, with a yearning toward something as effective as the syllabication approach; but the spelling method falls short of this desired solution, in that it shatters the word into meaningless, unpronounceable minutiae and, worse, gives to those parts sounds that are utterly alien to the sound of the word itself.

With the exception of the last mentioned, all the techniques of word analysis discussed in the foregoing paragraphs have their value to the reader.   Quick observation of general configuration, the first approach a beginning reader makes to a word, is the mainstay of rapid reading.   The more careful, more elaborate techniques learned as the reader encounters difficulties are necessary supplements at times to the quick look at word wholes.   The reader must feel the assurance of this variety of techniques and must be sufficient master of each of them to use one or another or, if need be, a combination of them in the recognition of a single word.   He should always check the proposed meaning of the word against the context, as an index of its correctness; and, in the case of a word strange to his whole experience, he needs the ability to interpret the diacritical marks opposite the word in the dictionary and to select, on the basis of context, the meaning appropriate to the passage he has been reading.

Errors of Recognition.   *Reversals and Inversions.*—A common error in word or phrase recognition in the beginning stages of reading is the reversal of letters or words or of the members of a phrase.   A word like "calm" will become "clam," the *l* and *a* being interchanged; the word "saw" will become "was," the entire word being reversed; or "the little red hen" will become "the red little hen."   Sometimes a reversal such as the above will be complicated by inversion: *p* and *d*, *u* and *n*, *m* and *w*, and the like will be confused.   An adult will make such errors occasionally, but the persistence of these patterns above the primary grades is abnormal.

Various causes have been attributed to these tendencies.   Those who have handled the reading cases of individuals manifesting them have held various theories.   One is that the disability is associated with handedness.   Some people hold with Orton (32) that a mixed dominance (left-eyedness and right-handedness, for instance) or delay in dominance of one or the other hemisphere of the brain is responsible for directional difficulties in reading.   For every exponent of a theory, however, there seems to be an investigator who knows of exceptions to the theory.

A study of the experimental literature dealing with handedness, eyedness, and reversals, which are often cited as evidence of mixed dominance, indicates that unilateral brain dominance may be significant in the case of a few individuals.   There is lack of evidence, however, that it is an important consideration in a reading program designed to meet the needs of all pupils.   For the majority of secondary-school and college students, progress in reading will depend on factors other than the diagnosis and treatment of mixed dominance, handedness, eyedness, and reversals.   Regardless of the theory, all clinical procedures for remediation seem to follow the same general pattern; all advocate a method of teaching reading that forces the issue of direction upon the child, makes him conform to the left-to-right movement.   Fernald's procedure in the case of the little boy who was a mirror writer—simply having him start writing so far over to the left-hand side of his paper that he couldn't possibly write in the wrong direction and stay on the sheet—was refreshing in its common sense and simplicity.   The kinesthetic approach is prominent as a means of correcting reversals.

Whatever the error involved in a reading-disability case, it is important that the tutor direct his energies not to a vague area but to the points of difficulty. If the problem is the confusion of "was" and "saw," his immediate work is to see that the student recognizes the distinctive characters of these two words; his concomitant work is to watch the student's reading for evidences of other errors of this, type. Noting the error "was" for "saw," he should not say, "Oh, reversals!" and then put the student through the gamut of all the reversals that might be made in a lifetime. A tutor should never assume that one ailment implies possession of them all. Neither should he take it for granted that perfect results on an isolated word or phrase drill can be considered certain proof of a cure. Drill should have the constant company of natural reading situations, not only as a check on the effectiveness of the drill but as an insurance policy against the adverse effects of any extreme, such as drill, upon reading experience.

Substitutions.—Substitution of one word for another in a sentence may range from something resembling the correct word in form or meaning to something else that apparently has no relation whatever to that word. Sometimes in an oral reading test a student, as though in horror of hesitation, will say something, anything, for the word that he does not readily recognize. Again, a person trying to solve a word by the spelling method will spell it out carefully under his breath, furrow his brow, and then pounce upon some word—any word—that to his puzzled brain seems a likely space filler. The word need have no resemblance in form to the correct one. In another case, a reader intent upon the content of what he is reading may substitute some other word for the proper one; in his certainty of the direction the thought is taking, he apparently becomes careless of the form of the word and calls it what he is sure that it must be. So "kittens" may replace "cats" "mittens" may be read for "gloves," etc. A student who has read widely with little supervision is liable to make this kind of substitution.

Then there are substitutions that may or may not bear a meaningful relation to the context but that do resemble the correct word in some element of form. "Bath" may become "baby" or "bear," in the case of a reader who attends to the beginning of the word and ignores the ending completely. It may become "ball" to one who notes not only the beginning, but also the general contour of the word. Ignoring the beginning of the word, a student may read "where" for "there." The same kind of error, except that it seems to make a concession to contour, is the confusion of "flown" with "thrown."

Substitution of "man" for "men," "call" for "cell," "salad" for "solid" are evidence of failure to observe the crucial mid-portions of words.

Sometimes word substitutions can be traced to a lack of appreciation of the phonetic possibilities in a letter or a combination of letters, or to ignorance of rules regarding vowels. Many students will call "plumes" "plums," evidencing confusion concerning the formation of the plural of *plum* and disregard of the silent *e*, which causes the *u* to assume the long sound. A student who calls "pail" "pile" is revealing his ignorance of the sound produced by the combination *a-i*. A child whose knowledge of the sounds of *e-a* is limited to words like "fear" will betray himself when "Goldilocks and the Three Bears" turns out to be a story devoid of beverage.

Mispronunciation may result when the student tries a type of word analysis that does not apply, or when he misapplies it. The dictionary is a much safer haven than the rules of phonetics when it comes to a word like "aisle," for instance. "Ache" is perhaps the best spelling for the sound of a sneeze, from the phonetic standpoint. The visual analysis of the word "cathedral" is rather unsatisfactory, since "cat" and "he" do not quite produce the needed result and since "the" (in this particular spot) does not have the *th* sound of the article "the." If the reader uses syllabication, he at least avoids the "cat" mistake.

Even though the syllabication and visual analysis attacks are inadequate for the complete solution of "cathedral," the reader who makes such attacks is likely to arrive at the correct word. The only important reason for his not doing so is ignorance of the meaning of the word. With all the variations in accent, syllabication, and phonetics in the English language, it is unreasonable to expect a person to pronounce a polysyllabic word correctly if the word as an idea and as a sound is foreign to him. If the student makes a good attack on a word that is strange to him—strange, as proved by his discussion of it after the reading—the concern of the teacher is not one of word attack but of vocabulary development. Likewise, if the student makes errors in his reading that are due to stuttering, lisping, speech habits stemming from a foreign background, or any other speech error, the problem is one of speech and not of substitutions in reading.

Except for the conditions described in the above paragraph, substitutions evidenced in oral reading indicate the kind of word analysis of which the reader is incapable. Through them the examiner can obtain clues as to the techniques that the reader has never mastered and can plan a remedial program to fill these particular needs. Again let it be said that a reader who makes substitutions in his reading is not a case of general disability in word recognition and attack, but a person who errs in recognition of certain words for certain reasons and who fails to attack certain words successfully for certain reasons. The particular reasons behind the particular errors are the specific clues to the specific needs of the individual. Any general attack on the problem of substitutions means a dissipation of valuable time and impetus in a remedial program.

Omissions.—The omission of words or parts of words in oral reading is sometimes evidence of hopeless haste over trouble spots, areas in the reading material in which the reader encounters considerable difficulty. It is as though the reader may feel that haste will make errors less noticeable, comprehension easier, guesses more accurate, and the total impression one of smooth, skillful reading. However, bad luck seems to pursue the poor reader. Unlike the skillful reader, he omits important words and portions of words and sometimes even fails to note crucial marks of punctuation. If the material is really suitable to one of his age and intelligence and background, an inferior sight vocabulary may be an important cause of the omissions. Proof of this cause may be obtained by taking inventory of the words for which he makes erroneous substitutions and by requesting that the reader review the omitted words to see how many he really knows.

Omissions sometimes occur when the reader is trying to rectify a previous error; miscalling one word, he may omit and miscall subsequent words in an attempt to make sense out of the nonsense that he has started. After the first error, he seems to see only what he wishes to see, what will fit in with his idea of the author's meaning. By checking over the words with him, the examiner can soon tell which words were really unknown and which were known but ignored or miscalled in the emergency.

A reader may be careless because accurate reading is not often required of him; because he is quite retarded and impatient of laborious, careful reading; because he is characteristically a careless person of low standards who is not sufficiently motivated to exert himself; because, having poor comprehension, he has little cause to know or care about his errors; or because his eyes, traveling ahead of his voice, center his interest on certain words and cause the lagging voice to omit others because of inaccuracy of memory and lack of concentration on them. The careless reader not only omits words but distorts them, omitting their endings, as in the case of "runs," "run"; omitting their beginnings, as in "attraction," "action"; and neglecting their mid-portions, as in "fastened," "fasted."

We know that the rapid, efficient silent reader does not fixate upon all the words in a given piece of material but, by a keen knowledge of structure and of crucial words, is able to select centers of importance for his attention. Such a reader may not have had sufficient experience with oral reading or sufficiently high standards in that skill to read an author's work with utter faithfulness. While inaccurate reading is not to be condoned, it should be pointed out that the omissions that a skillful silent reader may make in oral reading are not of so serious a nature as are the errors of the poor reader.

The primary work of the examiner in the case of omissions is to have the student return to the words omitted or shortened, to discover whether he knows them or can attack them. The result of this investigation will be knowledge of the student's need, whether that be an enlarged sight vocabulary, improved word attack, a higher personal standard of accuracy, more frequent experiences in prepared oral reading, or special attention to the meaning of what he reads. On the basis of the particular need, the remedial program can be planned.

Repetitions.—A common failing among poor readers is the repetition of words, phrases, and even sentences in oral reading. Ophthalmo-graph records show a similar failing in silent reading where the eyes retrace their progress across a line of print, the movement known as a regression. The repetition in oral reading may be a reflection of this ocular regression and is to be criticized for the same reason—it wastes reading time.

Actually there may occasionally be good reason for regressions. Skillful readers who are reading material strange in vocabulary and structure or difficult in concept sometimes pause to repeat certain passages, phrases, or words. We all are capable of labored reading and occasional repetition if the material is difficult enough. The problem of repetition is important only when it occurs in material that is supposedly suited to the reader's stage of development.

Thus, repetitions may indicate a temporary loss in the train of thought or a desire to make sure of an idea that has been stated. They may, however, be the result of a habit developed from over-experience with difficult materials; the reader becomes a professional weaver. Further, they may stem from concern for the next word, a kind of marking time until the following word is solved. In the expression "the big eagle" a child may read, "the big—big—eagle," hesitating on the "big" and more or less entertaining his audience with that word until he makes sure of the identity of the word "eagle." This kind of repetition is not fundamentally a habit of regression but a problem in sight vocabulary and word attack.

A type of repetition that is not really a reading problem is caused by nervousness over public reading. A child who was referred to a certain reading clinic read perfectly for the examiner, worked well in the small class and in the tutoring periods, improved as much as could be expected of her mentality and background, and returned to school, only to be referred again to the clinic. Her oral-reading problem was a problem in terror of the teacher and embarrassment before a large class. Her first reading for the clinician, whose business was to put children at ease, gave no clue to the disabilities that she had manifested in the school from which she had been sent. The security she needed could be given only by the teacher and the situation that had denied it.

Failure to Try to Pronounce a Word.—A poor reader encounters words that he does not readily recognize, can solve only partially, or cannot solve at all; in such cases he may halt, look hard, scratch his ear, clear his throat, by utterance or attitude indicating intense concentration on an impossible situation. The result is usually a respectful pause, a look at the examiner, who may furnish the word, and continuation of the reading.

In some cases, the reader feels completely cowed by a strange word. Long experience with inadequate word attack has discouraged him; so, when he comes to the hard word, he will simply stop dead, whether he is reading silently or orally. The reader who has been taught that guessing from context is a sin will make no attempt to determine its identity other than a futile pause for analysis of the word itself. Likewise, a reader whose reading has become a system of word calling, through too much difficult reading, attacks each word without context clue to its meaning. Thus, in the case of the reader who lacks confidence, the problem is to find out what he does know about word attack and to help fill out his sight vocabulary and his techniques of solving strange words; with him it is also a matter of building confidence through much easy reading. Readers who fail to use context clues to assist recognition of words should be given experience in the use of clues, as well as help in word recognition and attack. Readers whose attention is obviously not on the content of what they are reading, and who hence make no use of the context to suggest the identity of the strange word, need an emphasis upon comprehension of what they read.

If, however, the reader does make some partial attack upon the word, whether he gives the wrong sound to an initial *c* or makes an adequate attack upon the first syllable, the examiner should be careful to note it. Any attack whatever is evidence of what the reader does know or what he knows incorrectly. It is the starting point of an investigation of that word and of words resembling it, to find out where the trouble lies and what is the extent of the deficiency. Sometimes the difficulty is not inadequacy of techniques but lack of independence in the use of them. Encouraged by a few pointed questions from the examiner, such as, Do you see any words that you know in this word? or How would you divide this word into syllables? the student may be perfectly capable of solving the word, and the remedial work can be built to cultivate this independence.

Insertions.—An enjoyable deficiency, from the examiner's point of view—if any deficiency may be called enjoyable—is the insertion of words, an embroidering of the author's ideas. In its most attractive form it is found in the young reader who takes "the old lion" and makes of him "the great big hungry old lion." In oral reading, the evidence of ornamentation is right in the words of the child; in silent reading it is to be found in the child's interpretation of what he has read. This tendency as an evidence of keen appreciation of the material read is certainly to be cherished; in the extreme, however, where the child takes over and roves far from the author's wildest dreams, it is not the best exercise for comprehension. Besides, a standard of accuracy is, of course, desirable in oral reading.

Sometimes, as in the case of omissions, the insertion is merely a by-product of a previous error. The reader makes one mistake and then, in the interest of sense, adds and subtracts and modifies subsequent words. The problem is one of standards of oral reading or reading accuracy, as well as of improved word recognition and attack.

Much unsupervised silent reading and little check on accuracy will lead to a number of bad habits, of which insertion is one. The reader may become not only careless but unaware of his carelessness. To make the reader conscious of his error and to provide motive and experience for improvement are the remedial tasks.

Word-by-word Reading.—Word-by-word reading is the dead-level utterance of one word after another, with no grouping of words closely associated, such as words in a prepositional phrase; the spacing of the words in time is either uniform, without regard for meaning, or in violation of it. It may also be characterized by long pauses between certain words. Eye-movement records of word-by-word readers show numerous fixations on every line of print.

Phrased reading, which is characteristic of the skillful reader, is, on the other hand, reading in which words are grouped in time and read expressively to give to the listener a valid and vivid picture of the author's intent. Eye-movement records of phrased reading show fewer fixations per line of print. The advantage of phrased reading over word-by-word reading is that orally it does give the material in a more attractive and understandable form to the listener, and silently it takes less time, fewer fixations being made and more words being accounted for in each fixation.

We are all word readers when we encounter material much too difficult for us. In the case of the poor reader, material that should be suitable for him may be read word by word because of a meager sight vocabulary, the presence of words that he does not readily recognize. Encountering a strange word, he may be so inexperienced in independent word attack or so poorly equipped for it that he will read haltingly. These are problems in sight vocabulary and word solving.

Fairly good readers may retain a tendency toward word-by-word reading. In their early training they may have been urged along with reading matter very difficult for them and have become rooted in the habit of reading as though in difficulty. Sometimes word-by-word readers have been developed simply because that kind of oral reading was tolerated; because no standard, no feeling for the audience situation or the drama of the piece had been created. Sometimes embarrassment or timidity has driven all other feeling out of the oral reader.

Another cause for word-by-word reading is the lack of knowledge of or attention to punctuation marks. This, too, is a matter of emphasis and training.

If a student has had little experience in silent reading for the sake of comprehension, or if in oral reading he is made to give no account of the meaning of what he has read, he may read in a word-by-word fashion; he may fail to think of meaning as he reads. If too he is unfamiliar with the ideas expressed in the material, he may show the same tendency to read monotonously with no regard for meaning, or to read with expression that reveals his lack of understanding.

In order to determine which of several reasons may be the cause for word-by-word reading, the examiner should make use of information on previous schooling, the student's own account of his reading habits, and the student's explanation of the meaning of the material read.

Remedial Procedures for Errors in Word Recognition.—If the following suggestions for remedial work were bottled in a pharmacy, the pharmacist would surely label them "Poison: to be taken only as prescribed by physician." In all of living there seems to be a necessary balance; too much of any one thing leads to trouble. The physician who continues to administer his medicines without regard to their results is liable to find his patient supplanted by an X to mark the spot; the patient who swallows sixteen pills at once when the doctor has said to take two daily for eight days—well, poor fellow! Similarly, in a program of reading, any technique used to an extreme extent is harmful. In many cases, resistance to reading has been created or increased by drills applied by too persistent parents or teachers.

The three primary bases for deciding upon a remedial procedure are the kind of error made, the apparent reason or reasons for its being made, and the kind of person with whom we are working. We have discussed at length the common causes for various types of errors of word recognition, the oral reading test by which we may discover the student's typical errors, and the experimental method of deduction to determine which of several reasons may account for the error in each case. Before assigning a remedial task to the student, however, we have yet to consider the kind of person he is.

Considering his attention span and his physical condition, how long can we expect to confine him to a given task? Considering his interests, his level of reading ability, and his need for specific types of reading experience, what kinds of subject matter can we safely assign him? Considering his temperament and reliability, should his tasks be supervised or trusted to his own responsibility for their completion? Considering his mental ability, how concrete and how gradual must be the development of any unit of learning? Considering his will to achieve in reading, is his motivation adequate or need it be supplemented by the artificial stimuli of scorekeeping, testing, booklisting, the reading of prepared passages to a group, and other means of recognition? Considering his faith in our ability to improve his reading, does he need to be impressed by the use of the gadgetry of reading, such as the flashmeter, the metronoscope, and other devices whose mechanical nature inspires awe and gives objective evidence of improvement? Considering his whole constellation of difficulties, are there certain procedures for the elimination of one type of error that we should avoid using because of their detrimental effect with regard to another type of error? Considering his history of reading failure and the extent to which he associates that failure with certain materials and types of reading approach, do we need to start our reading program with an entirely new procedure, making a complete break with his past?   Considering his preferences for a visual, auditory, or kinaesthetic approach to learning, what devices may be used that emphasize his preferences or what devices can be so altered as to admit of their use?   These are some of the most crucial questions to be answered before the tutor decides upon a remedial program. None of them can be safely ignored.

Methods of identifying the best avenues of learning for an individual student vary.   It is usually fruitful to explore his previous school and home history, to note preferred activities and kinds of endeavor in which he has excelled, and to analyze these for their requirements of visual, auditory, or motor skill.   Dr. Marion Monroe's Reading Aptitude Tests (30) are so designed as to yield separate scores in these three aptitudes, so that the preference is clearly seen.   In her book *Remedial Techniques in Basic School Subjects* (19), Dr. Grace Fernald describes her method of approach to reading-clinic cases at the University of California as an exploration of visual, auditory, and kinesthetic associations with word symbols until the student's preference is clearly demonstrated by his success in learning word symbols through one or more of these avenues.

Sometimes a knowledge of the way in which the subject has been taught in school suggests the approach that has been ignored or slighted as the one most likely to produce results.   Schools that confine their early reading methods to comparisons of pictures and word forms (picture of a cat and printed symbol "cat") are favoring visual learners and penalizing auditory and kinesthetic learners.   Students who experienced long sieges of measles, chicken pox, mumps, and the like in the first or second grade at the time when their particular school systems were stressing phonics (saying "cat" and hearing "cat" at sight of the symbol "cat"; learning sounds to be associated with certain letters and letter combinations such as hard and soft *c*, the vowels long and short, and *sh*) may have difficulties, later, that stem from an ignorance of the sound facts about words.   Most schools have done little with the kinesthetic approach (tracing a word with the forefinger as one pronounces it by syllables), a fact which may have some bearing upon the large proportion of extremely retarded readers who have been found to benefit by that method.

Ideally, a remedial program should stress the phases of reading in which the individual is deficient, but it should not stress them to the exclusion of other aspects of reading that are essential to balance and natural development.   A remedial program may well be a combination of all aspects of reading.   Word or phrase drill, if it is necessary, should be only a matter of 5 or 10 minutes in the tutoring period, and should be supplemented, generally speaking, by some oral reading of a prepared passage, some comprehension exercise in silent reading, some speed drill with a comprehension check. Beyond this, it is desirable that the student have a diet of wide easy reading, outside the tutoring period, as well as experience with more challenging material during the period itself. In other words, the tutoring period should be varied, the techniques used should be varied, and every gain that drill may effect must be measured by success in normal reading situations.

Finally, we must remember that any remedial procedure is productive of certain new knowledge, certain new clues to the difficulties that beset the student and retard his progress. As we plan the remedial program with the student's help, we must not lay down so hard and fast a procedure that it cannot be altered, as new experiences with the student reveal different needs. The initial oral reading test does not reveal everything; we must constantly take cues from our experience with the student to sense new directions for our work. Only in this way can we make the most of our time and of the student's energy.

In addition to these suggestions for remedial work in general, specific exercises and procedures for correcting each type of word-recognition error will be helpful.

In Case of Reversals.—First, make sure what kind of reversal it is (letter, word, or phrase—"bran" for "barn," "saw" for "was," or "red little schoolhouse" for "little red schoolhouse." Then encourage appropriate sequence in the following drills:

1. Emphasize left-to-right attack in everything that the student does.
2. Have the student slide his finger over the letters of the word or phrase to get a kinesthetic impression of the sequence.
3. Have the student trace the form of the word printed or written large on a card, saying the word in syllables as he traces; then have him remove the card from sight and write the word from memory (19, Chap. 5).
4. If the student continues to copy the word backwards, have him begin, as Fernald suggests in the case of a mirror reader, at the extreme left-hand side of the paper, so that he cannot possibly write in the wrong direction.
5. Give exercise in the use of a dictionary, which involves awareness of the letter-by-letter sequence.
6. Give experience in the use of the typewriter.
7. Have the student make his own dictionary of newly learned words.
8. Give completion sentences in which the proper word must be inserted: He fed the cows in the _____ (bran, barn).
9. Have the student write sentences using the words that are confused, or make a point of using the words in their other written work.

10. Make completion rhymes:

> Give the bucket a tilt
> And the milk will be _____
>   (split, spilt).

11. Make flash cards of the words that have been confused.

In Case of Substitutions.—If the substitution has been a wild guess, with no bearing on the form of the word or the meaning in the sentence, the student needs exercise in word recognition and word analysis and in attention to the meanings of sentences (comprehension exercise).

If the substitution is a context guess, the student needs exercise in word recognition and word analysis.

If the substitution is partially correct, there is need for stress on the parts that the student was not successful in recognizing or analyzing. These parts may be the endings, middles, or beginnings of words; they may be certain phonic combinations (*ai, ea, ch, ing*); they may be a matter of visual analysis (seeing the "sat" and "in" in "satin"); they may be a matter of syllables that the student has skipped ("action" for "attraction"), and there may be a need for attack on words through division into syllables (practice known words until technique is acquired; then attack unknown words).

If the student made a substitution because he did not know the meaning of the word (ask him what it means), and because he did not know how to attack it, the problem is one of word recognition and word analysis, but primarily it is one of teaching him the meaning of the strange word.

If the substitution is a reflection of a speech difficulty, such as the substitution of *th* for *s*, *l* for *r* (check by engaging the student in conversation and seeing whether he makes such substitutions normally), the problem is one of speech correction and not corrective reading.

For improved *word recognition*, try some of the following:

1. Make flash cards of the words confused and of other words involving the same issue (such as words beginning with *b* and *k*). For a single student, the flash cards may be of calling-card size with the word printed in the size he normally encounters in the books he can read. For a whole class, the cards should accommodate larger print, with about 2-in. capital letters and 1-in. lower-case letters.

2. Make lists of the confused words, to be used only once or twice, the student reading them in sequence. If the lists are used often, the student tends to anticipate the words by their positions in the list rather than by their appearance.

3. If the word is common, introduce it into the spelling lesson.

4. Use the Fernald method of seeing the word, hearing it, saying it in syllables while tracing it with the forefinger, then writing and saying it while the copy is out of sight, then filing the card on which it is printed in a filing system of newly acquired words arranged in alphabetical order.

The above suggestions all represent word-recognition exercise through isolated word drill. The following suggestions involve thought settings, sentences in which the words are planted for recognition in a more normal environment.

5. For word beginnings, middles, or endings, make sentences in which the critical word must be completed:

> It was a beauti_____ day in May.
> The birds were sing_____.

6. Make completion sentences in which the word is to be inserted: He cut the roast with a _____ knife.

7. Give multiple-choice sentences in which the proper word is to be selected:

> He cut the roast with a curling knife.
> carving
> canning
> curving

8. Make rhymes that are to be completed with the troublesome word:

> The little dog sat by the road on the curb
> For the sign on the door had said, "Do not _____."

9. Have the student make sentences illustrating the troublesome word.

10. Have the student read aloud some prepared passages containing troublesome words.

For improved *word analysis*, the specific treatment depends upon the kind of analysis that the student is unable to do, but, in general,

1. Have the student develop lists of words bearing the characteristic that he has found difficult:

> a phonic feature such as *ai, ea, ch,* or
> a visual feature such as *ight, able, take,* or
> a common prefix such as *un, in, pre, per,* or
> a common suffix such as *ing, ible, ant, ent, ly*

Let each list start with a word he knows well, so that it will be a clue to the phonic solution, the visual solution of the other words as he meets them and adds them to his list.

2. After the student has read some material through successfully, have him skim through it to circle or underline the parts of words of which he is making a special study: all the *ate*'s, the *ing*'s, the *pre*'s, etc.

3. If the difficulty seems to come in attacking longer words, have the student practice syllabizing such words, beginning with words he knows well.

4. Have the student use the dictionary to improve his familiarity with prefixes, suffixes, and roots, with syllabizing, and with the pronunciation symbols.

5. Have the student make his own dictionary, thus to gain an appreciation of the likenesses and the differences in words.

6. After the student has seemed to gain mastery of certain elements of word attack through certain words, test his ability in analysis through flash cards and through sentences containing the difficult words. Actually, his success in this exercise will be chiefly on a recognition rather than on an analytical level. For certain proof that he knows the element that caused him trouble, he must demonstrate his attack on strange words all of whose parts are familiar to him with the exception of the element to be tested.

In Case of Omissions.—Having the student reread the passage in which an omission has been made, the examiner can tell whether the omission was a matter of carelessness or a matter of ignorance of the word. If the word is omitted this second time, the examiner should point it out and ask to have it read.

If the student cannot attack the word and if it is a very common word, the remedial work should include the word-recognition exercises suggested in the section, In Case of Substitutions. If the word itself is not very common, although the elements of it are, the teacher should use the exercises for improving word attack suggested under the same heading.

If the error was a temporary adjustment to rectify a previous error, the previously miscalled word should be treated as suggested in the sentences immediately preceding. If the error has been simply a matter of carelessness (*i.e.*, the student, rereading carefully, shows capacity to read the passage correctly), the following steps may be taken:

1. Have the student read prepared, short passages when the incentive for good performance is high: for instance, it may be a special report before the class, the parents, or the assembly; he alone in the class may have a piece of information of high importance from a reference book; a record may be kept of the excellence of his reading at frequent intervals and this, in itself, may be an artificial but potent incentive.

2. Have the student read silently to answer detail questions which, if possible, concern the kind of word he seems to ignore. For instance, if he

tends to miscall prepositions, the question may require the reproduction of an entire phrase.

3. Have the student or the class set up standards of oral reading and make a conscious effort to progress with regard to them.

In Case of Repetitions.—The examiner should see whether the student has made repetitions in the easier passages he has read and, if so, whether he can read easily the word that immediately follows each repetition. If he is unable to read these words easily and has to sound them out or fails utterly to identify them, the problem is probably one of word recognition and word analysis (see In Case of Substitutions).

If the student stutters or stammers and if the pattern of repetitions seems to reflect this speech defect, the problem is probably one of speech correction rather than of reading.

If the student makes repetitions when he is reading material in which he knows every word, the case is one of habitual repetition, for which the following may profitably be done.

1. Give the student easier material than that which he has been reading, material in which he is at ease with the vocabulary and the concepts, and which has high interest value for him. Have the student read this easy, interesting material silently for main ideas of chapters or general outline of plot.

2. Give the student opportunities to read aloud, chorally with a group, material easy for him. Emphasize phrasing, grouping of words into thought units.

3. In the entire reading program of the student, emphasize the easy, interesting, rapid silent reading with correspondingly less emphasis on material more challenging in word and thought analysis.

4. Have the student read an interesting account of something that he already knows well, so that the easy vocabulary will be accompanied by thoroughly familiar concepts, thus building up his confidence.

5. Give the student the opportunity of reading orally a short, prepared passage from easy, interesting material: let him read a part that he likes to the class or to the tutor. Emphasize smooth, phrased reading.

6. After the student has read a passage of difficult material and has become acquainted with all the words, have him practice (*a*) reading it silently in a short time and (*b*) reading it orally with smooth phrasing.

If the repetition occurs but seldom and then only in rather involved passages (longer sentences, harder ideas), it may be due to temporary loss of thought and an attempt to recapture the picture of the whole sentence through repeating a part of it. In this case,

1. Give the student experiences in easier material to offset what may become a habit.

2. Have him skim a passage to identify hard words, solve them, and then read for the meaning.

3. Prepare the student in hard, new ideas before he encounters them in his reading.

4. Give the student a better knowledge of the ways sentences that puzzle him are put together.

5. Give the student a progressive diet of sentences increasingly long and ideas increasingly hard. He is perhaps at the present time reading above the point where he should start.

In Case of No Attempt to Understand a Word.—The examiner should determine why the student made no attempt on the word. He can do this by returning to the word and asking the student to tell him what it is. If the student can make no attack upon the word at all, the problem is one of word recognition (in case of words that the examiner believes should be in the student's sight vocabulary) and word analysis.

1. For inadequate sight vocabulary, use the word-recognition suggestions in the section, In Case of Substitutions.

2. For inadequate word analysis, use the techniques suggested under *word analysis* in the section, In Case of Substitutions.

If the student can make a partial but inadequate attack in solving the words that he did not attempt,

1. Note the kind of attack that he does not know, and explore the extent of his lack. (For instance, if he misses the sound of *ch*, see whether he knows other important sound combinations.) Then give him exercises such as those suggested under *word analysis* in the section, In Case of Substitutions, to correct the difficulty, whatever it may be: observation of the word form from left to right, underlining familiar parts, sounding large units, syllabizing, spacing parts of the word, and, in as many ways as possible, drawing attention to the features of the word that make it distinctive.

If the student can solve all the words when he is prompted, the suggestion is that he lacks confidence or independence in word attack. In this case,

1. Give him drills on words that demonstrate the same characteristic but that are known to him. More and more, require him to solve words without help, complimenting him with a kind of "I knew you could do it" bolstering.

2. Prepare him for attack upon difficult words in his reading material, so that he will seldom experience failure.

3. Let him keep lists of the types of words solved, so that he can compare

these with new, hard words and feel that he knows an increasing amount about word solving.

4. Have him keep in a convenient place a list of questions or things to do in tackling a strange word, so that he will realize his power and versatility and will not stop trying when one kind of word analysis fails.

If the student attacks a word with all the necessary tools but fails of its solution because the word presents too many alternatives, there are only two possible solutions: the use of the dictionary and the use of the context (rest of the sentence) as a clue to the meaning of the word. There are seven most common types of context clue that the student should learn to use. They are

1. *Definition.*—In this case the unknown word is defined elsewhere in the passage; for example, "After they had crossed the mountains, they flew over a _____. This part of the land was very dry, for a _____ does not have much rain. There were no creeks or rivers, and the soil was dry dust and sand."[1] In this passage, the lack of rain, absence of rivers, and presence of dusty, sandy soil suggest the desert. They *define* the situation.

2. *Experience.*—Here the unknown is predictable from what the student knows of such situations through book or life experience; for example, "No one knows just how _____ and man became friends. At one time the _____ was as wild and as fierce as all the other beasts." Anyone who knows that dog and man are good companions will find this clue easily. (A third grader responding to this item, however, thought best to fill the blank with the word "woman.")

3. *Comparison and Contrast.*—The unknown here is likened to or contrasted with something known; for example, "Eskimos have _____ing eyes like those of the Chinese people." This item, too, of course, requires experience; but here a comparison is offered that yields the word "slanting."

4. *Synonym.*—This type of clue is a known synonym for the unknown word. The structure of the sentence is such that the author gives us the unknown word where we would expect the synonym to be repeated; for example, "When Jim heard that his bicycle would be ready that evening, he was _____. He was glad that he would have it in time for the trip with Tom the next day." The word "glad" stands in the same relative position as the missing word "delighted."

5. *Familiar Expression or Language Experience.*—This clue requires an acquaintance with common language patterns—expressions heard every day and easily anticipated before they are completed by the speaker. In this case, however, a strange word is substituted for one of the familiar ones; for example, "She laughed and said, 'We thought we had a _____ on you, but the _____ was on us, instead.'" No matter what word is substituted for "joke," we know what to expect in meaning.

[1] The illustrations of context clues are paraphrased from widely used intermediate-grade texts.

6. *Summary.*—Here the unknown word summarizes the several ideas that have preceded it; for example, "His knees shook and his eyes seemed to pop as he looked all around, for he was very much _____." If our knees shook and our eyes popped and we looked all around, we should realize that we were frightened. Those three facts would convince us.

7. *Reflection of a Mood or a Situation.*—Here the context has provided a situation or established a mood or a tone, and the unknown word reflects that kind of situation or that kind of mood; for example, "He hopped and skipped and danced about and whistled _____ly to himself." He sounds gay, and the way he whistled is bound to reflect this mood. The missing word must be "gaily" or something close to it in meaning.

With regard to context-clue analysis,

1. Give the student an examination in filling in blanks for different kinds of clues and find out by this means the clues that he fails to grasp. Then plan a program of practice for him.

2. Have him study with you passages containing words that baffle him and containing clues for their solution. If he can solve the word through observation of the context, have him tell in his own words what kind of clue it was that helped him. Have him keep a list of passages representing this kind of clue.

3. Give him passages containing blanks for the new words that he is to encounter, and have him determine the meaning and build the unfamiliar concept through context analysis.

4. Have him make up passages of his own, revealing the meanings of a new word that he has learned and illustrating different kinds of clues.

In Case of Insertions.—The examiner should notice whether the insertion follows an error in word recognition and serves to make sense out of the nonsense that the error has created. If so, the problem is one of correcting the difficulty in the previous word. If, however, the insertion is an imaginative elaboration of the text, without reference to a previous error, the student needs correction, lest he mistake his own interpretation for the words of the author. In this case,

1. Have the student answer questions on his silent reading that require the exact reproduction of certain phrases.

2. Give the student exercise in reading flashed phrase and sentence cards, duplicating and patterning after the phrases and sentences he has misread.

3. Have the student read to answer questions that draw attention to specific details: "Did the author say the lion was old? Prove your answer."

4. Give exercise in prepared, accurate oral reading in radio broadcasts, assembly programs, club meetings, special reports, where pride is involved. Have a little carefully prepared oral reading instead of such mediocre, inaccurate reading.

5. Have the student read a passage, then write down the details that he recalls, then check to see for himself what insertions he has made that the author did not give in the passage.

In Case of Word-by-word Reading.—The usual causes of word-by-word reading are several: inadequate sight vocabulary; inadequate word analysis; inadequate experience to meet the words and ideas of the author; inadequate concentration and maturity to follow an author's complicated style; embarrassment in the presence of the examiner or the class, so that word calling takes the place of thoughtful reading; and a deep-seated habit of word-by-word reading fostered by years of encountering too hard material and practiced without regard to the ease or the difficulty of the passage that is being read for the examiner. If the student has had to figure out each word as he has read along, the problem is one of sight vocabulary; if he has had to figure out each word and has been poor at doing so, the problem is one of word analysis; in either case, see the proper heading in the section, In Case of Substitutions.

If the student reads easier passages fluently but lapses into word-by-word reading with more profound material, attacks the words easily but reads without expression, and, on questioning, shows that he does not understand what he has read, the examiner should

1. Ask the student the meaning of certain key words, to see whether the weakness is a matter of concepts. If it is and if this is the type of material that he is having to read in classes, the job is one of anticipating new, hard words in the material, having him skim to help find them, and having him develop a personal system of finding the meanings of the words through the dictionary or through context; giving him illustrative material and having him make illustrative material to give greater vitality to the subjects about which he reads; and having him read about the same subject in a textbook that develops the new ideas more concretely and gradually, before he attempts to understand any lesson in the difficult textbook.

2. Find whether the student knows all the difficult words but has trouble understanding the long, involved passages and complicated structure of the author's style. If so, have the student take an easier text to read on the subject before he attempts to read the harder book. Have him take the complicated sentences, piece by piece, tell what each part means, and gradually piece the entire meaning together. If he knows sentence structure, have him do this by finding subject and predicate, expressing their meaning in his own words, and then adding, phrase by phrase and modifier by modifier, the meanings in his own words. When he has finished with such a sentence and knows what it means, have him read over the sentence silently and then aloud, showing by his voice the grouping and the meaning of ideas.

If the student appears to suffer embarrassment in oral reading and if no other cause seems responsible for his inexpressive reading, try to create more informality in the situations in which he must read aloud and give him more opportunities of this sort.   See to it that he is never asked to read without having prepared the material silently first.

If the student reads all material, regardless of ease, in a monotonous, word-by-word fashion; and if it is apparent that his reading experience has consisted of books too hard for him, among groups of children who were always ahead of him and always better, so that he has been dragged by the hair through continuously hard reading situations,

1. Use easier material than the silent-reading test score indicates.   If his ability is seventh grade, according to a standardized test, give him mature reading of sixth-grade difficulty.

2. Give him easier reading material that is highly interesting to him; if it is fiction, it should have a good, clear, exciting plot.

3. Give the student experiences in choral reading with the class, with emphasis on expressive phrasing.

4. Have the student read parts in book conversation, in which he must express emotion and carry the feeling and personality of the character with his voice.   Before he tries it, have him describe how the character would say it.   Let him try it privately before trying it publicly.

5. Emphasize much easy, interesting, silent reading, with little oral reading except in cases in which expression is paramount and preparation is careful.

STUDENTS WHO CANNOT READ

Nonreaders are found in every grade, from kindergarten to college. The material in this chapter should be of particular help in working with these exceptional cases of the high-school and the college level. In addition to the technical difficulties already discussed, the personality factors in these cases should be given special attention.

Some pupils are afraid of reading; they think of themselves as children who cannot read.   When a pupil in the junior high school cannot read, he is often considered "dumb," or thinks of himself as "dumb."   Parents and older brothers and sisters often initiate or reinforce this attitude.   With these pupils, the first step is to show them that they can read a great deal more than they think they can, that they know more than they think they know.   This is a problem of reeducation with respect to a habit and attitude pattern.

The following are some of the ways in which this negative pattern may be changed.

1. Letting the student take an appropriate reading test at his own rate of reading or giving the test first with standardized timing and then letting him see how much he can improve his score when he is given more time. This procedure also shows the teacher whether there is a basic difficulty with comprehension or only a slow rate of reading.

2. If a pupil's anxiety about reading is very great, he should be assured that reading is something that he may learn later, that it is not so terribly important right now. It is more important, first, to find out what his emotional needs are and to help him satisfy those needs.

3. If this negative attitude has been reinforced at home, and parents are putting pressure on him to read, instruction in reading should not be given by members of the family.

4. A teacher who has small classes and time for work with individuals may talk with the pupil about his subject and let him write his own textbook. This can be typed and will supply excellent beginning-reading material for him.

5. Other reading material that is meaningful to the pupil should be supplied. By a careful choice of material the pupil's interest in reading can be increased.

6. The attitude of certain mothers of retarded readers from one school may be changed if they visit another school to help retarded pupils under the direction of remedial teachers. This experience not only shows the mothers sound methods of teaching reading but relieves their anxiety about their own children, when they have come in contact with many others who read just as poorly.

7. Occasionally a very seriously retarded reader may, of his own accord, decide to begin at the beginning and go back to preprimer work, reading fluently the material on each grade level and "graduating" rapidly from grade to grade.

Students who cannot read need a patient and sympathetic teacher —one who will proceed with instruction slowly enough and simply enough to give them a feeling of success and to avoid increasing their confusion and frustration. He will employ all his understanding of the individual, of psychology, and of reading procedures in working with each student. He will help the student to set immediate realistic goals of achievement in reading that he can reach with reasonable effort. Thus the teacher will help these seriously retarded readers to realize their reading potentialities.

References

1. ALDEN, CLARA L., HELEN B. SULLIVAN, and DONALD D. DURRELL, "The Frequency of Special Reading Disabilities," *Education*, Vol. 62, pp. 32–36, September, 1941.
2. *American Council Psychological Examination* (since 1938), American Council on Education, Washington, D.C.

3. ANDERSON, IRVING H., "The Reading Problems of College Students," *University of Michigan School of Education Bulletin*, Vol. 12, pp. 126–29, May, 1941.

4. ANDERSON, IRVING H., "Research in the Psychology of Reading," *Journal of Exceptional Children*, extra issue, pp. 57–60, January, 1938.

5. BAKER, HARRY J., and BERNICE LELAND, *In Behalf of Nonreaders*, rev. ed., Public School Publishing Company, Bloomington, Ill., 1940, 40 pp.

6. BARRY, LINDA, MABEL MADDEN, and MARJORIE PRATT, "Reading Difficulties of High-school Pupils," *School Review*, Vol. 46, pp. 44–47, January, 1938.

7. BENDER, I. E., and others, *Motivation and Visual Factors*, Individual Studies of College Students, Dartmouth College, Hanover, N. H., 1942, xix + 369 pp.

8. BETTS, EMMETT ALBERT, *The Prevention and Correction of Reading Difficulties*, Row, Peterson & Company, Evanston, Ill., 1936, xiv + 402 pp.

9. BLANCHARD, PHYLLIS, "Reading Disabilities in Relation to Difficulties of Personality and Emotional Development," *Mental Hygiene*, Vol. 20, pp. 384–413, July, 1936.

10. BROOM, M. E., "The Reliability of the Reading Graph Yielded by the Ophthalmograph," *School and Society*, Vol. 52, pp. 205–208, Sept. 14, 1940.

11. *California Test of Mental Maturity*, California Testing Bureau, Los Angeles, Calif., 1938.

12. CHALLMAN, ROBERT C., "Personality Adjustments and Remedial Reading," *Journal of Exceptional Children*, Vol. 6, pp. 7–11, October, 1939.

13. *Chicago Tests of Primary Mental Abilities*, American Council on Education, Washington, D.C.; also, Science Research Associates, Chicago, Ill.

14. CONRAD, LAWRENCE H., "Intensive Vocabulary Study," *English Journal*, Vol. 29, pp. 794–799, December, 1940.

15. DAVIS, FREDERICK B., "The Interpretation of Frequency Ratings Obtained from 'The Teacher's Word Book,'" *Journal of Educational Psychology*, Vol. 35, pp. 169–174, March, 1944.

16. DEARBORN, WALTER F., and IRVING H. ANDERSON, "Aniseikonia as Related to Disability in Reading," *Journal of Experimental Psychology*, Vol. 23, pp. 559–577, December, 1938.

17. DEARBORN, WALTER F., and IRVING H. ANDERSON, "A New Method for Teaching Phrasing and for Increasing the Size of Reading Fixations," *Psychological Record*, Vol. 1, pp. 459–475, December, 1937.

18. *Detroit Advanced Intelligence Tests*, Public School Publishing Company, Bloomington, Ill. The analysis chart provides for separate age scores for each of the eight parts.

19. FERNALD, GRACE M., *Remedial Techniques in Basal School Subjects*, McGraw-Hill Book Company, Inc., New York, 1943, xv + 349 pp.

20. GATES, ARTHUR I., "The Role of Personality Maladjustment in Reading Disability," *Journal of Genetic Psychology*, Vol. 59, pp. 77–83, September, 1941.

21. GILKEY, BEULAH G., and FRANK W. PARR, "An Analysis of the Reversal Tendency of Fifty Selected Elementary School Pupils," *Journal of Educational Psychology*, Vol. 35, pp. 284–292, May, 1944.

22. GRAY, WILLIAM S., "Case Studies of Reading Deficiencies in Junior High School," *Journal of Educational Research*, Vol. 10, pp. 132–140, September, 1924.

23. GRAY, WILLIAM S. (editor), *Reading in General Education*, Chaps. IX and X, American Council on Education, Washington, D.C., 1940, xiii + 464 pp.

24. *The Harvard Films for the Improvement of Reading*, Harvard Film Service, Biological Laboratories, Harvard University, Cambridge, Mass.
25. HOSEY, G., "Personality Maladjustments Resulting from Retardation in Reading," *School and Community*, Vol. 23, pp. 273–275, October, 1937.
26. IMUS, HENRY A., JOHN W. M. ROTHNEY, and ROBERT M. BEAR, *An Evaluation of Visual Factors in Reading*, Dartmouth College, Hanover, N. H., 1938, 144 pp.
27. KENNEDY, HELEN, "A Study of Children's Hearing as It Relates to Reading," *Journal of Experimental Education*, Vol. 10, pp. 238–251, June, 1940.
28. *Kuhlmann-Anderson Intelligence Tests*, Educational Test Bureau, Minneapolis, Minn.
29. MATEER, FLORENCE, "A First Study of Pituitary Dysfunction in Cases of Reading Difficulty" (abstract), *Program of the Forty-third Annual Meeting, American Psychological Association*, pp. 80–81, 1935.
30. MONROE, MARION, *Children Who Cannot Read*, University of Chicago Press, Chicago, 1932, xvi + 205 pp.
31. MONROE, MARION, "Reading Disabilities—the Importance of Early Diagnosis and Prevention," in *Education and the Exceptional Child*, pp. 24–28, Proceedings of the Spring Conference of the Child Research Clinic of the Woods Schools, Langhorne, Pa., April, 1935, The Woods Schools, Langhorne, Pa.
32. ORTON, SAMUEL T., "A Neurological Explanation of the Reading Disability," *Educational Record*, Supplement No. 12, Vol. 20, pp. 58–68, January, 1939.
33. RUSSELL, DAVID H., "Note on a New Theory about Visual Functioning and Reading Disabilities," *Journal of Educational Psychology*, Vol. 34, pp. 115–120, February, 1943.
34. *Secondary Education Board Junior Scholastic Aptitude Test*, Secondary Education Board, Milton, Mass. (distributed and scored by the Educational Records Bureau, 437 West 59th St., New York 19, N.Y.).
35. SEIBERT, EARL, "Reading Reaction for Various Types of Subject Matter," *Journal of Experimental Education*, Vol. 12, pp. 37–44, September, 1943.
36. SPACHE, GEORGE, "Eye Preference, Visual Acuity, and Reading Ability," *Elementary School Journal*, Vol. 43, pp. 539–543, May, 1943.
37. STRANG, RUTH, and others, *Examiner's Diagnostic Reading Record*, Bureau of Publications, Teachers College, Columbia University, New York, 1939, 20 pp.
38. TAYLOR, EARL A., *Controlled Reading:* A Correlation of Diagnostic Teaching and Corrective Techniques, University of Chicago Press, Chicago, 1937, xxviii + 367 pp.
39. TRAXLER, ARTHUR E., "Value of Controlled Reading: Summary of Opinion and Research," *Journal of Experimental Education*, Vol. 11, pp. 280–292, June, 1943.
40. WITZEMAN, B. EVANGELINE, "An Experimental Study Using the Ophthalm-o-graph and Metron-o-scope in the Diagnosis and Treatment of Reading Defects," *Journal of Psychology*, Vol. 11, pp. 307–334, April, 1941.

CHAPTER X

SPECIFIC READING DIFFICULTIES (*Continued*)

Although the difficulties in word recognition discussed at length in the previous chapter are basic they are far less frequent in high school and college than are difficulties involving comprehension, interpretation, critical thinking, application, and memory. These latter problems are repeatedly mentioned by more mature students as their major reading difficulties. Slow reading, which is the most frequently recognized of all difficulties, has already been discussed as a symptom of some underlying inability (pages 46–48).

SOURCES OF VOCABULARY DIFFICULTIES

The teacher cannot correct vocabulary difficulties intelligently unless he recognizes the sources of the trouble. It is very easy for a teacher, in his zeal, to intensify a bad situation—to permit certain student attitudes to continue and certain conditions in the required reading to persist that will neutralize any remedial work attempted. For these reasons, let us consider the usual or possible factors that contribute to poor vocabulary.

Reasons for Poor General Vocabulary

1. Residing in the author
   a. Failure to recognize the difficulty of his own general vocabulary, since it is so much a part of himself
   b. Fact packing: ideas so close together that no perspective can be gained, no context clues are presented, no concrete illustrations or explanations are offered, and no idea is given of the relative importance of the various facts
   c. Figures of speech that are difficult to interpret
   d. Abstract words
   e. An abundance of synonyms, used to vary the wording, which "throw the student off"
   f. Varied wording, used for literary effect, that results in confusing, difficult sentences
2. Residing in the teacher
   a. A school program that does not give the student all the vocabulary-developing tools that he needs

276

    b. An elementary-school reading program confined to a well-controlled reader series, where every new word is carefully anticipated, instead of broad experience in independent, individual book reading, as well as basal reading

    c. The use of one textbook, one author's vocabulary

    d. The assumption that nothing specific need be done to help the student in vocabulary development

    e. The treatment of vocabulary building as an unattractive chore or punishment

3. Residing in the student

    a. Little voluntary reading

    b. Association with children and adults whose language holds nothing new for him

    c. Narrow interests in general and in books specifically

    d. Oral language handicaps

    e. The habit of skipping over hard words

    f. The habit of ignoring context clues

    g. The habit of depending on class discussion for enlightenment on hard words

    h. Abhorrence of the dictionary

    i. Low intelligence

Reasons for Poor Technical Vocabulary.—("Technical," here, means peculiar to a given subject or used in a special sense in that subject.)

1. Residing in the author

    a. Presentation of technical words in a difficult general vocabulary, so that the context reveals nothing except more difficulty

    b. The presentation, without warning, of a word having a common meaning in popular usage but a special one in this text

    c. Lack of definitions for the technical words used

    d. The absence of verbal illustrations to lend concreteness and vividness to the new word

    e. The absence of pictures, maps, or charts to illustrate the new word; or the use of incomprehensible illustrations

    f. No context clues

    g. No frequent repetition of the new word

    h. No clear presentation of its function, its relation to other things

2. Residing in the teacher

    a. Failure to provide experiences to pave the way for new words

    b. Failure to pay special attention to new words in class

    c. Failure to use the new words except exactly as used in the text (exactly the same sentence structure or phrasing)

    d. Failure to draw attention to common words that have a technical meaning in the text *e.* Failure to show the student how to use the illustrations and other vocabulary helps in the textbook

3. Residing in the student
   a. Failure to write or underline new words as he meets them
   b. Failure to note parts of the word that suggest its meaning
   c. Failure to clinch the definition of a new word
   d. Failure to learn the function of the new word—what it *does,* as well as what it *is*
   e. Failure to refer to other more explanatory references
   f. Failure to observe the illustrations provided in words, maps, charts, pictures, and their legends
   g. Failure to see relationships of this word to other topics
   h. Failure to make the new word his own through writing, discussion, illustration, experimentation
   i. Low intelligence

WAYS OF IMPROVING VOCABULARY

Word and thought are—or should be—inseparable. The Greeks, recognizing this fact, had one word, *logos,* for our two separate words. The skillful teacher helps students to make word and thought one in the reading process.

It is easier to do this if words are learned in natural situations when they are needed. The importance of firsthand experience justifies our emphasis on providing a variety of activities in which new and important words are illustrated, demonstrated, and used. Thus a visit to a modern dairy will provide a basis of experience for understanding "sterilize," "pasteurize," and other words relating to milk production. These newly introduced words should be pronounced and written on the board and in reports of the visit; they should be noted when they occur in books and articles, and should be used in conversation. For example, a teacher in a university high school takes his classes on trips to the cafeteria and its kitchens, the engine room, the horticultural laboratory, and other places of interest on the campus. Later they visit industries, police stations, electric plants, and other institutions in the community. Before going, they write a letter requesting permission to visit and make an outline of what they want to see and the questions they wish to ask. On the trip they take pencils and cards, on which they list the new words and expressions that they learn. Later they copy the new words in their notebooks and read books and pamphlets that have a bearing on the trip. Important technical words that will be encountered in the text may be illustrated from the students' own experience; by an experiment; by impromptu demonstrations, pantomimes, and riddles; by charts showing the relationship of the new concept to the subject as a whole. There is no substitute for learning new words through experience and use.

Next best to firsthand experience is the recall of experience. The teacher may write a few key words on the board and ask the students to share the experiences that they have had with each word—where they have heard it, in what connection, with what meaning. In this way the teacher discovers what degree of correct meaning the students are bringing to the printed symbol; and, besides, the word gathers rich associations and the students are impressed with the personal aspect of word meanings.

Another way of sharing word experiences is through a class dictionary. This is a large, loose-leaf notebook, in which one page is devoted to each word. The committee in charge of this dictionary receives contributions of sentences or paragraphs in which the word occurs, statements of its multiple meanings and derivations, and pictures or cartoons illustrating it. Looking for illustrative material and clippings gives students practice in skimming and encourages newspaper reading. Several words may be put on the bulletin board daily, and clippings and original drawings may be exhibited there before they are pasted in the class dictionary. A rotating dictionary committee may be appointed to look ahead for trouble and report to the class the new words in the next assignment. Members of the committee should represent varied vocabulary abilities so that all kinds of difficulties common in the class will be anticipated. Incidentally, this practice in skimming is excellent for the committee.

Some student may be interested in making a dictionary of his own or in keeping an individual record of new words learned. One form of individual vocabulary record is kept on a full-sized sheet with the headings used in the form on page 280. Students should use these words in themes. They may, also, present some of them to the class for study, as words especially worth knowing.

Closely allied to firsthand experience is the vicarious experience obtained from wide reading. This is the way most adults have acquired their large vocabularies. Each new book, each new field introduces words to the reader. He learns new words as he reads. Through the reading of much easy material, such as well-written, well-illustrated supplementary books, the few difficult words that are used ultimately become commonplace and meaningful. In more difficult books, the students may note the synonymous words that the author uses and the words in the author's vocabulary that will continually cause difficulty if not mastered.

New word	Phrase where I found it	Dictionary meaning	A sentence showing how I have used this new word
1.			
2.			
3.			
Etc.			

If the passing attention given to words as they are read is not sufficient to fix them in mind, the use of vocabulary cards may be helpful. As students read, they may lightly check important words with which they are unfamiliar. Later, they may go back and write each word on a 3- by 5-in. card. On the back of the card they write the sentence in which the word was used, the dictionary definition, and the derivation, if they wish. They use these cards for drill—looking at the word, trying to recall its meaning, then looking at the other side to see whether they are right. Junior-high-school students use these or other types of flash cards for playing games with one another, counting the number of correct responses as the score.

Although the teaching of words in isolation is usually wasteful and inadequate, the value of direct, systematic, well-planned drill on words in context selected from basic vocabulary lists (2, 6, 21) has been frequently demonstrated, and is necessary for seriously retarded readers who can make little progress without a basic sight vocabulary. The Dolch basic vocabulary of 220 words makes up 50 per cent or more of the reading matter used in elementary school (6). In one school, each department prepared a list of the words considered essential for comprehension of the subject and included in the final examinations a question on the meaning of these words. After a word is presented to the student, if he has difficulty in pronouncing it, instruction should be given in word recognition, as has been already described (pages 260–272), and the student's understanding of its meaning should be checked. Lists of new words that will be met frequently may also be presented by a committee and a contest may be staged to see which side can use the largest number of these words correctly.

Students may also be interested in unusual word origins (13), and in finding out which of our English words come from Latin, French, or Celtic sources. Many students read a syndicated newspaper column in which the strange history of a word is told each day. One gifted young teacher asked each of the students in a sophomore class in world history, where they had been studying hieroglyphics and cuneiform writing, to bring to class a simple message in a code or sign language of his own concoction. Their immediate response was that they couldn't do it, but when they were given a little guidance they produced amazing results. Each student wrote his message on the board and gave the class the key or alphabet with which to work it out. It was a thoroughly enjoyable procedure and helped the students to realize that written language is, after all, only a set of symbols to which we give meaning, and that the thoughts that these symbols evoke are not really in the symbols themselves but in our interpretation of them.

This general interest in words may lead to specific word study— the study of common prefixes, suffixes, and roots that suggest meanings; the study of synonyms and antonyms. After reading passages containing difficult words, the class may discuss the meanings suggested by the context, learning how to determine when it is safe to guess and when it is not, what constitutes a foolproof clue. Students may write paragraphs of their own containing new words, to be interpreted by the class. This exercise not only brings out words that the class does not understand but may also reveal misunderstanding on the part of the student who has written the paragraph.

Word study should be followed by use of the word in written and oral reports and in casual conversation. If the teacher uses the new words frequently, they become familiar to the students, who, in turn, are more likely to use them in the daily class discussions.

Numerous word games have been suggested for vocabulary building—making as many words as possible from a few common roots, such as *fero* to bear, *tendo*, to stretch; adding prefixes and suffixes to these stems to see how that changes their meanings; doing crossword puzzles; participating in vocabulary quiz programs and vocabulary "bees." Devices of this kind increase young students' interest in words, often lead to more frequent use of dictionaries, and make new words a challenge, instead of something to be feared or skipped.

It is also necessary to help some students realize how limited their vocabularies are—to what extent they are skipping or depending solely upon the context. One way to help them perceive this is to ask them to underline, on a page or two of reading, the words that they do not know; then give them a test on all the potentially difficult words in these pages. After they have marked the test, they compare the number of words marked as unknown with the number of those that were missed on the test.

To make the student more aware of the complexity of word meanings, Richards (14, page 12) suggested a set of scales—measures by which to mark a word's variations in meaning along a number of coordinates. The following exercises are suggested as ways of increasing the student's awareness of the wide range of meanings that a single word may have.

1. Collect all the diverse correct meanings that you can find for a given word.

2. Look up some words in an unabridged dictionary and count the number of different meanings that each word may have. How many of these meanings seem almost unrelated?

3. Make families of words related in some way; for example, words that show the different degrees of feeling with which one may regard a person: *tolerate, accept, like, love, adore.*

In many groups, the use of the dictionary should be taught. Very few students know all the fascinating kinds of information that can be found in a dictionary or have learned how to turn to words quickly. Some need help in recognizing the initial letters of words and in using the guide words at the top of each page. One method that indirectly helped to interest students in vocabulary was a dictionary unit for the ninth grade. After a thorough discussion of the different parts of the dictionary, copies of *Webster's Collegiate Dictionary* and mimeographed questions, with spaces for answers, and a space for the page number (of the dictionary) where each answer was to be found, were distributed to the members of the class. Accuracy and speed were factors in the completion of the exercises. When enough exercises had been given to acquaint the student with the dictionary (about 2 weeks' time was required), a contest was held in which students from different sections competed. Honor-roll students did not compete, but assisted in administering the tests by checking answers and scoring. The *Thorndike Century Junior Dictionary* (19) is popular with poor readers; in fact, it is the favorite book of some students.

Certain types of vocabulary tests, involving discrimination and interpretation of meaning, may be even more valuable for teaching than for testing. The following type of test is different from the ordinary multiple-choice test, in that each response, except the correct one, represents a certain kind of error—one is a completely wrong response; another is a correct dictionary definition, but not the correct meaning in the context given; the third is a word that is similar to the test word in form but different in meaning.

Vocabulary

(18, pages 411–412)

Directions: First try to guess the meaning of the word from its context in the sentence. If necessary, use other methods of word recognition to get the meaning. Then underline the response which you think is correct.

1. On the lay level an *astute* person may learn a great deal about a student's reading ability.

   discerning   stupid   abstract   crafty

2. Clinical procedure is not synonymous with *dexterity* in the use of instruments and devices.

   clumsiness   dextrality   skill   alertness

3. The purchase of a telebinocular and an *ophthalmograph* does not make a reading clinic.

   a machine for studying handwriting
   a kind of kinetograph
   an instrument for photographing eye movements
   an optometrist

4. The ideal is the use of the most *precise* instruments by the wisest and most capable persons.

   précis   exact   faulty   fastidious

5. Any list of reading deficiencies is *circumscribed* by the methods of study used.

   limited   created   independent of   circumvented

6. An important reading deficiency is lack of *flexibility* in adapting method of reading to different materials and purposes.

marked rigidity   felicity   ready adjustability   elasticity

7. The word *diagnosis* comes to us almost without change through Latin from the original Greek word.

> superficial observation of phenomena
> measures of reading ability
> recognition of disease
> accurate detection through a critical examination

Another type of test exercise encourages interpretation and calls attention to shifts in meaning by means of several questions.

Slow Motion Study of Words and Sentences

(18, pages 412–413)

1. "Reading may be one of life's inexhaustible pleasures and blessings, but may also become a mere habit, an escape from thinking or a drug."—Walter de la Mare, *Early One Morning in the Spring*, p. 316, The Macmillan Company, New York, 1935.
   Give the literal meaning (denotation) of this sentence.
   Who said it?
   What was his mood and purpose?
   When did he say it?
   To whom did he say it?
   Give your interpretation of the passage.
2. "He that uses words without any clear and steady meaning, what does he do but lead himself and others into errors?"—Locke.
   Give the literal meaning (denotation) of this sentence.
   Who said it?
   What was his mood and purpose?
   When did he say it?
   To whom did he say it?
   Give your interpretation of the passage.
3. "Language is an inventory of human experience."—L. W. Lockhart, *Word Economy, A Study in Applied Linguistics*, p. 56, Kegan Paul, Trench, Trubner and Company, London, 1931.
   Give the literal meaning (denotation) of this sentence.
   Who said it?
   What was his mood and purpose?
   When did he say it?
   To whom did he say it?
   Give your interpretation of the passage.
4. "I only took the regular course," said the Mock Turtle with a sigh.
   "What was that?" inquired Alice.
   "Reeling and Writhing, of course, to begin with," the Mock Turtle replied; "And then the different branches of Arithmetic—Ambition, Distraction, Uglification, and Derision."—Lewis Carroll, *Alice in Wonderland*.

Give the literal meaning (denotation) of this passage.
Who said it?
What was his mood and purpose?
When did he say it?
To whom did he say it?
Give your interpretation of the passage.
5. "He who reads and reads
And does not what he knows
Is he who plows and plows
And never sows."—Old Oxford motto
Give the literal meaning (denotation) of this passage.
Who said it?
What was his mood and purpose?
When did he say it?
To whom did he say it?
Give your interpretation of the passage.

Like other remedial measures, these exercises in vocabulary are to be applied when and where they are appropriate. Many other suggestions for improving vocabulary and other reading abilities will be found in the various workbooks and practice books in reading described in Appendix A, as well as in suggested exercises in Appendix C.

SPECIFIC SOURCES OF DIFFICULTIES IN COMPREHENSION

The remediation of comprehension difficulties, as well as of vocabulary difficulties, requires some appreciation of the reason for their existence. Besides, the remediation of comprehension difficulties depends upon their particular nature. We cannot work on comprehension in general and expect to get the best results. We must put our emphasis where it is needed. Hence, the following list was prepared to suggest the sources of difficulties in four main areas of comprehension.

Reasons for Comprehension Difficulties

1. Residing in the author
   a. Poor writing: poor organization, no stress to designate main points, unnecessarily involved expression and thinking, remotely placed modifiers
   b. Difficulty of concepts involved: if Einstein were to write in monosyllables on the theory of relativity, he would still leave most of us behind him
   c. Unfamiliarity of the topic discussed
   d. Unfamiliarity of vocabulary
   e. Lack of helpful illustrative materials
   f. Lack of appropriately placed and worded definitions

     g. Lack of concrete examples

     h. An overabundance of prepositional phrases

     i. Too many complex, compound, and inverted sentences

     j. The presence of many pronouns

2. Residing in the teacher

     a. Too much word drill, to the neglect of silent reading for understanding

     b. No specific helps in reading for different purposes in different content subjects

     c. The use of reading material too difficult for the student to read successfully for any purpose

     d. Ignorance as to the kind of reading the students' next assignments will demand

     e. Failure to discover disabilities in various types of reading; tendency to attribute all reading difficulty to low intelligence or lack of application

     f. Failure to identify the causes of disability

     g. Failure to develop in students the ability to concentrate for long periods of time (inability to concentrate on long passages will not show up on most reading tests because of the brevity of the passages)

3. Residing in the student

     a. Tendency to ignore unknown words

     b. Failure to suit reading technique to the purpose for which he is reading

     c. Inability to retain an orderly mental picture of the sequence of events or relationships of dominance and subordination among ideas

     d. Failure to apply active thought to matters such as pronoun reference and facts that should induce inferential thinking

     e. Tendency to skip over passages whose meanings are not clear

     f. Failure to make use of headings, footnotes, index, illustrations, questions, and other helps to meaning

     g. Failure to take notes on, underline, check, discuss, repeat, or otherwise reinforce the memory of the ideas read

     h. Failure to evaluate the author's point of view or emphasis, and to take account of these in order to fulfill his (the student's) purpose

WAYS OF IMPROVING COMPREHENSION

It is easy enough to say, "Learn to find the key words and the main ideas," but it is more difficult to give instruction as to how to do this. Paying attention to headings and italicized words is helpful, of course. The author may give a clue as to which words he thinks are most important, sometimes by using these words frequently and providing illustrations of them, and sometimes by his statements, as, for example, "The most important economic needs are food, shelter, and clothing."

An understanding of the structure of paragraphs is helpful to students in locating the main idea. A quick glance at the paragraph will show whether it presents the key idea in the first or the second sentence, or in a summary sentence at the end; whether it is a paragraph presenting two contrasting ideas, whether it contains nothing but an illustration of a generalization made in the previous paragraph, or whether it is loosely constructed without unity or emphasis. Given the topic, the thought may be developed in several ways—by repetition in other words to clarify abstract material, by negative repetition that denies the opposite point of view, by examples, by breaking the topic into parts and developing it detail by detail, by comparison or contrast, by the exploration of causes, or by a statement of its importance. These items, put in question form, may be used by students as a guide to the analysis of paragraphs. The reader should see clearly the relationship between details and weave a pattern of thought as he reads. A more detailed description of paragraph structure written in a form enjoyed by college students is given in *College Reading Skills* (11).

Practice in the efficient reading of paragraphs should be given in every subject. For example, the members of class may be given a mimeographed story or article and asked to underline the key ideas as they read. Before reading they should discuss the characteristics of key ideas and, after reading, discuss the methods that they used to find those ideas. The "headline" technique has been widely used to give practice in finding the main idea of a paragraph. First, students are asked to select the most accurate headline from several given; later they are asked to formulate a headline for each paragraph. A third step is to put in one column the main ideas of a series of paragraphs and in a parallel column the important details that support them.

The structure of a longer passage or chapter should be understood before it is read. Otherwise, the reader does not know what to select as important and what to pass over as unessential. A period spent on an exercise, such as the one that follows, designed for this purpose, has proved beneficial. "Turn to No. 2 of *Study Type of Reading Exercises*. You will have just 1 minute to get the structure of the exercise as a whole. Read the first page quickly to find out what the exercise is about; pay special attention to italicized words. When you have a hunch as to the probable structure of the passage, read the first sentence of each of the other paragraphs to see whether you are right." When the minute is up, the group will give their ideas of the structure of the passage and discuss the methods they used. During the period, the class may read three or four other passages in the same way and may summarize all the suggestions for obtaining quickly the structure of a chapter or a section. The next step is to use this newly acquired sense of structure in subsequent, more careful reading.

Questions that lead the student to think rather than merely to repeat content, questions that require critical analysis, questions that make the student look before and after his immediate assignment—all such contribute to deeper and broader comprehension (see pages 381–386). Finding and naming the various parts of a long selection is another valuable exercise. The structure of a book and its position in the course and in the individual's background should be studied in the same way.

Anticipation of what the author is going to say sharpens interpretation and usually increases concentration. Students like exercises of the following kind: "Before reading this chapter, think what you would say if you were the author writing it. Then read the chapter and find out how closely you and the author agreed."

Skimming is a useful but much abused technique for gaining certain kinds of information quickly. Skimming is not careless, inaccurate reading. Whatever the nature of the material or the purpose in reading, the reader should emerge with definite, correct ideas or impressions of the passage.

Skimming may be described in terms of a scale ranging from the least to the greatest amount of information to be obtained. At one end of the scale would be skimming to locate a particular date or name; next in order would be skimming to locate a particular fact; then, skimming to get the general structure or skeleton of the article or book, skimming to get all the facts or points of view bearing on a particular problem, skimming to "get the heart of the book," and skimming to get a fairly detailed pattern of the author's thought. Students may begin learning to skim by glancing rapidly over a page to find certain words; later, they may look for ideas expressed in phrases, sentences, or paragraphs.

The reader gains in facility as he becomes familiar with a certain kind of book. For example, a person who is "sophisticated" in reading novels can tell from very few clues what is coming next and how the story will probably "come out." The more background one has in a field, the easier will it be to skip and select judiciously.

Skimming is an active process. It is guided by a clear idea of the knowledge sought. Each new acquisition is checked against what the reader already knows. Impressions from one source are compared with those from another.

Paragraph outlining—writing one sentence only for each paragraph and attempting to link these sentences into a growing pattern of thought—helps many students to increase their speed by judicious selection of key ideas. They find that the topic sentence frequently tells all that they need to know.

Exercises using passages in texts, reference books, magazines, and newspapers as practice material may be easily prepared. The passage is selected and appropriate questions are formulated. Then the student is asked to skim the passage in order to find the answers. He may be timed or limited to a certain number of minutes. Exercises may be quickly prepared from newspaper clippings. Select clippings of interest to the students, prepare questions appropriate to the article, estimate the time needed for skimming. The article may be pasted on one side of a page and the questions written or typed on the other side. Students may get these loose sheets to read whenever they have spare time or whenever they feel the need for this kind of practice.

Remedies for Comprehension Difficulties

1. In general
   a. Taking an inventory after the first representative assignment in any class, seeing how fast the different students can read and who made which errors
   b. Having a successful reader tell how he got a certain answer
   c. Working on the general reading deficiency of the class—*i.e.*, a deficiency common to all
   d. Using another textbook that expresses the same ideas more simply or from another viewpoint
   e. Giving special exercise and help to the student handicapped in unusual respects in reading
   f. Differentiating the reading materials according to the students' demonstrated reading abilities in a given subject—easy books for poorer readers
   g. Frequently assigning a kind of reading in which the class needs special drill
   h. Providing a fairly balanced diet in the kinds of reading most important for a given subject; getting main ideas, drawing conclusions, getting a sense of sequence and outlining, inferring, skimming to locate answers to questions, and noting the details that are important to these purposes. For example, to cite an old friend of long standing, Goldilocks might lend herself to the following types of question:
      main idea: What other title would be a good one?
      conclusions: Do you think Goldilocks would ever visit the bears again? Why or why not?
      inference: How do you think the little bear felt about Goldilocks?

details: Prove your answer.

outlining: If you were to divide this story into three big parts, what would you call each of them?

skimming: (finding the proof required in the inference question)

    i. Providing opportunities to write the kinds of material being read: Would you have done exactly as Goldilocks did? Would you have entered the house? Would you have run when you saw them? Write the story as it would have happened to you.

    j. Teaching paragraph structure through reading and writing various types: for example, reading paragraphs whose main ideas lie in the first sentence in each instance, and having students write such paragraphs; in some cases, give the start—"The team played well Friday." Acquaint students with other paragraphs whose main ideas are in the last sentence or are complex, a combination of first and last sentences; teach them to recognize transitional expressions that sometimes precede main ideas and start the paragraphs: for example, "But there is another reason for the disagreement." The main idea is the next sentence, which tells what the reason is. The first sentence is a transitional expression connecting the previous paragraph with this one.

    k. Teaching the structure of a sentence in terms of the basic materials (subject, predicate) and the relationships of additional ideas to these

    l. Teaching the role of punctuation in suggesting word, phrase, and clause relationships

2. In main ideas

    a. Giving opportunities for précis writing: a sentence summarizing every paragraph in a given piece of material

    b. Having students underline the sentence or parts of sentences that best express the main idea of a paragraph

    c. Having students choose headlines for beheaded newspaper articles

    d. Conducting a classroom newspaper in which organized writing and titling are naturally involved

    e. Having committees present occasional programs to the rest of the class, each member taking one part of a given subject

    f. Having students proofread a paragraph in which an alien idea has been planted

    g. Having students write a sentence representative of the main idea of an article

    h. Having a student mix up a short, original paragraph containing a main idea and several details, and having another person identify the main idea

    i. Having students unscramble and organize a very simple scrambled outline: lamb, ewe, ram, sheep

    j. Making a group paragraph to which students contribute a main idea and details suitable to it

   k. Having some students pantomime an idea and the class write a paragraph about it, to show how details of the pantomime contribute: for example, "waiting for Father to come home for dinner."

   l. Having the class write paragraphs of details, to which other students are to attach main ideas

   m. Discussing a sentence as a unit of main idea and details, the simple subject and predicate being the main idea and the modifiers being the details, which make for greater vividness

3. In details

   a. Basing a mural, a map, a blackboard sketch, or an experiment upon a descriptive paragraph, to appreciate the array of details given

   b. Making a paragraph that describes a given object

   c. Distinguishing between the main idea and the details of a paragraph

   d. Outlining a paragraph to show the relationship of details to the main idea and to each other, thus revealing the relative importance of various details

   e. Outlining a chapter to show that the details of the main idea in the chapter are the main ideas of successive paragraphs, each of which, in turn, has its details (great fleas have lesser fleas)

   f. Taking a main idea and building details to support it

   g. Rearranging a jumbled outline or a jumbled list of related ideas

   h. Finding the details in a jumbled paragraph

   i. Finding the materials in a paragraph that are neither main idea nor details (transitional expressions tying up one paragraph with another or one detail with another)

   j. Contrasting two ideas by making parallel lists of contrasting details (Greek civilization versus Roman)

   k. Reading to answer questions of detail

   l. Reading to contribute details to a main argument: for example, "Are airplanes superior to dirigibles?"

   m. Writing on a controversial subject, presenting specific arguments on one side

   n. Passing around papers on each of which a different main idea has been written: "Jimmy's room always looked as though a cyclone had struck it"; each person writes a supporting detail and passes it on. A committee can think up the main ideas and check them with the teacher before proceeding; the subject matter can be based on actual classwork if desired.

   o. Having an oral class exercise, one student expressing a main idea about something that has been studied and other students offering supporting details

4. In outlining or sequence

   a. Having the class do the outlining of their discussions and of their work on the board at every opportunity; too often the teacher does the organizing "to save time" (for what?)

b. Having students take notes on a chapter, spacing the subtopics down their paper and jotting the main points under each as they read along; this technique is especially good for the student whose notes always outwrite the author in volume

c. Discussing the relationships of the subheads of a chapter to one another (sometimes they are not parallel in thought importance)

d. Rearranging the material along other lines than the author has taken: instead of "Populations have changed in the last 100 years," say "Industry has changed people's lives in a number of ways"; in other words, cutting across the author's material in a different way, so that the student must do his own organizing

e. Having the students prove to themselves by outlining that a given sentence is alien to a paragraph that the teacher has written or a student has submitted

f. Having the students read to find and express a few main points in a given passage and one or two supporting facts for each (panel discussion, debate)

g. Listing the class knowledge on a certain subject and then deciding, as a group, how to outline it before writing

h. Rearranging a jumbled outline

i. Rearranging a sequence of jumbled sentences in a paragraph

j. Having the students outline a lecture or a reading by the teacher; discuss differences and clarify relationships; recognize the legitimacy of differences of opinion in certain instances

k. Having a group of students make an outline for an oral discussion of a debatable question by the class

l. Setting up a faulty outline to be criticized with reference to logical relationships and the reading material on which it is based

m. Having students outline one another's themes and compare new outlines with the students' original outlines

n. Having the class decide on the big scenes that the movie of a book might have

5. In seeing relationships and drawing conclusions

a. Reading a passage up to a certain point and having the student guess the ending, with reasons to support a given conclusion

b. Listing known points and possible conclusions and discussing the unlikelihood of certain conclusions, the probability of others

c. Reading to answer a question requiring inferential thinking: Would the people in this country have a means of heating in their houses? Why?

d. Listing material on one subject, and having students list parallel material on another subject

e. Comparing or contrasting two sets of material in parallel columns to answer questions such as: "Were the Greek and Roman civilizations much alike?" "What contributions did they make to us in various fields?"

f. Having students read a passage and write down the facts that plausibly supplement the facts given: "The man stood at the car stop, swinging his arms to slap his shoulders and stamping his feet." In this situation, what else would be true?   (city, cold weather, etc.).

Another interesting and helpful procedure is to provide the members of the class with typewritten directions for games and request them to draw a diagram of the setting for each.   A somewhat similar plan is to give directions for setting the stage for a play and have the pupils diagram the stage.

The following procedures for improving comprehension were incorporated as part of an English course.

1. Using the historical background of the subject and the biography of the author, to create interest in the material and to prepare students for it
2. Having the reading done in the class period—supervised study
3. Tying up experiences in books with personal experiences
4. Reading and writing conclusions to stories that were partially read in class—perhaps, read aloud by good readers
5. Teaching the use of footnotes, appendix, etc.
6. In complicated stories like *Ivanhoe*, keeping a list or "cast of characters" to help in following the story
7. In blank verse, stressing the point that it should be read sentence by sentence, not line by line.

In reading in the field of history the following suggestions were made.

1. In reading, remember that actual men and women have made history and are making it today.   Try to put yourself in their places.   How would you have acted?   Compare "then and now," "here and there," repeatedly (mimeographed "stories" used in class).
2. Try to determine the effect of various events on people—see cause and effect.
3. Spend at least as much time in thinking about an assignment as in doing it.
4. Try to see each assigned unit in relation to the whole.
5. In class, practice drawing inferences, perhaps beginning with detective stories and present-day events: To what will this lead?   To what did that lead?
6. In the social sciences, work should be done in units and not allowed to pile up.
7. Use books giving a complete picture, such as *A Day in Athens*, etc.

The combination of procedures required in improving comprehension is well illustrated by this account:

The major reading problem of the students on the level on which I am working is their inability to comprehend the material in the particular text-book we are using.   This is in a course in economic geography.   In the first place, economic geography should be given on the eleventh- or twelfth-grade level, preferably the latter, and not in the ninth grade, as it is where I am. The students cannot comprehend the text, not so much because they are poor readers—which, of course, some of them are—but because they do not have enough background or enough supplementary knowledge of the subject to enable them to comprehend it.   They do not have a sufficient vocabulary of their own to understand the author's.   They are not familiar enough with words in the subject or material in the field to enable them to get the meaning of the word from the context.   Their reading of the text requires constant use of the dictionary and the slow reading which that entails is not conducive to comprehension.   This particular textbook does not contain many of the clues which are so often an aid to comprehension.   It has no paragraph head-ings, no italics, no marginal notations, et cetera.   The book is large and the lines are quite close together.   Very few of the pages are relieved by a picture, although there are many charts and maps.   It is not hard to see why it is hard for the students to comprehend it.   At the present moment, there is only one thing in the book which would be an aid to comprehension and that is a summary at the end of each chapter.

I am going to list in order some of the things I have previously done to aid the students in their comprehension of it and some of the things I have learned here:

1. Make definite assignments.   I put lists of items on the board for the students to look for in their reading.

2. I have them outline the most difficult chapters.   I assist them in outlining by putting a skeleton outline on the board.

3. I put a word list on the board—a list of words which they will find especially difficult in the next assignment.   Sometimes we go over them together in class and sometimes I have them look them up in the dictionary as an assignment.

4. I have plenty of bulletin-board space in my room and I put up as many pictures *re* the subject we are discussing as I can possibly find.   We take lots of magazines at home and I save all appropriate and suitable pictures —principally colored ones.

5. I send for just as much "free" illustrative material as I see advertised. There was a time not so long ago when companies weren't sending much of this out, but they are beginning to send out material again.   The students read and look at this material during the free period I give them during each class.   Our periods are 50 minutes long and I give them 10 minutes of that to look around at the material or just to relax.   They usually look at the material, because I arrange it as attractively as I can.

6. I give them specific questions to be answered by their reading.   Some-times these are to be answered orally and sometimes they are to be written.

7. I give them as extensive lists of outside reading as the school library and city library can provide the materials for.

I make the lists as full of interesting material as I can. Sometimes the material is to be found in books, sometimes in magazines.

8. When a movie covering some subject in economic geography comes to the local theater, I arrange with the management to have a private afternoon showing at a reduced rate. The transportation industry, lumbering industry, and finishing industry have been made more realistic in this way.

9. I read them interesting articles and stories in class.

10. I make just as many assignments in easier texts as I can get material for.

11. I have them make lists of bothersome words and keep these in their notebooks.

SOURCES AND CORRECTION OF SLOW READING

Speed is commonly thought of as divorced from comprehension and as dependent 99 44/100 per cent on proper eye movements. Actually, the person who regards slow reading as a matter of poor eye movements alone is not only putting the cart before the horse but is donning blinders to shut out all that is known about the reading process. In the following materials on the subject of speed of reading, the reader will find considerable duplication of previous ideas, chiefly because the authors feel that full recognition should be given the fact that speed is a function of comprehension and can be divorced from comprehension neither in theory nor in practical remedial or corrective work.

Reasons for Slow Reading

1. Residing in the author
   a. Difficulty of the material itself, which requires a careful type of reading: mathematics, poetry, recipes, etc.
   b. Vocabulary difficulty: through general or technical words, or through semantic variations
   c. Difficulty of concepts involved
   d. Difficulty of sentence and paragraph organization
   e. Insufficient direction of the reader's thought through headings, transitional expressions, etc.
   f. Failure to suggest the relative importance of ideas by the space devoted to them (the more space the more important), expressions of relationship, etc.
   g. Failure to connect steps in logic carefully; omissions that lose the reader in the middle of a sequence of ideas
   h. Small-sized type, long lines, poor spacing between words and lines, type that is not clear

      i. Fact packing: too many ideas within a given space

      j. Lack of concreteness and other interest factors

2. Residing in the teacher

    a. Failure to designate the purposes for which the student is to read a given piece of material

    b. Failure to give experience in reading for different purposes and therefore at different appropriate speeds; the result—everything at a snail's pace

    c. Failure to point out the importance of chapter headings, subheadings, marginal topics, transitional expressions, directional words ("on the other hand," "conversely"), and paragraph structure, to make for reading efficiency

    d. Overemphasis upon slow, analytical reading

    e. Overemphasis upon oral reading

    f. Assumption that all "slow" readers are physiologically slow or stupid

    g. Emphasis upon speed primarily, rather than upon the comprehension essential to meaningful speed

    h. Use of speed drills, such as flash cards, without provision of ample, easy, interesting materials in books, magazines, and newspapers, to give natural practice

    i. Failure to instill a love of reading, which gives practice and maintains skills

3. Residing in the student

    a. Unfamiliarity with the topic concerned

    b. Letting the mind wander from the material

    c. Inadequate knowledge of word meanings; only a "translation" acquaintance with harder words

    d. Lack of the comprehension skills essential to reading purpose

    e. Reading without a definite purpose in mind; hence, inefficiently

    f. Lack of interest in the subject

    g. Failure to appreciate the important as opposed to the unimportant ideas presented

    h. Native slowness of reaction (it is easy to think this about every slow student, if you wish!)

    i. An established habit of slow reading; a reading speed which, through inertia and comfort of habit, has not kept pace with comprehension power

    j. Devotion of most of the reading time to material requiring slow reading, such as mathematics, poetry, proofreading

    k. Reading carelessly or with only speed in mind, and having, through the consequent loss of thought, to make frequent regressions.

Remedies for Habitually Slow Reading

    1. Selecting materials that are simpler as to vocabulary, concept, sentence and paragraph organization; that are more direct in thought; that have well-

designated emphasis, so that important ideas are obviously important; more detailed in logic, with concrete illustrations (verbal and visual) to clarify and space difficult and strange new ideas; that contain subheads and other directional devices as clues to the direction the material is taking; that are printed in clear type of good size, well spaced and short of line; that comprise the kind of information that permits rapid reading (narrative or factual materials whose facts are well spaced by discussion and illustration)

2. Making assignments that clearly indicate the kinds of information wanted, and having students discuss ways in which the material must be read to achieve this information most efficiently

3. Offering frequent opportunity for a type of reading in which the class in general has been shown to be deficient

4. Giving exercises in locating information quickly by the use of such aids as chapter headings, subheadings, marginal topics, key words

5. Teaching the students the structural types common to paragraph form and to factual chapter or article forms, to aid them in locating and reading only the important ideas

6. Writing paragraphs illustrative of common types of structure: main idea first, main idea last, part of complex idea first and part last

7. Writing articles illustrative of common types of structure: statement of purpose, body, and evaluation or summary

8. Using supplementary materials such as newspaper, magazine, and narrative book reading, to give practice in the skills used in such a subject as social studies, in which rapid reading is often an important asset

9. Putting more emphasis upon silent reading

10. Giving frequent, short speed exercises in the type of material in which speed is desired: flashed words and phrases, metronoscope or film exercise in phrase reading, timed reading without mechanical means (students reading and looking up when they have finished, to see what number of minutes the teacher has written on the board; or reading for a length of time and then counting the number of words achieved)

11. Stressing excellence of comprehension in speed exercises, so that the student goes no faster than he can read successfully so as to be able to answer the questions pertaining to the material, and increases his speed only when he can show that his comprehension is suitable

12. Using individual charts of speed progress on timed reading exercises of uniform difficulty and length

13. Encouraging wide, easy reading of material interesting to students, through casual exchange of ideas on the books read in a class library club or on a class topic; relaxation of booklist standards to include books of slightly lower literary quality which, with careful guidance, will start the student on the way up; constant recourse in classroom method to attractive books whose stories are interwoven with the facts that the class needs to know (colonial stories with regard to early American history, cowboy stories and fictitious hero stories for facts on the opening of the West, biography and popular books such as those by Beebe for science information); exploration

of magazines and newspapers, with reports on features liked and interests met; taking an inventory of book interests and reading abilities, and making sure that each student is reading something significant and comprehensible to him; minimizing the formal-report aspect of reading, which encourages dishonesty and dislike and is liable to become a ritual, without enthusiasm or meaning

14. Cultivating the habit of reading only so long as one can read efficiently; trying gradually to increase the length of reading periods; interspersing them with other activities, resting the eyes, trying to recall important points read, jotting down notes to help retention

15. Increasing familiarity with words through exercises to develop under-standing of the different meanings of well-known words, keeping lists of newly acquired words and using them often, and other vocabulary-building activities

16. Preparing with the student a plan of attack for the reading of each type of assignment, perhaps a chart to which he may refer before starting a given task

17. Helping the student make a conscious attempt to find an interest in the subject he is reading about

18. Creating an interest in the subject to be read about by class discus-sions, experiments, illustrative materials, questions

19. Discussing and perhaps outlining the relative importance of things to be read about in the next assignment, so that the student is armed with the knowledge of what his purpose is, regardless of the author's emphasis

20. Helping the student make a conscious effort to read without regres-sions; if necessary, to skim first for hard words and clear up these meanings before he reads

21. Using choral reading to develop a sense of phrasing

22. Getting exercise in making a quick, general outline of material as it is read—a combination of noting headings, reading main ideas, and skimming (This can be done in light pencil in the margin of the book.)

23. Reading to answer a question of inference, so that "creative reading" is going on as the reader evaluates the facts

24. Reading to cite parallels from experience immediately after reading the passage; here, again, "creative reading" urges the reader on to find mate-rial for his answer.

WAYS OF IMPROVING INTERPRETATION

Most complex of all are the problems of interpretation of meaning that have been briefly presented in Chap. II. The reader's previous attitudes and prejudices; his knowledge of the author's intent, mood, and purpose; his understanding of the nature of words and their interpretation; and his own background of experience—all influence his interpretation of a given passage.

The printed page presents the same words to each reader, but each person emerges with a somewhat different impression of what the author has said. That previous attitudes do influence interpretation of reading material is clearly demonstrated by the diversity of written responses to the question What did the author say? that were given by a number of persons who had read a certain passage (17). "Man's predispositions affect his interpretations in reading as in other areas of living."

A nontechnical discussion of sentence structure is sometimes necessary, to increase a student's awareness of the uses that words serve. Grammar that emphasizes the functions of different parts of speech is one aid to interpretation in reading. The following account of instruction given to a foreign-born college freshman who had been in this country for about a year illustrates how composition may contribute to comprehension in reading.

Steve himself expressed concern about both reading and writing. One day, he brought a composition to the interview. The professor had criticized it as "lumbering in sentence structure; faulty in diction, punctuation, verb tenses, and use of the article." The worker's report is as follows:

I thought it might be helpful to work over sentences, taken from his composition, with all of these things in mind. One of the sentences which we worked over, as it was originally written in the composition, was

"Opinion of the majority would never had been followed blindly, as everyone was equal, by the people."

I thought that it might be helpful for Steve to see the possibility and importance of simple, clear expression of complex ideas. With this in mind, I asked him what the sentence was about. He said, "Opinion." When I asked what the sentence said about *opinion*, he quickly saw the function of the verb and said, "Would never had been followed." I suggested that these two parts represented the basic part of the sentence and that everything else would be draped on them, would modify them. Steve saw this and added the phrases which modified the subject and verb. He saw the importance of keeping the modifier close to the words which it modifies.

The fact that Steve had used the wrong verb tense provided the opportunity to discuss the contribution of tenses to the precision and clarity of sentence meaning. He saw that, since the sentence in question involved a relationship of past to present, the more appropriate tense might be the present perfect. At this point the sentence read:

"Opinion of the majority would never have been followed blindly by the people."

It was easy for Steve to see that the simplicity and clarity of his sentence would decrease if the main clause were to be interrupted by the dependent one. He decided that the dependent clause had more meaning at the beginning of the sentence. Steve looked up "as" and "since" in the dictionary and decided that the latter more aptly suited his purpose. The sentence in its final form read:

"Since everyone was equal, the opinion of the majority would never have been followed blindly by the people."

An hour had been spent working over one sentence. I wondered if it was worth while. It was gratifying to have Steve report 2 weeks later that he had raised his composition grade from a C to an A.

Exercises may be prepared to increase the students' appreciation of the way in which associated ideas, either in modifiers in the same sentence or in surrounding sentences, determine the meaning of a particular word in the sentence, as,

He _____ into the room.

With head high he _____ into the room.

With head high, like a king, he _____ into the room.

Any one of a large number of words might be inserted in the first blank. In the second blank, choice would be limited to such words as "strutted," "swaggered," or "strode." In the third sentence, the verbs that could be appropriately inserted would be still more restricted.

TEACHING SUSTAINED ATTENTION TO CONTINUOUS READING

In some corrective reading courses there is a tendency to base the instruction almost wholly on the reading of many short selections, accompanied by questions. In fact, certain reading textbooks and workbooks consist, in the main, of material of this kind. Reading of this type is desirable, because it provides for variety of content and thus appeals to the interests of all the pupils. Moreover, the discussion of short selections can be so thorough that there is little chance that the difficulties of individual pupils will be overlooked.

On the other hand, longer selections should have an important place in the corrective reading program. Many pupils are having reading difficulty partly because they have formed habits of fluctuating attention. In everyday language, they do not *concentrate* on the reading material. In order to become efficient readers, they need to learn to give their undivided attention to reading for many minutes continuously. A habit of this kind can be established only through much practice.

An aid to increased efficiency is the practice of sustained reading, uninterrupted by note taking, during which ideas important to the reader's purpose are reflected upon, mentally sifted, catalogued, and clinched by a quickly written statement of the salient points winnowed from the reading.

Not infrequently, mature pupils who are genuinely interested in helping themselves to become better readers can be led to undertake regular practice in sustained reading outside class. Such individuals may employ time intervals considerably longer than it is feasible to use in class, and record their progress in terms of number of pages per hour. Experience shows that self-administered practice of this kind two or three times a week may result in significant gains, not only in sustained attention but also in rate and comprehension.

PRACTICE TO IMPROVE METHODS OF THINKING WHILE READING

The improvement of thinking during the reading process may be fostered through practice in reading to answer thought questions, reading to discover implied as well as explicit meanings, reading and applying the content of the selections to new situations, reading for the purpose of solving problems, and through formal exercises in thoughtful reading, such as the syllogism. These kinds of reading are not very well represented in the textbooks that have been published for use in corrective reading. At present, teachers of reading must rely mainly upon materials prepared locally for training of this kind.

If concepts, meanings, and thinking are emphasized as objectives of a corrective reading program, it becomes apparent that all learning may be regarded as either training in reading or preparation for reading, insofar as it provides a background of experience. In a sense, therefore, all teachers—in fact, all persons who have anything to do with the education of young people—are teachers of reading. The instructors in the various departments of the school should be brought to a recognition of this fact and of the need for close cooperation with those mainly responsible for the corrective program, in order that the efforts of the whole faculty may be coordinated in the conscious and efficient performance of a function that all teachers inevitably carry on to some extent. Regardless of which department is mainly responsible for the reading project, the corrective teachers will necessarily depend to a great extent on the teachers in the different fields for assistance in such matters as teaching the concepts peculiar to the various subjects, for only specialists in each field are fully qualified to give this kind of instruction.

The student's attitude toward reading is important: "Read not to contradict, nor to believe, but to weigh and consider."

Clarity of thought is usually associated with clarity of phrase. This quality is developed by solving practical problems, testing the logical sequence of thought in a passage, noting aberrations caused by propaganda, and writing outlines and creative summaries.

WAYS OF IMPROVING READING INTERESTS

"No matter what the reading tastes of my friend are I must respect them, and not feel superior."

The student should not, however, be allowed to stagnate at his initial interest level. A boy or a girl may be stimulated to read, through a vital interest in boats, horses, or dramatics; but this interest should lead out into new and broader interests. Free reading should be graduated reading.

Sometimes work or extracurricular activities lead to reading interests. For example, a high-school senior taking care of twin girls after school became interested in reading on the subject of twins and wrote an excellent paper on it.

Range of choice grows with the experience of the reader, as his tastes change and are modified by firsthand experience. He moves out from the classroom library to the school library, to the town library, to the county library. An effective way of developing a reader's interest is to expose him to the tastes of others. Various ways of doing this have already been suggested. A further effective device is the use of contrasting materials, either by seizing upon natural classroom opportunities to have students contrast Little Sure-shot with David Balfour, or by setting contrasting selections side by side and having the students discuss their reasons for liking the one better than the other.

IMPROVEMENT OF STUDY HABITS

Growth in reading ability is not the only problem in the instruction of retarded readers. Many of these pupils would continue to do ineffective schoolwork even if their reading level were brought up to the average of their grade, simply because they do not use efficient study methods. Good study habits depend partly upon knowledge of the best methods to be employed in different situations and partly upon practice in sound procedures. Since the nature of the study situation varies with the kind of content, theoretically the best training in methods of study can be given by the teachers in different fields, provided that their interest and cooperation are enlisted. A considerable number of study procedures, however, are common to nearly all phases of schoolwork, and it is desirable to take these up in the corrective reading class.

One of the first steps in improving the study habits of the pupils is to have them check themselves on a study-habits questionnaire, so that they will be aware of their weaknesses. A series of individual and group conferences based on the checking should then be planned. Devices such as the Wrenn *Study Habits Inventory* (25) or the Traxler *Survey of Study Habits* blank (23) may be used in this connection. The score on an inventory of this kind is not highly valid, but the pupils' answers to the individual questions are useful as a starting point for corrective instruction.

It cannot be too strongly emphasized that the teaching of desirable methods of study until the pupils understand them is an important part of the process, but this is not enough. A definite corrective program of study should be planned for each pupil, who should put it into practice under guidance (22).

Students can improve their approach to the reading of assignments. General suggestions, especially relating to the importance of having a specific purpose in mind, have already been given. With a college student who was required to read Plato's *Republic*, the following approach was employed. A few minutes' conversation showed that she knew little about Plato and the period in which he lived; that she was not in the habit of skimming the assignment to determine its nature and the purpose with which it should be read. Instead, she usually began by reading every word. To correct these deficiencies she spent 5 minutes on a 12-page biographical sketch of Plato and another 5 minutes on the introduction, which gave information about Plato's writings. She was amazed at how much information she could gain in 10 minutes by judicious skimming and how much this knowledge helped her in reading the assignment efficiently and interpreting it accurately.

Any form of timing sets a standard of prompt attention to the work in hand. The warming-up period is practically eliminated by this timing mind-set. Thus if a student estimates that it will take an hour to read his history assignment or recognizes that he has only a half hour to spend on a certain story, he is likely to set to work promptly, concentrate more closely, and select more carefully. An exercise that has proved valuable with graduate students is the following: "Assume that you have only an hour to spend in reading a popular book you have heard mentioned frequently and are eager to read. See how much of value you can get from this short contact." The next week the students reported orally on the books that they had read and what they had got from the reading. Each had selected a different book and each had read selectively, according to the nature of the book. One student, who had read *The Last Puritan*, paid special attention to the philosophy of the chief character; another, who had skimmed through *Gone with the Wind*, obtained a general idea of the plot and remembered some especially dramatic scenes. One student, however, who had not abandoned his initial belief that every word of a book should be read, selected a very small book that he could read in his accustomed way within the time limit.

Another exercise that students have found valuable is to decide on a certain amount of time—½ to 1 hour daily—for doing certain required reading. Before beginning to read, they decided on their purpose, and afterward recorded the approximate number of words read in the period allotted. (The words may be estimated by multiplying the average number of words in about 10 lines by the number of lines per page to get the approximate words per page, and then multiplying that figure by the number of pages.) It is enlightening to the student to see the differences in rate of reading different kinds of material. The form Record of Reading has been used successfully for this purpose.

RECORD OF READING

(Thirty-minute periods)   Book or article:
Purpose of reading the material:

Date	Time of day	Total number of words read	Comprehension score	Reasons for improvement or lack of improvement

Students frequently need to give attention to the budgeting of their total time, as well as to the use of a particular study period. The best way is for them to keep a simple diary record, beginning with the time that they get up in the morning and continuing with each activity through the day until they go to bed. They can then examine this objective record and decide on changes that can reasonably be made in order to provide a better study schedule. Since habit revision is painful and difficult, they need encouragement and specific evidence, in the form of daily records, of their improved use of time. These daily records may take the simple form, Diary Record of Daily Activities.

DIARY RECORD OF DAILY ACTIVITIES

Date:
Day: Name

Hour	Description of activity	Remarks	Number of minutes
6 A.M.—			

The importance of a pupil's discovering for himself that he can succeed in reading cannot be overemphasized. In comparisons with previous performance, a growing list of words learned or a large pack of vocabulary cards mastered, charts or graphs of speed and comprehension scores on comparable exercises, the pupil has objective evidence of his own success.

Many of the procedures described in this chapter have been employed in a course designed for the improvement of the reading of students at Teachers College, Columbia University. The analysis made by one student may emphasize the relative value of different techniques.

Aside from the actual practice in reading, the virtues of this course, as far as I am concerned, can be classified as having sprung from two general sources.

In the first place, I found the *Study Type of Reading Exercises* to be extremely beneficial. Undoubtedly, they wrought certain benefits in the reading practice which they provided. An analysis of the time required for each exercise indicates a general reduction as the exercises continued. Certainly, this increase in speed cannot all be due to improved eye movements and comprehension. While this certainly must have played a significant part, I cannot but feel that much of the increase in speed was due to an increasing realization that I could read somewhat faster than I thought I could. That is, I found that by reading somewhat less thoroughly, I could still comprehend to the degree demanded by the end-exercises. Certainly, it is well to realize when to read with utmost thoroughness and when to practice a degree of skimming.

But it seems to me that the actual subject matter in the booklet was of even greater benefit than the practice which it provided. For example, the entire concept of reading different materials for different purposes, and therefore in entirely different ways, while mildly evident to me before, was here brought home so emphatically that already it influences my reading habits markedly. Again, the discussions on certain specific skills in reading, such as eye movements, improvement of vocabulary, learning to skim, and organizing the author's thought, have proved both interesting and beneficial. It is for this reason that I hope to keep the booklet on hand as a practical reference condensation.

The second general benefit in the course was in the class activities, including the various tests and exercises, as well as the group discussions, both in the class as a whole and in the smaller groups. The series of tests informed me that I was perhaps not so poor a reader as I had imagined—true, there is much room for improvement, but it appears that I am not quite at the bottom of the scale. Another significant piece of philosophy that permeates the course is the idea that a saturation point in reading skill does not exist for any one person, no matter how poor or how excellent he may be, and no matter what his deficiencies, there seems to be a lifetime of potential reading improvement stretching away before each person. Perhaps the most significant virtue of this was (and is) the encouragement which it lends to each individual. As another example, the discussions on how to get started on a given task of reading or studying were of great value. General hints in this line, such as budgeting study time, securing an appropriate place to study or read, and starting off with a "gusto" have proved beneficial in my own study habits. Also, the "15 minutes a day" technique for general reading appeals to me as being extremely practical.

It is difficult to evaluate negative results at so early a date. While there are activities of the course which, to me, seem to have produced no results, I realize that this may be because there has been no direct attempt to measure them specifically, or because it takes them a longer time to mature. The discussion of and practice in eye movements and the practice in outlining do not at present impress me as having been particularly fruitful; however, I do not deplore the time so spent for the reasons mentioned above.

Obviously, a course such as this should be but the beginning of reading improvement, not the end of it. My plans for the continuation of the spirit of the course group themselves largely around the method described as "improving reading by reading." I plan to supplement this with a modicum of reading books about reading, such as Adler's *How to Read a Book*. I hope to plan a reading diet which is sufficiently well balanced to provide a breadth of reading experience and a richness of reading content.

Fortunately, this fits in well with my planned activities for the coming year. I took this course largely because my next year's work will require a good background of many types of literature, and because I will have to keep up with current and professional material rather thoroughly. I had hoped that this course would constitute a preparation for this task. This it has done, but most important of all, to my way of thinking, it has demonstrated that by attacking this reading program thoroughly I will experience an improvement in reading technique which will improve the attack—and so on and so on in an anything-but-vicious circle.

Reading seems to provide its own practice for the mature student without specific mechanical difficulties.

It is both a means and an end.

PROCEDURES FOR SLOW-LEARNING STUDENTS

The procedures used in working with slow-learning students— those having Binet I.Q.'s ranging from 70 to 100—are not fundamentally different from the procedures used with average and superior students. They, too, profit by extensive reading; they, too, understand and remember better if they have had firsthand experience and if the ideas are made graphic; they, too, like to illustrate and dramatize what they have read. The difference is chiefly in the slower pace of progress and the need for much more activity and varied repetition for learning at each level. In one special class an abundance of suitable reading material was available—books illustrating summer adventures that the students had had, each page consisting of a picture and an explanatory sentence or two that the student had dictated and the teacher had printed; charts of "stories" the class had composed; six or seven different basic reading series, providing considerable repetition on the preprimer, primer, first-, second-, and third-grade levels; supplementary science, health, and social-science readers and many simple storybooks; scrapbooks with simplified captions; menus and recipes that were to be prepared that day; and various signs and directions.

Reading difficulties do not occur singly. Any specific difficulty is embedded in a total situation that may help or hinder its correction. For this reason, the case-study approach described in the next chapter is the most effective method of dealing with complex reading problems.

References

1. BETTS, EMMERT ALBERT, and THELMA MARSHALL BETTS, *An Index to Professional Literature on Reading and Related Topics*, American Book Company, New York, 1945, vii + 137 pp.
2. BUCKINGHAM, B. R., and E. W. DOLCH, *A Combined Word List*, Ginn and Company, Boston, 1936, 184 pp.
3. BURTON MARY, "The Hearing and Reading Comprehension of Vocabulary among High School Seniors," *School Review*, Vol. 52, pp. 47–50, January, 1944.
4. BUSWELL, GUY THOMAS, *Remedial Reading at the College and Adult Levels*, Supplementary Educational Monographs, No. 50, Department of Education, University of Chicago, Chicago, 1939, x + 72 pp.
5. "A Diagnostic Approach to the Reading Program," Part I, pp. vi + 26; Part II, pp. iv + 32, prepared by Division of Instructional Research, *Educational Research Bulletin of the Bureau of Reference, Research and Statistics*, Nos. 3 and 4, Board of Education of the City of New York, New York, 1942.
6. DOLCH, E. W., *The Basic Sight Vocabulary Cards*, The Garrard Press, Champaign, Ill.
7. GATES, ARTHUR I., and M. C. PRITCHARD, *Teaching Reading to Slow-learning Pupils*, Bureau of Publications, Teachers College, Columbia University, New York, 1942, 65 pp.
8. HILDRETH, GERTRUDE, "Individualizing Reading Instruction," *Teachers College Record*, Vol. 42, pp. 123–137, November, 1940.
9. KIRK, SAMUEL A., *Teaching Reading to Slow-learning Children*, Houghton Mifflin Company, Boston, 1940, xi + 225 pp.
10. McCAUL, ROBERT L., "Student Personnel Opportunities for the College Remedial-reading Teacher," *School Review*, Vol. 51, pp. 158–163, March, 1943.
11. McCULLOUGH, CONSTANCE M., *College Reading Skills*, Western Reserve University Bookstore, Cleveland, Ohio, 1941, v + 65 pp.
12. McCULLOUGH, CONSTANCE M., "The Recognition of Context Clues in Reading," *Elementary English Review*, Vol. 22, pp. 1–5, 38, January, 1945.
13. *Picturesque Word Origins*, G. & C. Merriam Company, Springfield, Mass., 1933, 134 pp.
14. RICHARDS, I. A., *Certain Notions on the Theory of Interpretation and Reading*, Official Report of 1940 Meeting, American Educational Research Association, May, 1940, pp. 10–14.
15. SHAFFER, VELMA R., "Remedial Reading Materials," *Peabody Journal of Education*, Vol. 20, pp. 162–165, November, 1942.

16. SHANNON, J. R., and MARIAN A. KITTLE, "An Experiment in Teaching Vocabulary," *Teachers College Journal*, Vol. 14, pp. 1–6, September, 1942.

17. STRANG, RUTH, *Exploration in Reading Patterns*, University of Chicago Press, Chicago, 1942, 172 pp.

18. STRANG, RUTH, *Problems in the Improvement of Reading in High School and College*, 2d ed., The Science Press Printing Company, Lancaster, Pa., 1940, 423 pp.

19. THORNDIKE, E. L., *Thorndike Century Junior Dictionary*, rev. ed., Scott, Foresman and Company, Chicago, 1942, xx + 940 pp.

20. THORNDIKE, E. L., *Thorndike Century Senior Dictionary*, Scott, Foresman and Company, Chicago, 1941, 1065 pp.

21. THORNDIKE, E. L., and IRVING LORGE, *The Teacher's Word Book of 30,000 Words*, Bureau of Publications, Teachers College, Columbia University, New York, 1944, xii + 274 pp.

22. TRAXLER, ARTHUR E., *The Improvement of Study Habits and Skills*, The Educational Records Bureau, New York, October, 1944, v + 37 pp.

23. TRAXLER, ARTHUR E., *Survey of Study Habits*, experimental ed., Grades 8–14, the author, New York, 1944, 8 pp. (Distributed by the Educational Records Bureau, New York.)

24. WESTOVER, FREDERICK, *Mechanical Control versus Practice Exercises in Reading as a Means of Improving the Reading Speed and Comprehension of College Freshmen*, Bureau of Publications, Teachers College, Columbia University, New York, 1945.

25. WRENN, C. GILBERT, *Study Habits Inventory*, Stanford University Press, Stanford University, Calif., 1935.

CHAPTER XI

CASE STUDIES OF STUDENTS HAVING READING DIFFICULTY

Although instruction in regular classes and in special reading groups can be individualized, there is an occasional student whose reading problem is so complex, whose resistance to reading is so strong, whose ability to learn in groups is so limited, that individual work with him is necessary. Individual conferences offer the best opportunity for the student to gain a new orientation, a more hopeful and realistic view of himself, an understanding of his reading difficulties and what to do about them; as well as for him to know the experience of a relationship with a person who accepts him as he is, recognizes his best potentialities, and expects him to assume responsibility for the improvement of his reading but is ready to use all available resources to help him do so.

REFERRAL FOR INDIVIDUAL WORK

The way in which the student is referred to the reading expert or clinic largely determines the success of the initial contact. After the teacher or the counselor is certain that individual help is desirable and available, he has the task of suggesting it to the student in such a way that he himself will consider it an opportunity and will make the decision to take advantage of the service. In order to give the student an idea of the kind of service offered, the teacher might say, for example, "Dr. X (the reading expert) tells me he has a free hour twice a week in which he could help you improve your reading. You know Marjorie, Bill, and others (mentioning some boys and girls whom the student admires) have taken advantage of this special opportunity and have learned to read more efficiently and thus save time for other things. Jean is working on her reading, too, with Dr. X and thinks it will do a lot to help her get off to a good start in college. Dr. X expects students who come to him to discover, with his help, what is interfering with their being better readers and to plan a program for improvement. It's up to you to decide whether you can fit 2 hours a week into your schedule and whether you really want to take advantage of this individual work."

The attitude of other students toward the individual reading work or clinic is equally important. If they feel that a student is lucky to get a chance to have this additional help, there will be no stigma attached to the remedial work. It will be considered a normal part of the school program.

Referral of an adolescent to a reading clinic is frequently suggested by an adult who knows him and is concerned about him. Initial contact with an adult who is concerned about the student's reading gives the worker an opportunity to obtain valuable case data, as is indicated in the following record of an interview with the father of a girl in the tenth grade.

MR. R.: We wanted to have her examined so that we would know what to do about it.

WORKER: What is it that concerns you?

MR. R.: She reads very slowly, and, in fact, far too slowly to get anywhere with her studies or anything of that sort. She passes her work, but it requires a great deal of her time on those things where there is much reading involved. We know that we should have done something about it much sooner. In her last year in grammar school she came home and reported to us that in the reading tests that they had given at the school, she was far below the average of the class and her speed of reading in the eighth grade was the equivalent of the fifth- or sixth-grade student.

WORKER: She hasn't been doing anything about it?

MR. R.: We thought at first that it was mainly because she hadn't done as much reading as she should have. When she was much younger, she was constantly urged to read more. She didn't enjoy reading and probably the reason for it was that she read slowly. By the time she got anywhere, she'd lose interest.

WORKER: Is it so bad now that it's causing very marked difficulty with her schoolwork?

MR. R.: Not a marked difficulty. We came to the conclusion that a step should be taken within a short period of time even if it meant a loss of a term of school now. If it were that serious it would probably be better to do it now.

WORKER: In what way do you mean? To concentrate on some particular work?

MR. R.: I don't know exactly what the procedure would be. We feel it would be worth while because we do hope to send her on to college. I think she is a bright enough child. For instance, she has an I.Q. of 120— considering the fact that so much of the intelligence tests is based on actual reading, too.

WORKER: Were those group tests? Then they would involve reading.

MR. R.: Yes. Maybe her I.Q. is even higher than that.

WORKER: Does she have to study longer than most of the girls in her class?

MR. R.: Yes.

WORKER: Is she conscientious?

MR. R.: Yes. It isn't that she just slides along with her work.

WORKER: Does she work too long and too hard?

MR. R.: Yes. As the matter stands now, she is just not able to complete the homework assignments that she is given.

WORKER: Does that upset her? Does it bother her when she can't do them?

MR. R.: Well, naturally it does. She is conscientious. It isn't that it's causing a psychological difficulty, if that is what you are driving at. I don't think it is causing her to become a psychological misfit.

WORKER: I don't mean anything abnormal. Worry does take away from one's energy. It is energy spent in a not very fruitful way. If she worries, then it takes energy away from her energy to do work. There is a wide variation in the amount people worry about things. Some people let others know that they worry and some people can hide it. I just wondered if that was a factor in this situation.

MR. R.: There is also the factor that the family may be farther away from New York in the spring. So we are anxious to have an examination and recommendations as to what should be done. At the high school they have a teacher who is quite interested in that sort of thing and they have actually purchased one of those machines.

WORKER: You mean some of the equipment for reading purposes? The metronoscope?

MR. R.: Yes. We went to see her first to find out just what they were doing and they made the recommendation also that she should be taken to a regular clinic somewhere for a complete diagnosis.

WORKER: Does she know about all these plans, and is she interested?

MR. R.: Yes.

WORKER: It's voluntary on her part, not at the instigation of her family?

MR. R.: Yes.

WORKER: Those things make a difference in how to approach the problem.

MR. R.: I'm sure that anyone making the diagnosis would have her complete cooperation. I think she is much older in her actions than most. She is more mature.

WORKER: What makes you say that? Could you give me a better idea?

MR. R.: She takes much greater individual responsibility than most girls do. She is quite a leader. I think it is because of home environment. She is the youngest of four, and enters into the family conversation on social, political, and other subjects.

WORKER: Is she the only one of your four who has had difficulty with reading?

MR. R.: Her sisters who went to the school to which she is now going made excellent records for themselves, and I do believe that she is under pressure a bit because of this.

WORKER: They make standards for her to follow? Is that it?

MR. R.: Sometimes the teachers throw it up to her. Even now, although it is some years since her sisters were there, some of the teachers that knew them expect wonderful things immediately upon seeing her in the class.

One sister was valedictorian. Both sisters are not only very capable in schoolwork, but were also leaders in extracurricular activities and were very popular there.

WORKER: Well, you say B— is also something of a leader; but not so outstanding?

MR. R.: I don't know. It's hard to make a comparison. Probably not quite so much.

WORKER: Do you think she does it more to follow in her sisters' footsteps, or does it come naturally to her?

MR. R.: I don't think she's consciously trying to be popular.

WORKER: She seems to be getting more satisfaction in the social field than academically?

MR. R.: Probably.

WORKER: I think B— sounds like a girl that would be very much interested in being helped and, if it is at all possible, we will try to arrange it. We especially like to have the student take a good deal of responsibility for her own reading program. There are a number of tests that are given— both intelligence and reading tests—and then, of course, we also try to determine something of the student's interests. In working out any remedial program her interests and personality are factors that have to be taken into consideration. If we feel there is something wrong with her eyes, we would recommend her seeing an oculist. Has she had her eyes examined?

MR. R.: Yes.

WORKER: And there is no difficulty?

MR. R.: The doctor gave her glasses for reading, although he did not think that she particularly needed them.

WORKER: Would it be possible for her to come here for appointments, and if so does it mean missing school, and is that all right?

MR. R.: How closely spaced are the interviews?

WORKER: That depends a little bit on her schedule and the schedule of the person who is working with her—usually once or twice a week. The arrangement about fees was discussed when you made your application. Is there anything else that you think it would be of help for us to know?

MR. R.: No, I think I've probably described her as well as I can. I do think that you would agree with me that she is much more mature than her age indicates.

WORKER: You said she is quite a leader, but I'm not quite sure what gives you that impression.

MR. R.: Her interests are quite mature interests. Of course, we have quite a group of young people about the same age. She conducts herself with much more decorum than the average. I mean, where it is necessary, for instance, almost to step on the necks of some of the kids to maintain any discipline, she will be the one to maintain the discipline. She has a more mature interest. She will take an interest in such things as a housing problem or a social problem, or things that the average person of that age isn't concerned with, and she will be able to discuss them fairly intelligently.

WORKER: Thank you very much for explaining it so clearly, and I'll write to you soon.

MR. R.: I'm happy to have had the chance to talk it over with you.

This conference with the father brought out many factors that might be related to B—'s reading difficulty. The father, perhaps, was relieved of some of his anxiety by talking about B— objectively in the presence of an understanding listener. He obtained an idea of the nature of the service offered and could present it to B— in a way to win her interest and cooperation. He also obtained the necessary specific information as to time, place, and fees. At the end of the interview the worker's word of appreciation strengthened the friendly relation that had developed during the interview.

INITIAL INTERVIEW WITH THE STUDENT HAVING READING DIFFICULTY

There is no one best approach. Every reading case follows a somewhat different pattern, depending upon many factors in the total situation. In the case just mentioned, the conference with the father in which so many background data were obtained enabled the worker in the first interview with B— to devote his attention to helping her to think through the question of what reading meant to her and why she wanted to improve her reading ability.

The worker's approach varies with the expectations and needs of the individual. If the client is antagonistic to reading or is deeply anxious about his inability to read, it is usually wise to avoid this problem area, which might associate the worker with strong negative emotions. In these cases, it is better to discuss the client's positive interests and abilities, his social success or achievement in sports or hobbies, his outstanding work in shop or art, or some other subject. This is, in general, a good approach when the worker does not know what the client's attitude toward reading is. If this approach is not feasible, beginning the interview with a test of vision may offer the worker a chance to establish a friendly relation. The Betts' tests of visual factors used in the Keystone Telebinocular are especially useful for this purpose. Few boys or girls fail to respond with interest to the forest scene that measures visual acuity and to the curious way certain numbers pop out in the test of depth perception. Regardless of the value of the telebinocular as a test of vision, it is often an effective means of relieving anxiety and establishing a good relationship between worker and client.

An approach that is effective with individuals who like books is to place a number of books on different subjects and of varying levels of reading difficulty on a table and let the client browse through them, while the worker ostensibly busies himself with something else, but actually notes the client's responses. After the client has examined the books, he may be asked to read a few paragraphs of the book in which he is most interested. If he reads this fluently, he can be tested on a more difficult book, until his level of reading ability is approximately ascertained. This procedure is valuable not only in establishing a friendly relationship and in supplying information on reading interests, attitudes, and ability but also in choosing a suitable standardized reading test. The discussion of these books may lead to conversation about interests in general, the student's use of time, and his reading difficulty as he sees it.

If the individual comes with the idea that he is to take reading tests and wants to know what his reading ability really is, the worker may begin the interview with an oral reading test and follow it with silent reading tests. If time permits in this interview—or if not, in the next—the worker can score the tests with the client, study the errors made, encourage him to analyze how he happened to make these errors, and give him a few suggestions as to how to read more effectively the kind of material that was used. The client is usually interested in the test results and eager to do something about them.

A mature, intelligent student may want to spend the first interview thinking through his reading problem for himself. The role of the worker then becomes that of a sympathetic listener who occasionally asks a question or offers an interpretation when the client seems ready for it.

The best approach with seriously retarded readers who are deeply discouraged about their reading but very anxious to improve may be to give them the experience of success in the first interview. This was done in the case of a boy seventeen and a half years-old, who had a good oral vocabulary and conversational ability but was practically a nonreader. The first interview, briefly reported, was as follows:

WORKER: Mr. L—tells me you're interested in learning to read.
E—: Yes. I'll be in the Army in about 5 months, and every time I go for a job, I have to do some reading and writing.
WORKER: Tell me some word in which you are particularly interested.
E—: "Guns," I guess. Guns are my hobby.

WORKER: Fine. Let's learn to write "guns." (Worker writes "guns" with crayon in large letters on card. E— traces letters with finger pronouncing the word correctly as he does so. He repeats this process several times—Fernald method.) Now you can write it without looking at the copy. (E— writes word correctly.) That's just fine. Now let's try "are." (E— traces this word four times and then writes it correctly. He does the same with "my.") The next word is "hobby."

E—: Oh, I don't think I can do that one.

WORKER: Sure you can. Try it. (Worker pronounces it clearly in syllables as she writes it. Then E— traces it five times.)

E—: Now I think I can write it. (Does so correctly.)

WORKER: That's *very* good. Do you want to write it again without looking? (E— does so correctly.) Now you know the whole sentence. You can write it all now.

E—: Without looking?

WORKER: Sure.

E—: O.K. (Writes entire sentence, omitting "my.")

WORKER: You left out one word. (E— puzzles over it a few minutes and then inserts "my.") That's just fine! You didn't make one mistake.

E—: Gee! Ain't we got fun! (E— goes on to tell about making a collection of gun catalogues.)

WORKER: That would make a good next sentence to learn, wouldn't it? —"I am going to make a collection." (Following the same procedure, E— learns all the words up to "collection.")

WORKER: That's splendid. You haven't made a mistake yet. Now try "collection."

E—: That's hard.

WORKER: (Writes it and pronounces it distinctly by syllables and E— practices as before.)

E—: Now I think I can do it. (Begins, but finds that he can't do it.)

WORKER: That's all right. If you trace it several times more, you'll be able to do it. (They study the three syllables, noting where the "tion" starts. E—writes it correctly.) Good! That's perfect.

They talk for a little while, E— telling about his collection of matches and the collection of gun catalogues that he made while he was in the hospital. He was hospitalized for a number of years because of infantile paralysis.

WORKER: Would you like to write another sentence today about getting the catalogues or would you rather wait until next time?

E—: Let's go. (Using the same method, he learns the words of the next sentence—"I had catalogues from every gun industry in the country.")

WORKER: Now, for the whole sentence. (E— writes the first two words and hesitates on "catalogues.") Just skip that and go on with the rest of the sentence. (He finished the sentence correctly except for putting *g* instead of *n* in "gun" and *nu* instead of *un* in "country." After practicing "catalogues" again, he writes it correctly.) Now the sentence is 100 per cent perfect. Will you file the cards while I have your three sentences typed?

E—: Sure. I know how to file them in the card catalogue. (He does this correctly.)

The worker has the three sentences typed in booklet form with the title "Guns" and the boy's full name on the outside page. The "book" reads

> Guns are my hobby.
> I would like
> to make a collection.
> I had catalogues
> from every gun industry
> in the country.

WORKER: Now, here's your book in typed form. Let's hear you read it just as though you were talking to me. (E— reads it fluently and with great pleasure.)

They talk for a few minutes about skeet shooting. The worker is interested and says she never knew so much about that before.

E—: Gee, you learned something, too.

The interviews that followed included more of the same kind of practice, using the material that E— suggested. At the beginning of the third period, he announced that he wanted to learn this sentence: "I particularly like semiautomatic rifles." Another time he wanted to write to his brother, who was in the Army. The worker furnished writing paper and envelope and E— wrote the following letter:

> January 10, 1944
> Hi, Bill,
> How's every little thing?
> I am going to Columbia University
> every Monday and Wednesday.
> As always,
> E—

In this case, the objective was to help E— acquire from the beginning a feeling of confidence and success in reading and writing, beginning with words of special interest to him, and gradually acquiring a knowledge of the basic vocabulary that constitutes so large a part of directions, books, and magazines. By using his own conversation as reading material, he gained a sense of reading fluency. Eventually he would make the transition to other simple reading material for which he had need. His interest and enjoyment in the learning process were indicated by such comments as

"Let's try every word once more."

"I can write it now."

"Now I want to make a list of the words I've learned."

"Yeah, I'm learning" (when the worker said after a review, "Good. I think you really know these words now.")

"Ain't we got fun!" (a remark repeated several times during each interview).

The casual conversation about his interests and future plans not only prevented fatigue but also helped to give him a sense of direction and a more accurate and hopeful appraisal of himself. The worker summarized her prognosis for E—briefly as follows:

"E— should be able to read and write fluently at about the fourth-grade level of difficulty. A changed attitude toward himself and his place in the world's work or friends who may arouse his ambition may at any time provide the drive necessary for him to put forth the effort that adult reading and writing demand."

These are only a few examples of the great variety of approaches to individual reading difficulty. There is no general principle except sensitivity to the individual who is being helped to realize his best potentialities.

THE READING AUTOBIOGRAPHY

A history of his reading development as the student views it— either orally or in writing, depending on which avenue of communication is preferred—often throws light on the best procedures to use. In some cases the autobiography may be limited primarily to reading per se; in other cases, as in the following, the understanding of the child's interests and family relationships has a most important bearing on her reading development.[1]

On June 1, 1929, a baby girl was born to a school principal and his wife. When the baby's sister, who was about ten, first viewed this little red ball, her reaction was a grown of disappointment. That homely, red, baby was I.

Of the town of my birth I remember very little as we soon moved to (another town). There I played in our great, big, yard for four years. I had short, straight hair and was seldom seen, when not wearing overalls. I did not play with girls, as boys games, and toys appealed to me more. The boy across the street, was my best pal. We played with his electric trains and made airplanes together.

I played mostly with boys until I was about eight years old when I joined the Sunshine Club. It was a girls' organization. They served cocoa every

---

[1] The same fifteen-year-old girl referred to in the conference with her father, pp. 311–314. Spelling, punctuation, and style are unchanged. Names have been changed and identifying details omitted.

meeting. That was the only reason I attended. It was always I that would not obey. Probably this was dew to the fact that the heads of the organization always told me to set a good example as I was the principal's daughter. I resented this very much and still do.

I attended Public School for eight years. I always had a dislike for education and teachers. Consequently, I would never obey them. I walked out of the class several times. I was sent out of classes by three different teachers. One teacher literally through me out. She took me by the neck, opened the door and gave me a shove. I can not account for my attitude toward teachers, except that one kept me untill four thirty, after school, telling me I should be good because of my father's position.

I have been brought up in a family that is mentally allert, a family of broad minded people. I have always eaten at a table at which, problems of economics were discussed often. I've heard my brothers discuse contriversial subjects by the hour. It is only natural that I too would be somewhat interested in these things.

When I was fourteen one of my sisters was engaged to be married. She asked me to be Maid of Honnor. The wedding was held in the church. I received my first evening dress and high heals. I had a permanent wave too. You would not have known me that day. At the wedding I met a boy who invited me to attend a formal dance with him. It was my first dance. That summer he took me other places too. By fall practically all of my tomboy characteristics had vanished. I believe my sister's wedding was the beginning of a great change in me.

Now I am in high school. There are a great many things I regret. I wish that I had not waisted my time, fooling in grammar school. If I could live those years over, I would attend school with the purpose of obtaining everything I could possibly receive from it. I would spend my spare time reading masterpieces and not trash.

Lately, I have held my sister as an ideal. She is so well poised. She has such a beautifull character and temperment. She is also very intelligent. I would like very much to be like her. I realize that a character such as hers must be developed. It is only recently that I have begun to try to better myself.

Within me there seems to be a desire to serve man-kind. I would like to do Social Service Work. If I did this, it would put me in a better position to do my part in abolishing slums. I realize this is a hard, depressing, task. I would like to give those people an ideal, a reason for living well. Perhaps to some of the homes I might bring a note of Religion. I feel that the making of a man, and of a nation is based upon a strong, enduring faith in God.

Social Service or perhaps Religious Education work, would be the occupation I would choose if any. But I don't think I am unlike any other girl, when I would like to have a home. Most any other person would like to own there home, and bring up a family they can be prowd of. This is something of course that cannot be counted on therefore I will train myself for Social Service. Unfortunately the future can not be foreseen.

This autobiography suggests the need for instruction in certain fundamentals that were neglected in the primary grades, reveals difficulties in spelling, and indicates interests and motives that can be used to reinforce instruction in reading. It helps to put reading instruction in its rightful place as part of the student's total development.

USE OF TESTS

Little need be added to the information about tests on pages 125–145. The same principles of selection, administration, and interpretation apply here. However, standardized tests may be used more flexibly in the clinical situation when the aim is to study the reading process rather than to obtain information on the student's reading proficiency. By means of analysis and introspection, more diagnostic information can be extracted from standardized tests than is usually obtained. The following report of two interviews with the girl to whom reference has already been made (pages 311–314, 318–319) illustrates one diagnostic approach through tests.

First Interview.—B—'s approach was friendly and spontaneous. The worker asked if she had ever taken a reading test. She said she had not since elementary school. She mentioned oral reading and interest in oral reading, so we passed directly to the oral reading tests.

Her interpretation of these tests showed several interesting tendencies: (1) to tie up the passage read with knowledge she already had, (2) to substitute occasionally a meaningless word for the correct word, and (3) to insert words that did not change the meaning (see Examiner's Diagnostic Record Blank).

Her comprehension of the third passage was better than the worker expected. She explained this by saying that she was taking a course in child psychology for Sunday-school teachers.

Her attitude was cheerful and objective; she showed no embarrassment when she came to difficult words, but said, "I don't usually have so many difficult words so close together."

She spoke enthusiastically of sports—swimming and skating. "I could spend all day skating." She had won several prizes in athletics recently. She said she had not joined clubs this year because she needed time for study. However, she was teaching a Sunday-school class as well as taking a course in child psychology given for Sunday-school teachers. She was also active in the Young People's Society.

When flash cards were used, she had difficulty in reading more than one word at a time.

Although the hour was almost gone, she was willing to take the

Traxler test. She said it was quite a long trip over and she'd like to stay a little longer.

Her conversation was somewhat mature, her vocabulary good, her expression coherent and a little more precise than ordinary conversation, as though she were quite conscious of her expression.

Second Interview.—B— was very cooperative in coming to the college a half hour earlier than was originally planned. The reason for this was to get a photograph of her eye movements. The worker introduced her to Mr. I—, who made a record of her eye movements. Her approach to him was friendly and social, and she followed the directions without any hesitancy or difficulty.

After the photographic record was taken, she was given the visual-perception tests of the Gates series of diagnostic tests. On the test of recognizing different figures she made a score above the highest elementary norms given in the test manual. This was also true of the selection-of-figures test. These results indicated that the errors in recognizing words that B— made on the oral reading test last week were probably not due to a general visual-perception difficulty. On the visual-perception test of different numbers her score was at 4.1 grade level. Of the six errors she made, four were caused by a confusion between the numbers 2 and 3. She said that she would have to get busy and learn the difference between a 2 and a 3, and also mentioned the fact that she was not very good in arithmetic, and remarked that some of the difficulty might be due to this inaccurate reading of numbers.

B— also mentioned that she had great difficulty with spelling and had made a large number of errors on a single composition. She said that her English teacher was glad she was coming over here because she thought she was "a baffling case." She said that she frequently wrote a word four or five times in order to see which form looked right. She said she misspelled the simplest words. In a letter to her brother, she said she spelled "sky blue" "skei blu." In self-defense she said she thought that spelling should be simplified and that words should be spelled the way they sound. "Thomas," for example, should be spelled "Tomas." There was no reason to have the h in there.

After the visual-perception test, the worker said to B—, "Suppose we go over the test which you took last week, to see if we can get any clues as to why you made some of the errors and how you managed to get the correct response in so many cases." Together the worker and B— went over the test, trying to find out what association was involved in some of the correct and incorrect answers. Some very interesting associations emerged. For example, she marked "auxiliary" correctly as "assisting" and said that she had thought of the Ladies' Auxiliary of the church and knew that they helped repair the church and did other useful things. "Deficiency" she marked incorrectly as "inferiority"; in tracing back the association, she said that she thought of a "spelling deficiency," which she considered a sign of inferiority, so she marked "inferiority" instead of "lack." The worker asked her at that point whether she had other associations with "deficiency," and she said, "Yes, I know there is a food deficiency, a water deficiency, and the like." The worker then suggested that she would be more likely to get the main meaning of the word if she recalled various associations and saw what idea was common in these various uses of the word. Similarly, in almost all the errors made, there was a logical reason for the response that she made. The responses were not illogical but rather seemed to involve a certain periphery, or derived, meaning rather than the central meaning of the word. An exception to this was in the case of "stile." She marked "fashion," instead of "steps," and the reason for the error was obviously a confusion of the two words, into which a spelling difficulty entered.

The errors on the paragraph reading were rather few in number and were of all different kinds. Few clues were obtained here as to the difficulties involved, because of the relatively small number of errors.

The rest of the time was spent in discussing B—'s next assignment in English, "The Specter Bridegroom," by Washington Irving. B— explained what the teacher expected them to get from their reading. The worker asked B— how she would go about reading this assignment. She said that she had read the preliminary pages, which had aroused her interest in the story, so that she would begin to read with a desire to know what the story was about. She read the first paragraph and the worker asked her what she got from it that would help her in getting the story. She said that the first paragraph was concerned with description of the castle. In response to the question "Did you find anything else of interest in the first paragraph?" she pointed out that the reader was given the idea that the owner of the castle was a proud man.

B— read the second paragraph and the worker asked her what else she had found out about the chief character in the story. She said that her idea of his being proud was confirmed. On further questioning, she noted that he was not only proud but also had the characteristic of being afraid of certain things.

The next paragraph contained a description of his daughter. When the worker asked what kind of girl the daughter was, B— said that she must have been a very ladylike girl, which was a good generalization. B— pointed out one particular phrase that was very well written, and this showed that she had a certain appreciation of literary style.

They then summarized the discussion by saying that in reading the story she would probably want to find out what kind of characters were in the story and what happened to them. In addition, she might find especially beautiful descriptions and some phrases or sentences that she would like to remember in the words of the author.

An appointment was made for the following week.

Third Interview.—B— came about three-quarters of an hour earlier than her scheduled appointment and had to wait a half hour. When the worker joined her, she said, "I wanted to read some of the Hazen Conference books that I saw here last week, but the books were gone. I'm devotional leader and want to get some new ideas." She went on to say that she had attended the Eastern Hazen Conference a year ago and enjoyed the outdoor evening devotional services.

B— read the first exercise in *Study Type of Reading Exercises*. The summary was good for the first part, but poor for the latter part of the passage. B— said that she had difficulty in remembering the last part, which the worker thought she read more rapidly than the first part.

The next day's assignment in biology, which she brought with her, was very difficult for high-school pupils—a condensed treatment of Mendel's laws, with no attempt to explain a large number of technical words introduced with great rapidity. B— said that she did well in biology and it seemed as though her slow, thoughtful type of reading was more appropriate to this short, difficult type of assignment than to other assignments.

During the hour, she passed her hand over her eyes a number of times, as though they bothered her, but she said they did not hurt.

The worker asked her what she would like the worker to do next. B— laughed, a little puzzled, and said she would like to know whether to begin trying to improve her spelling or her reading. The worker suggested the following procedure for improving her spelling.

Learning to spell is something you can do independently; you can teach yourself. Here are a few suggestions:

1. Underline all the misspelled words in your letters and written work. Ask someone to check your underlining to see that you have marked all misspelled words.

2. Study each of the misspelled words. Pronounce each correctly; write it one syllable at a time, saying the syllables distinctly as you write them; note parts of the word that are hard for you and give special attention to them; write the word several times, to get the feeling of how it is written correctly; close your eyes and write the word the way you feel it should be written, then check to see if you are correct; close your eyes and see if you can see how the word looked.   When you are sure that you know how to spell the word, write it and check the correctness of your written word. Practice until you have written the word correctly without help at least three times.   Test yourself again each week until you never make a mistake.

3. Form the habit of looking closely at unfamiliar words; break them into syllables that you can spell easily.

4. If certain letters or letter combinations give you special difficulty, make a column for each and fill the column with words that contain the troublesome letters, being sure that each is spelled correctly, as, for example, the following:

oa	al	a	ou
groan	alert	permanent	proud
moan	alternate	testament	loud

5. Play word-building games—anagrams, "hang man," combining small known words into larger words, doing crossword puzzles.

6. Overpronounce some words that cause special difficulty:

perm *a* nent
priv *i* lege

OTHER PROCEDURES FOR IMPROVING READING

Means of improving reading, including books and articles, instruction, practice exercises, machines and other equipment described on pages 235–238 and 335–347, can be adapted to work with individuals. Always the procedure is individualized to meet the needs and to arouse the interest and cooperation of the student. The following case is reported in some detail, merely to illustrate the kind of adaptation required in each individual case.

The subject was a college student, initially very low in reading ability.

First Period.[1]—Miss M— talked about herself: school history, family interests, aims, etc., and then took the Nelson-Denny test.

Second Period.—As Miss M— wanted to know the results of the Nelson-Denny test that she had taken in the previous period, the interview started with a further study of the test results. She discovered that one of the reasons for her low scores was that she had finished only a small part of the vocabulary and the paragraph-read-

---

[1] Each period was an hour in length, once a week.

ing tests. On the vocabulary test she had made perceptual errors, which she corrected easily when she looked more closely at the word. There were, however, many literary, educational, and scientific words with which she was not familiar. She accepted eagerly the suggestion that she put a light pencil check on unfamiliar words in the fields in which she was now reading and listening, look them up later, and record them upon cards, thus making a pocketbook file for study in odd moments.

Third Period.—Miss M— made an analysis of her paragraph reading on the Nelson-Denny test, to discover how she read material of that kind, where she made errors, and what kind of content was most difficult for her. In thinking back over her method, she decided that she attempted to "memorize everything," rather than to read for the author's pattern of thought. She had failed on every question that required an understanding of the central thought. When she reread for the related pattern of thought, she had no difficulty in answering the test questions.

The worker then suggested that she practice getting the author's pattern of thought in another kind of material. The *Study Type of Reading Exercises* were used for this purpose. Miss M— was given 1 minute to glance over one of the thousand-word passages, to find out what the author was attempting to do and to get the skeleton organization of the passage. After she had done this and reported on what she had gleaned from this quick survey of the material, suggestions were made for skimming more effectively for this purpose. She noticed, for example, in the first exercise she read (Hygiene of the Eyes) that the first page was introductory and the clue to what followed was given at the bottom of the page in a sentence to which the reader's attention was called by italics. This sentence suggested that the rest of the passage would be devoted to a consideration of the various rules of eye hygiene. A glance at the topic sentence of each paragraph confirmed this hypothesis and thus the structure of the passage as a whole became clear. The worker said that sometimes the author was still more helpful and enumerated at the beginning the main points that he was going to discuss. Miss M— applied these suggestions to her skimming of the next two exercises and was delighted to see how easily she could get the structure of well-organized material and how much she retained from such a small expenditure of time. She asked to take the booklet home with her for further practice. She read one exercise a day at home, according to directions, until the 20 exercises were completed.

She also expressed a desire for help in reading the scientific, philosophical, and abstract material that was assigned in one of the courses. The worker suggested that she bring in her assignment in that course at the next reading period and that they use it as practice material.

Fourth Period.—Miss M— brought in the syllabus outline of the course and some of the readings. The worker studied the syllabus with her to see what the main topics and subdivisions were, and they discussed the plan and purpose of the course.   Miss M— then glanced over the assignment for the day, to see where it fitted into the total outline and how it contributed to the purpose of the course. She noticed that the two readings assigned represented different points of view. She skimmed both for their general pattern of thought, then read them more carefully to weigh the evidence given by the two authors.

Miss M: This kind of reading is a sort of argument, isn't it?
Worker: That's a good way to put it.   There is two-way communication in any thoughtful reading—the author is communicating his ideas to you and you are communicating your thoughts about his ideas.
Miss M: That means I have to read with an active mind, doesn't it?—not just let the book come to me.
Worker: Exactly.

The rest of the period was spent in weighing evidence presented in the two passages and in drawing inferences relating to the problem under consideration. Miss M— felt that she had acquired a much better method of reading for this course than she had previously employed.

Fifth Period.—As an aid to the analysis of paragraphs, Miss M— read the four oral-reading paragraphs in the *Examiner's Diagnostic Record*. Her oral reading was excellent as to phrasing, expression, and enunciation, and her voice beautifully pitched and modulated. But the question "Tell me what the author said?" showed that Miss M— had not grasped the author's pattern of thought except in the first paragraph (see discussion of oral reading test, pages 238–246).   The rest of the period was spent in instruction in ways in which the pattern of these paragraphs could be obtained. For example, on rereading the second paragraph, the student discovered that the first sentence, "The earth has written its own story," and the last sentence, "The pages of the book are the layers of rock that lie one on top of the other," stated the central thought of the selection and that the intervening sentences helped to develop that idea through specific illustrations. Miss M— became interested in the structure of paragraphs and gained a much clearer idea of how paragraphs are built and how a knowledge of the general structure of a paragraph helps the reader to grasp its meaning quickly.

As Miss M— had brought a book assigned in another course, on which she was to write a report, the worker took a little time for discussing this with her.

Miss M: I have read this book quickly and I think I know what is important, but I don't know how to write a review.

Worker: What is your purpose in writing this review—to give (1) an abstract of the book, (2) a discussion of its theories and their relation to the problem you are studying, or (3) an appraisal of the author's style and his contribution to his field?

Miss M: I think the second purpose best describes the kind of review called for here.

Worker: Then suppose that you begin by writing in outline form the central ideas that stand out in your mind as you recall the book.

Miss M: Shouldn't I look at the table of contents for that?

Worker: Let's see what you have in mind first.

Miss M— proceeded to recall the main ideas, with some tendency to enlarge on trivial points. The worker questioned the latter and thus helped her to see their subordinate relationship. From this beginning, Miss M— wrote a good outline of the author's thought pattern and then considered how it was related to the problem under discussion in the course. She wrote the report later and said that it was the best and easiest review she had ever written.

Miss M— also mentioned her difficulty in finding time for everything, and the worker suggested that she jot down the reading she did during the next week.

Sixth Period.—Miss M— showed the worker her reading record and expressed dissatisfaction with her newspaper reading. "You see, I don't actually have time to read my newspaper thoroughly. I'd like to have help on that, because I feel that so many important things are happening and I'm just not 'up' on them." The worker asked her if she'd like to analyze her newspaper reading and radio listening according to a form that had been found helpful. This they did, the worker asking the questions and Miss M— answering them orally.

1. Do you read newspapers or a newspaper regularly?
2. What ones?
3. What parts of the paper do you find most interesting?
4. Do you read the editorials? If so, do you agree with the editor's opinion or question it?
5. Do you question the reliability of news stories?

6. Is there any signed column which you habitually read? If so, why?

7. Do you enjoy cartoons? Can you select *one* and describe your emotional reaction to it? Your intellectual reaction?

8. Do you enjoy comics? Why?

9. What weekly or monthly magazines do you read? What parts?

To help her to analyze her attitude with respect to reading, she was presented with the following exercise:

10. In your news reading which of the following most nearly describes your attitude?

    a. I accept what I read without question.

    b. I consider the reliability of the news presented.

    c. I sometimes recognize bias in the presentation of facts.

    d. I form, revise, or test my opinions by what I read.

    e. I am conscious of emotional overtones in such words as: (1) "free enterprise" (2) "capitalism" (3) "monopolies" (4) "C.I.O." (5) "coal strikes" (6) "radical"

    f. I skim (name) sections of the paper.

    g. I read (critically) _____ sections of the paper.
           (carefully)
           (analytically)

    h. I read news for information.

    i. I read news for cultural development.

    j. I read news to increase my value as a contributing citizen.

    k. I seldom read the _____ section of the newspaper.

What I Get from the Radio

11. I usually spend ____ minutes each day reading the newspaper.

12. I listen to any newsbroadcastors or commentators who happen to be on the radio.

13. I usually try to hear _____ (name of commentator) because

_____.

From this analysis, Miss M— discovered that she did not cover enough ground because she read everything equally carefully. She also did very little critical reading. Without a purpose for reading and listening, she did not select and remember important ideas.

Twenty minutes were spent in reading and discussing the sections in *How to Read the News* that she thought would be most helpful to her. Miss M— was particularly interested in the "Standards of Reading" section and said, "Do you think I can learn to read like that?" The worker replied, "I know you can make noticeable progress in a week if you try out your new reading skills in the right places. *Skim* the headlines to decide what you really want to read. *Appraise* the editorials as one man's opinion. Try reading one of the columnists and let me know how you like his or her style. Skim the foreign and domestic news for significant items. Then ask yourself, 'What have I read today that is significant for myself, for my job, for my community, my country, and the world?' "

MISS M—: How about clipping very good material and telling you why I want to keep it.

WORKER: A good idea. I'll do that, too, and we can compare clippings next time.

Seventh Period.—The newspaper session had apparently been very effective, for Miss M— said that she had learned how to read the newspaper quickly. "You wouldn't believe it, but I never enjoyed reading my newspaper before. *Now that I have a plan, it's fun.*" She read in 5 minutes a one-column editorial and made an excellent abstract of it. Her rate of reading was about 400 words a minute. Her selection of clippings was interesting. One clipping on strikes and another on educational budgeting she discussed with the worker for their social implications and related them to the course in social and educational problems that she was taking. As she had mentioned *The Reader's Digest* on the list of books and magazines that she particularly enjoyed, the worker used one of *The Reader's Digest* articles as an informal test. Miss M— read the article in 5 minutes and obtained a grade of 95 per cent on the comprehension test. The remaining time was spent on a course assignment, with special attention to note taking.

It was quite evident that Miss M— was convinced of her progress in reading and of her own ability to build on the skills that she had acquired, using them as they were appropriate in a flexible and efficient reading procedure. She also said that she had become less and less conscious of eye fatigue, which had always troubled her when reading. An oculist's examination showed no visual defects.

Miss M— said that she wished to plan a varied course of reading for the summer, including challenging material for thinking. She decided to read for a broader background. With the worker's help she selected books from the N.C.T.E. booklet in the fields of essay, biography, philosophy, religion, history, drama, fiction, poetry, science, and economics—one or two of the best in each field. She seemed eager to follow through her program and said, "I have a basis for good reading now, which I intend to perfect."

Outstanding Features in Treatment of This Case.—First of all, the procedure was to start with this student's recognized needs. As she suggested immediate reading problems, they were studied and instruction, practice, and follow-up were provided.

Second, important diagnostic material was obtained informally, through conversation, through the student's introspective reports on reading processes that she was using, by analysis of errors on the standardized test given, by observation of her method of reading different kinds of material.

Third, instruction and practice proceeded along with diagnosis, so that from the first period the student felt that she was gaining skills that were immediately helpful to her. This was particularly important, for the student was carrying a heavy schedule; spending time that did not seem to her to contribute to the accomplishment of her assigned work would have increased her anxiety and tension.

Fourth, the student took major responsibility for planning the remedial procedure. Because she was so active in making plans, the chances are that she will continue to exercise the same initiative after the periods with the worker are discontinued.

Fifth, objective evidences of progress were obtained that encouraged the student as well as checking on the procedure. The student's improved attitude toward reading and her satisfactions were considered fully as important as the results on standardized tests or timed exercises.

CUMULATIVE READING RECORDS

The majority of high-school students can be interested in keeping some kind of cumulative reading record, if the idea is properly introduced to them. In a discussion they will bring out the values of a reading record.

1. It is fun to see how many books they have read during high-school years.
2. It is an aid in improving their voluntary reading—filling gaps in content areas, introducing material other than fiction, providing for progression in quality and difficulty, suggesting sequences in their major field of interest.
3. It may be a means of interesting other students in books that one has liked.

The students may either work out their own forms or select a form that has already been developed. The *Cumulative Reading Record,* devised by Margaret M. Skinner and published by W. Wilbur Hatfield (2), provides space for records of 38 books. It is organized as follows:

CUMULATIVE READING RECORD OF _____
Devised by Margaret M. Skinner

Rölvaag	Giants in the Earth	9/8/33	2

Norwegian immigrants cross the trackless Minnesota prairie into Dakota and establish themselves as farmers. Through resourceful Per Hansa we realize the element of adventure in meeting the dangers and hardships; through his wife, Beret, we realize the bareness and lonely fears of this life.

Please record here *both* your voluntary and required reading. Follow the plan of the sample entry, giving author and title according to the scale below, and using the large space for a brief comment.

1. One of the best books I have ever read.
2. A good book. I like it.
3. Not so very interesting.
4. I don't like it.

Record of reading tests

Date Name Score of test

___ ___ ___
___ ___ ___
___ ___ ___
___ ___ ___

A more detailed analytical type of record suggested by Witty included the following items spaced on a normal-sized sheet of paper.

Name_____Div._____Date_____
Assignment_____Book_____
Story_____Pages_____
Did you like this story?   Write yes or no_____
If you did not like this story, tell why you did not like it._____
_____
_____

Put a ring around the words that tell what you think about the story.

    Vocabulary too   Vocabulary too   Story hard to
      difficult   easy   understand

Name the main characters in the story._____
_____
Write the main facts of the story._____
_____
_____
_____
List the difficult words in the story._____
_____
_____
_____
_____

A class chart is of value in showing each student's types of interest in books.   The rough chart shown on page 333 was made from an inventory of reading interests and was used during the first 2 weeks of school to help students in making reading selections taken from *The Children's Book Shelf*.

The stars showed the different types of reading that each child was doing and helped to broaden his reading interests.

As a means of unifying developmental and diagnostic information from various sources, the *Examiner's Diagnostic Reading Record* (8) is useful.   Information from standardized tests, school records of marks in each subject, items from health records, the student's own statement of his problem, facts about his reading history and present interests and reading habits, a record of his oral reading of four paragraphs and of his demonstrated ability to use the index and the dictionary may all be recorded and, in this unified form, more easily interpreted.   Thus a more precise and individualized basis for going ahead with remedial procedures is provided.

Pupil's name	Animals	Athletics	Adventure	Humor	Mystery	Romance	Science	College	Western
Carmen									
Clarence									
Elsie	*			*		*			
Ellison	*		*		*				
Steven			*		*	*			
Don		*	*				*		*
Mary				*			*		*
Marion		*			*			*	
Larry		*			*				*
James				*				*	
John	*		*	*					
Elmer		*		*			*		
Susan		*				*	*		
Rose			*			*		*	

References

1. GRAY, WILLIAM S., with the cooperation of Delia Kibbe, Laura Lucas, and Lawrence W. Miller, *Remedial Cases in Reading:* Their Diagnosis and Treatment, Supplementary Educational Monographs, No. 22, Department of Education, University of Chicago, Chicago, 1922, vii + 208 pp.
2. HATFIELD, W. WILBUR, "Cumulative Reading Record," W. W. Hatfield, Chicago, 1939.
3. KEYES, ROWENA K., *Students' Reading Report Book*, Noble & Noble, Publishers, Inc., New York, 1939.
4. MONROE, MARION, *Children Who Cannot Read*, University of Chicago Press, Chicago, 1932, x + 172 pp.
5. NOLTE, K. F., "Case Record of Jerry, a Non-reader," *Elementary English Review*, Vol. 21, pp. 66–70, February, 1944.
6. ROBINSON, HELEN M., "Treatment of Severe Cases of Reading Disability," *Journal of Educational Research*, Vol. 32, pp. 531–535, March, 1939.

7. ROBINSON, HELEN M., and JEAN F. SAVERY, "A High-school Freshman Learns to Read and Write," *Education Digest*, Vol. 8, pp. 42–44, December, 1942.

8. STRANG, RUTH, and others, *Examiner's Diagnostic Reading Record*, Bureau of Publications, Teachers College, Columbia University, New York, 1939, 20 pp.

9. STRANG, RUTH, *Exploration in Reading Patterns*, University of Chicago Press, Chicago, 1942, x + 172 pp.

10. STRANG, RUTH, "Records of Reading Ability, Habits, and Interests," *Handbook of Cumulative Records*, pp. 44–52, U.S Government Printing Office, Washington, D.C., 1945.

11. SYLVESTER, EMMY, and MARY S. KUNST, "Psychodynamic Aspects of the Reading Problem," *American Journal of Orthopsychiatry*, Vol. 12, pp. 69–76, February, 1943.

12. YOUNG, R. A., "Case Studies in Reading Disability," *American Journal of Orthopsychiatry*, Vol. 8, pp. 230–254, April, 1938.

APPENDIX A

READING MATERIAL FOR THE SECONDARY SCHOOL AND COLLEGE

One of the first problems of the teacher of reading at the high-school or college level is the selection of materials to be used in the group. Prior to 1930 there was available to teachers of reading very little material that was specially designed or selected for use in reading instruction in the high school. This type of material was nonexistent in the college. Consequently, it was necessary for teachers of reading to spend much time locating and duplicating material that was suitable for their objectives.

In recent years there has been a rapid multiplication of reading materials for the high school. Some of these materials are suitable for use with college freshmen, and in addition a few workbooks have been issued specifically for college students. The use of a large amount of supplementary material rather than dependence on one reading workbook or textbook alone for the classwork is highly desirable, if the teacher can find sufficient time and energy to search for and organize the supplementary reading selections. This procedure keeps the work of the reading course from becoming too narrowly stereotyped and routinized and enables the teacher to take account of individual interests and needs.

The kinds of sources of materials for remedial, corrective, or developmental reading in the high school and college are as follows: (1) reading workbooks, (2) reading textbooks for the secondary school or college, (3) textbook series, (4) materials for vocabulary building, (5) study-habits workbooks and guides, and (6) books for free reading. Let us consider each of these sources and note some of the titles that are available in each category.

READING WORKBOOKS

Secondary School.—Most workbooks in reading for the secondary school are of fairly recent origin, but one set of booklets that has been widely used for nearly 20 years is the series of *Standard Test Lessons in Reading*, by McCall and Crabbs (27). These booklets are designed for the elementary school, but experience has shown that books IV and V in the series are difficult enough for retarded readers throughout the junior high school. In fact, Book V has been employed with success in remedial reading up to the tenth grade and even in the case of an occasional college student. Each lesson in the McCall-Crabb booklets consists of a paragraph followed by 10 multiple-choice questions. Three minutes are allowed for a lesson. The number of questions answered correctly is translated into a G score. The G scores on

335

the various lessons are designed to be equivalent. If the pupils keep graphic records of achievement on the lessons, they usually take much interest in their progress from day to day.

A somewhat similar, but more advanced, series of exercise booklets was published by McCall, Cook, and Norvell (26) in 1934. This series, which is entitled *Experiments in Reading* and consists of three books, is designed for high-school use. Each lesson is centered on a particular reading problem. The raw scores on the different lessons may be changed into G scores.

A booklet entitled *Study Type of Reading Exercises*, by Strang (43), consists of work-type reading materials for senior high schools and colleges. An unusual feature of this booklet is that each of the 1,000-word reading exercises is based on description and explanation of good reading habits, and thus the student learns about reading procedures while practicing reading. The uniform length of the exercises makes them an easily administered speed test.

A little book published in 1937 by Mack, McCall, and Almack (25) may be classified as a workbook, although it is in a cloth binding. This book, *Roads to Reading*, is designed to teach six basic reading skills: skimming, word meaning, following directions, understanding stated facts, following the main thought, and comprehending implied facts. There are 44 lessons, each of which stresses one or two of the skills. Among the titles of the lessons are Treasure Trove, Who Was Surprised?, The San Francisco-Oakland Bay Bridge, Elephants, A Narrow Escape, and Around the World in Seventeen Days. There are a number of multiple-choice questions on each lesson. The authors state that the lessons range in difficulty from the fourth to the seventh grade, but that they are on a ninth-grade interest level.

Among workbooks that consist of series designed to cover a fairly wide range of grade is *Getting the Meaning*, by Guiler and Coleman (13). Book I is planned for the seventh or the eighth grade, Book II for the ninth or the tenth grade, and Book III for the eleventh or the twelfth grade. The authors, however, indicate that the books should be adapted to the needs of any grades or groups, depending upon the levels of reading ability. Each booklet contains 36 lessons, each of which consists of a short passage, usually two or three paragraphs, followed by six types of questions relating, respectively, to getting word meanings, choosing the best title, getting the main idea, getting the facts, making an outline, and drawing conclusions. The questions are objective and average scores for various grades are given in connection with each lesson. The more difficult words in each passage are defined in a glossary below the passage.

Another set of workbooks is the *Developmental Reading Series*, by Simpson and Gilmer (39). Books II and III are designed for developmental reading in the upper elementary grades or for corrective reading in the junior and senior high school. According to the authors, the reading level is that of news and feature stories in the daily press. There are two parts to each booklet: a story section, which contains the reading materials, some supplementary reading materials, and a word list; and the exercise section, which contains a pretest, the practice exercises, and some supplementary practice exercises. There is also a separate booklet of scoring keys and a separate retest.

The authors state that these workbooks are aimed at the development of a variety of abilities, including rate, comprehension, noting details, interpretation, finding the central thought, supplying supporting details, following directions, making inferences, locating facts and information, locating dispersed ideas, and word study. The titles of some of the lessons in Book II are Trapping in the Yukon, Aboard an Ocean Liner, The Black Widow Spider, Hawaiian Animals, and The Mighty Sahara. The reading material in each lesson covers about a page. The questions in the exercise section are fairly objective, although some of them are of the completion type.

A series of *Diagnostic Reading Workbooks*, by Eleanor M. Johnson and others (21), contains workbooks for grades 7 to 12, as well as for the elementary grades. There is a set of achievement tests to be used with the workbooks. In addition to the regular series of workbooks, there is a hectograph edition, which may be used in duplicating copies at the school.

College.—Several reading specialists with experience at the college level have prepared reading manuals for college students. Blair's *Manual of Reading* (3) is designed to provide instruction and practice in serious reading and its integration with writing. The book contains a wide variety of practice materials. A large part of the manual is devoted to training the student in the analysis of different types of writing.

McCallister's *Purposeful Reading in College* (28) stresses growth in reading ability through adjustments in the student's regular reading activities. The manual does not consist of an extensive compilation of reading selections, as does Blair's book, but introduces only a sufficient number of reading selections to illustrate appropriate reading practices and to serve as the basis of testing. The illustrated materials are drawn from the fields of English, social science, biological science, and physical science. The manual, which contains many practical suggestions organized according to the main reading needs of college students, is designed for use in English classes, orientation classes, and special reading classes.

College Reading Skills, by McCullough (29)—a booklet of materials for college freshmen that was developed in an experimental English course at Hiram College—deals with the following topics: reading for the main idea, reading speed, outlining, reading for propaganda, reading for inference, reading for plot, reading for organization, reading for technique, library activities, reading for academic acceptability, and reading for survival. The last topic concerns reading in preparation for examinations. This is a brochure explaining different types of reading and offering suggestions for the students, rather than a workbook containing practice materials.

Triggs (47) has published a manual of remedial reading exercises for college students entitled *Improve Your Reading*, which contains an explanation of the nature of reading and reading procedures in five sections and provides

25 specific assignments for the students. The five sections deal with the following topics: what is good reading, streamline your reading, get acquainted with strange words, to understand what you read, think as you read.

A manual for college students by Wilking and Webster (49) stresses organizational and associational skills. The reading materials in the exercises were taken from college textbooks and from typical primary sources that college students should be able to read. The exercises have been used in remedial reading work at Harvard.

Students in colleges and technical schools who have difficulty with the reading of scientific and technical material will find help and practice in a manual, *How to Read Science and Technology*, by Howland, Jarvie, and Smith (18). The material is of genuine college difficulty. There is need for more material of this kind designed to develop reading skills in specific fields.

READING TEXTBOOKS

Within the last 10 years, a new kind of secondary-school textbook has made its appearance. This is the type of book that is planned to meet the needs of reading classes that are set up as an integral part of the curriculum. Several such books are now available. One of the most widely used—*Following Printed Trails*, by Carol Hovious (19)—contains 15 long reading selections and some 350 short selections, which together provide enough material for a year's course in reading. The three parts of the book, arranged in order of difficulty, are divided into several chapters each, every chapter dealing with a separate reading skill. Among the skills covered are finding main ideas, remembering important details, connecting reading with what is already known, seeing the writer's plan, skimming, and understanding and enjoying figures of speech.

This book is written in a lively style, designed to catch and hold the interests of high-school pupils. The material is of suitable maturity for the high-school level. Fourteen tests placed at intervals throughout the book are planned to measure progress in reading. A teacher's manual and a key to the test exercises accompany the book.

In one of the chapters, entitled Eye Stretchers, there is some highly mechanical material that may not be entirely sound from a psychological point of view. However, in the teacher's manual the author has recognized the limitation of the chapter and has warned that it should be used with caution. As a whole, the book is well written and contains much excellent material. A more recent and somewhat easier book by Miss Hovious is *Flying the Printways* (20).

Another reading textbook is *Reading for Skill*, by Broening, Law, Wilkinson, and Ziegler (4). Designed to improve the reading ability and the library skill of pupils in junior and senior high schools, this book has four parts. Part I tests various reading and library skills. Part II contains practice exercises selected from classical and contemporary sources and is arranged to provide continuous practice in reading for exact meaning, skimming, reading rapidly, determining appropriate reading method, and remembering what is read. Part III consists of exercises that give training in such library skills as using a card catalogue; using a title page, a preface, or a table of contents; using an unabridged dictionary; using an atlas; using magazine indexes; using encyclopedias; and using dictionaries of biography and history. Part IV contains tests for the reading and library skills similar to the tests in Part I. There are progress tests after each practice period. The entire book is well organized, and the materials seem well chosen to represent the kinds of content and the levels of difficulty that high-school students encounter. The fact that the book makes provision for training in both reading skills and library skills adds to its value for use in reading courses in the high school.

A book that serves a purpose somewhat similar to that of the two works just discussed is *Read and Comprehend*, by Knight and Traxler (23). It is a little more difficult than the other two and contains a larger proportion of literary selections. Its two parts are designed, respectively, to provide practice in extensive reading and intensive reading. The chapters in Part I are directed toward the following questions: How much fun can you find in books? How rapidly do you read? Can you skim? Do you need winged words? Can you get the best of the dictionary? and How shall we read the newspaper? Those in Part II have these challenges: Can you find the main idea? Can you get a bird's-eye view of the whole? Are you curious? Can you grasp details? Do you believe all you read? and Just imagine! The book is issued in a cloth-bound edition and in a paper-backed edition of the workbook type. There is a separate booklet containing a teacher's manual and an answer key. This book can be used in developmental reading courses for normal readers in the ninth and tenth grades and in corrective or remedial work with retarded readers in the eleventh and twelfth grades and at the college-freshman level.

A later and easier book by the same authors—*Develop Your Reading* (24), published in 1941—is planned for developmental reading in grades 7 and 8 and for remedial reading in grades 9 and 10. In organization and purpose the newer book resembles *Read and Comprehend* in most respects. However, it contains no chapter on reading the newspaper: instead, it has a long chapter designed to give practice in oral reading. It is accompanied by a workbook and a teacher's manual and answer key.

Each of the topics just mentioned—reading the newspaper and oral reading —is treated separately in an interesting book. The first of these books—*How to Read a Newspaper*, by Edgar Dale (9)—has its chapters organized in three parts: What is a Newspaper?, Getting Behind the News, and Looking Ahead. The second part contains useful chapters on how to improve the technique of newspaper reading and how to judge newspapers. Near the end of the book there is a separate section dealing with photography of the news, comic strips and cartoons, columnists, and the newspaper as a critic.

Tresidder's *Reading to Others* (46) provides helpful suggestions and training for oral reading. The 13 chapters are concerned with interpreting meaning, interpreting emotion, how the voice works, the sound of speech, controlling volume and pitch, improving tempo and quality, movement and manners, information reading, dramatic and narrative reading, across the footlights, before the microphone, in chorus, and enjoyment of reading aloud. There is an extensive appendix, in which special problems in voice improvement are discussed and prose for oral reading is provided.

A book considerably more elementary than any that has been mentioned thus far is *Improving Your Reading*, by Wilkinson and Brown (50). It is intended for pupils in the intermediate grades of the elementary schools and for those in the junior high school who are seriously retarded in reading. The first of the four parts contains two units, called Introducing You to Reading and Experimenting in Reading. The experiments are in reality tests, but the word "test" has been avoided, to reduce the possibility of emotional stress. The second part is devoted to oral reading. There are five units which cover Making New Word Friends, Learning the Sound, or Phonetic Clues to New Words, Learning to Phrase, Training Your Eyes to Move from Left to Right across the Page, and Learning to Read the Author's Words. The third part, which is on silent reading, contains three units: Understanding and Enjoying What Is Read, Remembering What We Read, and Finding What We Want to Read. The fourth part includes experiments or tests to show improvement and an appendix containing a key to the exercises in the book.

A book that emphasizes comprehension in study situations is *Reading for Understanding*, by Bessey and Coffin (2), which derives its objectives and organization from *An Experience Curriculum in English*, published by the National Council of Teachers of English. It contains more than three hundred selections for practice in work-type reading. The selections are accompanied by explanations of the study method, questions, and exercises planned to improve reading skills. Designed as a textbook for remedial reading courses in the ninth and tenth grades, this book is divided into two parts, called Reading for Comprehension and Re-expressing the Thought. The material in the book is sufficiently varied to keep up interest. The authors state that the vocabulary of the selections has been checked with the Thorndike wordbook.

A book written in somewhat more popular style than the other reading textbooks and workbooks is *Learning How to Learn*, by Pitkin, Newton, and Langham (31). The purpose of this book is not training in reading alone, but the emphasis is on reading. There are six units, as follows: Learning Is Determined by Self-understanding, Learning Is Determined by Self-mastery, Learning Is Determined by Efficiency in Reading, and Learning Is Determined by One Vocational Goal. Each unit contains explanatory reading and experiments. On the whole, this work is perhaps more suitable for individual use by students on their own initiative than for use as a textbook in classwork.

There is a book by Buell and Strawinski (5), entitled *Reading with Clues*, which is planned for average students in high school. The first part contains

20 stories and the second part, 20 articles. Each part is preceded by a guide to study. Each story or article is followed by questions in three areas: understanding, language appreciation, and social appreciation. There are also questions that apply to any story and questions that apply to any article. Although most of the stories and articles have little literary merit, they are interesting, and they should appeal to high-school boys and girls. The authors state that there is more than enough material in the book for a term of 8 weeks.

Another book suitable for use in high school is *Reading in High Gear*, by Mabel V. Cage (6). Part I, entitled Pointing the Way, contains lessons on how to read. Part II, called Reading Practice, provides practice material, with directions and tests intended to promote different kinds of reading skills. Most of the reading exercises are short. The tests are very informal. A brief appendix contains suggestions for teachers. There are some lists of reading references and a list of suggested tests, but these lists include only a small fraction of the available titles.

TEXTBOOK SERIES

A series of books with an especially attractive format is *Let's Read*, by Roberts and Rand (33). Whereas some of the reading textbooks, such as those by Hovious and Bessey and Coffin, contain a large number of very short selections, the four books under the title *Let's Read* contain interesting stories and articles, each of which is several pages in length. Each selection is followed by instructions to the student on what to do and by questions. The number of words is given at the end of each selection in order to make it easy for the student to find his reading rate. The materials in the books seem to be very well chosen to appeal to the interests of high-school pupils. In case some other book is used as the basic text, the *Let's Read* series could well be employed for supplementary work or be placed on the list for free reading.

A series of textbooks by Center and Persons (8) is planned to cover the 6 years of the junior and senior high schools. The titles of the books are *Experiences in Reading and Thinking, Practices in Reading and Thinking,* and *Problems in Reading and Thinking.* The third book is intended for college students and adults, as well as for high-school pupils. This is probably the most comprehensive series of reading textbooks thus far available for the secondary school. The selections are interesting and the photographs are excellent. The level of the material is probably suitable for normal readers, but it seems difficult for retarded pupils. Whether the third book should be used at all in remedial work in the secondary school is doubtful. Each of the books is introduced with discussion and illustrations of eye movements. The instructions for the various reading selections in the first two books are organized under "target" and "how to hit the target."

An attractive two-book series, entitled *Growth in Reading*, was published by Pooley, Walcott, and Gray (32). These books are intended for a developmental program of reading in grades 7 and 8. The material in the books seems to combine high quality with appeal to the interests of junior-high-school pupils. There is a self-test workbook, entitled *Read and Think*, which is planned to accompany Book I.

A *For Better Reading* series of three books, planned for pupils in junior and senior high schools, was prepared by Herzberg, Paine, and Works (16). The titles of the books are *Quests*, *Ventures*, and *Rewards*. The materials seem to be well chosen and the exercises carefully worked out.

MATERIALS FOR VOCABULARY BUILDING

Within the last few years, a number of books and pamphlets containing useful vocabulary teaching materials have been made available. One of the most thorough books of this kind is *Vocabulary Building*, by J. M. Steadman (42), which is intended for high-school and college use and contains 94 detailed sections. These may be organized by the teacher into seven units, including meaning; spelling; pronunciation; word formation and the history of words; idioms, standards of correctness, and levels of English usage; how to use the dictionary; and style and diction. Much emphasis is placed on word formation and the logical analysis of words. The students are encouraged to keep their own word lists and to try to add 10 new words each week. The textbook is paralleled by a pupil's workbook.

A rather mature book, suitable for use in senior high schools and colleges, is Gilmartin's *Building Your Vocabulary* (12). This book challenges the student in the very beginning with Sixty Snags in Pronunciation, and then takes up a great variety of procedures for improving vocabulary.

Another interesting vocabulary textbook is *Twelve Ways to Build a Vocabulary*, by Archibald Hart (14). An attractive little book, designed for use in both high school and college, it contains 12 chapters, some of which carry such intriguing titles as Weary Words, The Poisoned Well, Malapropisms or What Did She Mean? and Fun with the Dictionary. There are chapters on synonyms, antonyms, definitions, the use of the dictionary, slang and idioms, prefixes, and three chapters on word derivations. Ten multiple-choice vocabulary tests appear near the end of the book.

A newer book by Hart and Lejeune, entitled *The Growing Vocabulary* (15), is intended for pupils twelve to sixteen years of age. The word list is based on the *Thorndike Century Junior Dictionary*.

Among the materials dealing with the vocabulary of certain fields of study, there is a booklet by Dix (10) that is devoted entirely to the vocabulary of the social studies. In addition to a basic vocabulary of 500 words, it includes exercises to aid in learning the meaning and uses of the words, as well as test exercises.

Secondary schools attempting to correlate instruction in reading with the teaching of spelling may be interested in a *Vocabulary Building Speller* by Meyer (30). In this book the spelling lists are accompanied by definitions and illustrations of the use of the words, and most of the words are repeated several times in the definitions of other words.

STUDY-HABITS WORKBOOKS AND GUIDES

Closely related to reading textbooks and workbooks are certain workbooks and aids in the field of study habits. Perhaps the best-known workbook for training in study habits in the secondary school is *Better Work Habits*, by Salisbury (35). This book contains many detailed practice exercises on a variety of work and study skills. It is planned especially for the ninth grade, but it may be used in the senior high school as well. The book begins with very easy exercises and is practically self-administering, so that it is suitable for independent individual work, as well as for group classwork. The workbook is divided into three parts, called Finding Plans and Making Plans, Making Notes, and Work Materials. Within the parts are units on The Elements of Thinking, Reading to Grasp the Point, Selecting Detail, Making the Most of the Textbook, Making Summaries, Planning Compositions, Note Making in the Book, Note Making on Paper, Combining Sources, and Writing Examinations. There is a separate answer key for the exercises.

Salisbury has also prepared a workbook for college students, entitled *Better Work Habits in College* (36). The organization of the high-school and college workbooks is similar and some of the exercises are identical.

Another extensive and well-organized workbook is *Diagnostic and Remedial Techniques for Effective Study*, by Francis P. Robinson (34). This workbook was developed in how-to-study programs with college freshmen, but it could probably be used with students in the upper years of high school. An admirable feature of the book is close coordination between diagnostic tests and remedial materials.

A second type of booklet designed to help pupils study better consists not of practice exercises, but of a series of practical suggestions concerning methods of study in different fields. A recent guide of this kind is *Best Methods of Study*, by Smith and Littlefield (41). The booklet, which contains 18 brief chapters, covers the main fields of study in senior high school and college.

A somewhat similar booklet containing helpful suggestions for the senior-high-school or college student is *Improvement of Study Habits*, by Edward S. Jones (22). Among the aspects of study discussed in the 10 chapters are reading, note taking, improving one's memory, use of the library, the habit of concentration, reasoning in mathematics and science, mental hygiene, and preparing for and taking examinations. In the appendix there is a form that the student can use in scoring himself on study techniques.

One of the most thorough among the study guides that have yet appeared is a *How to Study Handbook*, by Robert W. Frederick (11). This book, which is based on several years of experimentation in a junior-senior high school, contains a multitude of detailed suggestions for study procedures. These are classified under 40 headings, such as how to read by the block method, how to use the index, how to read graphs, how to read a newspaper, how to use the library, how to keep notebooks, and how to prepare for tests and examinations. It is suitable for use either as a textbook in how-to-study classes or as a reference book for students.

Of several brief study handbooks that were prepared for use by the students in individual secondary schools and that are available in printed form, one of the most interesting is *Doing Your Work Well*, by Robert N. Hilkert (17). This booklet grew out of the need for guidance in work habits and study skills among the students of The Hill School, Pottstown, Pa. The straightforward, practical, "man-to-man" style makes it especially suitable for distribution to fairly mature high-school pupils.

Two other study handbooks containing well-organized, definite suggestions for secondary-school pupils are *How to Study*, by Roy R. Shrewsbury (38), of The Pingry School, Elizabeth, N. J., and *Hints on How to Study*, by Wilburt R. Walters (48), of The William Penn Charter School, Philadelphia, Pa.

BOOKS FOR FREE READING

One of the greatest needs at present is that of very easy, interesting material for seriously retarded readers in high school. A bibliography for adolescents who find reading difficult was prepared by Strang, Checovitz, Gilbert, and Scoggin (45). This bibliography, *Gateways to Readable Books*, includes many titles of about fifth-, sixth-, and seventh-grade level of difficulty, but few below the fourth-grade level.

For very handicapped students, *The Army Reader* (1) begins at the first-grade level and moves along through second- and third- to fourth-grade difficulty. The content—about Private Pete's life in the Army—is interesting to the older boys and suggests other similar material that might be produced. Another volume, *Meet Private Pete* designed to orient Private Pete to civilian life was prepared and should be very useful when made available to schools.

Specific titles that should be in the class libraries of social-studies teachers of mentally retarded junior-high-school students were selected by Carpenter and Whitted (7) on the basis of the reactions of 175 pupils to almost 300 books. Their report, "Readable Books for Slow Learners," published in *Social Education*, is an excellent source of titles of books appealing to a wide range of interests, books having the characteristics of simplicity and concreteness, and illustrated books.

For pupils of average and superior reading ability, the reading lists published annually by the Secondary Education Board (37) are very helpful. It is also desirable for teachers of reading to note what books are recommended for free reading by the authors of some of the reading textbooks, since usually the lists given by these persons will be based on a wide background of experience. As a rule, the free-reading book list is weighted rather heavily with collections of short stories for young people.

Thus far, few books have been written especially to serve as a basis for independent reading in connection with instruction in the secondary school. Two little books of this kind, however, have been made available by Strang, Burks, and Puls (44). They are *Seven Days at Sea* and *Here and There and Home*, and they contain an account of the travel experiences of four young people. No work material interrupts the continuity of the reading, but there are some test exercises at the end of each book. It is to be hoped that a larger amount of such material will gradually become available.

The following list of reading materials and bibliographies of books for young people is by no means exhaustive, but it is extensive enough to cover nearly all kinds of reading undertaken at the secondary-school level and to convince schools that they need no longer hesitate to undertake a reading program because of lack of suitable materials. So many sources of remedial, corrective, and developmental reading material are now available that good teachers should refuse to confine themselves and their pupils slavishly to any one, but should search through the different books and workbooks for the selections that best serve their own purposes and the needs and interests of their pupils.

References

1. *The Army Reader*, U.S. Government Printing Office, Washington, D.C.
2. BESSEY, MABEL A., and ISABELLE P. COFFIN, *Reading for Understanding*, D. Appleton-Century Company, Inc., New York, 1936, xiv + 325 pp.
3. BLAIR, WALTER, *Manual of Reading*, Scott, Foresman and Company, Chicago, 1943, viii + 279 pp.
4. BROENING, ANGELA M., FREDERICK H. LAW, MARY S. WILKINSON, and CAROLINE L. ZIEGLER, *Reading for Skill*, Noble & Noble, Publishers, Inc., New York, 1936, xiii + 399 pp.
5. BUELL, LEONARD W., and WILLIAM E. STRAWINSKI, *Reading with Clues*, Benj. H. Sanborn & Co., Chicago, 1940, ix + 459 pp.
6. CAGE, MABEL V., *Reading in High Gear*, Harper & Brothers, New York, 1938, x + 347 pp.
7. CARPENTER, HELEN MCCRACKEN, and DOROTHY J. WHITTED, "Readable Books for Slow Learners," *Social Education*, Vol. 7, pp. 167–170, April, 1943.
8. CENTER, STELLA S., and GLADYS L. PERSONS, *Experiences in Reading and Thinking*, xi + 395 pp.; *Practices in Reading and Thinking*, xiii + 473 pp.; *Problems in Reading and Thinking*, xiii + 657 pp.; The Macmillan Company, New York, 1940.
9. DALE, EDGAR, *How to Read a Newspaper*, Scott, Foresman and Company, Chicago, 1941, xii + 178 pp.
10. DIX, JOHN P., *Vocabulary Booklet in the Social Studies*, Carthage Press Publishing Company, Carthage, Mo., 1938, 12 pp.
11. FREDERICK, ROBERT W., *How to Study Handbook*, D. Appleton-Century Company, Inc., New York, 1938, xxvii + 442 pp.
12. GILMARTIN, JOHN G., *Building Your Vocabulary*, Prentice-Hall, Inc., New York, 1940, vi + 281 pp.
13. GUILER, W. S., and J. H. COLEMAN, *Getting the Meaning*, Books I, II, and III, J. B. Lippincott Company, Philadelphia, 1940, 80 pp. in each book.
14. HART, ARCHIBALD, *Twelve Ways to Build a Vocabulary*, E. P. Dutton & Company, Inc., New York, 1939, 183 pp.
15. HART, ARCHIBALD, and F. ARNOLD LEJUNE, *The Growing Vocabulary*, E. P. Dutton & Company, Inc., New York, 1940, 156 pp.
16. HERZBERG, MAX J., MERRILL P. PAINE, and AUSTIN M. WORKS, *For Better Reading*, a three-book series, Houghton Mifflin Company, Boston, 1940.

17. HILKERT, ROBERT N., *Doing Your Work Well*, Department of Personnel Study, The Hill School, Pottstown, Pa., 1940, 54 pp.

18. HOWLAND, HAZEL POPE, LAWRENCE L. JARVIE, and LEO F. SMITH, *How to Read Science and Technology*, Harper & Brothers, New York, 1943, xi + 264 pp.

19. HOVIOUS, CAROL, *Following Printed Trails*, D. C. Heath and Company, Boston, 1936, x + 371 pp.

20. HOVIOUS, CAROL, *Flying the Printways*, D. C. Heath and Company, Boston, 1938, xii + 525 pp.

21. JOHNSON, ELEANOR M., and others, *Diagnostic Reading Workbooks*, Education Press, Columbus, Ohio, 1939.

22. JONES, EDWARD S., *Improvement of Study Habits*, Foster and Stewart, Buffalo, N. Y., 1939, 112 pp.

23. KNIGHT, PEARLE E., and ARTHUR E. TRAXLER, *Read and Comprehend*, Little, Brown & Company, Boston, 1937.   (Now published by D. C. Heath and Company, Boston.)

24. KNIGHT, PEARLE E., and ARTHUR E. TRAXLER, *Develop Your Reading*, Little, Brown & Company, Boston, 1941, vi + 376 pp.   (Now published by D. C. Heath and Company, Boston.)

25. MACK, REBA G., WILLIAM A. McCALL, and JOHN C. ALMACK, *Roads to Reading*, Harcourt, Brace and Company, New York, 1937, vi + 89 pp.

26. McCALL, WILLIAM A., LUELLA B. COOK, and GEORGE W. NORVELL, *Experiments in Reading*, Books, I, II, and III, Harcourt, Brace and Company, New York, 1934.

27. McCALL, WILLIAM A., and LELAH MAE CRABBS, *Standard Test Lessons in Reading*, Books IV and V, Bureau of Publications, Teachers College, Columbia University, New York, 1926.

28. McCALLISTER, JAMES M., *Purposeful Reading in College*, D. Appleton-Century Company, Inc., New York, 1942, v + 170 pp.

29. McCULLOUGH, CONSTANCE M. (with the collaboration of Ruth M. Strang and Mary Louise Vincent), *College Reading Skills*, Edwards Brs., Inc., Ann Arbor, Mich., 1941, v + 60 pp.

30. MEYER, A., *Vocabulary-building Speller*, The Macmillan Company, New York, 1939, vi + 160 pp.

31. PITKIN, WALTER B., HAROLD C. NEWTON, and OLIVE P. LANGHAM, *Learning How to Learn*, McGraw-Hill Book Company, Inc., New York, 1935, vii + 194 pp.

32. POOLEY, ROBERT C., FRED G. WALCOTT, and WILLIAM S. GRAY, *Growth in Reading*, Books I and II, Scott, Foresman and Company, Chicago, 1938.

33. ROBERTS, HOLLAND, and HELEN RAND, *Let's Read*, a four-book series, Henry Holt and Company, Inc., New York, 1937.

34. ROBINSON, FRANCIS P., *Diagnostic and Remedial Techniques for Effective Study*, Harper & Brothers, New York, 1941, ix + 318 pp.

35. SALISBURY, RACHEL, *Better Work Habits*, Scott, Foresman and Company, Chicago, 1932, viii + 219 pp.

36. SALISBURY, RACHEL, *Better Work Habits in College*, Scott, Foresman and Company, Chicago, 1932, viii + 179 pp.

37. Secondary Education Board, *Junior Booklist and Senior Booklist*, Milton, Mass., published annually; last number, May, 1944.

38. SHREWSBURY, ROY R., *How to Study*, the Author, the Pingry School, Elizabeth, N. J., 1941, vii + 49 pp.

39. SIMPSON, ROBERT G., and ELLEN C. GILMER, *Developmental Reading Series for Improving Reading Habits*, Books II and III, Educational Test Bureau, Minneapolis, 1940.

40. SMITH, ELMER R., MARION EDMAN, and GEORGIA E. MILLER, *Invitation to Reading*, Book II, Harcourt, Brace and Company, New York, 1944, x + 534 pp.

41. SMITH, SAMUEL, and A. W. LITTLEFIELD, *Best Methods of Study*, Barnes & Noble, Inc., New York, 1938, 132 pp.

42. STEADMAN, J. M., *Vocabulary Building*, Turner E. Smith and Company, Atlanta, Ga., 1938, xiii + 199 pp.

43. STRANG, RUTH, *Study Type of Reading Exercises*, Bureau of Publications, Teachers College, Columbia University, New York, 1935, 128 pp.

44. STRANG, RUTH, BARBARA BURKS, and HELEN PULS, *Seven Days at Sea* and *Here and There and Home*, Bureau of Publications, Teachers College, Columbia University, New York, 1938, viii + 117 and vi + 120 pp.

45. STRANG, RUTH, ALICE CHECOVITZ, CHRISTINE GILBERT, and MARGARET SCOGGIN, *Gateways to Readable Books*, The H. W. Wilson Company, New York, 1944.

46. TRESSIDER, ARGUS, *Reading to Others*, Scott, Foresman and Company, Chicago, 1940, xiii + 529 pp.

47. TRIGGS, FRANCES O., *Improve Your Reading*, University of Minnesota Press, Minneapolis, 1942, vi + 127 pp.

48. WALTERS, WILBURT, R., *Hints on How to Study*, Extra-curricular Publishing Company, Keokuk, Iowa, 1938, 32 pp.

49. WILKING, STEPHEN V., and R. G. WEBSTER, *College Developmental Reading Manual*, Houghton Mifflin Company, Boston, 1943, 363 pp.

50. WILKINSON, HELEN S. S., and BERTHA D. BROWN, *Improving Your Reading*, Noble & Noble, Publishers, Inc., New York, 1938, xiii + 361 pp.

APPENDIX B[1]

USEFUL INFORMATION ABOUT COMMON PREFIXES, SUFFIXES AND ROOTS

PREFIXES

Prefix	Meaning	Examples
a (ab)	from, away	abnormal, abdicate, avert
a (an)	without, not	aseptic, anesthetic
ad	to, toward	adjust, adjourn, administer
ambi (amphi)	around, both	ambidextrous, ambiguous, amphibious
ante	before	anteroom, antedate
anti	against, opposite	antithesis, antagonist
bi	two, twice	bisect, bicycle, biscuit
circum	around	circumscribe, circumvent
con (co, col, com)	together, with	concur, connect, contend, combine, collect
contra (counter)	against	contradict, contraband
de	from, down from	dejected, delegate, degrade
dis (di)	apart, not	dispatch, dismiss, dishonor
dia	through, around	diameter, dialogue
epi	upon	epitaph, epiphenomenon
eu	well	euphemism, euphony
ex	out of, from	expel, exodus, exhume
hetero	different	heterodox, heterogeneous
hypo, hyph	under, below	hypothesis, hypocrite
in (il, un, ir)	into, not	inconsistent, inelegant, illegible, irreverent
in, en	in, into, among	invade, include, entice
inter	between	interpose, interurban
intro	within, against	introspective, introduce
mono	single, one	monograph, monorail
non	not	nonalcoholic, nonentity
ob	against	obtrude, obstruct, object
pan	whole, all	Pan-American, pantheist
per	fully, through	peruse, perturb
peri	around, about	perimeter, peristyle
post	after, behind	postpone, post-mortem
pre	before	precede, prelude
pro	for, forward, in front of	propose, program

[1] RUTH STRANG, *Problems in the Improvement of Reading in High School and College*, rev. ed., pp. 376–377, The Science Press Printing Company, Lancaster, Pa., 1940.

Prefix	Meaning	Examples
re	back, again	renew, reiterate, repress
retro	backward	retrospect, retrograde
se	aside	seclude, secede, segregate
semi	half, partly	semicircular, semiannual
sub	under	subway, subnormal, subject
super	over, above	supercilious, superfine
syn (sym)	together with	synthesis, syntax, sympathy
trans	beyond, across	transgress, transatlantic
tri	three, thrice	trisect, triangle, triplets
ultra	beyond	ultramontane, ultramarine
un	not	unkind, unnecessary

SUFFIXES

Suffix	Meaning	Examples
-able, -ible	capable of being	serviceable, credible
-ace, -acy } -ance, -ancy }	state of being	disturbance, intimacy
-age	act or condition	dotage, marriage, bondage
-al, eal, -ial	relation to, that which, on account of	judicial, credentials, elemental
-an, -ean, -ian	one who, relating to	American, statistician
-ant	adj.: being	resonant, vacant
	noun: one who	attendant, servant
-ar, -er	relating to, like	lunar, vulgar, solar
-ary	adj.: relating to	residuary, contrary
	noun: one who	dignitary
	place where	sanctuary
-ate	adj.: having quality	fortunate, desolate
	noun: one who	prelate, advocate
	verb: to make	celebrate, agitate
-cle, -acle } -icle, -cule }	little	animalcule, particle molecule, pinnacle
-ee	one who is (object of action)	trustee, employee devotee
-eer	one who does	pamphleteer, auctioneer
-en	(1) little	maiden, kitten
	(2) made of	earthen, olden
-ence } -ency }	state or quality	independence, violence dependency
-ent	adj.: being	dependent, patient
	noun: one who	resident, student
-et, -let	little	lancet, leaflet
-fic	causing, producing	soporific, terrific
-fy, -ify	to make	magnify, simplify
-hood	state, condition	motherhood, manhood
-ic	like, made of	plastic, magic
-ice	that which, quality or state of being	artifice

Suffix	Meaning	Examples
-id	pertaining to, being in a condition of	squalid, placid
-ile	relating to	puerile, imbecile
-ion	act, or state of being	coercion, fusion
-ity, -ty	state	unity, vicinity
-ist, -ite	one who	optimist, theist
-ive	relating to	legislative, decorative
-ise, -ize	to make	colonize, memorize
-kin	little	napkin, lambkin
-less	without	hopeless, worthless
-ment	state of being, act	amendment, development
-or, ar, -e	one who, that which	elector, engraver
-ory	{ relating to / that which / pertains to place of serving for }	dormitory, factory / commendatory, explanatory
-ose, -ous	abounding in	verbose, grandiose, gracious
-some	full of	troublesome
-tude, -itude	condition	beatitude, aptitude
-ule	little	capsule, globule
-ward	turning to, in direction of	heavenward, forward
-wright	doer, worker	cartwright, shipwright

SOME COMMON LATIN ROOTS

acer, sharp
ager, field
ago, agere, egi, actum, to rouse or stimulate
albus, white
alter, other
amare, to love
ambulare, to walk
amicus, friend
amor, love
annus, ring or year
aqua, water
arare, to plough
audio, audire, audivi, auditum, to hear
aurum, gold
avis, bird
bene, good or well
bonus, good
bos, bovis, ox
brevis, short
cado, cadere, cededi, casum, to fall
canis, dog
cantare, to sing
capio, capere, cepi, captum, to take
cedo, cedere, cessi, cessum, to go

celer, quick
centum, a hundred
cor, cordis, heart
corpus, corporis, body
crux, crucis, cross
dexter, right
deus, god
dominus, master
domus, house
dormire, to sleep
duo, two
dux, ducis, leader
ego, I
eo, ire, ivi, itum, to go
facio, facere, feci, factum, to do or make
felix, happy
fero, ferre, tuli, latum, to carry
fidus, faithful
finis, end
fortis, strong
frater, brother
habeo, habere, habui, habitum, to have or hold
homo, hominis, man
juvenis, young

lac, *lactis*, milk

lego, legere, legi, lectum, to read or to pick out

leo, leonis, lion

lex, legis, law

liber, book

liber, free

lingua, tongue

locus, place

lux, lucis, light

magister, master

mater, mother

manus, hand

mare, maris, sea

medium, middle

mirare, to wonder

miser, wretched

mitto, mittere, misi, missum, to send

navis, ship

niger, black

nihil, nothing

novus, new

nox, noctis, night

pater, father

pendo, pendere, pependi, pensum, to hand

pes, pedis, foot

plicare, to fold

pono, ponere, posui, positum, to put, to place

scribo, scribere, scripsi, scriptum, to write

senex, old

soror, sister

spirare, to breathe

sto, stare, steti, statum, to stand

terra, earth or land

traho, trahere, traxi, tractum, to draw

umbra, shadow

unus, one

urbs, urbis, city

velox, swift

venio, venire, veni, ventum, to come

veritas, truth

verto, vertere, verti, versum, to turn

video, videre, vidi, visum, to see

vir, man

virtus, strong

vivo, vivere, vixi, victum, to live

APPENDIX C

Test Items from *A Survey of European Civilization, Ancient Times to the Present*, by Wallace K. Ferguson and Geoffrey Bruun, Houghton Mifflin Company, Boston, 1942–1943.[1]

Selection 1, p. 221

"The series of dependent relations established between the tenant laborers and the owners of large estates, and between the fighting landholders and their lords, which formed the framework of social feudalism, were the natural
5 results of the break-up of the state and central government. Society was split into smaller units and men were forced to seek protection where they could find it. The actual form taken by this process, however, was conditioned by the existence of somewhat similar Roman and Germanic institu-
10 tions at an earlier date. In the late and unsettled period of the Roman Empire, it was not uncommon for a freeman, who could not hold his land under the pressure of hard times and taxation, to give his land to a rich landowner, while continuing to work it as a tenant. Also poor men frequent-
15 ly sought the protection of a wealthy man, giving in return services as clients. The former relation is called precarium, the latter patrocinium. But these implied no military service, nor the bond of personal loyalty to be found in the relation between the feudal warrior and his lord. For an
20 earlier model for this institution we must go back to the Germanic past, to the comitatus, the band of warriors who swore allegiance to their chief, fought for him and in return were provided with the necessities of life. The extent to which these institutions influenced the growth of
25 feudalism is doubtful; but so far as feudalism did draw its origins from the past, it may be said to have been a combination of Roman methods of landholding and of Germanic methods of military service."

Selection 2, p. 345

"The guild system offered many advantages to the medieval worker and consumer, but there were also disadvantages

[1] By permission of Houghton Mifflin Company, Boston.

which became more apparent as the economic life of Europe assumed larger proportions and as the need for protective
5 associations became less acute. The system maintained a high standard of quality of goods produced, guaranteed honest value to the purchaser, and at the same time ensured a fair living to the guildsman, with little chance, it is true, of becoming wealthy, but also with little chance of
10 being ruined. On the other hand the minute supervision of work, and the innumerable regulations tended to check individual enterprise and retarded invention or progress of any kind. Even the social solidarity of the guild was not an unmixed blessing to society. The guildsmen helped each
15 other, but they were intensely jealous of other guilds which infringed on their monopoly, and they suppressed ruthlessly all competition from those who were not members. One modern historian has compared the guild in a vivid metaphor to a feudal castle, which protected but imprisoned those
20 it sheltered, and which might easily degenerate into an instrument of tyranny over those without."

Selection 3, p. 39

"The Greek peninsula, broken by mountains and valleys, has a long indented coastline. This topography played a large part in the development of the Greeks. Separated from its neighbors by mountains, each community, however
5 small, became a separate political unit. The city, center of government and trade, together with the surrounding countryside, constituted a city-state or polis, in which there grew up political institutions different from those of the kingdoms of the East. The coastline favored the
10 growth of maritime trade, and to it the Phoenicians brought with the goods they offered for sale manufacturing techniques, decorative designs with an oriental flavor, and the alphabet.

"In the organization of commerce and industry the
15 Greeks contributed little that was startlingly new. They introduced variations, they extended commercial operations encouraged by the many colonies they founded throughout the Mediterranean world, and through them the use of coined money was spread. But there had been great mer-
20 chants in the past and eastern craftsmen had worked with extraordinary skill. The political institutions of the

city-states, the evolution of democracy, and even moderate
oligarchy, were, however, peculiar to the Greeks. And
to their genius we owe a great heritage of art, litera-
25 ture, science, and philosophy."

Questions and Vocabulary for Selections from Ferguson and Bruun, *A Survey of
European Civilization*

Directions

A. Answer the following *questions*, rereading the selection concerned, if
necessary.
B. Write after each *listed word* the meaning which best fits its use in the
selection.

Selection 1

State the main idea of this paragraph in one sentence.

_____

_____

_____

Words
dependent (line 1)_____
tenant (line 2)_____
feudalism (line 4)_____
conditioned (line 8)_____
clients (line 16)_____
bond (line 18)_____
allegiance (line 22)_____
origins (line 26)_____

Selection 2

List the advantages and disadvantages of the guild system.
Advantages_____
_____
_____
Disadvantages_____
_____
_____

Words
guild (line 1)_____
medieval (lines 1–2)_____
consumer (line 2)_____
proportions (line 4)_____
guildsman (line 8)_____
minute (line 10)_____
individual enterprise (line 12)_____
solidarity (line 13)_____
infringed (line 16)_____
monopoly (line 16)_____
suppressed (line 16)_____
degenerate (line 20)_____

Selection 3

What were the outstanding features of the Greek civilization? List under "political," "economic," and "cultural."

Political_____Economic_____
_____   _____

Cultural_____
Words
  peninsula (line 1)_____
  indented (line 2)_____
  topography (line 2)_____
  polis (line 7)_____
  maritime (line 10)_____
  techniques (line 12)_____
  commerce (line 14)_____
  evolution (line 22)_____
  oligarchy (line 23)_____
  peculiar (line 23)_____
  heritage (line 24)_____

As soon as you have finished answering these questions and giving the meanings of words, give both the selections and your answer sheets to the examiner.

From memory of the material you have just read, list the advantages and disadvantages of the guild system.

Advantages_____
_____
_____

Disadvantages_____
_____
_____

As soon as you have finished, give this sheet to the examiner.

Test Items from *Foundations of Biology* by Lorande Loss Woodruff, 6th ed., The Macmillan Company, New York, 1941.[1]

Selection 1, pp. 25–26

"The average composition of the human body, including cellular and intercellular material, is about as follows:

Oxygen	65.00%
Carbon	18.00
Hydrogen	10.00
Nitrogen	3.00
Calcium	2.00
Phosphorus	1.00
Potassium	0.35
Sulfur	0.25

[1] By permission of The Macmillan Company, New York.

Sodium.............................. 0.15
Chlorine............................ 0.15
Magnesium........................... 0.05
Iron................................ 0.004

"At first glance there is nothing very striking about this
list of elements. They are all common ones with which the
5 chemist is familiar in the non-living world. The materials
of a man's body are worth less than one dollar! Furthermore, quantitatively the most important compound is
nothing more complex than WATER (H2O). It composes
more than two-thirds of the human body. But there are
10 combinations of the elements which are highly significant and
characteristic, and result from the capacity of carbon, hydrogen, and oxygen, or carbon and hydrogen together, to form
the numerous complex compounds which in turn supply the
basis for intimate associations with other elements. As a
15 matter of fact, the bulk of protoplasm is composed of carbon,
oxygen, hydrogen, and nitrogen associated with each other
in an apparently infinite series of relationships, in which the
carbon seems to play the leading role—the indispensable
bond that links all other elements in organic unity. Some of
20 these compounds are relatively simple, but the majority
consist of elaborate atomic arrangements and not a few
represent molecular complexes of hundreds and even thou-
sands of atoms."

Selection 2, p. 239

"The eggs of the fresh-water Clams, or Mussels, are fer-
tilized by sperm entering the mantle cavity with the in-
halent water current, and the larvae develop in the gills,
which act as temporary brood-pouches. Eventually as tiny
5 clams, known as GLOCHIDIA, they escape, settle on the bottom of the pond or river, and die unless they come into
contact with a fish. In this event, each glochidium becomes
attached to a fish and as a parasite obtains free food and
transportation for several weeks until it has developed suffi-
10 ciently to drop off, settle to the bottom, and shift for itself."

Selection 3, pp. 298–299

"As a summary of this general outline of the structure of the
vertebrate body, we may emphasize three characters which
are of prime diagnostic importance.

"In the first place, whereas the skeletal structures of Inverte-
5 brates typically consist, as in the Crayfish, of an exoskeleton
of hard, non-living materials deposited on the surface of the
body, the chief function of which is protection, the vertebrate
skeleton is primarily a living endoskeleton. It is an organic
part of the organism which, although it affords protection
10 for delicate parts, provides adequately for support and
supplies muscle levers, and thus makes practicable the
relatively large bodies of the higher animals. The notochord
is at once the foundation and axis of the vertebrate internal
skeleton and either persists throughout life as such, or simply
15 long enough to function as a scaffolding about which the
vertebral column is built. It is in recognition of the prime
importance of the notochord that the Vertebrates and their
nearest allies, such as Amphioxus, are known as Chordates.

"In the second place, it will be recalled that the central
20 nervous system of the Earthworm and Crayfish consists of
a nerve cord running along in the body cavity below the
digestive tract, except at the anterior end where it encircles
the pharynx to form a dorsal brain. The position of the
vertebrate brain is similar, though the spinal cord is not a
25 'cord' but a nerve tube which lies in the vertebral canal
embedded in the muscles of the body wall *above* the digestive
tract and, of course, outside of the coelom. Thus the spinal
cord itself and its location are highly characteristic.

"The third fundamental characteristic is a series of perfora-
30 tions or slits through the throat and body wall. In the lower
forms the gill slits provide an exit for the current of water
entering by the mouth and, being richly supplied with blood,
afford the chief means of respiratory interchange between
the animal and the surrounding medium. In the higher
35 Vertebrates the gill slits are present merely during a transient
phase in the development of the individual, since the function
of aerating the blood is taken over by the lungs."

Selection 4, pp. 474–476

Galton's Studies:
"The statistical treatment of biological data as a method of
studying inheritance was first brought prominently to the
attention of biologists by the work of Galton, a cousin of
Darwin, during the closing decades of the last century and

5 started the widespread investigation of genetic problems. In particular, his work on the inheritance of characters in man, such as stature and intellectual capacity, is a biological classic judged by the discussion it evoked. As a result of these studies, Galton formulated two principles of heredity 10 which may be briefly stated as follows:

"*Ancestral Inheritance.* The two parents contribute between them, on the average, one-half of each inherited faculty; each of them contributing one-quarter of it.   The four

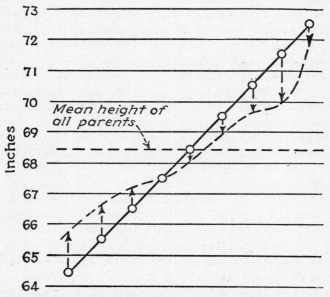

Fig. 317.—Scheme illustrating Galton's law of filial regression, as shown in the stature of parents and children.   The circles represent the height of graded groups of parents and the arrow heads show the average heights of their children.   The length of the arrows indicates the amount of 'regression' toward mediocrity.   (From Walter.)

grandparents contribute between them one-quarter, or each of them one-sixteenth, and so on.

"*Filial Regression.* On the average any deviation of the parents from the racial type is transmitted to the progeny in a diminished degree; the deviation from the racial mean being two-thirds as great as that of the parents. (Figs. 317, 20 394.)

"These so-called laws, taken by and large, undoubtedly express general truths—offspring inherit much more from

their immediate than from their remote ancestors; and offspring of gifted or deficient parents, judged by the average
25   standard of a mixed population, regress toward mediocrity:
that is, toward the population average. But the 'laws' are
not particularly helpful in arriving at the fundamental
principles involved in heredity because the data upon which
they are founded include indiscriminately both inheritable
30   variations, and modifications. The individual's somatic
characters, which form the data, belie in many cases the
underlying germinal constitution—what will be transmitted to the progeny. Thus, for instance, experiments on
plants and animals show that when the *germinal* make-up
35   of all the members of a group is the same with regard to a
character in question, the regression is complete, no matter
how far the particular parents may diverge *somatically* from
the group average. The somatic divergence represents
modifications which are not inherited. Conversely, when
40   the divergence of the parents from the population average
is due to characters which represent expressions of their
germinal constitution, then there is no regression."

Selection 5, pp. 38–40

"In short, Protococcus takes materials from its surroundings in the form of simple compounds, as carbon dioxide,
water, and mineral salts, which are relatively stable and
therefore practically devoid of available energy, and, through
5   the radiant energy of sunlight, shifts and recombines their
elements in such a way that products rich in potential energy
result. Protococcus thus exhibits the prime distinguishing
characteristic of green plants—the power to construct its
own foodstuffs.
10   "The key to this power of chemical synthesis by light—
PHOTOSYNTHESIS—resides in a highly complex chemical
substance called chlorophyll which consists of two very similar but distinct pigments. Chlorophyll is segregated in special
cytoplasmic bodies, the plastids, and gives to Protococcus
15   during its active phases and to the foliage of plants in general
their characteristic green color. Plastids bearing chlorophyll grow and divide and are known as CHLOROPLASTS.
The chlorophyll arrests and transforms a small part of the
energy of the sunlight which reaches it, in such a way that

20   the protoplasm can employ this energy for food synthesis. . . .
      "Protococcus thus takes the raw elements, so to speak, of
      living matter and by the radiant energy of sunlight, which
      its chlorophyll traps, constructs carbohydrate, protein, pro-
      toplasm.   In other words, the green plant is a synthesizing
25   agent, building up highly complex and unstable molecular
      aggregates brimming over with the energy received from the
      sun. So the green plant, whether Protococcus or Elm, by
      this AUTOTROPHIC method manufactures its own food for
      itself as well as for the living world in general.   And inci-
30   dentally, as it were, replenishes the available supply of free
      oxygen without which plants and animals could not exist."

Questions and vocabulary for selections from Woodruff's *Foundations of Biology*

*Name:*_____

Directions

A. Answer the following *questions*, rereading the selection concerned, if necessary.
B. Write after each *listed word* the meaning which best fits its use in the selection.

Selection 1

Of what four chemicals does protoplasm largely consist?
_____

What is the apparent function of carbon in protoplasm?
_____

What is true of the chemicals as they exist in living protoplasm?
Words
    intercellular (line 2)_____
    compound (line 7)_____
    protoplasm (line 15)_____
    indispensable (line 18)_____
    atoms (line 24)_____

Selection 2

List in order the five steps in the development of the fresh-water clam.
    _____
    _____
    _____
    _____
    _____

Words
    inhalent (lines 2–3)_____
    sperm (line 2)_____
    larvae (line 3)_____
    gills (line 3)_____
    parasite (line 8)_____

Selection 3

Name the three outstanding characteristics of vertebrates as differentiated from invertebrates.

_____

_____

Words

skeletal (line 4)_____

exoskeleton (line 5)_____

function (line 7)_____

endoskeleton (line 8)_____

organic (line 8)_____

levers (line 11)_____

notochord (line 12)_____

vertebral column (line 16)_____

anterior (line 22)_____

dorsal (line 23) _____

respiratory (line 33)_____

surrounding medium (line 34)_____

transient (line 35)_____

aerating (line 37)_____

Selection 4

Copy from this passage the simplest expression of Galton's finding on ancestral inheritance.

_____

Studying Fig. 317, explain what is meant by "regression toward mediocrity."

_____

Why do Galton's laws fail to explain inheritance completely?

_____

Words

statistical (line 1)_____

genetic (line 5)_____

heredity (line 9)_____

filial (line 16)_____

progeny (line 17)_____

mediocrity (line 25)_____

somatic (line 30)_____

germinal (line 32)_____

diverge (line 37)_____

Selection 5

What is the power of chemical synthesis or photosynthesis (define)?

_____

Where does chlorophyll reside in the plant?

_____

What does chlorophyll do?

_____
_____
_____

Words
    compounds (line 2)_____
    stable (line 3)_____
    potential (line 6)_____
    synthesis (line 10)_____
    pigments (line 13)_____
    transforms (line 18)_____
    aggregates (line 26)_____

As soon as you have finished answering these questions and giving the meanings of words, give both the selections and your answer sheets to the examiner

From memory of the material you have just read, list in order the five steps in the development of the fresh-water clam.

_____
_____
_____
_____
_____

As soon as you have finished, give this sheet to the examiner.

APPENDIX D

EXERCISES FOR THE RECOGNITION
OF CERTAIN STUDY TECHNIQUES AND THE IMPROVEMENT
OF READING SKILLS IN REGULAR CLASSES

TABLE OF CONTENTS

NOTE: The symbols E, S, G, H, and M indicate the appropriateness of the suggested reading or study technique to *English*, *Science*, *Geography*, *History*, or *Mathematics*.

NOTE: The symbols E, S, G, H, and M, representing *English, Science, Geography, History,* and *Mathematics,* indicate the appropriateness of a suggested technique to those subjects. The absence of a given symbol before a given technique does not prohibit the teacher of that subject from using the technique if he sees the desirability of it in his subject. The majority of techniques here described may be applied to or translated to any level or grade from the beginnings of reading through collegiate work.

Reading for the Main Idea

E—Summary of situation, plot, character, author's thought, mood; headlines

1. Give in a sentence the event in a given scene or situation: "The wolf ate Grandmother."
2. Give in a sentence the character or nature of a situation: "The air was alive with friction."
3. Give in a sentence the personality or general appearance of a character: "Frank was friendly, generous, optimistic, utterly unaffected."
4. Give in a sentence the point of view of the author as expressed in the book or article: "All men must learn to practice democracy if mankind is to survive."
5. Give in a sentence the mood that is expressed in the action, situation, and characters of a book as a whole: "*Ethan Frome* is permeated with the inevitability of tragedy."
6. Give in a sentence the author's thought as expressed symbolically or otherwise in a poem: "Guard the life of this valued friend." (Millay's "To the Wife of a Sick Friend.")
7. Choose alternative titles for a story, news article, magazine article, or poem: "A Surprise Visit with a Surprise Ending" ("Goldilocks and the Three Bears").
8. Choose alternative titles for scenes in a play (substitute titles suggestive of the action rather than of the setting).
9. Select a revealing name for a character (Miss Prim, Mr. Blowhard).
10. Pantomime briefly a book, character, or scene to be guessed.
11. Send a telegram repeating the events of a crucial scene in the story; keep it cheap!
12. Read a summary or title and have the class guess which event or situation or character it is.
13. Match headlines to a decapitated news article.
14. Select headlines and subheadlines for news articles, original or decapitated.
15. Give a beginning sentence to a news article whose beginning (main idea) has been removed.
16. Write an account of a day spent and then decide on the best topical sentence and title for it: "Twelve Hours in Twelve Directions" or "Frustration, Thy Name Is Busyness."
17. Write summarizing sentences for every paragraph in an article and fit them together in a more brief account.

SGH—Chapter headings, subheadings, marginal headings, introduction, summary, and questions

18. Read the chapter headings, subheadings, and marginal headings, in turn, and try to gather from these the kind of material and topic your author

has to offer.   Put your impression into a sentence: "This first chapter is about the development of science, from primitive superstitution, through the attempts of the Greeks to systematize knowledge."

19. Look at the questions at the end of the chapter to see the kind of thing you are to expect and read for.   Tell in a sentence: "I'm to notice what kinds of people the characters are."

20. Read the introduction at the beginning of the chapter and the summary at the end to get the scope and purpose.

21. After reading the material under a marginal heading, state or write in a sentence the main idea.

22. After reading the chapter, think of a sentence that might express the content better than the title does.

23. Find the sentence in the chapter which best expresses the author's main idea of the subject.   (This is likely to be in the summary.)

24. Find the sentence in the chapter which best expresses what material is covered.   (This is likely to be at the beginning.)

S—Summary of experiment: purpose or result

25. Express the purpose of an experiment in one or two compact sentences: "The test is to determine the relative speed with which water will pass through sand, clay, and loam."

26. Express the finding of an experiment in one sentence: "Water passes most easily through sand, then loam, then clay."

27. Express the utility of this finding in one sentence: "Plants requiring rapid drainage should not be confined in a bed of clay unless an outlet is provided."

28. Find the author's statement of the purpose of an experiment.

M—First general reading of a verbal problem

29. Read the verbal problem to see in general what kind of problem it is. Express the situation in a general way, such as, "With time and rate given, the distance is to be found."

30. Go carefully through a verbal problem, picking out the general words which suggest the character of the problem (time, rate, distance, inverse proportion).   Translate other words into these terms (that is, translate "minutes" or "hours" into "time").

31. Read the problem to find the unknown.

32. Find the author's statement of the problem involved in a given example or problem or chapter.

33. State in your own words the problem with which an example or a chapter deals.

ESGH—Main idea stated specifically in a paragraph

34. Underline the author's statement of the main idea of a chapter or section, if he gives it in so many words.

35. Interpret the author's statement of the main idea in your own words.

36. In sequence, read the main ideas you have underlined in a chapter to get an overview of the ground you have covered.

37. Model from the underlined ideas a main idea of the whole chapter in a single, original sentence.

38. Underline the main ideas in several paragraphs in your textbook.   Where is the main idea usually found?   What do the other ideas in the paragraphs do for the main ideas?

39. Find a paragraph whose main idea is explained by the details.

40. Find a paragraph whose main idea is justified by the details.
41. If the main idea is in the second sentence of a paragraph, what does the first sentence do? How can you tell that the first sentence is not main? What words in it suggest the author's purpose in putting this sentence there instead of starting with the main idea?
42. Write a paragraph giving a main idea. Give the paragraph to another person, who must find the main idea.

ESGH—Main idea, not stated in so many words, to be inferred
43. Find some paragraphs in which the main idea is not stated in any one sentence or two sentences.
44. Give titles to these paragraphs.
45. Give in a sentence the main idea of each paragraph.
46. What do you have to do mentally to get the main idea of such a paragraph?
47. List briefly the kinds of information you are given in a paragraph. Prove that all these add up to the main idea you have selected.
48. Write a paragraph with the main idea in mind but not stated. See whether someone else can gather from the things you have stated what your main idea is.
49. From someone else's statement of the main idea in a paragraph, think of and list details to explain or justify it. Then compare your details with those given in the original paragraph. How well do they agree and why? Was the main idea stated too broadly? Was your experience too limited for you to guess all the details?

SGH—Keynote paragraph, which sets the purpose of the whole chapter or section
50. Summarize the introductory section or paragraph of a chapter.
51. What kind of information does this paragraph give you? Does it tell the importance of the topic, the phases of the topic?
52. List the things you have known before about the topic.
53. What sentence or sentences give you the best idea of the topic to be discussed? What do the other sentences do for the topic?
54. If you were going to write an introduction to this topic, what things would you tell to interest the reader in it and what would you say to explain exactly what the topic is about?

Reading for Sequence or Outline

E—Plot sequence
55. In a news report of an incident, what is usually told first? Prove your answer with more than one clipping. Why do you suppose the story is started in this way?
56. Rewrite in your own words a short newspaper article, telling the story from first to last. How is the order of events in your story different from that in the newspaper story? What is better about your way? About the newspaper way? How were you able to tell in the newspaper story which event really happened first?
57. Take a story that you have written and rewrite it as a news article.
58. Read a chapter of a book, in which a number of things happen. List the 2, 3, 4, or 5 big things that happen in the order that they happen. What could these be called as a group (chapter heading or original

heading)? Do any of these happen at the same time? How can you list these to indicate that they happen simultaneously?

(II. At Twelve O'Clock
    A. The Hero's Venture
    B. The Villain's Conniving)

In each of these events, who are the actors, what do they do, and what are the results? List these points under the heading of each event.

(III. The Drawing-room Episode
    A. The Characters
    B. The Action
    C. The Result)

59. Plan a play. Give it a title. List the things that you would have happen. Make another list of the scenes and the kinds of things you will need for each. (Scene I. The Living-room Furniture—4 straight-backed chairs, a sofa, a large table, etc.)

60. If you were to produce as a play a story that you have read, what would you need?

    Make an outline entitled: The Requirements for the Production of _____ As a Play.

    What kinds of items will be your main headings? (characters, costumes, scenery, committees for costuming, lighting, etc.). List under each of these main headings the items that you will need of each kind.

61. Make a time line of a story as it is told. Some stories go from beginning to end chronologically: _____

    beginning   end

Some start toward the middle of the period concerned, go back to the beginning of the time, lead up to the starting point, and continue to the end.

                                  start

    beginning of time   end

62. Find remarks by the author suggesting coming events ("But had he gone home as they were led to suppose?")

63. Find a conversation in your story that makes the plot move (tells you about something that has happened or something that is going to happen).

64. Find a description of something that has happened and see whether you can turn it into a conversation that will tell the same thing.

65. In a ballad (such as "Clementine"), in what parts of the ballad does the action take place? What does the rest of the story do for the ballad as to thought?

66. Tell the story of a ballad as a straight story.

67. Write the ballad story as a news item.

E—Character change or development in a story

68. Describe a character in the beginning of a story. Make another description of him as he was at the end. How did he change? What did he learn?

69. List, step by step, the people and things and events that made a character change during a story.

E—Organization

70. In a sonnet, what does the first group of lines do?   What does the second group of lines do?   What does the second group do for the first?

71. In a limerick, what do the first two lines do?   What do the last three lines do?

72. As you read a story, notice in what order the author takes up his different topics or events.   (Dickens's chapters are parallel in time but deal with different characters, who are united in a subsequent chapter.   Some books are divided into large parts in which chapters dealing with a given area are united.   Sometimes a chapter is concerned completely with setting the stage for character and action in a subsequent chapter.)

73. In a biography, what topics has the author given to various sections of the person's life?   How do these topics show what the author considers to be significant about these sections?

74. In a play, list the scenes and tell why you suppose the author chose those particular scenes.   Tell what each does for the story.

75. In a nonfiction book, notice the part and chapter headings in the table of contents.   What does this inspection tell you about the author's train of thought?   How are the parts or chapters related to one another?

EH—Logic of article or argument

76. List the steps that the author of an article gives to prove his point.   In them, does he assume as true anything which is questionable?   (All Athenians are liars; therefore, Socrates is a liar.)

Is any of them suggested rather than arrived at in a straightforward manner?   (A politician says that his party was not in office during a certain critical time.   The suggestion for the reader is that his party would have made these critical times better times.   The real evidence may be that the party as a unit opposed the reforms that would have made the times good, or failed to have a constructive plan.)

Does the selection of words itself influence the reader for or against a given opinion?   (They refused to cooperate with the press, *vs.* They were not available for comment.   They battled bravely, *vs.* They engaged in wholesale murder mercilessly.)

Is there an emotional appeal that can cause the reader to judge the ideas not on their merit but on his own blood pressure?   (Dear old Mother, gray hair and shaking fingers, etc.)

Does the choice of facts show careful avoidance of those which would certainly spoil the author's argument?

Is ridicule used to make the reader laugh his way through indefensible leaps in logic?

Is there a generalization based upon insufficient data?   (My white rabbits have white tails.   My brown rabbits have white tails.   Therefore, all rabbits have white tails.)

To prove a point, is an analogy or story introduced which actually is not comparable to the situation under consideration?   (Don't change horses in the middle of the stream.)

Are arguments on the "other side" given brief treatment which does not do them justice?

Does the author emphasize the shortcomings of the "other side" in order to hide the lacks of his side?

Does the author trace a set of facts or a situation to a false origin, ignoring the real origin? (During this man's term of office, 6,000 businesses closed down yearly. Therefore, he was bad for business. Here the coincident factor of a depression or whatnot is not given.)

Does he attach an idealistic appeal?

Does he label a person, an action, or an idea as a means of damning him or it, when actually there are no facts to validate the label? (This is *heresy*.—The man is a *radical* of the worst sort.—This *mossback* would propose to lead us to a new world order.)

Are there threats of consequences unwarranted by the data? (This can only lead to the ruination of our country.)

Does he use the chummy appeal? (*You and I* know better than this.)

MS—Steps in an experiment or a problem

77. Note the steps you must take to carry out an experiment. Translate the author's words carefully into your own in a list of the things to be done. Read the list you have made to see why each step is necessary, noting especially the order in which the steps occur.

78. Using the example of a mathematical process, make two columns on a sheet of paper; list in one column in your own words and in order the steps required for solution; in the second column translate these steps into mathematical symbols. Placing a sheet of paper next to these lists of steps and symbols, work a problem of the same kind, step by step, according to your description in the lists.

GH—Topical outline of a complex situation

79. Taking the author's discussion of the geography of a country, make columns entitled Climate, Topography, Housing, Agriculture, Industry, etc., and put into these columns the facts that you find on each subject. If you do this for several countries in turn, you will have a means of quick comparison:

Country	Climate	Topography	Housing	etc.
Japan		(facts)		
China		(facts)		

Now set these up in an outline, making the topics your Roman numerals (I, II, III) and the facts under each topic your capital letters (*A, B*).

80. Make charts showing the influence of the physical features of a country (minerals, for example) upon the lives of the people. Have one chart for agriculture, one for housing, one for industry, etc.

minerals	soil	etc.	etc.

mining	shipping	etc.

Make an outline of these entitled, "The Influence of Physical Factors upon _____." Make the Roman numerals (I, II, III) the factors, and the capital letters (A, B, C) the kinds of industry, for instance. The arabic numbers (1, 2, 3) under the capital letters will be the specific effects of the physical factors, such as the making of jewelry or china, or the production and shipping of raw materials.

81. Outline in history the steps that a man took to gain office. Roman numerals would include such steps as Appeals to the People, Appeals to Political Groups, Appeals to Foreign Interests, Military Exploits. The A, B, C under these would be the actual things he did.

82. List in history the steps leading to a certain event, such as the factors contributing to the Civil War.

83. List in history the results of a certain event or condition.

84. List in history the contributions of a previous civilization to ours.

85. Taking an author's discussion of a civilization, make columns entitled Political, Social, Religious, Intellectual, etc., and write in each the facts about that phase of civilization that the author gives. Make an outline similarly organized.

86. Make a chart showing the influence of various groups or public figures upon the life of the people. (Such influences as those of a queen, a religious sect, etc.)

Q. Victoria		*Anglican church*	
.	.	. . .	
.	.	.	.
(effects)			

Make an outline of these, organized similarly and entitled, "Influences on the Lives of the People of _____ in the _____ Era."

SH—Chain of Events:

87. List the chain of events from a first incident to a culmination (the assassination of an archduke and the outbreak of a world war; the history of Queen Elizabeth's relations with Spain and the resultant attack of the Spanish Armada upon England).

88. List the chain of events leading to a scientific discovery (steps by which Mme. Curie and Pierre Curie isolated radium; steps by which a series of scientists discovered the factors governing falling bodies).

Reading for Details

NOTE: Details are never important in themselves but only in relation to a main idea, a sequence, a conclusion. It is desirable that detail exercise always be identified with arriving at a main idea or a generalization, getting a sense of sequence, or drawing a conclusion. Exercises whose only plausible justification seems to be an insatiable curiosity on the part of the teacher fail to qualify under the heading of purposeful reading.

E—Technique

89. From a story or poem, select a passage that you think is very vivid. What has the author done to make it vivid?

How many things does he give you to see?

What does he tell you about them?

Has he described them as to appearance or as to their resemblance to other things (analogy, simile, metaphor)?

Has he told you of their position or how they look in relation to each other?

Make a picture or a diagram showing exactly what the author has made you see.

90. Select a character that you like.   What has the author done or had him do to make you like him?

91. Select a character that you dislike.   What has the author done or had him do to make you dislike him?

92. List the things that happen on a few pages in your book.

Does the author tell you about them
through his own comment?
by having the characters act them through?
by having the characters tell what happens?

Use a similar technique in a story of your own.

93. Select a trait that you think a certain character has.   Go through the story to see whether the author reveals this trait:
by the author's word that the character has it.
by the character's actions.
by the character's words.
by the testimony of other characters.

Use similar techniques in a story of your own.

94. Select one of the ideas about life that you feel a story has suggested (virtue is rewarded; evil will out; never live with a mother-in-law). Go through the story to find out in what ways the author has made you feel this.

95. As you read a story or an article and find yourself having certain emotional reactions to it, try to note the things that the author has done to produce this effect upon you.

E—Description (for plot, character, setting)

96. List the events that occur in a story, a play, or a narrative poem, in preparation for
Judging their plausibility or truth to life as you know it.
Seeing how the author has built up to a climax.
Seeing whether the events justify the ending.
Summarizing the events in a general statement of the story's content, such as, boy meets girl, the lost is found, a quest succeeds despite difficulties.

97. List the details that the author gives you about a character, in preparation for
Drawing a picture (physical features).
Inventing a scene that the author omitted, demonstrating the character's traits.
Writing a letter such as this character might have written to another, showing what kind of person he is.
Discussing the consistency or inconsistency of the author's portrayal.
Showing the monotony of the author's repetitious descriptions or the variety of ways he has of saying the same thing.

Making a comparison of this character with someone you know.

98. List the details in the description of a room, a landscape, or some other setting, in preparation for

Drawing a model of it.

Painting a picture or making a mural of it.

Planning to dramatize the story.

Comparing the author's description with that of another author or with your own of the same place or a similar place.

Noticing the things that give the description a mood of gloom, gaiety, impending doom, mystery, etc.

E—Sentence inversion (especially in poetry)

99. "There in the gloom where the willows stood were two shining eyes." What does the author achieve by turning sentences around, putting the subject (the thing talked about) last? (suspense, variety in sentence structure, fluency of style, emphasis, rhyme ending, etc.). Rewrite an inverted sentence as it would be if the author put the most important thing (two shining eyes) first.

As you have it written, what does it mean? Tell it in your own words.

100. Find the subject of the inverted sentence. (It will be toward the end.) Find the predicate. (It is the expression that tells what the subject did or was.)

Take each phrase and decide, by studying its meaning, whether or not it refers to or explains the word next to it, or some other word.

Notice the commas; a comma between a word and a following phrase frequently means that the phrase refers to some other word previously mentioned.

Rewrite the sentence, putting the subject and its modifiers (words and phrases) first and the predicate and its modifiers second.

Write in your own words what the sentence means.

E—Sentence length and complexity

101. If the meaning of a long sentence is troublesome, two reasons are usually that retention of a long passage is difficult and that the sentence has two or more related thoughts in it.

The sentence above, for example, starts with a dependent (stage-setting) clause, is continued by an independent clause (the act), and is prolonged by the presence of two substantive clauses (the "that" clauses). The comma shows the separation of the dependent and independent clauses. Take a sentence that is long and puzzling. See what the punctuation tells you (commas, semicolons, colons). Try to identify the clauses as dependent (stage-setting) or independent (the act). Find the subjects and predicates of the clauses. Decide what the other words and phrases modify in the sentence and what they do for the sentence.

102. Write a statement of fact in two words. (It rains.)

Write before it a dependent (stage-setting) clause telling *when* this fact may be. (When the stars do not shine, it rains.)

Separate the clauses with a comma.

Add to the dependent clause a phrase telling *where* it may be. (When the stars do not shine in Podunk, it rains.)

103. Make collections of dependent clauses and phrases until you begin to recognize the words that commonly introduce them.

104. Take an old newspaper and pick out or underline the dependent clauses and phrases.

105. Practice condensing dependent clauses into phrases
(When the stars do not shine—on a starless night.)   Similarly you can mentally shorten the long sentences that trouble you.

EMSG—Compact writing:

106. In a poem in which every word is burdened with meaning,
Read the sentence carefully, trying to get the whole meaning.
If this fails, find the subject and the predicate and then decide which phrases and words modify each.
Reread the sentence, rearranging the phrases and words, if necessary, to clarify their relationships to the subjects and predicate.
If the sentence still defies understanding, notice each word and phrase again to see whether a different meaning may be attached to any of them: (a) through the application of a different dictionary meaning, (b) through taking the words in a figurative sense (the bird and the flower—the lover and his beloved), or (c) through looking up certain words whose historic or literary meanings have escaped you (Zeus, the cypress, the olive branch).

107. In a verbal mathematics problem, in which you must know every word meaning and word relationship in order to solve the problem,
Read the problem through to decide on the method you will have to use to solve it and on the nature of the unknown.
Reread, noting each expression (the product of 2 and 10, decreased by 4) and translating each into mathematical equivalents $(2 \times 10, -4)$; if in doubt concerning an expression, consult the example or previous problem for an interpretation of it.
Reread for the relationships among these terms, noting the clues in punctuation (a comma between parts that are not to be attached to each other) and the statement of equality (which groups of relationship are said to be equal to which other groups).

108. In scientific definitions and laws, notice the qualifying words: the descriptive words, the phrases that narrow the application of the law or the scope of the thing defined.
Study the meanings of these descriptive words and phrases to be sure that you know what they mean.
Rewrite the definition or law in a paragraph instead of a sentence, making each sentence in your paragraph explain fully the meaning of a descriptive word or phrase in the definition or law.

E—Circuitous language

109. Notice the parts of the sentence that seem to cause difficulty.
Often this is a negative or a double negative: "Thou art not unlike an onion." "Not" is one negative; "un" is another; the two cancel each other and produce "Thou art like an onion." But the two negatives are a form of caution and seem a little less plain-spoken and assured.
Sometimes it is the presence of many qualifying phrases: "even the best of them," "such as _____," "regardless of _____," "more than any other _____," etc.
These expressions are usually set off from the rest of the sentence by commas. Look for such signs of their presence. Read the sentence without these qualifying phrases and say in your own words what the

meaning of that much of the sentence is. Then approach each qualifying phrase individually and add its meaning to the meaning of the sentence. Sometimes it is the presence of many qualifying clauses: "when he is sure no one is about," "while the breath of life remains," etc. These are usually set off by commas. Use the same technique as that suggested above for phrases. In addition, translate these clauses into shorter phrases: "certain of being alone," "till death."

Sometimes it is the presence of interrupting words, phrases, or clauses which do not contribute to the main thought but comment upon it: "assuredly," "indeed," "without doubt," "on the other hand," etc. Use the same technique as that suggested above for phrases. Then determine what prestige the author's "asides" have given the meaning of the sentence or in what way the sentence has been related to previous sentences by means of the "asides."

Sometimes it is the avoidance of a shorter and more common expression in favor of a less common or more poetic expression: "They left the place" avoided in favor of "They undertook to evacuate the place"; or avoidance of a longer and more common expression for a shorter, less common one: "He had no other possible choice" avoided in favor of "He had no alternative."

Translate these less common expressions into the equivalents to which you are more accustomed, "the words you know better."

Sometimes it is the presence of certain figures of speech: "just as the gull in his flight . . . ," etc. These expressions are intended to enrich meaning but actually present an obstacle to it if they are long and frequent. Use the same technique as that suggested for phrases.

Sometimes it is the presence of phrases and clauses that make very fine distinctions and thus keep the reader's mind running from one comparison or contrast to another, drawing lines of fine distinction, the while: "A slice of corned beef, neither too hot nor too cold, served with just a dash of mustard, which in excess is most unpalatable but in moderation is a delight, . . ."

Use the same technique as that suggested for phrases.

E—Facts to substantiate headlines

Because of the prevalence of newspaper headlines that purposely or unintentionally violate the standard of impartiality in reporting, it is important for the reader to find the actual facts on which the headlines are based. Such facts, such as direct quotations, are often buried toward the end of the article. Students must learn to distinguish between the actual quotations or occurrences stated in the article and opinions (arising from hearsay) or generalization.

110. Read a newspaper headline and write a sentence putting the thought it contains more fully. Jot down two or three facts that you think must be in the article in order to justify the headline. Then read the article to find the facts on which the headline is based. Check these facts as you go along; a check in the margin will do. Then return to them and compare them with your own first guess of two or three facts. Are the reporter's facts sufficient justification for the statement in the headlines? If not, what effect has the headline on the reader (overoptimism, hate, righteous indignation) and why might the newspaper have wished to produce this effect?

111. Go through a newspaper article underlining every statement which either tells exactly what happened or quotes a responsible source. Reread these statements and see whether they justify the headlines.

112. Read a newspaper article on a controversial issue and underline the words that prompt you to a favorable or unfavorable reaction to a given side of the issue: "Pickets *harried* and *threatened* the workers who *refused to break their word*"—"harried" and "threatened" suggest disagreeable action, while "refused to break their word" suggests honorable action. Contrast this with: "Pickets *tried in vain to dissuade* strike *breakers* from *deserting* the cause." Do the words you have underlined suggest a definite bias or partiality for one side on the part of the author?

See "How to Read the News," *National Defense Bulletin* No. 16, U.S. Office of Education, 1942.

MS—Conversion of words into symbols, phrases into symbols

113. Underline the words or phrases in a problem that are to be converted into mathematical or scientific notation. Over each of these write the symbol that represents it.

114. Write the appropriate symbol after each of the expressions in the problem whose symbols you know. If there is a symbol that you do not know, look back into previous problems or examples to see whether the expression has occurred before. Note the symbol used on this previous occasion. Put this expression and its symbol in your vocabulary notebook for special attention.

MSG—Drawing a figure

115. Read the description of the figure very carefully, noting the objects that are to be in it. Write the names of these objects, and draw the symbols for them next to their names.

Next, study carefully the relationships among the figures—where one thing is in relation to another and what the relative sizes are. Indicate these relationships lightly on the symbols or briefly in words.

Next, draw the complete figure, constantly referring to these notes. (If a student's drawings are already acceptable most of these steps may be performed mentally.)

MS—Laws

116. Read the law carefully, getting a clear picture of the meaning of the words and phrases involved.

If it includes any words that you do not know, look for them in the glossary or in a dictionary, but be sure to use the dictionary definition labeled "sci." or "math.," if there is one so labeled.

Reread for the relationships among these words and phrases. Try to put the law into your own words.

Try to think of a practical example of the law.

Look at the verbal and pictorial illustrations in the textbook for other suggestions of its practical meaning.

HMSG—Definitions

117. Read the definition carefully for the general meaning.

Look up any words that trouble you.

Put the definition into your own words.

Read additional material which tells what the thing referred to does (what its function is), what it is good for or bad for.

Make some special note of the definition, underlining it, writing the word and its definition in the margin, putting the word with a statement of its characteristics and its function into a vocabulary notebook.

118. Write the definitions and functions of several new terms on separate cards and on the backs of the cards write the terms referred to. Read through the cards, seeing whether you can identify the term from the description.

MS—Formulas

A formula is most meaningful if its derivation is clearly understood.

119. Read through the explanation of the derivation of the formula. See whether you can follow the reasoning that leads to its final form.

120. Read the verbal description of the formula and see that that is understandable to you, referring to the dictionary, if necessary. Compare the verbal description with the formula, to see how the different concepts are represented.

121. Note the examples and read the text to find out to what kind of situation the formula is appropriate.

122. Work a problem through, to experience the effectiveness of the formula.

123. Notice what precautions must be taken in the use of the formula, especially the relationships or proportions that must be maintained among the factors.

HSG—Characteristics or members of a group

124. When the author enumerates the characteristics of a group, underline the name of the group and the characteristics, saying them over.

125. Try to remember from your own experience as much as you can of proof of these characteristics. If the group is strange to you, try through pictures and mental imagery to visualize it.

126. Make a set of cards for the characteristics or members of the group, putting the name of the group on one side and the characteristics or members on the other. Read the characteristics or members and guess the name of the group. Or read the name of the group and try to name all the characteristics or members.

127. Think of each characteristic in turn, trying to visualize it, and then try to think of other groups that have this characteristic also.

128. List the characteristics of two groups in two separate columns in preparation for making a comparison.

MSGH—Names

129. As you meet a new name that you wish to remember,
Look at it for any feature which will make it easy to remember.
Think of the situations, characters, or events with which it is connected.
State in a sentence why it is worth remembering.
Put it in an outline of the events or situations or characters discussed, so that you will have a record of its bearing on the subject.
Make a family tree or chart suggesting its relationship to other topics.
Put it in a time line of events, thus relating it to a period of time or sequence.

H—Steps in a chain of historical events

130. As you come to an enumeration of steps in a chain of historical events,
Underline the steps.
Notice the words that suggest the introduction of another step: "then"

"finally," "second," "another," "subsequently," "in response to this," etc.

Compare the thought of each sentence with that of the previous one to see whether the new sentence contains a new thought and a new addition to the chain of events or still refers to the last thought.

Try to visualize each step, studying carefully the author's description of it and thinking of similar events that you have known or heard of.

Try to see how one step leads to another.

Close the book and try to recall the steps as they came.

Review the steps in your own words.

S—Steps in an experiment

131. Note the purpose of the experiment and, as you read, anticipate what will be done; see how the steps are related to the purpose.

Notice the kinds of words that suggest the introduction of a new step: "then," "to this, add—," etc.

Number the steps as they are given.

Underline or write down the important words of each step so that you have the essentials for each.

Reread each step underlined and try to visualize it or draw a diagram of it.

Try to see the relationship of each step to the next and of each to the purpose of the experiment. Ask yourself, "Why do we do this?" and "Why does this step come here instead of sooner or later?"

Close the book and try to enumerate the steps and their details; open the book and compare.

S—Steps in a life cycle

132. Be sure you know the identity and classification of the plant or animal whose life you are to read, its family tree, and where you are likely to find it. Recall, if possible, your experiences with it.

Note the words that introduce the descriptions of each new phase in the life: "then," "the seed," "the egg," "in the earliest stage," etc.

Number the steps in the life. Try to see the relationship of one step to another, how one leads to another.

If a title to each of these stages is not given, write in the margin a title for each (egg, larva, pupa, etc.).

Underline or write the important characteristics of each stage.

Close the book and try to enumerate the stages. Open the book and compare.

With the book closed, enumerate the essentials of each step in sequence. Open the book and compare.

S—Steps in the life of a scientist

133. Be sure you know the general placement of the scientist: the time he lived, his country, the field to which he contributed. Try to recall in what connection you have ever heard of him.

Note the words ("then," "his chief contribution," etc.) or the forms (new paragraph) that introduce new steps in his life.

Underline or write the important events in his life. Number them.

In the margin, give a name to each discovery or event.

Note the methods that he used in his studies, if those methods are important.

For each discovery, notice what the author has to say about its value or significance to scientific thought and to our lives.

Try to think of ways in which each of this scientist's discoveries has affected your thinking or your life.

Close the book and enumerate the events or discoveries and give the important details of each. Open the book and compare.

SHG—Selectivity in details

134. In material that has too many facts for you possibly to remember,

Decide how many things you can remember; that is, roughly set limits to your goal of assimilation.

Notice the ways in which the author indicates, if he does, the relative importance of these facts, so that you will remember only the most noteworthy

By giving more space to the discussion of one fact than to another.

By the use of introductory remarks, such as "above all," "pre-eminent," "the chief factor," "probably the most crucial."

By organization (paragraphs in which a big fact is illustrated or supported by a lot of little facts; marginal headings to point out the big facts).

By questions at the beginning of the chapter, or at its end, to call attention to the most important facts.

By a list of important words at the end of the chapter.

By a summary at the end of the chapter or section.

By the use of italics.

By pictures or other illustrative material.

Otherwise, note by yourself the relationships among the facts and choose the key facts among these.

Compare the facts in the text with the kind the teacher seems especially anxious for you to note, and select those which he likes to emphasize. (What kinds of facts does he usually require in his questions in class, in his tests, in his assignments?)

Underline or write the facts selected by the above methods.

Review them, noting their relationships to the whole topic and to each other.

Close the book and try to write or repeat these facts. Open the book and compare.

Compare questions and answer them with these facts, or see how many of the author's or teacher's questions you can answer with the facts you have selected.

G—Description of physical conditions and life

135. Before you read such material, try to recall the things that you have heard or read about such life or conditions, and try to anticipate imaginatively the information you will be given.

Look at the illustrations of the life or conditions.

Underline as you read, or write, the important characteristics given. Rereading these, see whether you can group them under certain headings (mining, housing, agriculture, etc.). Write these titles in the margin, unless the author has already done so. Number these for the sake of knowing how many kinds of information you have.

Close the book and enumerate the kinds of information and the details of each, or draw a diagram or rough picture including all you know. Open the book and compare.

E—Evidences of emotion or feeling in a character

136. Given the character in a situation to which he will show a feeling or emotional response,

The reader's objective is to piece together the evidences of this feeling or emotion and determine its nature—anger, despondency, joy, grief, the mixture of love and sorrow at parting, etc. The feeling or emotion is the main idea of the passage, and is to be comprehended by means of the several evidences or clues.

The first task, then, is to note these clues; the second is to piece them together, perhaps by imagining one's own reactions in a similar situation, and to generalize them into an emotion or feeling. The first task is to read for details; the second is to infer and to generalize, asking the questions: Why does the character think or do these things? What feeling or emotion might prompt all these thoughts or acts?

The author will give these evidences or clues through

What the character says or does.

What the character is said to think.

What other characters say or do about the character or in reaction to him.

Symbolism in the environment (gray day—gloomy mood).

Sometimes what the character says is

A direct expression of emotion: "I hate you!"

An expression from which the emotion may be inferred: "He is such a little boy," meaning "I am his mother and should stay with him; yet I must go,"—hence love and regret; or, "Evidently there is no basis on which we can reach an agreement," meaning, "You are being difficult and I am impatient with you."

Sometimes what the character does is

A direct expression of emotion: a slap, a stamping of the foot, a kiss, tears.

An expression from which the emotion may be inferred: bringing father's slippers or straightening his tie—concern for his welfare, and hence love; crushing a flower (symbolic)—suggesting the desire to destroy someone or something else beautiful but hateful.

The character may think aloud or the author may tell how he feels and what he thinks.

Other characters may discuss the character's situation: "I don't see how he puts up with it"; the character's actions: "Did you notice how he looked at it?" or words, interpreting them to suggest how the character must feel.

In an effort to discern a character's feeling or emotion, note the ingredients of the situation and imagine how you would feel in his place; notice what he does and says, what, according to the author, he thinks, what other characters have to say about him and how they act toward him, points about the environment that seem to have no significance unless taken as symbolic of the character's feeling or emotion.

Reading Creatively: Inferring, Drawing Conclusions, Seeing Relationships

(the skill that makes the difference between thinking Americans and fact-reading sheep)

EH—Predicting events

137. Considering the background events, the situation, the characters involved, and what is said and done, decide what is likely to happen next.

138. Comparing our present situation with a previous one in history, decide what is likely to happen next. What disparate factors may justify another result than the one you have predicted? (For instance, it is possible to suppose that we shall fail of world organization this time as we did 25 years ago; but the disparate, hopeful factors are that now we have had more experience in cooperation, know more about internationalism, realize more fully the desperate need for peace among men, and are better informed about and more alert to world problems.)

139. Considering the character involved in a situation, his disposition, his feelings, and his motives, what action do you anticipate?

140. In a situation of strife or indecision, what do you think will happen? Why?

141. From the author's description of a place, what kinds of activity or problems would you expect to arise? Give your reasons.

142. What hints do you find in a conversation that suggest how a character's opinions are changing or what his future actions may be? Give your predictions about these opinions or actions.

EMSG—Comparison with own experience

143. Comparing the expressed feelings of the poet with your own in a like situation, tell how his reaction is similar to yours or different, and what it offers as a suggestion to your living. (For instance, he may be philosophical about a loss; you, rebellious.)

144. Recall a situation which you have faced, similar to one that the author presents.

145. Tell to what extent your feelings would be the same as or different from those of a character in a given situation, and give reasons.

146. Think of a place you know that is like the one described in a story. Tell why you think the story might or might not have taken place in the situation you know.

147. In a newspaper or magazine article, do the facts stated as true seem convincing to you? What in your experience makes you distrust or trust them? What about the sources of information makes you believe or disbelieve them?

148. Tell the experience you have had with a principle or an object discussed in your science text.

149. On reading a description of a certain country in geography, tell how it compares with or differs from the places you have seen. To the extent that it compares with your experience, tell what activities, housing, etc., you would expect to find in such a country.

EH—Propaganda

150. Compare what the author says with what you know in an area you have explored. See whether his idea seems plausible. If not, think of the reasons he might have personally for promoting a false idea.

151. From the novelist's or playwright's portrayal of a situation, a character, a plot, draw conclusions about situations, people, and the way life develops. What does the author make you think about the situation, about people, about patterns of life or the lack of pattern in life? What do you think he thinks about these things?

152. If an author presents two sides of a problem and draws a conclusion, observe the facts carefully to see whether he does justice to both sides. In what ways, if any, does he slight the arguments that favor the side he opposes? Can you think of any favorable arguments that he has overlooked?

153. In an article on a debatable issue, notice the facts given and the opinions that the author bases on these facts. Are all the facts you know of, bearing on the subject, given? Taking all the facts you know, do you arrive at his conclusion or at another? Does the author state as fact something you know to be debatable and really a matter of opinion?

EH—Author's point of view

154. An author of a story makes his point of view evident by the way he makes his characters act and speak, by the things he causes to happen to them, by outright statements of his opinions, and sometimes by the title of the story.

An author of an expository article states his opinion openly, usually in the introduction and/or the conclusion of the paper, and sometimes the wording of the title.

Give the evidence and draw conclusions as to the opinions of an author of a story or an article.

E—Structural relationships

155. Read a newspaper article and notice how many times the story is told. What are the differences among the ways in which it is told? What justification is there for each retelling, i.e., what contribution does each reiteration make?

156. In a poem of several stanzas, what happens in each stanza? Is each stanza in some way a unit in thought?

157. In a sonnet, decide what the first stanza does for the second, what the second does for the first.

E—Figures of speech

When the author likens someone, something, or a situation to something that it really is not, he is actually making a comparison helpful to the reader's appreciation of the person, object, or situation:

"Thou'rt like unto a lovely flower.

So fair, so graceful, and so pure," clearly states the way in which the maiden reminds the poet of a flower.

"We have given our hearts away, a sordid boon," suggests that we have freely rid ourselves of a quality most essential to our being. The poet considers this quality so vital that he compares it to the heart itself.

158. To benefit from the author's full meaning, consider his figures of speech and determine the qualities that he finds alike in the two situations, people, or things. "The road was a ribbon of moonlight"—the quality that a road and a ribbon might have in common would be smoothness, slenderness, length, and gentle curves; the quality of the road and the moonlight would be a silver cast and glow.

159. Find places in which the author helps you to see something more clearly by means of such figures. Show how the object is described indirectly by the comparison.

E—Comparison of two arguments

160. Read two articles discussing the same topic. How is each organized? Tell how they differ in organization. What are the arguments of each? How do the facts differ? How does one author's interpretation of the facts differ from that of the other? Do both authors' giving the same fact present it with equal fullness and comparable point of view? How does the treatment of each fact suggest the author's point of view toward it?

M—Statement of equality, relationship of the parts of a problem

161. Read the mathematics problem to note the statement of equality, *i.e.*, what group of elements is equal to what other group of elements under what conditions. Notice what alterations in one set of elements or another are required for a status of equality, *i.e.*:

$$X \quad - \quad 10 \quad = \quad 2\times \quad (2 \times 12)$$

(a certain number) *decreased by* ten (is equal to) *twice* (the product of two and twelve.)

Such alterations are suggested by terms like "decreased by," "diminished by," "reduced by," "increased by," "is greater by," etc.

162. Read a problem of the type for which there is a standard formula such as $d = rt$. In the sentences that comprise the problem, find the elements to represent d, r, and t, and substitute them in the formula.

If two situations are compared in such a problem, note the conditions of comparison. For instance, the distance train X travels is twice the distance of train Y. Train X goes 70 miles per hour. How far could train Y go in an hour?

The first sentence gives the basis of comparison: $d' = 2d''$. If this is true, then $r't' = 2r''t''$. The second sentence requires this second formula, as the comparison is shifted from distance to rate and time: $70 \times 1 = 2(r'' \times 1)$. The equation becomes a comparison of two situations for which the condition of equality was set ($d' = 2d''$).

SHG—Significance of a finding

163. In a science experiment,
Note what you are trying to find out.
Note what the possible results will be.
Perform the experiment.
Note the results of the experiment.
Decide what the results of this experiment mean to the farmer, to conservation, to industry, or whatever other area of life it may affect. Does it change the things people do, the way people do things, the ideas people have about a certain thing?

164. In science, from the description of a bird, for instance, decide what its eating habits, etc., must be. (Long bill, long legs, webbed feet, would suggest what about the food, nest, habits, kind of life?)

165. In history, when an important event is described, such as a change in government, the end of a war, a new invention,
Think of all the things such an event changes.

Think of all the ways in which these changes will affect groups of people.

List any results that the author gives for a certain event and try to think of others that might plausibly be given.

166. In geography,

List the conditions of life in a given area.

Decide what kinds of commerce, occupation, housing, etc., the people in that area have.

Guess what kinds of previous events in the earth's history made the land and the water the way it is in this area.

Predict the future of this area on the basis of its present status and the conditions affecting it (depletion of natural resources, erosion, floods, etc.).

EHSG—Cause and effect

167. In a story, notice the feelings of the characters, the way they act, and the situation.

What are the possible results of this situation?

What do you think the most likely result, considering the way the characters feel and the way they usually act?

How do you think such-and-such a character felt in a given situation? How does his feeling have bearing on what happens later?

Note the factors that led to a certain result.

From the description of a room, what do you expect the owner to be like?

From the description of the country and climate in which the characters of the book live, what kind of people do you expect the characters to be? (poor, uninformed, agricultural, lazy?)

From the description of the situation in the beginning of a story, do you expect the story to be funny, sad, gloomy, frightening?   Why?

168. In history,

List the factors that led up to or contributed to a certain event.

List the things that happened before a given event.   Then check each one to see whether it might have helped cause the event.   Present your reasons for thinking it helped.

Find situations in history similar to the present one.   List the points that make them alike, the points that make them different.   Decide whether the points that make them different will make the result of this present situation different, or whether the likenesses warrant a like result.

169. In science,

List the phases in the life of a mosquito (for instance).   Then list the conditions that make those phases possible (stagnant water, etc.)

Given a diet of certain foods, list the content of these foods and note the deficiencies or excesses, if any.   Decide what effect this diet would have on an individual in health, energy.

Show how a bee's life (for instance) is perfectly suited to his limitations and skills.

170. In geography,

Note the effects of the nature of the seasons on occupation, housing, clothing.

Note the effects of the habits of a river on the land and people.

Note the effects of wind and water in a certain area.

If certain conditions continue (drouth, erosion, lumbering, etc.) in a certain area, what can be expected as a result?

SGH—Comparing two countries, peoples, types of life, groups of any kind

171. In science,

List the attributes of two kinds of animals, plants, inanimates, and tell what the chief differences are, what the chief likenesses.

As you read about one kind of animal, plant, or inanimate object, think of another like it that you know in your reading or experience. How are they alike? How are they different?

172. In geography,

Compare the appearance of two countries, listing the characteristics of each and then noting likenesses and differences.

Taking two countries that are very much alike in appearance (Norway and Switzerland in parts), note the differences in occupation and account for them.

As you read about one country, what other country does it remind you of? List the likenesses and differences.

How is the country you are reading about like your own? How is it different?

173. In history,

Compare the world of the sailing vessel with the world of the airplane. List points with regard to each and compare.

Compare a civilization that you are reading about with our own. List points with regard to each and compare.

Compare a civilization that you are reading about with one you have already studied. List points with regard to each and compare.

List all that your know about the rule of a certain monarch. Point for point, put down all you know about his successor or another ruler, as you read about him. Compare these points and decide the relative merits of each.

List all of the things you think should typify good government. Then compare two types of government on these points.

SGH—Marginal headings that do not show relationship to each other

NOTE: Sometimes marginal headings are not equally important but are written in the same sized type. It is important for you to know whether they are of equal importance or not.

174. Read the marginal headings under a topic. As you read each, decide exactly what it means (in some cases this requires a reading of the section itself, but in many cases not).

Compare each heading with the next. Are they parts of the same idea ("Pekinese" and "collie" would be such headings, parts of the idea "dog")? If so, they may be considered of equal importance to the topic ("dog") and read with equal care.

Is one dependent upon another ("dogs," "Pekinese")? If so, read the more important one with greater care, as it is probably the more important to remember. Usually, the dependent idea ("Pekinese") is of less importance in the author's mind, even though his marginal headings give it stress equal to that of the more general heading ("dogs").

H—Relating dates and characters to something to make them memorable
175. When you come to a date which you think you must remember,
Compare it in time with a date you do know well, *i.e.* "This was ten years after the death of Queen Elizabeth."
Think of some other event happening at the same time.
Think of the date in connection with the characters with whom it is associated in time, *i.e.* "This was during the reign of _____."
Look up from your reading and repeat the dates and the situations and people involved, if you think you will otherwise forget them.
Write notes on the event.
Make a couplet, rhyming the date with the event: "Back in 1849, People went out West to mine." This is silly, but it works.
176. When you come upon a person or event you think important to remember,
Write a note about it.
Look up from your reading and try to say all that you know about this.
Think of the ways in which this person or event resembled another.
Think of the ways this person or event was associated with another.

Vocabulary in the Special Fields

177. General: Try to determine the meaning of a strange word from its appearance.
Notice the unknown words that the author uses over and over again.
Look up the meanings of them in a dictionary, and find the meanings that fit the author's use.
Underline or check the strange words that the author repeatedly uses and that seem important to the meaning of the passage. See whether you can guess the meanings from the way the words are used. Consult a dictionary.
Make a list of these unknown words, with their definitions, and use them in sentences.
Write these words on cards, the word on one side, the meaning on the other. Read through these cards until you know the meanings.
Technical: Known words used in a special way in history, science, geography, or mathematics
178. Underline or check the known words that the author seems to be using in a new way for this special subject (consumption, trunk, mouth, etc.)
Note whether the new meaning is suggested by the way the word is used or by its appearance.
Note whether the author gives a definition.
Note whether any pictures, diagrams, charts, and the like, illustrate the meaning.
Write these words down on cards, with the word on one side and the meaning and a use on the other. Use these for practice. Whenever possible, use the words in discussion and writing.
Technical: Words new to you and used only in this special field
179. Underline or check the new words that seem to be special to this subject (oligarchy, phylum, topography, quotient).
Note whether the meaning is suggested by the way the word is used, or by its appearance.

Note whether the author gives a definition.

Note whether any pictures or other illustrations are given.

Write these words down on cards, the words on one side and the meaning and use on the other. Practice defining the words. Use the words in discussion and writing whenever possible.

Write these words in a notebook, each with its definition. Every time the author uses one of these words, put in the notebook the new knowledge you have of its meaning and use. In this way, you will know not only the meaning of each word but the place of the word in your subject. Every time the author uses this word, write it in the margin and try to recall the other things you know about it.

E—Dialect

180. Look carefully at the strange words used.

See first whether they are short forms of words you know.

If not, see whether you can sound them out.

Determine from the sound and the position of the word in the sentence, the word or combination of words that it must represent.

181. If certain puzzling words are used over and over, study them carefully and learn to respond quickly to them. If necessary, write and say them.

E—Figurative speech

Figurative speech is comparison of something with something else, either by use of words of comparison, such as "like" and "as," or by direct statement which confesses no comparison.

182. When "like" or "as" is used, as in the expression, "I feel like a bird."

Decide from the passage how the person might feel.

Think of the way in which this is like a bird.

Think of the usual meaning of this comparison. (Usually, to feel like a bird is to soar in a spiritual sense. But perhaps in this particular setting there is a special meaning, such as that the food being served is no better than bird seed!)

183. When no word of comparison is used, you usually have to rely on detecting the figure by the seeming irrelevance or untruth of the statement ("I am walking on air.")

Think what the usual meaning of this figure is, if it is one you have heard before.

Think of the character of the situation or of the object to which it is applied.

Think of the character of the figure itself, and imagine what the situation or condition described would be (what would it be to "walk on air"?).

Study of this kind should make the value of the figure clear, and the figure should give you a better understanding of the situation or object, through its vividness or exaggeration of the case.

E—Literary allusions

Literary allusions may be proper or common names (Apollo, the cypress), or even quoted phrases or sentences that have their origin or special meaning in a literary work other than the one being read. In making a literary allusion, the author assumes that we know what he is referring to, and he is trying to make his meaning vivid and rich by the suggestiveness of the allusion. The only trouble is that we often do not know nearly so much as the author assumes, and the allusion means nothing to us. For instance, "Thanks to Apollo, we have vegetables," doesn't mean that the Greek grocery boy has delivered them, but that the sun (Apollo being the sun god) has been shining and growing our vegetables.   When someone has been "living in the shadow of the cypress since her husband's death," she has not been sitting under a tree but has been in mourning, the cypress representing mourning.

184.   When you come upon a proper name that does not allude to the character or place in the book that you are reading,
See whether the passage suggests the meaning in any way.
Think in what connection you have heard that name before.
If you do not recall it, look up the word in the pronouncing gazeteer, the biographical section, or the general section of a dictionary.
Decide, from what the dictionary has to say about the word and from the way the word is used in your sentence, in what sense it is used.

185.   When you come upon a noun such as "the cypress," "the rose," "the dove," "the money-changers," not apparently referring to anything previous in the story or article or poem,
See whether the passage suggests the meaning in any way.
Think of the connections in which you have previously seen the word.
Look in the dictionary to see whether the word has an established symbolic meaning.

186.   When you come to a quoted phrase or longer passage whose meaning is not in itself of value to you, it is possible that this is a mere suggestion of a larger literary piece that contributes to the thought the author is trying to give.   "The world is too much with us" offers little unless the reader is familiar with the main thought of the whole poem.
See whether the passage in which the quotation is used suggests the meaning.
Think of the places you have seen it before, to what it refers, who wrote it and what he believed.
Look it up in a reference book, such as Bartlett's *Familiar Quotations*.
The best cure for difficulty with literary allusions, of course, is to become acquainted with as many as possible of the thoughts and writings of the past.

GSM—Symbols and formulas

Certain letters and odd marks stand for certain things in mathematics and science.   The letter t, for example, often means "time," and v means "velocity."   In order to think well in mathematics or science, you must attach these meanings to the letters and odd marks as they are given in the text.

187.   When you come to a symbol in the text,
Note the definition that is given for it.
If no definition is directly given, reread the preceding sentences to determine what is must stand for.
Write the symbol on one side of a card and the definition on the other.
Looking up from the text, try to repeat the symbol and its meaning.
Write down the symbol and its meaning in a notebook or on a card.

188.   When you come to a formula that is important to remember,
Underline it.
Write it and its meaning and use in a notebook.
Write the formula on one side of a card and its meaning on the other.
Looking up from the text, try to repeat the formula and its meaning.
Tell what it is used for and give it a name: "formula for —."

EGHSM—Abbreviations

189. Refer in a dictionary to the section entitled, "Abbreviations Used in Writing and Printing." Jot down the abbreviation and its definition if you are not sure that you will remember it.

190. When a notation like "see Fig. 17" refers you to another page, put a check in the margin beside your place and keep your finger or a slip of paper in the page so that you can easily find your place again. Much time is lost if you do not do this.

EH—Abstract words

These are words, like "democracy," that are hard to define because they mean a great many things. You have to meet such a word in many places before you learn much of what it means. Everybody's idea of "democracy" is a little different from everybody else's because everybody has met the idea in his own several ways. The word "sweetness" is an abstract word, too, because its full meaning depends on your meeting it in all of its applications. When you meet a new, general term, a word that isn't the name of a visible object but a general name applying to many situations and describing a quality in those situations.

191. Write it down in your notebook along with a definition, if the book gives one, or a definition that you invent from noting the use of the word in the text.

Every time you meet the word again, either in its first form (democracy) or in another (democratic), add in your notebook any new definition.

If you have been studying about a democracy, look up from your text and try to say all the characteristics that it seems to have.

List in your notebook a group of things that a democracy is not, if the author gives you contrasts to help form the meaning of the word.

Remember that sometimes the abstract word does not apply to the whole situation but just to a part of it—for instance, a country may be a democracy politically but not economically and socially, or a democracy economically but not politically and socially—so, as you find the use of these abstract words, notice what one or more phases of the concrete situation are always mentioned in connection with the word.

EH—Emotional words

Some words have in addition to their primary meaning another meaning which arouses one emotionally. For instance, "mother," in the expression "mother country," means the origin from which another country sprang. But, in addition, it arouses in one the feeling of respect and love normally accorded a mother. By using the expression "mother country," the historian arouses a feeling of devotion in the reader, which tends to blot out or minimize other aspects of the relationship between the new country and the old. We should be aware of the power of such words, lest they distort our opinions and the truth. At the same time, as readers of fiction, we should appreciate the power of such words to build the emotional character of a scene.

192. When you feel aroused by a piece of writing,

Look through the passage and try to identify the words that carry the emotional power. Could other words be substituted just as well for these? Make the substitution and see whether the feeling you had has any justification in the thought that remains.

Think of the possible partisan views of the situation described.

See whether the author seems to choose his words to favor one side.

Find out what you can about the author and the possible reasons he has to take sides, consciously or unconsciously.

The Reading of Illustrations

HMSG—Labeled figures

193. Read what the text itself has to say about the figure.

Read the caption of the illustration. Think what it means in relation to what you have been reading. Say it in your own words.

Look at the figure, keeping the legend in mind. Notice the items that the legend suggests are important.

If the figure is especially important for you to remember,

Read the labels and notice the parts carefully. Close your eyes and try to visualize the figure and name over the parts.

Jot down the labels and try to describe these parts or draw them. Compare with the original.

Try to draw the whole figure from memory.

HMSG—Charts or graphs

194. Read the legend and try to put it into your own words.

Notice any key to the meaning of different colors; different kinds of lines, figures, etc.

Notice the location of each of these on the chart.

Look at the bottom and left-hand margins of the chart and read the labels.

Trace the fluctuating lines of the chart and generalize on the kind of movement they have and what it means.

Pick out a given point on one axis (margin) of the chart and find the point on the other axis (margin) that indicates the location of the line. State in your words the meaning of this point on the line. Practice using the chart in this way.

If the text mentions a given point or feature of the chart, locate it.

HMSG—Tables

195. Read the legend and put it into your own words.

Read what the text has to say about the table.

Look at the headings of each column and each row across the top and down the left-hand margin.

Pick out a number in the table and interpret it according to its placement in column and row.

Looking over the table and comparing the numbers in the rows and columns, make a general statement as to any tendency to large amounts or small amounts in a given category.

HMSG—Maps

196. A map cannot show everything. The first concern of the reader is to find out what it claims to show.

Notice the label of the map, the area concerned, and the dates during which the given political boundaries or physical conditions are valid. Is this a political map, an economic map, a topographical map? Notice the lines of longitude. If they are fairly straight toward the North and South poles and give the map a flat appearance, the map is making the areas north and south of the equator appear wider than they really are. If they are curved to give a global effect, it is a global map whose distances are probably more true to fact. If the map shows a curve of the earth's surface as though you were looking at it from an airship in the stratosphere, the areas toward the outer regions of the curve—probably toward the edges of the map—are given in perspective and look smaller than they really are.

Notice the entire map. Is there a break in it, indicating that a portion of the earth has been omitted? Is there an insertion, a square or oblong marked off for the insertion of another map, usually enlarging a region already shown or adding a portion that normally would extend beyond the edges of the page?

Read the key. (This is usually in the lower left corner, middle, or right corner.) Use it to identify the nature of certain areas and to gauge the distances between places.

Notice how the mountains, states, cities, rivers have been labeled. See whether you can find the labels for any that you choose.

See whether you can tell the latitude and longitude of a given place. Compare distances between places you are reading about.

Read the text itself to see what the author wishes you to notice about the map. Study the map until you find the things he mentions. Remember to use the key for help in this.

If you must memorize the map, half close your eyes and study the big areas: the shapes of the continents, the shapes of the seas and oceans, the paths of the great rivers and the lines of the mountains. Try to copy these from memory before you try to remember any more detail. Close your eyes and try to picture the map as you say over to yourself the important facts about the placement of the items in it.

EHMSG—Pictures

197. Read the legend of the picture and put it into your own words.

Think of the way the picture is related to the topic you are reading.

Decide, on this basis, whether it is important to see all the details in the picture or the few big objects.

Scan the picture for the items suggested by the legend.

See what the text itself has to say about the picture.

If the picture is supposed to give you a comprehensive idea, such as kinds of occupation or the way people live or the kinds of land in a given country, look at all the details. Follow a system of looking for these details so that you will not miss any. Close your eyes and repeat all that you have seen.

If it is a picture that has only one important thing for you to remember (such as that some trains scoop water up from the track as they travel along), look carefully for that one thing and then put its description into a sentence.

Locating Material in a Book

HSG—The use of the Table of Contents

When you first approach a textbook, an important practice is to read the title and put into your own words the probable content of the book. See also who the author is and what he has done to qualify as an authority on the subject. Then look at the Table of Contents.

198. Read each topic to determine what it means, if you can. If there are comments after each topic as to the content of the chapter, read these. Try to put each topic into your own words.

199. Read the topics down the page to determine in what sequence the author has written, how he has organized the material.   Express this organization in a sentence.
200. Think of certain topics in this field that interest you especially.   See under what headings they might come.

Whenever you are assigned a new topic in a strange book, use the Table of Contents to find the page numbers and to locate the material, especially if the topic is a large one that is likely to be treated extensively in the book.

HSG—The use of the Index
201. Turn to the Index and look up a topic about which you have a question. Turn to the page recommended and look rapidly (skim) down the page for the shape and beginning letters of the name of the topic.   It will surely be in one of the sentences, but if you are lucky it may be in a marginal heading.   In either case, read the area in which it is.   Does it answer your question?   If not, look at the other pages mentioned in the Index after the name of the topic.
202. Read the preface for hints you are given of what the author intends to do in his book.   Take one big topic that he mentions and ask yourself a question about a part of it.   Look in the Index for the topic.   If it is a big topic in the book, it will probably have several subheadings. Think of the way a subheading about your question might be worded. Then, read the subheadings, comparing each with your idea.   Choose the subheadings that might refer to your idea, and look up the page references, one after another, until you find your information.

Whenever you are assigned a new topic that is not indicated in the Table of Contents, look in the Index for it.   *Don't let anyone tell you where it is* or you may become eternally dependent upon someone else's good work habits.

HSG—The use of the Glossary
203. If your book has a glossary and you come to a hard word in your reading, put a marker in the place you are reading and look in the Glossary until you find the word.
Look at the pronunciation recommended for the word.   If you do not understand the way the pronunciation is indicated, look for a key that will explain (usually at the beginning of the Glossary or at the foot of each page).
Read the definition of the word.   Turn back to the page you have been reading and substitute this definition in the sentence to get the meaning of the sentence.
Put the word on a card with its meaning.   A word in the Glossary is often a word that you should learn to know very well.
Put a little check beside each word that you look up in the Glossary.   If you have to look the word up a second or a third time, these checks will show you that it is time you really learned the word.

APPENDIX E

APPROACHING THE READING PROBLEM THROUGH STUDY HABITS

The following questionnaire may prove helpful in an analysis of study difficulties in a given school and may indirectly serve the purpose of making the school aware of reading difficulties.

In what ways do study habit deficiencies reveal themselves
1. In the study hall?
2. In the classroom?
3. In the home?
4. In college or adult life?

How prevalent are the deficiencies
1. Among special students?
2. At special times of year?
3. In special classes?
4. In special types of assignment?

What measures have been taken to meet the deficiencies
1. Through tests?
   a. Administration of reading tests?
   b. Administration of mental tests?
   c. Tests in the uses of books as they are required by teachers (index, table of contents, etc.)?
   d. Pretests to determine
      (1) Ability to read a given subject?
      (2) Previous knowledge of subject?
2. In the classroom
   a. Study helps in the classroom?
   b. A study sheet for the preparation of assignments?
   c. Care in the wording of the assignment?
   d. Discussion of the assignment?
   e. Note taking?
   f. Student illustration so that the meaning is clear?
   g. Talks on how to study (of little use if not followed up)?
   h. Analysis of time demands of different assignments?
   i. Motivation of assignments?
   j. Differentiation of student assignments according to abilities, experience needs, and interests or talents?
3. In the study hall
   a. Equipment in the study hall?
   b Study-hall conditions for study—lighting, accoustics, arrangement, time of day, etc.?

4. In the library
   a. Advance arrangements for material on certain mass assignments or committee reports?
   b. Careful instruction in the use of the parts of the library important to a given course?
5. In the home
   Home conditions for study—quiet, lack of interruption, time of day?

In what respects and to what extent have these measures appeared to help? Teachers may respond to a questionnaire of this subject or hold a group meeting preceded by careful consideration of the problem by each teacher. The drawback to a group meeting is that it so often becomes a contest among strong and weak personalities—the aggressive versus the meek—in the course of which someone usually feels called upon to defend what he interprets as a public assault upon his teaching ability.   For this reason perhaps individual written responses followed by a general meeting to consider the mass of findings, would be more fruitful.

For a given teacher:

Do your assignments always demand the same general approach in study and reading skills?
Give one example for each type of assignment that you commonly make in which the students come poorly prepared.   In what respects do they fail to fulfill the assignment in each case?

Questions and activites of this type are almost certain to result in better teaching and better reading and therefore in better attitudes on the part of students throughout the school.

INDEX OF PERSONS

SUBJECT INDEX

A

Activity record, 305

Adults, remedial program for, 220–221, 223–224

American Council on Education Psychological Examination, 58

Aniseikonia, 230–231

Army literacy program, 201, 222–223, 344

Attention span, 300–301

Attitudes of nonreaders, improvement of, 272–273

Auditory difficulties, 231

B

Beginning reading, Chicago method of, 106
stage of, 87–88

Book lists, 148, 344–345

C

California Test of Mental Maturity, 56–58

Carroll Prose Appreciation Test, 171

Case studies, 310–334

Chicago method of beginning reading, 106

Chicago Reading Clinic, 221

Chicago reading program, 16–17

Chicago Reading Tests, 125–126

Choral reading, 109

Class size, 98–99

College reading, 91–92

College reading test, 192–195

College students, remedial program for, 218–220

Columbia College reading program, 24–29

Communication and reading, 38–39

Comprehension, exercise in, 371–380

Comprehension, questions on, 109–112, 288
reasons for difficulty in, 285–286
sources of difficulty in, 285–295
speed of, 46–48
ways of improving, 286–295, 365–385

Cooperative Reading Comprehension Tests, 23, 24, 128–129, 170, 210

Cooperative Test of Literary Appreciation, 24

Cost of remedial reading, 201–202

Creative reading, 292–295, 301, 381–386

Curriculum revision, 96–97

D

Details, exercise in comprehension of, 371–380
overemphasis on, 109–111
reading for, 291

Developmental program, need for, 115–117
suggestions for, 118–168

Dictionary, use of, 282–283

Directions, reading of, 68

Drill, 104–105

Durrell Oral Reading Test, 240

Durrell-Sullivan Reading Capacity and Achievement Tests, 128

E

Eames eye test, 235

English in a reading class, 171–180

Experience and reading, 37–38

Eye-movement records, 235–238

F

Fernald method, 265, 315–318

Films, 238

Fixations, 235

Flash-card drill, 104

401